Ius Gentium: Comparative Perspectives on Law and Justice

Volume 144

Ius Gentium is a book series which discusses the central questions of law and justice from a comparative perspective. The books in this series collect the contrasting and overlapping perspectives of lawyers, judges, philosophers and scholars of law from the world's many different jurisdictions for the purposes of comparison, harmonisation, and the progressive development of law and legal institutions. Each volume makes a new comparative study of an important area of law. This book series continues the work of the well-known journal of the same name and provides the basis for a better understanding of all areas of legal science.

The *Ius Gentium* series provides a valuable resource for lawyers, judges, legislators, scholars, and both graduate students and researchers in globalisation, comparative law, legal theory and legal practice. The series has a special focus on the development of international legal standards and transnational legal cooperation.

Ioana Maria Costea
Editor

Legal Interpretation in Motion

Rights, Institutions and Regulation in Contemporary Legal Change

Springer

Editor
Ioana Maria Costea
Faculty of Law
Alexandru Ioan Cuza University of Iaşi
Iaşi, Romania

ISSN 1534-6781 ISSN 2214-9902 (electronic)
Ius Gentium: Comparative Perspectives on Law and Justice
ISBN 978-3-032-32947-9 ISBN 978-3-032-32948-6 (eBook)
https://doi.org/10.1007/978-3-032-32948-6

This work was supported by Universitatea „Alexandru Ioan Cuza" din Iaşi.

This Springer imprint is published by the registered company Springer Nature Switzerland AG
The registered company address is: Gewerbestrasse 11, 6330 Cham, Switzerland

Preface

"All things are subject to interpretation; whichever interpretation prevails at a given time is a function of power and not truth."—Friedrich Nietzsche

Nietzsche's observation remains profoundly relevant for contemporary legal thought. Law is never applied in a vacuum of pure objectivity. Every legal norm passes through the filter of interpretation, institutional authority, historical context, and social transformation. Yet, the role of legal interpretation within a democratic society is precisely to prevent power from becoming arbitrary by subjecting it to reasoned argument, constitutional values, procedural guarantees, and judicial accountability.

Law does not exist merely in the text. It exists in the space between text and meaning, between norm and reality, between certainty and doubt. Every legal system is ultimately sustained not only by rules, but by interpretation, by the continuous intellectual effort through which societies attempt to transform abstract formulations into living justice.

Interpretation gives law its movement. Without interpretation, legal norms would remain static formulations incapable of responding to the complexity of human relations, technological transformation, constitutional tensions, or social evolution. Through interpretation, however, law becomes dynamic without losing coherence, adaptable without abandoning stability, and responsive without dissolving into arbitrariness. The interpreter therefore occupies a paradoxical position: neither creator of the law nor passive executor of it, but rather the mediator through whom legal meaning emerges.

This volume is grounded in the conviction that interpretation represents one of the most profound dimensions of legal thought. Far from being a merely technical operation, interpretation is an exercise in legal philosophy, institutional reasoning, democratic legitimacy, and social responsibility. The chapters brought together in this collective work explore interpretation not only as a doctrinal method, but also as a mechanism through which legal systems negotiate uncertainty, protect fundamental rights, and confront emerging realities.

The book reflects the diversity and complexity of contemporary legal interpretation. The contributors examine constitutional adjudication, criminal law, budgetary regulation, civil liability, consumer protection, procedural cooperation, digital regulation, forensic science, legal technology, and European legal integration. These analyses reveal that interpretation functions simultaneously as a tool of coherence and a source of transformation. It preserves continuity with legal tradition while allowing the law to adapt to evolving social, economic, and technological conditions.

Several chapters engage directly with foundational questions concerning legal rationality and constitutional values, highlighting how interpretation shapes the understanding of the rule of law, governmental responsibility, and fundamental rights. Others investigate the delicate balance between restrictive and extensive interpretation in criminal law, the role of teleological reasoning in forensic science, or the evolving legal understanding of family and vulnerability in private law. The volume also addresses contemporary challenges generated by digitalization, online advertising, legal tech companies, and the increasingly complex interaction between national legal systems and European regulatory frameworks.

A recurring theme throughout this book is the tension between stability and openness. Modern legal systems must preserve predictability and legal certainty while remaining capable of responding to realities that legislators themselves could not always anticipate. Interpretation becomes, therefore, the bridge between permanence and change. It allows the law to maintain its authority while avoiding rigidity. At the same time, interpretation also carries risks: over-interpretation may distort the normative framework, while under-interpretation may render law incapable of protecting those it was designed to serve. The chapters in this volume repeatedly illustrate that legal interpretation is inseparable from responsibility.

The Romanian legal experience offers a particularly fertile terrain for such reflections. Situated at the intersection of continental legal tradition, European integration, constitutional transformation, and rapid digital development, Romanian law continuously negotiates multiple layers of normative influence and institutional adaptation. In this context, interpretation acquires not only doctrinal significance, but also cultural, constitutional, and societal importance. Romanian legal scholarship increasingly demonstrates that interpretation is not simply about identifying meaning, but about constructing legal coherence in a fragmented and rapidly changing world.

This collective work therefore seeks to contribute not only to Romanian legal doctrine, but also to broader international discussions concerning the nature and future of legal interpretation. The plurality of perspectives assembled here reflects the plurality inherent in law itself. Interpretation does not eliminate complexity; rather, it renders complexity intelligible. It transforms ambiguity into argument, conflict into reasoning, and abstract principles into practical justice.

Ultimately, this volume invites the reader to reconsider interpretation as one of the defining forces of legal civilization. Law survives not because its texts are immutable, but because interpretation enables them to remain meaningful across generations, contexts, and transformations. In this sense, interpretation is not secondary to law, but it is the condition of its existence.

Iaşi, Romania Ioana Maria Costea

Contents

Introduction

Ioana Maria Costea

Legal interpretation is often presented as a technique. This volume proceeds from a different premise: interpretation is not external to law, but constitutes the condition through which law acquires meaning, stability and effect across different institutional layers.

The opening section addresses the conceptual foundations of interpretation. Codrin Codrea frames interpretation as structurally embedded in legal reasoning, showing that legal thought operates within conditions it cannot fully neutralise. Despina-Martha Ilucă brings this structural insight to the level of legal definitions, highlighting how classificatory thresholds determine access to legal regimes. Mihai Dunea explores the limits of interpretation in criminal law, where legality constrains interpretative expansion, while Carmen-Ecaterina Ciobăcă demonstrates that even core legal notions depend on linguistic and comparative reconstruction across legal systems.

The second section focuses on the operational dimension of interpretation. Nicolae-Horia Țiț shows that interpretation is inseparable from procedural design, where cooperation between judge and parties sustains the coherence of adjudication. Ancuța Franț complements this perspective by analysing teleological reasoning, illustrating how interpretative purpose intervenes in contexts where legal norms encounter factual complexity.

The third section turns to fundamental rights, where interpretation functions as a mechanism of adjustment and delimitation. Alina Gentimir examines the influence of European standards on national law, while Lucia Irinescu analyses the adaptive reinterpretation of family structures. Andra Iftimiei explores the interpretative construction of religious freedom, showing how legal orders balance internal conviction and external regulation.

I. M. Costea (✉)
Faculty of Law, Alexandru Ioan Cuza University of Iași, Iași, Romania
e-mail: ioana.costea@uaic.ro

I. Maria Costea (ed.), *Legal Interpretation in Motion*, Ius Gentium: Comparative Perspectives on Law and Justice 144,
https://doi.org/10.1007/978-3-032-32948-6_1

The fourth section situates interpretation within private law and emerging regulatory markets. Carmen-Tamara Ungureanu highlights the transformation of litigation through legal tech actors, while Aura Amironesei shows how digital advertising requires interpretative coordination across fragmented regulatory frameworks. Codrin Macovei analyses the vulnerability of consent under conditions of influence, and Luiza-Cristina Gavrilescu addresses contractual balance, where interpretation directly redistributes economic burdens.

The final section introduces a shift from private interactions to institutional structure. Ioan-Dumitru Apachiței examines the liability of public officials, showing how interpretation defines the limits of authority and responsibility within constitutional systems. Building on this institutional dimension, Ioana-Maria Costea reconstructs the concept of the budget as a structural element of public law, where interpretation no longer resolves isolated questions but organises a system of allocation of resources, power and obligation.

The volume thus follows a continuous movement: from the conceptual conditions of interpretation, through its procedural articulation and its operation in rights and markets, to its role in structuring public authority and, ultimately, public resources. Legal interpretation appears not as a discrete act, but as a process through which law produces, stabilises and distributes meaning across normative and institutional levels.

Conceptual Foundations of Legal Interpretation

Legal Logic, Aporia and Structured Openness: A Theoretical Account of Legal Interpretation

Codrin Codrea

Abstract In this chapter, I propose a reframing of legal interpretation through the notions of aporia, legal logic, and structured openness. I argue that what appears as heterogeneous difficulties in interpretation can be seen as a structural condition of law, called aporia, which varies in visibility across interpretive contexts. I begin by contrasting two paradigms: structured legalism, exemplified by Hans Kelsen's model of norm-governed interpretation within a hierarchical legal order, and iterative hermeneutics, associated with Jacques Derrida's emphasis on singularity, undecidability, and the openness of meaning, each resting on particular assumptions about law and language. Classical methods of legal interpretation—grammatical, systematic, historical, and teleological—appear not as neutral techniques but as strategies that simultaneously rely on their own specific presuppositions but can still be reshaped by each paradigm. To account for their interaction, I propose legal logic not as a fixed deductive scheme but as a meta-theoretical framework for structuring legal interpretation under various conditions of aporia. Drawing on a range of non-classical logics responding to the internal dimensions of aporia, I argue that the notion of structured openness can explain how law can remain rational and institutionally accountable while remaining receptive to plurality, contestation, and change.

1 Introduction

When Nietzsche suggested that *we are all interpreters of interpretations, as it was later phrased* (Vattimo 1997, p. 26), he expressed, in a condensed philosophical aphorism, a foundational idea, that meaning is never given, only mediated (Nietzsche 1966, §22). This insight would later define modern hermeneutics, which, beginning as *"hermeneutica sacra"*—the exegetical reading of sacred texts—was transformed by Schleiermacher and Dilthey into a general methodology for understanding

C. Codrea (✉)
Faculty of Law, 'Alexandru Ioan Cuza' University of Iași, Iasi, Romania
e-mail: codrin.codrea@uaic.ro

I. Maria Costea (ed.), *Legal Interpretation in Motion*, Ius Gentium: Comparative Perspectives on Law and Justice 144,
https://doi.org/10.1007/978-3-032-32948-6_2

human experience, and reoriented by Heidegger and Gadamer as a condition of human existence itself (Grondin 1994; Gadamer 1989/2004).

This layered nature of meaning to which Nietzsche refers is equally relevant in the legal domain. Legal norms, although expressed in natural language, and perhaps precisely because of that, do not contain fixed meanings awaiting retrieval, but rather require interpretation within institutional, linguistic, and historical contexts (Dworkin 1986, pp. 86–87). My claim is that interpretation is not an auxiliary feature of legal practice, but one of its structural conditions of possibility. The Renaissance jurists such as Guido (Guy) de la Pape, Aloisius de Albertis, Philippus Decius, and Petrus Paulus Parisius were the early proponents of the principle later expressed in the maxim *interpretatio cessat in claris* (Schott 2001, pp. 155–189), a maxim which rested on the presupposition that clarity is an unmediated property of the legal text (Grabowski 2015, pp. 67–97).[1] However, what counts as "clear" is always the result of an interpretive decision: a decision that resolves ambiguity by establishing a single norm, a single usage, a single function as dominant over others. In this sense, interpretation is the rule not the exception, since even when legal language appears semantically transparent, such clarity is often the result of cumulative prior interpretive acts, of the abstraction of a general situation of application, without which no legal norm can possess any meaning (Codrea 2023, p. 251). Given this pervasive interpretive mediation, if legal meaning always passes through interpretation and interpretation is always involved, the main issue is how law can follow reasons, standards, methods, and institutional constraints while relying on continually shifting semantic grounds.

The answer I argue in this chapter is that legal logic can mediate aporia through structured openness, allowing legal reasoning to preserve consistency without losing its capacity for adaptation. As a meta-theoretical framework, legal logic incorporates formal logical instruments capable of regulating interpretation without reducing it to deductive schemes in a strict logical sense. By aporia, I refer to the structural condition of legal reasoning in which interpretation becomes both necessary and problematic, when the application of a legal rule is simultaneously required and underdetermined, making aporia internally differentiated and externally variable in its visibility across interpretive contexts.[2] Structured openness, in turn, designates the juridical condition that results from this mediation, a condition in which law preserves normative continuity while remaining open to reinterpretation but in which coherence is achieved rather than presupposed, as a revisable outcome rather than a settled premise.[3]

[1] The maxim circulated in related formulations such as *clara non sunt interpretanda* and *in claris non fit interpretatio* and the idea can be traced to Roman rhetorical discussions in Cicero and Quintilian (Masuelli 2002, pp. 401–424).

[2] Watson frames the debate over legal interpretation as a meta-interpretive question, but his remedial answer locates interpretive theory primarily at the point where the law runs out. The present account differs by treating aporia not as a residual problem of gaps, hard cases, or discretion, but as a structural condition of legal reasoning itself (Watson 2025, pp. 1407–1456).

[3] See also Hinz (2009), who argues for a normative orientation capable of reconciling universal human rights with the legal traditions of culturally diverse communities, especially within African

The chapter sets out by contrasting two paradigms: one which I call "structured legalism" with Hans Kelsen's approach to interpretation as a model, and, at the other end of the spectrum, a paradigm which I call "iterative hermeneutics" relying on the approach of Jacques Derrida. Kelsen understands interpretation as a rule-bound, hierarchical process logically constrained by a normative order culminating in the *Grundnorm*.[4] In contrast, Derrida's deconstructive theory reveals that every application of a legal norm involves a singular decision, shaped by *différance* and the context-dependence of meaning.[5] These divergent perspectives rest on

plural legal systems. In his account, the relevant structure is institutional and intercultural: it lies in balancing overarching human-rights principles with respect for local legal consciousness, thereby remaining open to plural sources of legitimacy while preserving a core normative framework. By contrast, the concept of structured openness developed here concerns an internal epistemology of legal interpretation rather than an intercultural negotiation. It designates the rational tension within legal reasoning between structured legalism and iterative hermeneutics, where the "structure" is logical and normative, and the "openness" refers to the inexhaustibility of interpretive application.

[4] Not just Hans Kelsen, but the broader orientation I call structured legalism can be reconstructed as a long-standing tendency in legal theory to treat interpretation as becoming especially necessary when normative clarity breaks down. H. L. A. Hart distinguished between a "central core of undisputed meaning" and a "penumbra of doubt" where only the latter required judicial interpretation (Hart 1961, pp. 12, 119–126). Antonin Scalia advances a comparable orientation in his textualist approach, treating the ordinary meaning of the enacted legal text as normally controlling and the recourse to broader interpretive considerations as exceptional rather than regular (Scalia 2018, pp. 17–24, 29–30). Even legal realists such as Karl Llewellyn retained the view that much legal decision remains reasonably reckonable within the doctrinal apparatus, while interpretive judgment becomes more prominent where uncertainty or contestation arises (Llewellyn 1960, pp. 20–25, 179–180). This orientation also finds expression in more qualified or mediated forms in theories that preserve a distinction between ordinary rule-application and more explicit interpretive or justificatory reasoning under conditions of indeterminacy, conflict, or argumentative contestation: Joseph Raz argues that authoritative directives are meant to pre-empt further deliberation and thereby to constrain interpretation (Raz 1999, pp. 35–48; Raz 2009, pp. 140–142); Aulis Aarnio also distinguishes routine or isomorphic legal application from decisions of discretion (Aarnio 1987, pp. 1–5, 47–60); Jaap Hage distinguishes normal rule-application from interpretive reasoning about the content and validity of rules, especially where legal sources admit competing interpretations (Hage 1997, pp. 95–98, 197–202); Andrei Marmor treats interpretation as distinct from ordinary application, becoming necessary where conventional meaning leaves the issue underdetermined (Marmor 2005, pp. 9–21, 95–97, 115–116); Neil MacCormick distinguishes relatively straightforward rule-application from harder cases involving interpretation, classification, and relevancy, while resisting the view that all legal reasoning is interpretive through and through (MacCormick 1978/2003, pp. xii–xvi, 19–33, 140–141, 176–177); and Robert Alexy distinguishes relatively simple cases of subsumption from more complex cases requiring external justification and interpretive argument (Alexy 1989, pp. 222–227, 230–250).

[5] A series of thinkers, although diverse in vocabulary, scope, and method, can be read as converging on the view—most forcefully articulated in legal theory by Derrida—that legal meaning is never simply applied but is always mediated through interpretation; it is on this basis that I refer to this orientation as iterative hermeneutics. Judith Butler's theory of performative repetition echoes this understanding by treating normative structures as produced through iterative citation (Butler 1997). Drucilla Cornell reworks this logic into a deconstructive jurisprudence that affirms law's ethical openness to singularity (Cornell 1992). Julia Kristeva contributes to this strand through her theory of intertextuality, in which meaning emerges from a differential network of texts rather than from any inherent textual stability (Kristeva 1980/2024). Peter Goodrich advances a literary-legal

conflicting presuppositions on the importance, scope and role of interpretation to legal meaning, grounded in distinct theoretical assumptions about what law is, and which will be further analyzed.

I further argue that classical methods of legal interpretation—grammatical, systematic, historical, and teleological—already in their conventional form hold certain presuppositions about language and law. Reframed through these paradigms, they are not neutral as often presented in legal doctrine, but interpretive strategies whose significance varies depending on whether law is treated rather as a closed system, as in the structured legalist view, or an open discursive field, as in the iterative hermeneutics perspective. This raises several questions on the epistemological and methodological levels: does legal cognition capture fixed semantic content, or is it inherently a constructive process shaped by historical and institutional norms of justification, and if so, can interpretation produce valid legal knowledge? Considering the mediated nature of meaning, can a framework account for how legal reasoning works, as inferential, defeasible, and dynamic, while avoiding formalist inflexibility and the unbound interpretive flux?

Positioned between the two paradigms, this account reframes their relation at a higher level of analysis from which the theories of Hart, Raz, Dworkin, and Alexy can be read as answering to different manifestations of the same aporetic structure while confronting separate limited problems. Legal logic becomes necessary here as a second-order account since it addresses this structural tension, which, once treated as epistemically transparent, can render legal interpretation disciplined and legally consistent, answering to the drive toward systemic coherence, and to the imperative of contextual responsiveness, corresponding to each of the two paradigms.[6]

To substantiate this view, I incorporate contemporary formal logical instruments—non-monotonic reasoning, dynamic epistemic logic, deontic and paraconsistent systems, semantic logic, and formal argumentation theory—which formalize the very conditions under which legal interpretation operates: revisability, context-sensitivity, norm conflict, and semantic plurality. Through these formal instruments,

hermeneutics that rejects the rigidity of doctrinal interpretation in favor of interpretive multiplicity and semiotic engagement (Goodrich 1996). Cornelia Vismann interrogates the infrastructural and archival conditions of legality, showing that law's interpretive space is shaped by media technologies and material files (Vismann 2008). Costas Douzinas and Ronnie Warrington, drawing on Derridean and Levinasian ethics, argue that justice always exceeds the legal text, requiring interpretation to remain open to alterity (Douzinas and Warrington 1994). Robert Cover, writing within constitutional theory, likewise treats legal interpretation as not merely epistemic but narrative and world-creating in nature (Cover 1983).

[6]This second-order orientation connects the present account to recent meta-interpretive debates. Watson frames the meta-interpretive question as concerning what theories of legal interpretation are theories of, while Urbina approaches interpretive choice by asking what kinds of reasons can justify methods of interpretation. The present account shares this meta-theoretical orientation, but shifts the focus from the choice among interpretive theories or methods to the legal-logical mediation of aporia as the structural condition under which interpretation becomes both necessary and underdetermined (Watson 2025, pp. 1407–1456; Urbina 2024, pp. 1661–1740).

legal logic operates descriptively, methodologically and prescriptively, showing patterns of legal reasoning that deduction alone cannot adequately explain, allowing one to reconstruct and evaluate how interpretation responds to a particular form of aporia and providing second-order criteria for assessing whether the chosen mode of reasoning is appropriate to the form of aporia being mediated.

Ultimately, I argue that through legal logic as I propose it, legal interpretation, while still dependent on choice, becomes less opaque and more traceable in its internal unfolding, becoming the conceptual space where legal challenges posed by various forms of aporia can be addressed in such a way that makes it possible to think of law as rational and coherent. The issue that runs throughout the chapter is how interpretation is constrained by the legal structure, and how, in return, the legal structure itself is constituted and transformed through interpretation while remaining rationally intelligible.

2 Divergent Paradigms and Classical Legal Methods of Interpretation

Two influential models of interpretation can be contrasted that differ fundamentally in their assumptions about both the object of interpretation and the nature of the interpretive act itself. The first, which I refer to as the structured legalist interpretation, exemplified by Hans Kelsen's "Pure Theory of Law", conceives legal interpretation as a constrained activity governed by a hierarchical system of norms, culminating in a presupposed *Grundnorm*. In this approach the logic of the system serves as both a guide and a constraint, structuring the relationship between norms in a way that seeks to minimize indeterminacy. The second theoretical approach, which I refer to as iterative hermeneutical interpretation, emerges from Jacques Derrida's deconstructive philosophy of law, which reveals that the act of applying a norm is always a moment of decision, invention, and irreducible singularity. For Derrida, legal meaning cannot be logically deduced from a rule alone, because every rule encounters the unpredictability of context and the infinite deferral of meaning inherent in language.

Although these two perspectives are radically different in their assumptions about the nature and structure of law, they both address the problem of the necessity and scope of interpretation, and it is on this shared concern that I propose legal logic as an appropriate conceptual framework for interpretation.

2.1 Structured Legalism: Hans Kelsen and Interpretation as Normative Derivation

Hans Kelsen's "Pure Theory of Law" offers the most illustrative model of what I call structured legalism and, although his account is arguably more nuanced than presented here, I treat his approach to *Stufenbau der Rechtsordnung* (hierarchical structure of the legal order) as an ideal-type reconstruction. In his theory legal interpretation is presented as a disciplined, methodical process operating entirely within the framework of an autonomous legal system. According to Kelsen, "law is a system of norms regulating human behavior", a system of ought-propositions and its scientific study must remain uncontaminated by extralegal domains such as politics, morality, or sociology (Kelsen 1967, pp. 1, 4–5). The legal order, as he conceives it, functions through a hierarchical structure in which each norm derives its validity from a superior one, culminating in the *Grundnorm* (basic norm), the foundational presupposition that grounds the unity and validity of the system as a whole (Kelsen 1967, p. 31).[7]

This hierarchical structure resembles that of a formal axiomatic system. In such systems—paradigmatically those of logic or mathematics—a foundational set of axioms, considered given, provides the basis for deriving further theorems through strictly defined rules of inference. Similarly, in Kelsen's theory, the legal system is composed of a set of normative propositions whose validity is derived from higher norms in accordance with the hierarchical structure of the legal order, with the *Grundnorm* holding the position of a transcendental axiom, which is not enacted or enforced, but presupposed, functioning as a transcendental-logical necessity, the point of origin that renders the legal system coherent and unified (Codrea 2020, pp. 368–375).

Just as an axiomatic system is defined by internal coherence and completeness, contradictions being impossible and every valid statement being derivable from axiomatic premises, in a similar way the Kelsenian legal order can be understood as aiming to preserve consistency on all normative levels, ensuring that no legal norm validly produced from the system contradicts another and that every legal situation can, in principle, be governed by norms derived from higher norms.

Within this model, legal interpretation can be understood as functioning in a manner analogous to the derivation of a theorem, rather as a logical process governed by internal criteria and not an act of external or discretionary invention of the system. Interpretation, under this view, serves not to innovate but to determine which specific applications are permissible within the parameters set by the norm in question. Kelsen's distinction between *authentische Auslegung* (authentic interpretation) which is binding and performed by legal institutions and *wissenschaftliche Auslegung* (non-authentic or scientific interpretation) which remains explanatory, is central to his framework. Both, however, are circumscribed by the *Spielraum der Auslegung* (frame of interpretation) which is the interpretive space within which valid meanings must be derived from superior norms: as Kelsen explains, law already contains a finite set of meanings which can be logically identified and the law-creating organ can choose one of the possible meanings of the general norm,

---

[7] "An 'order' is a system of norms whose unity is constituted by the fact that they all have the same reason for their validity; and the reason for the validity of a normative order is a basic norm (…) from which the validity of all norms of the order are derived. A single norm is a valid legal norm, if it corresponds to the concept of "law" and is part of a legal order; and it is part of a legal order, if its validity is based on the basic norm of that order" (Kelsen 1967, p. 31).

and the norm it creates is legally valid if it remains within the frame of interpretation (Kelsen 1967, p. 351). Therefore, this interpretive space is not unbound, it does not imply discretionary freedom in searching for meaning and Kelsen insists that the decision is legal insofar as it stays within the frame set by the higher norm (Kelsen 1967, pp. 351–355). Judges also are not free creators of law but agents of its systematic application, tasked with selecting among legally derivable meanings without departing from the logic of the normative structure. "The idea (...) that the determination (of the legal act to be performed) not rendered by the norm that is to be applied could be gained by some cognition of the existing law, is a contradictory fallacy because it is incompatible with the presupposed possibility of an interpretation" he argues, but still interpretation is not a matter of free invention, but a function determined by the legal order itself (Kelsen 1967, p. 353). Therefore, even in those cases where interpretation is necessary, it must nevertheless operate within the structural logic of the legal system, reinforcing its coherence and procedural regularity and any flexibility granted to interpreters must remain functionally subordinated to the internal criteria of the legal order.

Therefore, Kelsen's theory presents interpretation as a limited, norm-governed practice rather than free creation, restricted by logical considerations deriving from the normative hierarchy. Legal meaning is not discovered through external reasoning or sources outside law but unfolds immanently, even if through acts of will, from the architecture of the system itself. The perspective on law held by structured legalism is one in which law tends towards closure if not a complete closed system, where meaning is authorized by form and position within a hierarchy allowing for juridical self-reference and securing the autonomy and internal legitimacy of the legal system (Codrea 2023, pp. 338–341).

2.2 Iterative Hermeneutics: Jacques Derrida and Interpretation as Creative Rearticulation

Iterative hermeneutics advances a contrasting view on legal interpretation, asserting that meaning does not preexist the act of interpretation but is instead generated through it. Jacques Derrida exemplifies this approach, which embraces contextual variation, resists closure and highlights the open-ended nature of meaning. Central to Derrida's philosophy is *différance*, a term that unites "differentiation" and "deferral". Meaning arises from the relational differences between signs and their constant postponement, not from a direct correspondence between word and referent. As he argues, the signified concept is never present in and of itself in a sufficient, autoreferential presence and it is always already inhabited by the trace of another sign which never appears as such (Derrida 1982, pp. 11–13).[8] Since any sign carries a

[8] "It is because of différance that the movement of signification is possible only if each so-called "present" element, each element appearing on the scene of presence, is related to something other

trace of another sign, no meaning is ever fully present or self-contained, never fully transparent, and it is always interwoven with other meanings.

If traditional theories treat words as carriers of fixed meaning, Derrida challenges this assumption of any intrinsic essence in linguistic signs. Meaning is constructed relationally, emerging through distinctions from other signs and through temporal deferral: there is no linguistic sign before *différance*, and *différance* is not another word, but "the possibility of conceptuality", of language, and of meaning (Derrida 1982, pp. 10–13). The notion of a final, stable interpretation is thus unsustainable, since every act of reading brings forth new contexts and associations, and meaning is always "in play": a signifier gains meaning not through itself, but only through its relation to other signifiers and it is this chain of connections that produces meaning (Derrida 1982, pp. 11–13; Lacan 1978/1998, pp. 20–21, 45–46). Therefore, in order to understand a word, for example, as a particular kind of sign, it is always required to relate to other words and meanings in a process which is never entirely closed or complete—an unlimited semiosis, as Umberto Eco would explain (Eco 1976, pp. 15, 69–72).

In the legal context, this particular view implies that legal texts are not static sources of meaning but are perpetually open to reinterpretation. As he argues, to apply a rule is to transform it, to follow it is to interpret it anew, in a unique and singular context that the rule did not and could not foresee (Derrida 1992, pp. 17, 23–27).[9] Thus, Derrida suggests that law's authority may be inseparable from the interpretive act which continuously shapes and redefines the legal norm.

This perspective challenges the notion of law as a closed, self-sufficient system since legal texts acquire force only through their engagement with specific contexts and meaning arises through the dynamic encounter between text and interpreter. Legal texts, on this view, do not encode pre-determined meanings but serve as sites of ongoing interpretation, shaped by historical, institutional, and social contexts and as he paradoxically suggests, the authority of law is derived from the performative moment when a decision retroactively legitimates itself (Derrida 1992, pp. 12–15, 36–37). Each judicial decision, therefore, is not merely the application of an abstract norm but a creative act that adapts the law and legal interpretation is not the tracing of a line from a higher norm to a lower one, as in Kelsen's model, but the enactment of a decision in the face of undecidability. Derrida argues that a genuine decision, to be just, must arise in a moment of undecidability, so if the outcome is already pre-determined by prior norms, no true decision would ever occur, but merely logical deduction (Derrida 1992, pp. 24–27). Law, therefore, simultaneously requires this paradoxical compliance and reinvention, since every application of a norm is in a

---

than itself, thereby keeping within itself the mark of the past element, and already letting itself be vitiated by the mark of its relation to the future element, this trace being related no less to what is called the future than to what is called the past, and constituting what is called the present by means of this very relation to what it is not" (Derrida 1982, p. 13).

[9] See also Henderson (2018), especially her reading of *Hamdi v. Rumsfeld,* 542 U.S. 507 (2004) as an instance in which judicial interpretation both repeats and alters an existing legal-discursive framework.

way a revision, an alteration of law, through a decision that cannot be fully derived from prior norms and must nevertheless present itself as consistent with previous iterations. Each interpretive act reopens meaning, exposing its apparent stability to contingency and responsiveness to context and Derrida insists on this persistent tension between singularity and norm: "Each case is other, each decision is different and requires an absolutely unique interpretation, which no existing coded rule can or ought to guarantee absolutely" (Derrida 1992, p. 23).

Thus, iterative hermeneutical interpretation holds a certain perspective on law as a dynamic process of ongoing rearticulation and not as a closed system, a process in which legal meaning is not fixed but emerges through continuous engagement with norms, and where each act of application redefines the norm, contributing to the ongoing development of legal meaning. Interpretation here is not a flaw in the system to be minimized, but the very essence of legal intelligibility, since law persists and evolves precisely because interpretation is always at work.

2.3 Theoretical Assumptions of Classical Legal Methods of Interpretation

The classical methods of legal interpretation—grammatical, systematic, historical, and teleological—are often presented by legal doctrine and more often in legal practice as neutral tools of textual analysis, each serving to make legal norms clear and understandable by appealing to different facets of a text or its context. In spite of developments in contemporary methodology, this presumption of neutrality frequently goes unanalyzed and these methods are still used as instruments, a sort of set of algorithmic steps detached from any particular purpose, free from any underlying assumptions, a number of transparent techniques employed "scientifically" to uncover a meaning that remains obscure due to some regrettable circumstance. However, each of these methods relies on its own epistemological and philosophical presuppositions, which implicitly shape how legal meaning is understood and justified by locating aporia in a specific register and proposing a corresponding mode of mediation.

The grammatical method considers that the meaning of a legal text can be ascertained by scrutinizing its language, by looking at its syntax and vocabulary according to the ordinary usage. It privileges what is often termed "the plain meaning of the text" as the common sense codified in dictionaries and grammatical rules with the underlying assumption that language has, to begin with, this capacity of conveying a definite meaning when examined properly. On this ground, legal norms are best understood in their actual formulation with minimal recourse to extratextual factors. Legislators are presumed to have chosen their words carefully and reading those words in their ordinary sense reveals the intended meaning of the legal norm (Scalia and Garner 2012, pp. 33–41, 56–58). This approach enjoys a favored position in many legal systems, especially those of continental European law, influenced by formalist or positivist traditions, since the appeal to fidelity to the text is thought to guard against subjective judicial improvisation. As it was stated in legal doctrine, the grammatical method must form the starting point of any interpretive inquiry and every interpretation begins with the wording, since one cannot interpret what one has not first read (Larenz 1991, pp. 320–324, 343).

The systematic method requires that the interpretation of a particular legal provision must take into account the wider legal order to which it belongs, assuming that the legal system as a whole is internally coherent. No provision should be understood in isolation, but interpreted in harmony with other legal texts, with the general principles of law and with the architecture of law as a system. When contradictions between norms or provisions arise, the method seeks to resolve them by situating the contested provision within the wider normative network, so that the resulting interpretation preserves the logical unity of the legal order (Larenz 1991, pp. 324–328). Systematic interpretation plays a central role in civil-law traditions, due to their focus on legal dogmatics grounded on comprehensive codes, embedded in a more general organic vision of law.

The historical method emphasizes the origins and formation of legal provisions, attempting to reconstruct the intent of the legislature or the meaning of a provision at the time of its enactment, relying on extratextual sources such as legislative debates, preparatory works (*travaux préparatoires*), historical commentary, and other records of the drafting process. The premise is that the insight into the proper interpretation of law today is assured by uncovering what lawmakers aimed to achieve, or how a norm was originally perceived by its contemporaries. In this perspective, interpretation is not merely an act of decoding a static text but a recovering of the historical life that informs it. The assumption on which this method operates is that anchoring interpretation in the original intent or original understanding can prevent arbitrariness and constrain judges by the authority of the past (Larenz 1991, pp. 328–333). The method has a venerable tradition through the historical school of jurisprudence, which viewed the legal system as an organic whole evolving through history bound by rational consistency (von Savigny 1867, pp. 8–9) and gained prominence through Friedrich Carl von Savigny and the nineteenth century *Historische Rechtsschule*, the German historical school, which held that law is an expression of a people's spirit, *Volksgeist*, and must be interpreted with reference to its historical development (von Savigny 1867, pp. 11–15, 171–173).

The teleological or purposive method, *interpretatio secundum finem*, directs attention to the aims or values that a legal norm is designed to promote. It assumes that one cannot fully understand a law without grasping the end it serves or the problem it addresses. The interpreter is allowed to go beyond the literal text and consider the broader purpose or function of the norm within its social, ethical, or constitutional context. This method often requires making value-based judgments and normative evaluations about what outcome would best further the general objectives of a legal norm. A judge using this method asks: What goal or purpose does the norm serve? What social setting or problem-situation does it presuppose? What ratio of law or underlying system of goals gives the norm its point? And how should the interpretation of the norm reflect the values and purposes that guide legal decision-making (Aarnio 1983, pp. 19, 47–50, 245–249)? In legal systems with strong constitutional traditions or comprehensive human-rights commitments, this method is used in aligning legal interpretation with fundamental principles, where courts might interpret provisions in light of constitutional values like human rights or democracy, preferring the reading that best realizes those values.[10] This approach is grounded in the idea that law is not an end in itself but a means to achieve societal goals, thus, the key to applying a legal norm correctly lies in discerning its objective (Larenz 1991, pp. 333–339, 343–346). Presupposing that interpretation is an engagement with the future-oriented dimension of legal norms, this perspective stands in some tension with strict textualism or rigid formalism. However, considering that legal rules are parts of larger projects, the method often infuses legal interpretation with a normative dialogue about ends and means.

With this outline of the classical methods in their conventional usage, with their own specific assumptions, the way in which each method is reframed can be further examined under the two competing paradigms—structured legalist and iterative hermeneutics.

3 Legal Logic: Mediating Aporia in Interpretation

3.1 Reframing Classical Interpretive Methods by the Two Divergent Paradigms

Examining the classical methods through each of the paradigms will show both affinities between the assumptions of each method with a particular paradigm, and how, nevertheless, each paradigm can reorient those methods according to its own underlying presuppositions.

From a structured legalist perspective, with a closure-oriented view on law, the methods become tools for reinforcing internal coherence, hierarchy, and the formal integrity of the legal system. Legal language is assumed to be relatively stable, and the use of the methods must keep interpretive outcomes tied to authoritative texts and to the legal order as a whole. The grammatical and systematic methods are particularly consistent with this paradigm since they also treat language as a reliable

[10] The German Federal Constitutional Court, for example, often employs a value-oriented approach, invoking the idea of an "objective value order" (*objektive Wertordnung*) in the constitution to guide the meaning of laws. See BVerfG, 15 January 1958, 1 BvR 400/51, BVerfGE 7, 198 (Lüth). The Court of Justice of the European Union likewise interprets EU law considering general principles and fundamental rights, including democracy and the rule of law. In *Internationale Handelsgesellschaft* (Case 11/70, 17 December 1970), the Court held that EU law prevails over conflicting national constitutional law, while respect for fundamental rights forms part of the general principles of EU law. In *Kadi and Al Barakaat International Foundation v Council and Commission* (ECJ, Joined Cases C-402/05 P and C-415/05 P, 3 September 2008), the Court annulled EU measures implementing UN sanctions on the ground that they violated fundamental rights, thereby affirming the autonomy of the EU legal order.

medium of meaning and see legal texts as internally transparent once each provision is situated in its proper logical and structural context. Under this paradigm, the grammatical method ties interpretation to the wording of the legal text, while the systematic method ties that wording to the hierarchy of the legal system. However, the historical and teleological methods have a more uncertain place and are regarded with caution, since they are most prone to importing uncontrolled external meaning through historical sources or policy-oriented purposes whose legal relevance is not self-evident from the text or from the internal criteria of legality. As such, they are considered acceptable to the extent that they are authorized by superior norms or used in a manner circumscribed by the rules of the legal system. For example, a judge might rely on legislative history only if the applicable norm explicitly permits reference to preparatory materials or if there is a superior norm allowing resort to such resources to clarify ambiguities. Similarly, teleological reasoning would be considered legitimate when the purposes have been formally codified or can be derived from constitutional or legal principles. Therefore, under this paradigm, interpretation functions as an exercise in containment. Every interpretive move must be traceable to the established legal bases, so that no new meaning enters the system without permission from within the system itself. From a logical perspective, this requirement gives legal reasoning a closure-oriented form, analogous to a monotonic model, in which once a conclusion follows from accepted premises, it remains stable unless further considerations are explicitly recognized by law.

The iterative hermeneutic paradigm changes the function of the methods, revealing that none can predetermine its own application, and, instead of closing interpretation, may leave more than one legally plausible path open. The grammatical method is not immune to difficulties since words often carry multiple meanings which raise the problem of polysemy, and the evolution of linguistic conventions over time makes the attempts to reach a singular static sense unreliable when confronted with vagueness or unforeseen usage of terms. The appeal to the "plain meaning" of the text inevitably encounters the inherent instability of language itself, and apparently simple terms can prove contestable, while efforts to clarify them can show that their meaning is not determined by convention alone, but continually shifts with context, and the passage of time. What structured legalism sees as a secure starting point, relying on syntax and vocabulary, iterative hermeneutics sees as another site of interpretive dispute, a place where meaning can proliferate. The pursuit of a unique "correct" interpretation may fail since focusing on plain meaning may not resolve ambiguity so much as it may expose the play within language—each attempt at clarification through this method can uncover new layers of significance and open a field of interpretive variation in which meaning is continually deferred rather than decisively settled. Therefore, what this method presents as clear and objective can, under this paradigm, reveal itself to be contingent and debatable.

In a similar way, the systematic method intended to ensure coherence may, instead, expose latent contradictions and gaps within the legal order, since a thorough attempt to harmonize one provision with the rest can highlight fractures or ambiguities in higher norms. Whenever the parts of the system do not seamlessly fit, it becomes necessary to innovate, to adjust doctrines or recognize exceptions, at which point, interpretation can no longer rely on the coherence of the system but must reconstruct it, requiring creative reconciliation not specifically provided by law as such. Various applications of this method reveal this critical aspect and what structured legalism would treat as an anomaly to minimize is, in fact, indicative of a deeper logical flexibility. In effect, legal reasoning has a defeasible character: general rules apply "all else being equal" but still they can be overridden when special circumstances, countervailing principles, or superior norms arise. In this light, the logic of law is not a deductive abstract mechanism as in the structured legalist paradigm, but defeasible, allowing conclusions to be withdrawn or modified as a result of new premises, such as updated or additional facts or higher norms. Also, the emphasis on internal coherence within this method can lead to circular reasoning since interpreting each part by reference to the whole, and the whole by reference to its parts, may obscure tensions rather than resolve them. Nonetheless, systematic interpretation remains central to legal practice precisely because of the aspiration and often the need for coherence in law, and, as Ronald Dworkin points out, an interpretation that does not consider norms as part of a totality and disregards the holistic context risks undermining the integrity of law itself (Dworkin 1986, pp. 176–180, 225–234, 239–254).

The historical method seeks an authoritative origin to restrain interpretation, however, every turn to history is itself an interpretive act. Depending on which historical sources are considered relevant and selected, and depending on how they are understood, the past can be read in dramatically different ways. As such, interpretation becomes less about recovering a singular intent and more about constructing a narrative that connects past and present in a plausible way. Philosophical hermeneutics—particularly as developed within the post-Heideggerian tradition by thinkers such as Hans-Georg Gadamer, Paul Ricoeur, and Gianni Vattimo—argues that every act of historical interpretation is conditioned by the present context and the "horizon" of the interpreter, which, while never objective, constitutes the very condition that makes understanding possible, while pure access to original intent becomes illusory (Gadamer 1989/2004, pp. 301–305; Ricoeur 1981/2016, pp. 131–140; Vattimo 1997, pp. 4–6, 13–14, 39–40). To understand the past, we inevitably do so through the lenses of the present and this condition turns the very effort to be faithful to history into an act colored by current perspectives. From an iterative hermeneutic perspective, since there is no immediate access to former events, but rather they are selectively reassembled in light of the historical, linguistic, and institutional horizon, any appeal to an original meaning is already an interpretive move. In seeking to limit interpretation, this method paradoxically introduces new uncertainties: whose historical account, and which aspect of the multifaceted "intent" should take precedence? The search for an authentic historical meaning often uncovers a plurality of plausible intentions and understandings, revealing that even origins are contestable.

Finally, the teleological method used to clarify a norm by looking at the goal it supposedly must achieve raises the prior question of which purpose should count as legally decisive. Laws often serve multiple aims, those aims can evolve and different interpreters may disagree on which one should take precedence. The method cannot guarantee a singular outcome since it has to broaden the debate: one judge might see the purpose of a legal norm as protecting individual rights, while another may emphasize public safety, leading to divergent applications of the same text. From a structured legalist perspective, the openness of this method to policy and principle can let judges infuse their personal preferences under the guise of discerning objectives, thereby subverting legislative intent or the separation of powers. Meanwhile, from an iterative hermeneutic perspective, assuming a single aim can be misleading, since legal texts frequently embody several competing goals. In complex legislation, different stakeholders may have had different objectives and even the intent of a single legislator can be multifaceted or indeterminate. Thus, what is presented as the unique purpose of a legal norm might mask a plurality of goals or values and deciding which of those to prioritize is itself an act of interpretation, and often one exposed to contestation.

From this standpoint, the very interpretive methods that structured legalism uses to resolve ambiguity are recast as moments of interpretive invention in the face of various dimensions of aporia in law. A Derridean insight helps explain why this inversion remains permanently possible: no textual structure, no discursive configuration can exhaust the potentiality of its own interpretation, "no context can entirely enclose it. Nor any code"; every sign "can break with every given context, engendering an infinity of new contexts in a manner which is absolutely illimitable" (Derrida 1988, pp. 9, 12). No matter how clear or settled a legal text may appear, it can never completely determine how it will be interpreted in every future instance, because there is always a gap between rule and application, an undecidability that the interpreter must bridge, thereby extending or transforming the meaning in the process. Iterative hermeneutics embraces this impossibility of complete closure instead of trying to minimize or eliminate it and recognizes interpretation as a creative act through which law continuously reconstitutes itself. Every method of interpretation appears in this perspective as a site where new meanings can be generated instead of a neutral instrument for recovering a preexisting significance.

Thus, the classical methods of interpretation have no intrinsic authority in isolation, and their function depends on the paradigm in which they are employed.[11] Structured legalism uses them to contain and secure meaning, whereas iterative hermeneutics uses them to highlight uncertainty and spur the evolution of meaning. While the first employs them as instruments of constraint and determinacy, the second reveals those same methods as sites of rupture and reinvention. If, from a Kelsenian perspective, each method is explicitly directed to the project of normative stability with grammatical and systematic interpretation ensuring fidelity to the text and the system, whereas historical and teleological interpretation are kept on a short leash to avoid introducing extrinsic ideas, from a Derridean perspective, the same methods demonstrate the impossibility of sealing law off from the play of

[11] Sunstein's claim that there is nothing that interpretation "just is" supports the point that no interpretive method is self-authorizing: each method mediates differently the tension between closure and responsiveness (Sunstein 2015, pp. 193–212).

interpretation, even when grammar and system try to secure a determinate meaning, while history and purpose only multiply interpretive possibilities. In short, what is a mechanism to reinforce normative order for Kelsen is, for Derrida, a means by which law remains open and continually rearticulated.

Since the very same technique can serve either to narrow or expand interpretive possibilities, depending on the orientation of the interpreter, these methods are not only non-neutral, but also function as meta-normative means through which different visions of what law is and what interpretation ought to do are expressed and enacted. The contrast between the two paradigms with their divergent demands reveals a somewhat paradoxical aspect, that every act of legal interpretation simultaneously relies on the stability of law and contributes to its change. Thus, the question becomes whether and how the requirement of structured legalism that law is and should be logical can still be fulfilled given the iterative hermeneutics perspective on legal meaning. If, however, aporia is structural rather than exceptional, these dimensions of legal reasoning cannot remain analytically discrete, but must be brought into relation within a level of analysis capable of accounting for their interaction.

3.2 *Legal Logic as a Meta-theoretical Framework*

At this point the framework I advance must be distinguished from other influential jurisprudential approaches that likewise seek to move beyond the opposition between the two paradigmatic approaches. My account shares with Dworkin the view that law is not a system of rules whose meaning is given prior to interpretation, but the main purpose of my framework is not to ground legal rationality primarily in the constructive identification of the morally best interpretation of legal practice (Dworkin 1986, pp. 87–101, 225–254), but to identify the formal and meta-theoretical conditions under which interpretive plurality can remain rationally structured even where no single interpretive outcome is guaranteed in advance. In a similar way, although it converges with Alexy's theory in rejecting deductive formalism and in treating legal reasoning as constrained by requirements of internal and external justification (Alexy 1989, pp. 1–8, 221–234), it does not situate rationality chiefly within discourse-theoretical justification alone (Alexy 1989, pp. 188–194), nor within principles and balancing (Alexy 2002, pp. 47–51, 66–69), but tries to articulate a broader logical framework at a different level capable of accounting not only for justificatory practices, but also for defeasibility, semantic instability, normative conflict, and the revisability of legal conclusions. More generally, if post-positivist theories have convincingly shown that law operates through the interaction of the two paradigms, they usually approach this relation through one particular register rather than as a structural problem spanning those dimensions. At times, this has also led to treating this difficulty primarily as a methodological or doctrinal problem arising within adjudication. These theories nevertheless capture essential aspects of legal rationality, but they do not fully explain how semantic instability, defeasibility, normative conflict, and institutional plurality interact and reinforce one another within legal practice.[12] Without developing here a complete account of these interactions, I argue, nevertheless that this tension, through its various dimensions these theories address, is constitutive of legal rationality itself.

For example, in my reading of Hart's theory of "open texture" of law (Hart 1961, pp. 124–132, 140–144), with legal rules that possess a "central core of undisputed meaning" surrounded by a "penumbra of doubt", within which judicial discretion becomes necessary (Hart 1961, p. 12), the "penumbra" is only the visible manifestation of a deeper structural condition inherent in rule-governed practices (Hart 1961, pp. 119–123) while the apparent stability of the "core" itself depends on prior interpretive stabilization, which obscures the mediation required to sustain it. What Hart identifies as semantic uncertainty at the margins can be reinterpreted as the local visibility of a broader structural issue, the fact that although legal rules must guide application, they cannot completely determine in advance the contexts in which they are to be applied. Aporia arises from the gap between rule and application, which Hart's distinction reveals only in part, while his theory addresses the problematic of semantic instability of legal language.

Kelsen's approach to interpretation, which I have already engaged with, conceives legal reasoning as operating within a hierarchical system of norms, where interpretation occurs within a legally authorized range of possible meanings (*Spielraum der Auslegung*), judges selecting among permissible interpretations grounded in higher-order norms. However, the very existence of such a range implies that the relation between norm and application is not entirely determined by the norm itself (Kelsen 1967, pp. 351–355) and, in order to preserve the appearance of derivation, Kelsen tries to contain this plurality within the institutional form, treating it as bounded and pre-structured. The *Spielraum* appears, nevertheless, from my perspective, as the juridically organized expression of an aporetic condition since the hierarchy cannot eliminate the competing demands of determinacy and contingency. What is presented as bounded interpretation presupposes that the norm must be both general enough to belong to a legal order and concrete enough to govern singular cases but still cannot achieve both without interpretive mediation.

Raz's service conception of authority offers a further instructive case, since legal authority provides "exclusionary reasons" that pre-empt individual deliberation, enabling subjects to better conform to reasons that already apply to them (Raz 1999, pp. 35–48; Raz 2009, pp. 136–146). Law replaces first-order reasoning with authoritative directives; nevertheless, identifying the content, scope, and interaction of

[12] See also Henderson (2018), who brings legal interpretation into a Derrida–Dworkin encounter and describes law as marked by "structured undecidability". The present account develops a broader second-order framework by treating legal logic as the meta-theoretical structure through which this tension can be rendered rationally intelligible. If "structured undecidability" designates the irreducible underdetermination of legal meaning, "structured openness" designates the juridical form through which that underdetermination is mediated. The former names a condition of interpretation at the level of meaning; the latter the juridical form of its rational mediation.

those directives already requires interpretation, and their application remains subject to exceptions, conflicts, and changing circumstances. This, on the one hand, suggests a defeasibility that cannot be contained within a strictly monotonic model, and on the other, an already implied openness that the coordinating function of authority seeks to discipline, since authority must both terminate interpretation and depend upon it.

Alexy's theory of principles and balancing is probably one of the most explicit attempts to reconcile legal rationality with interpretive openness. Principles function as optimization requirements (Alexy 2002, pp. 47–48), and the conflicts between them are resolved through balancing guided by proportionality (Alexy 2002, pp. 49–51, 66–69). However, the need for balancing arises precisely because principles do not determine their relative weight in advance. The aporia is generated by the aspiration of legal reasoning to rational justification while it has to confront competing norms whose relation cannot be established prior to application. Since principles have only prima facie priority and acquire concrete weight only through proportionality analysis in light of the factual and legal possibilities of the case, the relations of precedence established by balancing remain conditional rather than absolute; in this sense, balancing has a non-monotonic structure. As such, it can be understood as a modality of legal logic concerned with the argumentative management of normative conflict as a specific form in which aporia appears, making such conflicts unavoidable.

This brief overview supports the idea that the apparent fragmentation of legal theory can be read as a series of responses to the same structural difficulty, which becomes visible with differing intensity depending on the interpretive context. Each theory isolates aspects of semantic indeterminacy, hierarchical constraint, authority, or justificatory balancing as a distinct dimension of legal rationality while relying on a tension it cannot fully absorb within its own terms. The concept of aporia makes explicit precisely the necessity of decision under conditions in which no single dimension of legal reasoning can, by itself, predetermine the outcome.

To further develop this approach, logical instruments capable of modeling revisability, conflict, and contextual sensitivity are required. Contemporary developments in logic already offer several tools for this purpose, but they have often remained tied either to the reconstruction of particular types of legal inferences or to domain-specific applications. The conception of legal logic I advance differs from this orientation by treating it not as a specialized instrument, but as a framework which operates on a level of analysis at which different logical instruments can be integrated in order to capture how legal reasoning remains coherent without presupposing closure.

Legal logic thus appears not opposed to interpretation, but as the means through which its necessity and its mode of operation can be clarified and assessed. If the same interpretive methods can stabilize legal meaning in one setting and unsettle it in another, legal logic must explain how that movement remains rationally manageable. This becomes possible once legal reasoning is framed as an interaction between system and event, rule and application, structure and meaning, interactions which imprint on legal inference a non-monotonic character: outcomes are not irrevocably fixed by initial rules or facts but remain open to recalibration as new normative grounds or contextual information emerge. Unlike monotonic logical systems, closer to a Kelsenian model, where additional premises can never overturn prior conclusions, legal logic must allow revision and sustain adaptability without sacrificing coherence or structural integrity (Codrea 2024, pp. 319–335).

Since legal logic mediates aporia at a meta-theoretical level, it is at this level that the two paradigms can co-constitute the practice of legal reasoning, accounting for both the drive toward closure and for the inevitability of interpretive openness.[13] These apparently irreconcilable approaches can be encompassed by structuring their relation, which is not a compromise in the reductive sense, but rather a deeper methodological stance: a framework through which the internal differentiation of law can be made comprehensible without collapsing into either rigid formalism or unrestricted relativism.

It can manage this gesture by recognizing that law is a normative practice that aspires to consistency and legitimacy while operating within historically contingent, socially pluralistic, and linguistically open contexts. As such, the formal conditions under which normative structures operate in such contexts can be formulated, a task that requires both formal criteria and interpretive judgment, as well as instruments capable of navigating ambiguity rather than eliminating it.

First, the relation between rule and application can be clarified at the level of legal logic. If in structured legalism, this relation is conceived in broadly deductive terms, where application follows from the norm and interpretation is reduced to identifying a pre-existing meaning, in iterative hermeneutics application becomes a site of meaning-production, a moment in which the rule is not merely followed but instantiated in a singular context. Applying a rule can therefore introduce new considerations that reshape the outcome, in a manner analogous to non-monotonic reasoning, where conclusions evolve as additional premises come to light. As a mediating space, legal logic can acknowledge both that norms must be general and logically structured in order to function, and that their meaning remains underdetermined without the event of application. Closely connected to this is the difficulty posed by the generality of norms and the singularity of cases. In structured legalism, the norm governs because it is abstract and universally applicable and generality is prioritized. In iterative hermeneutics, singularity disrupts abstraction, since each case brings with it a context that resists generalization. Legal logic can regulate this tension without resolving it, showing how law can treat similar cases alike while remaining responsive to particularity. Interpretation thus appears not only as a matter of choice, but of rational positioning of the case within the norm, while remaining open to the possibility that the case reshapes the scope of the norm.

Second, the rationality of legal interpretation is preserved in the face of plurality by setting out criteria through which interpretive acts can be judged, justified, and situated within broader discursive practices. The aim of legal logic is disciplined

[13] In Urbina's terms, the two imperatives at work here may be redescribed as competing normative reasons internal to legal interpretation (Urbina 2024, pp. 1661–1740).

openness, not closure, and as such, it can structure the way in which interpretation proceeds without dictating in advance what the outcome must be. Thus, it can transform interpretation from arbitrary subjectivism into a reasoned activity accountable to shared legal standards, even when those standards are themselves contestable.

Although inseparable from hermeneutics it is not reducible to it, since legal logic operates on a distinct plane. If interpretation is the condition under which meaning becomes intelligible, legal logic can function as the epistemic and normative structure that makes interpretation institutionally relevant and conceptually constrained by defining which interpretive acts count as legally relevant or admissible within a normative legal order. In this sense, it would operate not within hermeneutics, but on hermeneutics, as a meta-hermeneutic framework that formalizes the conditions under which interpretive plurality remains coherent within institutional discourse. In this way, the fluidity of meaning is disciplined through formal logical instruments, making legal interpretation both rationally sound and normatively bound.

These tensions are managed through an internal plurality of instruments within legal logic, including those yet to be developed insofar as they perform the same theoretical function, a plurality that embodies the spectrum between closure and openness. As shown earlier, the grammatical and systematic methods strive for stability, whereas the historical and teleological methods invite sensitivity to change; moreover, each can function differently depending on the interpretive stance adopted. Legal logic can therefore offer a symmetrical spectrum, a scalable framework with its own parallel formal instruments through which the classical methods can be assessed and prioritized since it is not the methods themselves that determine the outcome, but the logic through which they are integrated into a coherent structure.[14] Legal logic can be understood then as a reflective practice in which multiple possible inferences and interpretive moves are evaluated within a unified reasoning structure. Ensuring that novel arguments or exceptions are incorporated through rational analysis rather than opaque intuition or simple acts of decision, flexibility is transformed from a threat to law's coherence into one of its structural features.

Finally, legal logic can accommodate both structured legalism and hermeneutical iteration by taking institutional dialogue into account, considering that courts interpret the law in relation to past judgments, legislative texts, scholarly commentaries, and evolving social expectations. Even the most formal decisions draw on prior interpretations, while the most innovative rulings seek to remain comprehensible and generally coherent within the tradition they transform. This apparent circularity constitutes the actual institutional dimension of law to which legal logic can provide a conceptual account and a formalized language.

Both paradigms can be encompassed within legal logic because it is not committed to one pole of the dichotomy, but to the articulation of their relation. It does not

[14] Vermeule's account of interpretive choice shows that the selection of interpretive doctrine does not follow directly from any single theory of legal authority, but depends on institutional capacities, empirical uncertainty, decision costs, and comparative doctrinal effects. The present account reframes this problem as a second-order mediation of aporia through legal logic (Vermeule 2000, pp. 74–149).

eliminate the necessity of interpretation, nor does it deny the importance of form, rather, it frames the conditions under which both form and interpretation can interact rationally within law. Understood in these terms, it is a logic of legal reasoning under conditions of indeterminacy, not opposed to interpretive openness, but its rational form.

3.3 Formal Logical Instruments for Modeling Legal Interpretation

Since aporia is internally differentiated, manifesting itself as semantic instability, defeasibility, norm conflict, contradiction, epistemic update or justificatory contestation, legal logic cannot force interpretation into a single inferential model.[15] Legal reasoning does several different things at once: it revises conclusions, updates meanings, handles duties that conflict or depend on context, continues reasoning despite inconsistencies, and weighs arguments that defeat or modify one another. No single logic captures all of this, and the plurality of instruments is required by the plurality of the difficulties themselves. The classical methods remain the ordinary language of legal interpretation, but the symmetrical spectrum of formal logical instruments explains why the problems they try to address do not call for the same kind of reasoning. The relevance regarding aporia is in rendering its differentiation more explicit, traceable, and accountable at the level of legal logic itself. Even where it appears substantively or doctrinally plausible, legal interpretation may be rationally defective if it mediates aporia through a form unsuited to its structure: a defeasible question treated deductively, a clash of normative requirements treated as though it were exhausted by semantic clarification, or a contradiction prematurely dissolved rather than governed. What legal logic makes visible, therefore, is not maximal closure, but the rational force of an interpretation that mediates aporia in a manner responsive to its form. The criterion of legal logic is the intelligible correspondence between the dimensions of aporia and the interpretive mode through which it is addressed.

In actual interpretation, these dimensions of aporia are often intertwined, since interpretation may begin from what seems to be a semantic difficulty and reveal that the decisive issue is one of normative conflict, or proceed from an apparent conflict and show that part of it was produced by semantic ambiguity. Interpretation does not begin by consciously sorting cases into fixed categories in advance, but legal logic can reconstruct the structure of aporia by identifying what remains unresolved

[15] Fallon's central insight is that legal meaning is not fixed by a single privileged referent: semantic or literal, contextual, real conceptual, intended, reasonable, and previously interpreted meanings may each be legally eligible in different contexts (Fallon Jr 2015, pp. 1235–1308). This plurality of eligible referents appears here as an expression of aporia. Legal logic mediates among them at a second-order level, preserving the legal constraint of meaning without collapsing it into either prelegal linguistic fact or unconstrained normative judgment.

once successive modes of interpretation have been exhausted. As such, it cannot abolish decision, but it can discipline it, narrow it, and make explicit why this closure, rather than another permissible one, is being adopted. Where first-order interpretation leaves more than one solution equally justified, legal logic does not uncover a uniquely correct solution but stabilizes one lawful closure by subjecting the remaining possibilities to second-order demands of appropriateness, coherence, competence, and justificatory transparency.

In order to make explicit the dynamics that rationally sustain the claims of law to coherence, adaptability, and normative force, given the tensions between the two paradigms, legal logic must engage with formal instruments suited for mediating the various dimensions of aporia. It can draw on the developments in formal logic that allow for defeasibility, epistemic update, semantic modeling, and reasoned contestation through instruments such as non-monotonic logics, dynamic epistemic frameworks, advanced deontic systems, paraconsistent theories, formal argumentation structures, and semantic logic, whose contribution lies in its ability to make variation in meaning understandable and formally accountable.[16] As I previously showed, such instruments do not replace interpretation but clarify the inferential conditions under which interpretation remains rationally accountable, each primarily disclosing a dimension of aporia identified above, while their combination provides the formal resources through which legal logic can function as a genuinely meta-theoretical framework. Accordingly, the relation between aporia and formal instruments is diagnostic rather than classificatory, since a single interpretive difficulty may require several instruments, while one instrument may illuminate different difficulties depending on the legal context. Taken together, these formal instruments can address interpretive challenges across the full range of classical methods of legal interpretation, even though each of those methods tends to align more closely with one paradigm than the other.

Various types of non-monotonic logic are relevant to legal interpretation because they explain how a conclusion can be legally warranted while remaining defeasible, thereby connecting the demand for systemic integrity with the emphasis on contextual responsiveness of each paradigm. A conclusion may follow from the available facts and applicable norms, then lose its force once an exception or a higher-order norm becomes relevant. This occurs regularly in legal reasoning, where general rules are applied to concrete cases and where the initial legal result may have to be suspended, limited, or displaced by further considerations.[17] These types of logic

[16] For a useful technical overview of formal approaches to legal reasoning, including non-monotonic logic, argumentation theory, and formal semantics, see Bench-Capon and Prakken (2008). I use their discussion mainly as a point of reference for the formal tools involved, but my concern here is different: not the technical reconstruction of legal inference as such, but the way these tools can help clarify the tension between stability and revisability in legal interpretation.

[17] For a context-sensitive and conditionally revisable approach in EU jurisprudence, which seems similar to non-monotonic reasoning in its capacity to reconsider prior conclusions while preserving systemic coherence, see CJEU, 20.03.2018, *Criminal proceedings against Menci*, C-524/15, where the Court held that the *ne bis in idem* principle may be limited when a duplication of proceedings pursues objectives of general interest and satisfies requirements of coordination and pro-

allow legal outcomes to depend on a determinate normative background while remaining open to further specification, making it possible to account for revision without treating it as a failure of legal rationality (Gabbay and Woods 2007, pp. viii–ix; Bochman 2007, pp. 557–559).

The juridical landscape is marked by evolving precedents, interpretive shifts, and institutional reactions to social transformation which reveals the temporal dimension of legal knowledge. Dynamic Epistemic Logic (DEL) can model the ways in which epistemic states, and, by analogy, legal-interpretive positions, are updated within discourse through informational and communicative events (Moss 2015, pp. 261–312; van Ditmarsch et al. 2007). The need for such updating is inherent to the diachronic nature of law, since law can be considered as a system at a given moment in time and through the ongoing reinterpretation and reshaping of norms (Ricoeur 1988, pp. 104–126, 230–235). Legal logic must therefore internalize temporality by registering changes in information as well as the institutional memory through which law preserves its intelligibility and authority across historically variable contexts. Through DEL, it can supply the formal account for a meaning which is neither static nor self-sufficient but is recalibrated as new judgments, legislation, or doctrinal developments appear.[18] These recalibrations are in line with the hermeneutical understanding of legal reasoning as a historical practice, while preserving the structured legalist concern that such changes are integrated and traced to a broader system.

Deontic logic, particularly in its dyadic and input/output forms, enhances legal logic by providing more nuanced models for legal obligations, permissions, and prohibitions, especially when these are conditional or contextually bound (Carmo and Jones 2002, pp. 265–266; Makinson and van der Torre 2000, pp. 383–408). If classical deontic logic has long struggled to address the problem of contrary-to-duty obligations and norm conflicts, the newer variants allow for layered normativity, representing the interrelation of rules that govern both primary and secondary obligations triggered

portionality; CJEU, 29.06.2016, *Criminal proceedings against Kossowski*, C-486/14, in which the Court determined that a decision not to prosecute in one Member State precludes further proceedings in another only where it reflects a final determination adopted after a sufficiently detailed investigation; and CJEU, 24.10.2018, *XC and Others*, C-234/17, where the Court clarified that national procedural autonomy does not require the reopening of proceedings for every alleged infringement of EU law, thereby illustrating that revisability within the system remains conditional rather than unlimited.

[18] For the Court's responsiveness to societal realities, illustrating the evolving interpretation of legal meaning over time, see ECJ, 11.07.2006, *Chacón Navas v Eurest Colectividades SA*, C-13/05, where the Court initially adopted a restrictive interpretation of "disability" under Directive 2000/78/EC, later refined in CJEU, 11.04.2013, *HK Danmark*, Joined Cases C-335/11 and C-337/11, in light of the UN Convention on the Rights of Persons with Disabilities; CJEU, 5.06.2018, *Coman and Others v Inspectoratul General pentru Imigrări and Ministerul Afacerilor Interne*, C-673/16, where the Court recognized same-sex spouses for the purposes of freedom of movement, reflecting the change in the interpretation of "spouse" in light of fundamental rights and changing social context; and CJEU, 24.06.2019, *Commission v Poland (Independence of the Supreme Court)*, C-619/18, reaffirming and developing the principle of judicial independence in response to novel rule-of-law challenges.

by violation (Carmo and Jones 2002, pp. 265–343).[19] Therefore, deontic logic offers a methodologically precise means of accounting for both the structured command orientation favored by the structured legalist paradigm and the layered, context-sensitive duties identified in an iterative hermeneutical reading of legal discourse.

Paraconsistent logic responds to the fact that legal systems regularly confront internal contradictions or "legal dialetheias", whether in constitutional conflicts, overlapping jurisdictions, or transitional legal regimes (Priest 2006, pp. 182–188). Where classical logic would collapse under contradiction through *ex contradictione quodlibet*, paraconsistent logic allows reasoning to proceed when norms or judgments are in tension within such conflictual legal settings (Priest 2006, pp. 117–122, 221–225).[20] The possibility of sustaining legal reasoning in these circumstances corresponds to the practical functioning of legal systems, in which coherence is often provisional or incomplete, disputed and revisable, and providing it a formal expression can account for the iterative hermeneutical critique of consistency as a metaphysical ideal, while simultaneously preserving the structured legalist project of a legal system whose validity is not wholly undermined by conflict (Carnielli and Coniglio 2016, pp. 1–28).

In practice, law requires a discursive space in which competing readings are proposed, challenged, modified, and either defeated or upheld within institutional procedures. Formal argumentation theory clarifies this process by representing the justificatory force of an interpretation in terms of its supports and vulnerabilities: its grounding in precedent and principles, the procedural conditions under which it is advanced, burdens and standards of proof, admissibility constraints, conflicts between rules and assumptions, applicability claims, and priority relations such as *lex specialis*, *lex posterior*, and *lex superior* (Dung 1995, pp. 321–329; Prakken and Sartor 1996, pp. 332–338; Bench-Capon and Prakken 2008,

[19] For the Court's layered and context-sensitive reasoning in reconciling obligations, permissions, and prohibitions, which can be seen as applications, in a reconstructive sense, of modern deontic logic, see ECJ, 5.04.1979, *Pubblico Ministero v Ratti*, Case 148/78, where the Court held that, once the period for implementation has expired, a Member State may not rely on its failure to implement a directive in order to impose obligations on individuals contrary to that directive, thereby expressing the conditional binding force of legal norms; ECJ, 19.01.2010, *Kücükdeveci v Swedex GmbH & Co KG*, C-555/07, in which the Court required the disapplication of a national rule conflicting with EU fundamental rights, demonstrating normative hierarchy and conflict resolution; and CJEU, 26.02.2013, *Melloni v Ministerio Fiscal*, C-399/11, affirming that Member States may not apply higher national fundamental-rights standards where these undermine the primacy, effectiveness and unity of EU law.

[20] See ECtHR, 11 April 2019, *Mariyka Popova and Asen Popov v Bulgaria*, 11260/10, where the Court acknowledged deep and persistent divergences in national case law but, given the existence of legal mechanisms for resolving them, found no violation of Article 6 § 1, illustrating how legal systems may remain operational despite a degree of inconsistency; and ECtHR, 6 December 2007, *Beian v Romania* (No 1), 30658/05, where the Court held that incoherence in domestic jurisprudence on statutory entitlements violated Article 6 § 1, affirming that systemic inconsistency, if left unaddressed, may breach the right to a fair trial.

pp. 1–7).[21] By tracking the argumentative movement within legal procedure, these instruments bring the two paradigms into relation, acknowledging that rational determination cannot replace the act of judgment required by moments of undecidability.

Lastly, semantic logic, understood broadly as the formal analysis of meaning, reference, and truth-conditions, is perhaps the most foundational of the logics considered here. It operates not at the level of rules, but at the level of meaning itself, redirecting the focus from syntactic validity to the interpretive operations through which legal terms acquire content within particular settings (Tarski 1944, pp. 341–355). It is therefore essential for understanding both the classical methods and their reframing under the opposing paradigms. From a structured legalist perspective, it clarifies how legal norms maintain their identity through stable reference, enabling abstract and general rules to be applied consistently, while from an iterative hermeneutical perspective, it formalizes the dependence of meaning on institutional and linguistic variation. It also allows the classical methods to be understood as distinct but interconnected operations upon semantic content (Alexy 1989, pp. 234–250) where grammatical and systematic methods seek coherence within a presumed semantic field, while the historical and teleological methods recontextualize that field in light of temporal and purposive dimensions. Rather than treating these methods as hierarchically ordered or externally imposed, semantic logic shows that they are internal modalities of sense-making, each of which can be modeled and evaluated in light of its contribution to the organization of legal meaning.[22]

These formal instruments provide not merely additional techniques, but a rational, scalable architecture capable of modeling, regulating, and stabilizing the interpretive process, without, however, imposing a specific decision as its final outcome. In this respect, they fulfill the same function as the classical methods of interpretation, which have historically served to discipline legal meaning within institutional

[21] See ECtHR, 30 June 2005, *Bosphorus Hava Yolları Turizm ve Ticaret Anonim Şirketi v Ireland*, no. 45036/98; ECtHR, 29 June 2007, *O'Halloran and Francis v United Kingdom*, nos. 15809/02 and 25624/02; and ECJ, 20 February 1979, *Rewe-Zentral AG v Bundesmonopolverwaltung für Branntwein* (*Cassis de Dijon*), Case 120/78. Each case requires a choice between competing arguments and the legal reasoning used for ordering rival considerations can be reconstructed through formal argumentation models: the relation between EU obligations and Convention review in *Bosphorus*, the right to silence and public-safety regulation in *O'Halloran and Francis*, or market freedom and national regulatory autonomy in *Cassis de Dijon*.

[22] See ECJ, 12.11.1969, *Stauder v City of Ulm – Sozialamt*, Case 29/69, which resolved interpretive ambiguity across language versions through contextual and purposive interpretation, illustrating the interaction between textual meaning and broader normative considerations; ECJ, 16.07.2009, *Infopaq International A/S v Danske Dagblades Forening*, C-5/08, which held that even short textual extracts may be protected where they reflect the "author's own intellectual creation", thereby highlighting the legal significance of minimal units of expression; and ECJ, 17.11.1983, *Firma E. Merck v Hauptzollamt Hamburg-Jonas*, Case 292/82, ECLI:EU:C:1983:335, para. 12, where the Court held that, in interpreting a provision of Community law, it is necessary to consider not only its wording, but also the context in which it occurs and the objects of the rules of which it forms part.

practice. However, whereas these classical methods operate heuristically and remain fundamentally vulnerable to the unaccountable theoretical commitments of the interpreter, as previously shown, as well as to the implicit and sometimes opaque contingencies of historical and institutional traditions, the application of formal logical instruments clarifies and explicitly organizes interpretive rationality, ensuring that within the use of any classical method there unfolds a verifiable, traceable, and accountable inferential process. Moreover, even if not explicitly used in legal practice, these formal logical instruments successfully model patterns of legal reasoning confronting aporia which are already visible in case law.

4 Conclusions

The conceptual tension between structured legalism illustrated by Kelsen's theory and iterative hermeneutical openness exemplified by Derrida marks the boundaries of law constituted by two incompatible but interdependent imperatives: the imperative for closure, for a law that speaks with the force of logical necessity, and the imperative for responsiveness, for a law that encounters each case anew. Since legal meaning is not self-given, interpretation is not a secondary device activated only in moments of obscurity, but the primary mode through which law acquires effectiveness and normative force. As Ronald Dworkin observed, law is "an interpretive concept" shaped and sustained by the interpretive stance adopted toward it (Dworkin 1986, pp. 45–68, 87–92). But such a stance must itself be framed by a logical structure if it is to remain accountable and coherent, even though that structure cannot be static in the way the structured legalist perspective assumes.

I argued that legal logic is not reducible to deductive logical schemes, nor is it a repository of discretionary methods, but functions as the framework that enables interpretation to unfold within a space that maintains both structure and generality on the one hand, and openness and singularity on the other. Interpretation becomes intelligible and legally relevant when guided by a logical architecture capable of sustaining this double movement—toward coherence and toward responsiveness. Even the classical methods of legal interpretation do not function autonomously and their normative force derives from the legal logic that binds them into a rational practice: if structured legalist interpretation uses them to preserve consistency and hierarchy of law and iterative hermeneutical interpretation reactivates them in light of new contexts and evolving discourses, legal logic encompasses both: not by collapsing the differences between the two opposites, but by enabling their generative, constructive potential. As such, it recognizes that rules structure the space of decision, that each decision, in turn, gives meaning to the rule and that legal logic, within this oscillation, mediates aporia not by closing it, but by formalizing the structures through which it is reasoned and decided. Thus, legal logic can structure aporetic mediation by becoming the framework within which interpretation can be rationally organized without becoming rigid, and flexible without becoming arbitrary, transforming the plurality of methods into a more coherent practice and turning legal interpretation into a form of disciplined normativity that would otherwise be exposed either to uncritical application or to unfettered discretion.

The formal instruments of legal logic are not supplementary to legal interpretation but disclose and clarify the underlying conditions under which interpretation takes place, answering, in the end, to the enduring juridical demand that law remain rationally intelligible, even where that intelligibility can no longer be understood as immediate or purely deductive. Legal logic is not a single formal system, but its unity lies in its function, operating as a second-order structure through which different inferential regimes— defeasible, deontic, paraconsistent, semantic, epistemic and argumentative—can be coordinated because aporia itself is internally differentiated. Understood in this way, it allows for thinking interpretation as what it always already is: not a deviation from the path of law, but the act by which that path is drawn and through which law becomes not a closed system, nor an open text, but a structured openness for which legal logic provides a rational framework, a meta-theoretical architecture through which various dimensions of aporia must nonetheless always be decided.

References

Aarnio A (1983) Philosophical perspectives in jurisprudence. Acta Philosophica Fennica, vol 36. The Philosophical Society of Finland, Helsinki

Aarnio A (1987) The rational as reasonable: a treatise on legal justification. Law and philosophy library. D. Reidel Publishing Company, Dordrecht

Alexy R (1989) A theory of legal argumentation: the theory of rational discourse as theory of legal justification. Translated by Ruth Adler and Neil MacCormick. Clarendon Press, Oxford

Alexy R (2002) A theory of constitutional rights. Translated by Julian Rivers. Oxford University Press, Oxford

Bench-Capon TJM, Prakken H (2008) Introducing the logic and law corner. J Logic Comput 18(1):1–12

Bochman A (2007) Nonmonotonic reasoning. In: Gabbay DM, Woods J (eds) Handbook of the history of logic, vol 8: The many valued and nonmonotonic turn in logic. North-Holland/Elsevier, Amsterdam, pp 557–632

Butler J (1997) Excitable speech: a politics of the performative. Routledge, New York

Carmo J, Jones AJI (2002) Deontic logic and contrary-to-duties. In: Gabbay DM, Guenthner F (eds) Handbook of philosophical logic, vol 8. Springer, Dordrecht, pp 265–343

Carnielli W, Coniglio ME (2016) Paraconsistent logic: consistency, contradiction and negation. Logic, epistemology, and the unity of science, vol 40. Springer, Cham

Codrea C (2020) The externality of law: Kelsen, Kant, and Nietzsche in a hermeneutic circle. J Romanian Lit Stud 23:368–375

Codrea C (2023) Logică juridică: Curs universitar. Hamangiu Publishing House, Bucharest

Codrea C (2024) Judicial syllogism: integrating non-monotonic logic in a deductive logical form. Eastern J Eur Stud 15(2):319–335

Cornell D (1992) The philosophy of the limit. Routledge, New York

Cover RM (1983) The Supreme Court, 1982 term—foreword: Nomos and narrative. Harv Law Rev 97:4–68

Derrida J (1982) Différance. Translated by A Bass. Margins of philosophy. University of Chicago Press, Chicago

Derrida J (1988) Signature event context. Translated by S Weber and J Mehlman. Limited Inc. Northwestern University Press, Evanston

Derrida J (1992) Force of law: the "mystical foundation of authority". Translated by M Quaintance, D Cornell, M Rosenfeld, DG Carlson (eds) Deconstruction and the possibility of justice. Routledge, New York, pp 3–67

Douzinas C, Warrington R (1994) Justice miscarried: ethics and aesthetics in law. Harvester Wheatsheaf, Hemel Hempstead

Dung PM (1995) On the acceptability of arguments and its fundamental role in nonmonotonic reasoning, logic programming and N-Person games. Artif Intell 77(2):321–357

Dworkin R (1986) Law's empire. Belknap Press of Harvard University Press, Cambridge

Eco U (1976) A theory of semiotics. Indiana University Press, Bloomington

Fallon RH Jr (2015) The meaning of legal "meaning" and its implications for theories of legal interpretation. Univ Chic Law Rev 82(3):1235–1308

Gabbay DM and Woods J (eds) (2007) Handbook of the history of logic, vol 8: The many valued and nonmonotonic turn in logic. North-Holland/Elsevier, Amsterdam

Gadamer H-G (1989/2004) Truth and method, 2nd rev edn. Translation revised by Joel Weinsheimer and Donald G. Marshall. Continuum, London

Goodrich P (1996) Law in the courts of love: literature and other minor jurisprudences. Routledge, London

Grabowski A (2015) Clara non sunt interpretanda vs. omnia sunt interpretanda: a never-ending controversy in Polish legal theory? Revus: J Constitutional Theory Philos Law 27:67–97

Grondin J (1994) Introduction to philosophical hermeneutics. Translated by J Weinsheimer. Foreword by H-G Gadamer. Yale University Press, New Haven

Hage JC (1997) Reasoning with rules: an essay on legal reasoning and its underlying logic. Law and philosophy library, vol 27. Springer Science+Business Media, Dordrecht. Originally published by Kluwer Academic Publishers

Hart HLA (1961) The concept of law. Clarendon Press, Oxford

Henderson LM (2018) Deciding to repeat differently: iterability and decision in judicial decision-making. Eur J Leg Stud 11(1):97–127

Hinz MO (2009) Human rights between universalism and cultural relativism? The need for anthropological jurisprudence in the globalising world. In: Bösl A, Diescho J (eds) Human rights in Africa: legal perspectives on their protection and promotion. Macmillan Education Namibia, Windhoek, pp 3–32

Kelsen H (1967) Pure theory of law. Translation from the second (revised and enlarged) German Edition by Max Knight. University of California Press, Berkeley

Kristeva J (1980/2024) In: Roudiez LS (ed) Desire in language: a semiotic approach to literature and art. Translated by Thomas Gora, Alice Jardine, and Leon S. Roudiez. Columbia University Press, New York

Lacan J (1978/1998) The seminar of Jacques Lacan, Book XI: the four fundamental concepts of psychoanalysis. Edited by Jacques-Alain Miller. Translated by Alan Sheridan. W. W. Norton & Company, New York. First American edition 1978; first Norton paperback 1981; reissued 1998

Larenz K (1991) Methodenlehre der Rechtswissenschaft, 6th revised edn. Springer, Berlin

Llewellyn KN (1960) The common law tradition: deciding appeals. Little, Brown and Company, Boston

MacCormick N (1978/2003) Legal reasoning and legal theory. Clarendon Press/Oxford University Press, Oxford

Makinson D, van der Torre LWN (2000) Input/output logics. J Philos Logic 29(4):383–408

Marmor A (2005) Interpretation and legal theory, 2nd edn. Hart Publishing, Oxford

Masuelli S (2002) 'In claris non fit interpretatio': Alle origini del brocardo. Rivista di Diritto Romano II:401–424

Moss LS (2015) Dynamic epistemic logic. In: van Ditmarsch H, Halpern JY, van der Hoek W, Kooi B (eds) Handbook of epistemic logic. College Publications, London, pp 261–312

Nietzsche F (1966) Beyond good and evil: prelude to a philosophy of the future. Translated by Walter Kaufmann. Vintage Books, New York

Prakken H, Sartor G (1996) A dialectical model of assessing conflicting arguments in legal reasoning. Artif Intell Law 4:331–368

Priest G (2006) In contradiction: a study of the transconsistent, 2nd expanded edn. Clarendon Press/Oxford University Press, Oxford

Raz J (1999) Practical reason and norms, 2nd edn. Oxford University Press, Oxford

Raz J (2009) Between authority and interpretation: on the theory of law and practical reason. Oxford University Press, Oxford

Ricoeur P (1981/2016) Hermeneutics and the human sciences: essays on language, action and interpretation. Edited, translated and introduced by John B. Thompson. Cambridge University Press, Cambridge

Ricoeur P (1988) Time and narrative, vol 3. Translated by Kathleen Blamey and David Pellauer. University of Chicago Press, Chicago. Originally published as Temps et récit, vol 3, Paris: Seuil, 1985

Scalia A (2018) Common-law courts in a civil-law system: the role of United States federal courts in interpreting the constitution and laws. In: Gutmann A (ed) A matter of interpretation: federal courts and the law, new edn. Princeton University Press, Princeton, pp 3–47

Scalia A, Garner BA (2012) Reading law: the interpretation of legal texts, 1st edn. Thomson/West, St. Paul

Schott C (2001) "Interpretatio cessat in claris" – Auslegungsfähigkeit und Auslegungsbedürftigkeit in der juristischen Hermeneutik. In: Schröder J (ed) Theorie der Interpretation vom Humanismus bis zur Romantik – Rechtswissenschaft, Philosophie, Theologie. Franz Steiner Verlag, Stuttgart, pp 155–189

Sunstein CR (2015) There is nothing that interpretation just is. Constitutional Commentary 30(2):193–212

Tarski A (1944) The semantic conception of truth and the foundations of semantics. Philos Phenomenol Res 4(3):341–376

Urbina FJ (2024) Reasons for interpretation. Columbia Law Rev 124(6):1661–1740

van Ditmarsch H, van der Hoek W, Kooi B (2007) Dynamic epistemic logic. Springer, Berlin

Vattimo G (1997) Beyond interpretation: the meaning of hermeneutics for philosophy. Translated by David Webb. Stanford University Press, Stanford

Vermeule A (2000) Interpretive choice. N Y Univ Law Rev 75(1):74–149

Vismann C (2008) Files: law and media technology. Translated by Geoffrey Winthrop-Young. Stanford University Press, Stanford. Originally published as Akten. Medientechnik und Recht (2000)

von Savigny FC (1867) System of the modern roman law, vol I. Translated from the German by William Holloway. J. Higginbotham, Madras

Watson B (2025) What are we debating when we debate legal interpretation? Boston Univ Law Rev 105(5):1407–1456

Excluded by Definition: The Oversight in Romania's SME Legislation

Despina-Martha Ilucă

Abstract The role of small and medium-sized enterprises (SMEs) in economic growth is widely acknowledged both at the European and national levels. In Romania, however, the legislative framework defining SMEs has given rise to significant practical challenges. Using different methods of interpretation, this study examines the inconsistencies between the intended purpose of SME legislation and the restrictive interpretative practices that result in the exclusion of some enterprises from the benefits granted by law. This is a consequence of an inadequate transposition under the Romanian legislation of the Commission Recommendation regarding the definition of SMEs. When available, the case-law of the European Court of Justice, as well as several soft law instruments, are also analyzed as possible aid for a less restrictive interpretation. Arguments favoring a more inclusive normative interpretation are formulated based on the indirect effect of EU norms and on the *Grimaldi* doctrine. More broadly, the study illustrates how legal definitions may generate exclusionary effects when formal legislative imports diverge from the functional purpose of EU regulatory instruments.

1 Introduction. Legal Framework and Interpretative Approaches to SME Definition

Legal definitions do not only describe social or economic realities but determine the scope of rights and obligations. In this sense, legal classification operates as a 'gatekeeping' mechanism through which access to specific legal regimes is granted or denied. Definitions therefore possess an implicit exclusionary dimension: while they should simplify administrative application and enhance legal certainty, they may simultaneously exclude borderline situations that correspond to the purpose of the norm. The present study analyses such a situation in the Romanian SME

D.-M. Ilucă (✉)
Faculty of Law, 'Alexandru Ioan Cuza' University of Iaşi, Iasi, Romania
e-mail: despina.iluca@uaic.ro

I. Maria Costea (ed.), *Legal Interpretation in Motion*, Ius Gentium: Comparative Perspectives on Law and Justice 144,
https://doi.org/10.1007/978-3-032-32948-6_3

legislation, where the very structure of the legal definition produces outcomes that appear inconsistent with the economic reasoning underlying both national and European SME policy.

The role of small and medium-sized enterprises (SMEs) in economic growth is widely acknowledged both at the European and national levels as the 'backbone of the economy'. However, the concept of 'SME' remains largely unclear, due to a lack of a clear contemporary definition, excessive variability in public policies regarding SMEs and a correlation between weak definitions and policies with vague objectives (El Madani 2018, pp. 104–105). Even though our study will focus on Romania and the impact of European SME legislation, similar barriers were observed in other countries, such as Japan (Tsuruta 2020, pp. 1067–1106), Pakistan (Dar et al. 2017, pp. 46–70) or the United States of America (Anastasia 2015, pp. 88–99). In a broader view, there are at least three general models of definitions for SMEs that coexist with striking differences, proposed by the World Bank, the Organisation for Economic Cooperation and Development and the European Commission (El Madani 2018, pp. 106–107).

In Romania, the legislative framework defining SMEs, and more importantly its interpretation, has given rise to significant practical challenges. This study examines the inconsistencies between the intended purpose of SME legislation and the restrictive interpretative practices that result in the exclusion of some businesses from the benefits granted by law.

The legal scholarship in Romania has already identified several inconsistencies generated by the coexistence of multiple SME definitions across different branches of law. In tax law, for example, Costea (2022, pp. 302–303) underlined the fragmented use of the notion of 'microenterprise' and the practical difficulties arising from divergent fiscal and commercial criteria. Similarly, Ilucă (Ilucă 2018, pp. 123–136) emphasized the limits of SME classifications resulting from the coexistence of European and Romanian criteria. Building on these contributions, the present study focuses more specifically on the interpretative consequences of the Romanian import of the Commission Recommendation and on the possibility of resolving the resulting inconsistencies through the indirect effect of EU law and the *Grimaldi* doctrine.

Romanian SME legislation largely mirrors the European Union's framework, yet its adaptation and interpretation within national practice remains predominantly formalistic. Therefore, we begin by exploring the legal definitions of SMEs in Romania, their main elements, to underline how the prevailing interpretative approaches—particularly literal readings—contribute to a narrow application of the norm.

Prior to the current framework, the definition of SMEs in Romania was provided for by Law no. 133/1999 on stimulating private entrepreneurs for the establishment and development of small and medium-sized enterprises (Official Gazette of Romania, no. 349, 23.07.1999). Given the multiple amendments and additions this law was subjected to, in preparation for the accession to the European Union, the Romanian legislator opted to reassess the topic and adopt a new piece of legislation, in line with the European Commission Recommendation of 3 April 1996 concerning the definition of small and medium-sized enterprises (Official Journal of the European Union, L 107, 30.4.1996), replaced by the Commission Recommendation 2003/361/EC of 6 May 2003 concerning the definition of micro, small and medium-sized enterprises (Official Journal of the European Union, L 124, 20.5.2003; hereinafter, 'the Commission Recommendation'). To this end, Law no. 346/2004 on stimulating the establishment and development of small and medium-sized enterprises (Official Gazette of Romania, no. 681, 29.07.2004; hereinafter 'Law no. 346/2004') was adopted by Parliament on July 14th, 2004, and has been amended and supplemented several times since its adoption. To the purposes of our study, the most significant amendment was made in 2006 and has generated an inexplicable exclusion of some enterprises, as we will discuss below.

Even though both the Commission Recommendation and Law no. 346/2004 contain several provisions on more difficult issues, such as determining whether an enterprise is autonomous, partnered or linked to another enterprise—which we will address in the following section—or rules on how to determine the staff headcount and the financial amounts, what generates the first practical exclusion is the very definition of SMEs in the current form of Law no. 346/2004, as it was inadequately adapted from the Commission Recommendation.

The definition of micro, small and medium-sized enterprises in the Commission Recommendation is structured convergently from the general category of SMEs, as being made up of enterprises which employ fewer than 250 persons and which have an annual turnover not exceeding EUR 50 million, and/or an annual balance sheet total not exceeding EUR 43 million, under which small enterprises employ fewer than 50 persons and have an annual turnover and/or annual balance sheet total that does not exceed EUR 10 million, and microenterprises employ fewer than 10 persons and have an annual turnover and/or annual balance sheet total that does not exceed EUR 2 million.

On the other hand, the definition of micro, small and medium-sized enterprises in Law no. 346/2004 starts from an identical approach towards the general category of SMEs, however, shifts towards slightly different definitions of each individual enterprise. To the purpose of Law no. 346/2004, microenterprises employ no more than 9 persons and have an annual turnover or total assets that do not exceed the RON equivalent of EUR 2 million, small enterprises employ between 10 and 49 persons and have an annual turnover or total assets that do not exceed the RON equivalent of EUR 10 million, whereas medium-sized enterprises employ between 50 and 249 persons and have an annual turnover that does not exceed the RON equivalent of EUR 50 million or total assets that do not exceed the RON equivalent of EUR 43 million.

To better illustrate the difference between the two approaches, a mirrored comparison is designed in Table 1.

The most notable difference comes from the Romanian legislator's choice of imposing a minimum threshold for the staff headcount in comparison to the European approach of only imposing maximum thresholds. Even if at a first glance such a creative choice does not seem to fundamentally affect the logic from the Commission Recommendation, in practice there are enterprises that 'fall between

Table 1 Author's comparative synthesis based on Commission Recommendation 2003/361/EC and Law no. 346/2004

	Commission Recommendation			Law no. 346/2004		
Type of enterprise	Staff headcount	Turnover	or Balance sheet total	Staff headcount	Turnover	or Total assets
Micro enterprise	<10	≤ € 2 m	≤ € 2 m	≤9	≤ € 2 m	≤ € 2 m
Small enterprise	<50	≤ € 10 m	≤ € 10 m	10–49	≤ € 10 m	≤ € 10 m
Medium enterprise	<250	≤ € 50 m	≤ € 43 m	50–249	≤ € 50 m	≤ € 43 m

the cracks' of the definition and are impossible to be placed in a category under Law no. 346/2004. More specifically, it is the case of enterprises with a staff headcount that fits them into one category, but with a turnover or total assets corresponding to the superior category. For example, an enterprise with 8 employees and an annual turnover of EUR 3 million meets the staff headcount criterion for a microenterprise and the turnover criterion for a small enterprise. Similarly, an enterprise with 48 employees and an annual turnover of EUR 11 million is a small enterprise based on its headcount, but a medium enterprise based on the turnover. Finally, an enterprise with 248 employees and an annual turnover of EUR 51 million falls outside the scope of the definition of an SME, even if by staff headcount it is a medium enterprise.

A legitimate question would be how such an oversight is even possible. A case could be made in favor of the Romanian legislator from a normative history point of view. The initial form of Law no. 346/2004 defined SMEs based solely on the staff headcount criterion, as follows: microenterprises employ up to 9 persons, small enterprises employ between 10 and 49 persons and medium-sized enterprises employ between 50 and 249 persons. Therefore, under those provisions no enterprises would be excluded by the definition.

However, the amendments brought by Government Ordinance no. 27/2006 (Official Gazette of Romania, no. 88, 31.01.2006), which as per its preamble was meant to ensure a 'full alignment with the definition of small and medium-sized enterprises in the Commission Recommendation', turned out to have an opposite effect, despite the fact that the verb 'to amend' comes from the Latin *emendo,-are*, which means to free from faults, to correct, to improve. More specifically, the changes consisted of adding to each definition the same turnover or balance sheet total that was provided for by the Commission Recommendation. This ought to have been correlated with the elimination of the minimum threshold in the number of employees, either as an oversight or due to an inexplicable and unneeded dose of legal creativity on behalf of the Romanian legislator, has not happened. This has led to the current conundrum of framing SMEs in the definition, a problem yet to be addressed by the Romanian legislator, even though nearly 20 years have passed since that amendment.

The fact that the criteria for staff headcount and turnover or balance sheet total are cumulative is supported by the case-law of the General Court within the CJEU. In *Calestep* (ECJ, ECLI:EU:T:2015:711, T-89/13, 2015), the Court resorted to a grammatical interpretation of the Commission Recommendation and noted that

> 40. It is clear from a literal reading of that provision that the criteria relating to the staff headcount of the enterprise ('the staff headcount criterion') and to the financial ceilings ('the financial criterion') are cumulative criteria within the context of Article 2(2) of the Annex to Recommendation 2003/361. That is clear from the use of the coordinating conjunction 'and', which indicates the cumulative nature of the criteria, unlike the use of the conjunction 'or', which indicates an alternative nature (…)

This confirmed cumulative nature of the staff headcount and financial criteria, which *mutatis mutandis* is applicable under the provisions of Law no. 346/2004 as well, is what fuels the objective impossibility of placing some enterprises within the Romanian definition of SMEs.

An attempt to reach a satisfactory result in interpretation by using a systematic or holistic approach is also superfluous, since other provisions in Romanian legislation—such as those in Law no. 227/2015 (Official Gazette of Romania, no. 688, 10.09.2015; hereinafter, 'the Romanian Fiscal Code')—define SMEs fundamentally differently (Costea 2022, pp. 302–303). More specifically, to the purposes of tax law, microenterprises are Romanian legal persons which cumulatively meet the following criteria, assessed December 31st of the previous tax year: have an annual turnover of less than EUR 250,000 (starting January 1st 2026, the threshold lowers to EUR 100,000), have at least one employee, are owned by persons other than the state or administrative-territorial units and these shareholders own more than 25% of participation shares to no more than one legal person decided by the shareholders to apply microenterprise tax provisions, are not in dissolution followed by liquidation and have filed the annual financial statements on time.

Most notably, in comparison to the definition in Law no. 346/2004, the provisions in the Romanian Fiscal Code have substantially lower thresholds for the annual turnover and impose several other conditions in terms of ownership, legal status and fulfillment of legal obligations. As a result, even more confusion can be fueled by these different approaches, since a Romanian legal person can be a microenterprise to the purposes of Law no. 346/2004, but not meet the criteria for microenterprises to the purposes of tax legislation. For a simple example, a Romanian legal person with an annual turnover of EUR 1 million and 5 employees is a microenterprise as per the definition in Law no. 346/2004, but it is not considered a microenterprise by the Romanian Fiscal Code and, therefore, cannot apply the provisions regarding microenterprise income tax, which depending on the company's profile can be more favorable than those in terms of profit tax.

To further entangle the issue of systematic interpretation, despite defining microenterprises, Romanian tax legislation does not define small enterprises or medium ones. However, there are exemptions deriving from the VAT Directive (Council Directive 2006/112/EC of 28 November 2006 on the common system of value added tax, Official Journal of the European Union, L 347, 11.12.2006) for the supply of goods and services by small enterprises. To this end, should a Member State choose to exempt small enterprises from the VAT burden, it can impose an annual turnover threshold attributable to such supplies that is no higher than EUR 85,000 or the equivalent in national currency. The Romanian legislator opted for a slightly inferior threshold of RON 395,000 (approximately EUR 78,000), which leads to an even more confusing and surprising conclusion: small enterprises in terms of VAT have lower annual turnovers than microenterprises in terms of microenterprise income tax.

Furthermore, there are provisions for qualifying taxpayers as medium or large, based on general eligibility conditions, doubled by specific and basic selection criteria. To this end, specific selection indicators are typically determined by the activities carried out by the taxpayer and by the single tax group criteria, whereas the basic criteria are the annual turnover, the amount of declared tax debts and the amount of personnel expenses.

The common denominator that can be extracted from the above analysis of Romanian legislation is that the annual turnover seems to be the determining factor in defining SMEs, as it is a criterion present in all definitions, more so than the number of employees, which is currently less relevant—even irrelevant—under tax legislation (Costea 2022, p. 300). We will revert to these intermediary conclusions further on in the present study.

2 Practical Consequences of Restrictive Interpretation

Although the basic SME framework is designed to support entrepreneurial activity, the restrictive interpretation of legal definitions can exclude categories of businesses whose economic activity would justify inclusion.

To start with, a particularly cumbersome situation arises in the case of partner enterprises and linked enterprises (Raczyńska 2019, pp. 176–180). That is because according to the Commission Recommendation and to Law no. 346/2004, when assessing whether an enterprise is a microenterprise, a small enterprise or a medium one, its relationship with other enterprises needs to be considered, based on capital, voting rights and the right to exert a dominant influence. By these criteria, there are three types of enterprises, namely autonomous enterprises, partner enterprises and linked enterprises. Their definitions in Law no. 346/2004 largely mirror those in the Commission Recommendation, with the same general reasoning: there is a presumption that enterprises are autonomous, unless they are partner enterprises or linked enterprises, whereas partner enterprises are those not classified as linked enterprises. Therefore, from a legal standpoint, autonomous enterprises represent 'the rule' or the genre, and as more criteria are added, the enterprise falls either under the narrow category of partner enterprises or under the even narrower category of linked enterprises.

More specifically, an autonomous enterprise is defined by Law no. 346/2004 as any enterprise which is not classified as a partner enterprise or as a linked enterprise, if it holds less than 25% of the capital or voting rights of another enterprise—whichever is higher—or another enterprise holds less than 25% of its capital or voting rights. Exceptions to these thresholds are provided for certain types of investors, such as business angels, universities and non-profit research centers, institutional investors and autonomous local authorities.

The narrow category of partner enterprises describes all enterprises which are not classified as linked enterprises and between which there is the following relationship: an upstream enterprise holds, either solely or jointly with one or more linked enterprises, 25% or more of the capital or voting rights of the downstream enterprise.

Finally, the narrowest category of linked enterprises is represented by enterprises which have any of the following relationships with each other: an enterprise has a majority of the shareholders' or members' voting rights in another enterprise; or an enterprise has the right to appoint or remove a majority of the members of the administrative, management or supervisory body of another enterprise; or an enterprise has the right to exercise a dominant influence over another enterprise pursuant to a contract entered into with that enterprise or to a provision in its memorandum or articles of association; or an enterprise, which is a shareholder in or member of another enterprise, controls alone, pursuant to an agreement with other shareholders in or members of that enterprise, a majority of shareholders' or members' voting rights in that enterprise.

Even though most of these conditions are objective and leave little margin for interpretation, particularly in the case of autonomous and partner enterprises, the issue of exercising a dominant influence in linked enterprises is a rather subjective matter, as is the circumstance when the aforementioned relationships occur through a natural person or group of natural persons acting jointly, in which case those enterprises are also considered linked if they engage in their activity or in part of their activity in the same relevant market or in adjacent markets.

This issue was addressed by the Court of Justice of the European Union in *HaTeFo* (ECJ, ECLI:EU:C:2014:114, C-110/13, 2014), where it was called by a German national court to assess whether only enterprises which, through one or more natural persons acting jointly, have any of the relationships described in the Commission Recommendation must be regarded as 'linked', or whether the existence of that link can also be inferred from an overall economic analysis during which in particular the intention of those persons to circumvent the SME definition is established. The national court also sought to determine the conditions in which natural persons are regarded as acting jointly and in particular whether, for that to be the case, they must be linked by contractual relations.

The ECJ outlined its reasoning using teleological interpretation and considering the objective behind the definition of linked enterprises, which

> 31. (…) aims to gain a better understanding of the economic position of SMEs and to remove from that qualification of SMEs groups of enterprises whose economic power may exceed that of genuine SMEs, with a view to ensuring that only those enterprises which really need the advantages accruing to the category of SMEs from the different rules or measures in their favour actually benefit from them.

Even though not explicitly, the ECJ applied the principle of substance over form and ruled in *HaTeFo* that enterprises may be regarded as 'linked'

> where it is clear from the analysis of the legal and economic relations between them that, through a natural person or a group of natural persons acting jointly, they constitute a single economic unit, even though they do not formally have any of the relationships referred to in the first subparagraph of Article 3(3) of that annex.

Furthermore, by implicitly using the principle of economic content prevalence over legal form, the Court stated that

> [n]atural persons who work together in order to exercise an influence over the commercial decisions of the enterprises concerned which precludes those enterprises from being regarded as economically independent from each other are to be regarded as acting jointly for the purposes of the fourth subparagraph of Article 3(3) of that annex. Whether that condition is satisfied depends on the circumstances of the case and is not necessarily conditional on the existence of contractual relations between those persons or a finding that they intended to circumvent the definition of a micro, small or medium-sized enterprise within the meaning of that recommendation.

The Court's ruling in *HaTeFo* also underlines one of the main arguments for a restrictive interpretation of SME definition, as these types of enterprises can be eligible for advantages which in most cases are exceptions to the general rules, and since exceptions are of strict interpretation, such a result is warranted. For example, had HaTeFo been considered in isolation and not as linked to the other enterprise, it would have been eligible for an increased subsidy instead of the basic subsidy for investment allowances.

The stakes for correctly assessing an enterprise as an SME are not only relevant for subsidies but are also visible in terms of certain fees owed to public authorities. For example, in *Fertisac* (ECJ, ECLI:EU:T:2018:118, T-855/16, 2018), the applicant stated that it was a medium-sized enterprise, which enabled it to receive a reduction of the fee due under the REACH Regulation (Official Journal of the European Union, L 396, 30.12.2006). However, self-assessments of SME status are not infallible, as the European Chemicals Agency found that the applicant was a large enterprise and could not benefit from the reduced fee, a decision upheld by the General Court within the CJEU. In its ruling, the General Court opted for a literal interpretation of the norm which led to a restrictive result based on the parent-subsidiary relationship between the enterprises.

In terms of mediate outcomes, such differences in the assessment of SME status, namely the difference between self-assessment and the assessment of public authorities, can lead to cumbersome financial consequences for the enterprise, which could be significantly affected in its functioning: fees can be higher, subsidies can be lower, sums of money received as grants for co-financing projects might be reduced and subjected to reimbursement (Raczyńska 2019, pp. 181–183).

Furthermore, as self-assessments are made by the company's administrator using forms of self-declaration, issues regarding criminal liability for false statements can also arise. To mitigate such risks, most procedures and guidelines expressly stipulate that the method of calculating the financial and employee data of an enterprise in cases where it is partnered or linked to another enterprise will be carried out according to Law no. 346/2004 and to the SME Definition User Guide developed by the European Commission.

However, this raises another unexpected risk. The Romanian version of the SME Definition User Guide uses the term 'affiliated enterprise' (ro. *întreprindere afiliată*) instead of 'linked enterprise' (ro. *întreprindere legată*), as per the norms in Law no. 346/2004 and in the Commission Recommendation. This poses a risk of confusion with another legal concept in the Romanian Fiscal Code, that of 'affiliated persons'. According to these provisions, a person is affiliated with another one if their relationship falls under one of these circumstances: a natural person is affiliated with another natural person if they are spouses or relatives up to the third degree inclusively; a natural person is affiliated with a legal person if the natural person holds, directly or indirectly, including the holdings of affiliated persons, at least 25% of the value or number of shares or voting rights of a legal person or if they effectively control the legal person; a legal person is affiliated with another legal person if at least the latter holds, directly or indirectly, including the holdings of affiliated persons, at least 25% of the value or number of shares or voting rights in the other legal person or if it effectively controls that legal person; a legal person is affiliated with another legal person if a person holds, directly or indirectly, including the holdings of its affiliated persons, at least 25% of the value or number of shares or voting rights in both the first legal person and the second or if it effectively controls them (Ilucă 2018, pp. 134–135).

A comparative analysis of the definition of 'linked enterprises' with that of 'affiliated persons' shows an imperfect overlap between them, with at least two substantial differences. Firstly, natural persons can be 'affiliated' with one another, whereas they cannot be considered 'linked' to one another, since the latter concept only applies to enterprises. However, it is worth noting that authorized natural persons (as well as individual enterprises and family enterprises) fall under the scope of Law no. 346/2004, hence, can be 'linked'. Secondly, considering the thresholds, 'affiliated persons' under the Romanian Fiscal Code can be both 'partner enterprises' and 'linked enterprises' under Law no. 346/2004. This proves once again the inadequacy of a systematic approach when interpreting the Romanian SME definitions, as cross-referencing other normative acts—despite acknowledging their different scopes—is puzzling and futile.

Conversely, in Romania's legislative framework there are numerous other examples that highlight the practical importance of correctly assessing SME status, as it provides access to certain benefits unavailable for other categories of companies. In the national economic context, where access to EU-funded programmes represents a significant source of financing for developing enterprises, restrictive interpretations of SME status may generate exclusionary effects that go beyond mere classification difficulties. For instance, there are programmes for stimulating the establishment of SMEs under the general title 'Start Up Nation Romania' that allocate entrepreneurs *de minimis* financial aids for founding new SMEs (Official Gazette of Romania, no. 243bis, 20.03.2025), with special schemes to promote entrepreneurial culture within groups of female managers (Official Gazette of Romania, no. 726bis, 24.07.2024); grants co-funded by the EU for SMEs promoting sustainable aquaculture activities, as well as the processing and marketing of fishery and aquaculture products (Official Gazette of Romania, no. 274bis, 28.03.2025) or for the restoration and conservation of resources by building fishing shelters (Official Gazette of Romania, no. 1128bis, 08.12.2025); grants awarded by the EU via Member States through shared management for SME investments for the production of electricity from renewable sources (Official Gazette of Romania, no. 472bis, 21.05.2025); *de minimis* aids for SMEs in the smart growth, digitalization and financial instruments programme (Official Gazette of Romania no. 100, 06.02.2026); *de minimis* aids for supporting crafts and handicrafts carried out through SMEs (Official Gazette of Romania, no. 834bis, 21.08.2024). State funding that meets the criteria in article 107 of the Treaty on the Functioning of the European Union (Official Journal of the European Union C 202, 7.6.2016) constitutes state aid and is typically required to be notified to the European Commission. However, the Treaty provides for situations of exemption from the notification requirement, such as the case of aid for SMEs (Foster 2019, pp. 386–390; Horspool et al. 2018, pp. 521–523). Therefore, a restrictive interpretation of SME definition is also needed for Member States to comply with Treaty provisions.

3 Interpretative Flexibility Deriving from EU Law

When faced with such a legal conundrum of interpretation, one can turn to European legislation and case-law in hopes for a solution. As a preliminary point, we should note that when assessing SME status, even though the criteria are cumulative, as we underlined above, they are not equally important for the purposes of the Commission Recommendation. According to recital 4 in the preamble of the Recommendation, the staff headcount criterion is decisive and takes prevalence over the financial one:

> (4) The criterion of staff numbers (the ‘staff headcount criterion’) remains undoubtedly one of the most important, and must be observed as the main criterion; introducing a financial criterion is nonetheless a necessary adjunct in order to grasp the real scale and performance of an enterprise and its position compared to its competitors. However, it would not be desirable to use turnover as the sole financial criterion, in particular because enterprises in the trade and distribution sector have by their nature higher turnover figures than those in the manufacturing sector. Thus the turnover criterion should be combined with that of the balance sheet total, a criterion which reflects the overall wealth of a business, with the possibility of either of these two criteria being exceeded.

However, this statement is depleted of content by the further wording of the definitions in the Recommendation, as there is no express difference made between the definition of SMEs in the trade and distribution sector and of SMEs operating in the manufacturing sector, nor is there a formula through which the staff headcount criterion gains more legal ‘weight’ than the financial one. An enterprise that exceeds the financial threshold for a category will fall under the superior category, even if the staff headcount criterion would still make it eligible for the inferior category. As a consequence, using a teleological approach to the definitions by appealing to the preamble of the Commission Recommendation can be easily annihilated by the lack of consistency in embedding that reasoning further in the definitions.

Turning to an even 'softer' law instrument, based on the Recommendation, the Internal Market, Industry, Entrepreneurship and SMEs Directorate-General within the European Commission developed a User Guide to the SME Definition to serve as general orientations for both entrepreneurs and other interested parties when applying the SME definition. However, as per the disclaimer listed at the very beginning of the guide, it has no legal force and it does not bind the Commission in any way, since the Recommendation is the sole authentic basis for determining the conditions for qualifying an enterprise as an SME. Despite this, the guide underlines key elements behind the definitions in the Recommendation, as SMEs are the backbone of European economy, but are also faced with particular issues, such as market failures and structural barriers. Therefore, in an attempt to aid them without creating competitive distortions, identifying the enterprises which are truly SMEs is important because they need assistance that other enterprises do not.

In terms of qualifying SMEs, the User Guide highlights that 'size isn't everything' (European Commission 2020, p. 4), in the sense that the size determined by applying the employee headcount criterion and the financial one can be overruled when the enterprise has access to significant additional resources based on ownership, partnerships or linkages, in order to align to the 'spirit' of the Recommendation, namely to a teleological reading of its provisions.

The User Guide also encourages a logical interpretation of the legal norm, as it explains that the staff headcount criterion is considered the primary one because it should be the first applied when determining the size of an enterprise. Observing this criterion is compulsory and when met, the second question is the choice between the turnover and the balance sheet total as the financial criterion. In this regard, the essential element is that an enterprise does not need to satisfy both financial requirements and may exceed one of them without impact on its SME status. The reason behind the existence of such a choice is to reflect the difference between enterprises in the trade and distribution sector, which have high turnover figures, and those in the manufacturing sector, which could have a higher overall wealth reflected by the balance sheet total. Therefore, the logical equation that provides for the size of an SME can be synthesized as:

$$SME\,size = Staff\,headcount\,AND\left(Turnover\,OR\,Balance\,sheet\,total\right)$$

To further aid the application of the definition in the Recommendation, the European Commission developed a so-called SME Wizard on its EU funding and tenders' portal, which works as a self-assessment tool.[1] Gathering comprehensive information about the enterprise, such as data about the current organization, shareholders, participation, other relationships and data for partner organizations, the

[1] SME Wizard, available at: https://ec.europa.eu/info/funding-tenders/opportunities/portal/sme/public/organisation-name.

wizard helps qualify an enterprise in the definitions provided for by the Commission Recommendation. However, the caveat presented as a disclaimer on the portal is that the outcome is solely based on the input provided, therefore '[n]either the outcome nor any assessment based on it, is (…) binding the Commission in any way'. Furthermore, even if it is a valuable tool in terms of determining the size of an enterprise, it still does so only based on the definitions in the Commission Recommendation and cannot be customized to provide answers based on national legislations that transpose the Recommendation differently, as is the case of Law no. 346/2004.

Regarding the differences between the Commission Recommendation and Law no. 346/2004, we previously made an inquiry via email to the European Commission asking for interpretative guidance in terms of the prevalence between the criteria in the SMEs definition. The reply from the DG for Internal Market, Industry, Entrepreneurship and SMEs, Unit H1—COSME Programme, SME Envoys and Relations with EASME underlined the same algorithm as the one in the Commission User Guide, with no reference to the inadequacies of the Romanian legislation:

> The SME definition as described in Recommendation 2003/361/EC has 3 main criteria: 1 compulsory one (staff headcount) and 2 financial ones out of which 1 can be chosen (balance sheet total or turnover). (…) In practice you need to start by looking at the headcount: this determines the 'lowest' level an enterprise can be in. Then you check the financial data: as long as one of the matches this category, you're ok – if not, you move up to the appropriate level.

Therefore, what is currently the solution that allows us to place the aforementioned 'fall-between-the-cracks'-enterprises in at least one category of SMEs? The answer lies within the indirect effect of EU law theory and in the *Grimaldi* doctrine.

Firstly, to better understand the indirect effect theory, we ought to begin with the concept of direct effect of EU law, which was notoriously recognized by the ECJ in the *Van Gend en Loos* decision (ECJ, ECLI:EU:C:1963:1, C-26/62, 1963). Based on the Court's reasoning, legal scholars further outlined that the direct effect of EU law designates the ability of such norms to directly create rights and obligations for individuals, as well as the individuals' right to invoke these norms in cases brought to national courts, if certain conditions are fulfilled (Morano-Foadi and Neller 2018, pp. 264–283; Foster 2019, pp. 170–177; Woods et al. 2017, pp. 114–137). For EU legislation that does not meet the requirements for direct effect, the ECJ coined in *Von Colson* (ECJ, ECLI:EU:C:1984:153, C-14/83, 1984) and later refined the concept of indirect effect. Currently based on the principle of sincere cooperation provided for by article 4 of the Treaty on European Union (Official Journal of the European Union C 202, 7.6.2016), the indirect effect theory now requires the national judge faced with a conflict or contradiction between EU law and national norms to interpret the national norms in the light of the wording and the purpose of the specific EU provision that in the given case cannot generate a direct effect (Morano-Foadi and Neller 2018, pp. 283–289; Horspool et al. 2018, pp. 191–193).

Secondly, the ECJ was called to decide whether recommendations can create an indirect effect, given their 'soft law' nature (Morano-Foadi and Neller 2018, p. 145; Berry et al. 2019, p. 113). Since recommendations are not legally binding, the Court swiftly noted in *Grimaldi* (ECJ, ECLI:EU:C:1989:646, C-322/88, 1989) that they cannot have a direct effect:

> 16. In these circumstances there is no reason to doubt that the measures in question are true recommendations, that is to say measures which, even as regards the persons to whom they are addressed, are not intended to produce binding effects. Consequently, they cannot create rights upon which individuals may rely before a national court.

However, not having a direct effect (Berry et al. 2019, p. 127) does not equate to having no legal effect, particularly when recommendations served as basis for national legislation or when they are created to support the application of binding EU norms:

> 18. (…) in order to give a comprehensive reply to the question asked by the national court, it must be stressed that the measures in question cannot therefore be regarded as having no legal effect. The national courts are bound to take recommendations into consideration in order to decide disputes submitted to them, in particular where they cast light on the interpretation of national measures adopted in order to implement them or where they are designed to supplement binding Community provisions.

Sometimes referred to as 'the *Grimaldi* obligation', it has been argued that since recommendations are non-binding, they can at most only be considered to resolve ambiguities in domestic law (Woods et al. 2017, p. 136). However, this doctrine thoroughly fits the arguments needed to answer our question above considering the following specific reasons:

- Commission Recommendation 2003/361/EC of 6 May 2003 concerning the definition of micro, small and medium-sized enterprises cannot create rights upon which individuals may rely before a national court, therefore, has no direct effect, but could have an indirect effect if it was created to support the application of binding EU norms or if it served as basis for national legislation.
- The previous version of the Commission Recommendation was designed to supplement and support binding Community provisions at the time, namely those in Commission Regulation (EC) No 70/2001 of 12 January 2001 on the application of Articles 87 and 88 of the EC Treaty to State aid to small and medium-sized enterprises (Official Journal of the European Union, L 10, 13.1.2001). *Mutatis mutandis*, the reasoning stands for the current version of the Commission Recommendation and even more when referring to structural and cohesion funds that can be accessed by SMEs.
- Law no. 346/2004 was expressly amended in 2006 to ensure alignment with the definition of SMEs in the Commission Recommendation and therefore meets the condition of being adopted to implement the recommendation.

Applying the *Grimaldi* doctrine to the problem addressed by our study leads to a sole possible outcome, which is that even though the Commission Recommendation does not have a direct effect, it binds national courts to interpret Law no. 346/2004 in the light of the wording and the purpose of the recommendation. This translates into ignoring the minimum threshold imposed for the staff headcount criterion and thus eliminating the risk of some enterprises being impossible to fit into a category of SMEs.

4 Conclusions and Recommendations for a More Inclusive Approach

Considering the identified challenges, it becomes necessary to reconsider the interpretative or normative approach applied to SME legislation in Romania, either through a more teleological, purpose-driven reading of the relevant norms, either by amending the legislation, aiming to better align it with economic realities and policy objectives.

In a circumlocutory manner, if we are to divide the threshold of the annual turnover to the threshold of employee headcount, the Commission Recommendation establishes a presumption that an employee can generate an input in the annual turnover of up to EUR 200,000. This operates as an irrebuttable presumption, since proof of the contrary cannot lead to qualifying the enterprise in an inferior category of SMEs, but only in a superior category, when one of the thresholds is exceeded (Ilucă 2018, p. 126). Regarding the adequacy of such a presumption, our correspondence with DG for Internal Market, Industry, Entrepreneurship and SMEs, Unit H1—COSME Programme, SME Envoys and Relations with EASME revealed that '[t]he colleagues who wrote the SME definition years ago were aware that any ceiling that was set would always be arbitrary and up for discussion. However there was need to set the ceilings somewhere and data collection showed that over 99% of all enterprises in the EU fall under the SME definition'. In addition, the SME Definition User Guide states that '[t]he average European enterprise employs no more than six people (...)' (European Commission 2020, p. 7), a relatively small growth since 2005, when the average European business provided employment for four people, including the manager (Lukács 2005, p. 5). It should be also noted that 'no criterion can be considered absolute, which is unfortunate for such a definition' (El Madani 2018, p. 112) and proposals were advanced for a revision of the definition in the Commission Recommendation (Crehan 2020).

As it is apparent that Romania was not considered when the statistics that substantiated the definition of SMEs in the Commission Recommendation were compiled, given that it was yet to become a Member State, we believe this should have at least determined the Romanian legislator to question whether the thresholds in the recommendation are adequate. The reason why the European Commission opted for a recommendation and not a legally binding act was to specifically allow Member States to adapt the definition of SMEs to the realities of the national economic climate. This means that in developing countries the annual turnover could take prevalence over the staff headcount in determining the size of the enterprise, as there are businesses that employ a significant number of people and have a relatively low annual turnover because they operate in an underdeveloped, scarce or poor market.

The fact that the Commission is constantly monitoring SME growth in the EU and through its Recommendation (EU) 2025/1099 of 21 May 2025 (Official Journal of the European Union, L 2025/1099, 28.5.2025) has created a new category of small mid-cap enterprises that employ fewer than 750 persons and have an annual turnover not exceeding EUR 150 million or an annual balance sheet total not exceeding EUR 129 million should serve as inspiration to the Romanian legislator to adopt a similarly proactive approach and amend the legislation when it becomes obsolete. If such action is deemed too cumbersome, at least a minimal intervention is warranted to eliminate the current oversight, by repealing the minimum threshold in the number of employees in each definition.

To conclude, the current restrictive interpretation of SME definitions under Romanian law results in significant exclusions that undermine the legislation's purpose. A shift toward a more functional definition or at least a more flexible interpretation would not only enhance legal coherence but also foster a more dynamic and inclusive economic environment. Beyond the limits of the Romanian case, we notice how in areas governed through soft law mechanisms, there is a broader tension between formal legal classification and the functional objectives pursued by European regulatory instruments.

References

Anastasia C (2015) Exploring definitions of small business and why it is so difficult. J Manag Policy Pract 16(4):88–99

Berry E et al (2019) Complete EU law. Text, cases, and materials, 4th edn. Oxford University Press, Oxford

Costea I (2022) Asociatul unic între optimizare fiscală şi abuzul de drept. Sci Ann 'Alexandru Ioan Cuza University' Iaşi Jurid Sci Ser 68(2):299–313. https://doi.org/10.47743/jss-2022-68-3-18.

Crehan P (2020) Reflections on a revision of the definition of the EU SME. Publications Office of the European Union, Luxembourg. https://doi.org/10.2760/602855

Dar M et al (2017) Small and medium-size enterprises in Pakistan: definition and critical issues. Pakistan Bus Rev 19(1):46–70

El Madani A (2018) SME policy: comparative analysis of SME definitions. Int J Acad Res Bus Soc Sci 8(8):103–114. https://doi.org/10.6007/IJARBSS/v8-i8/4443

European Commission (2020) User guide to the SME definition. Publications Office of the European Union, Luxembourg. https://doi.org/10.2873/255862

Foster N (2019) Foster on EU law, 7th edn. Oxford University Press, Oxford

Horspool M et al (2018) European Union law, 10th edn. Oxford University Press, Oxford

Ilucă D (2018) Limite şi provocări în clasificarea întreprinderilor. Criterii europene şi criterii naţionale. Limits and challenges in the classification of enterprises. European criteria and Romanian criteria. Sci Ann 'Alexandru Ioan Cuza University' Iaşi Jurid Sci Ser 64(1):123–136

Lukács E (2005) The economic role of SMEs in world economy, especially in Europe. Eur Integr Stud 4(1):3–12

Morano-Foadi S, Neller J (2018) Fairhurst's law of the European Union, 12th edn. Pearson Education Limited, Harlow

Raczyńska M (2019) Definition of micro, small and medium enterprise under the guidelines of the European Union. Rev Econ Bus Stud (REBS) 12(2):165–190. https://doi.org/10.1515/rebs-2019-098

Tsuruta D (2020) SME policies as a barrier to growth of SMEs. Small Bus Econ 54(4):1067–1106. https://doi.org/10.1007/s11187-018-0119-0

Woods L et al (2017) Steiner & Woods EU law, 13th edn. Oxford University Press, Oxford

Reflections on the *in mala partem* Analogical Interpretation in Criminal Law

Mihai Dunea

Abstract "*Poenalia sunt strictissimae interpretationis*" (= the criminal law is of strict interpretation) is a well-known and generally accepted interpretation rule in criminal law. Criminal law is a regulatory field with a maximum of restrictive potential towards a human being's fundamental rights and freedoms, therefore it needs to operate with precise and punctual norms. The interpretation and application of these norms must be strict and as accurate as possible, to limit an arbitrary stance of the state. The fundamental principle of legality of the criminal law norm forbids the incrimination by analogy and usually does not allow the *in mala partem* interpretation of a criminal law disposition (the extensive interpretations of the norm made at the expense of the accused person). However, we argue that some situations can be identified when the criminal regulations should not be (logically) interpreted strictly in *a bona partem* manner. This is usually the case when the analyzed disposition can be interpreted in two or more ways, of which one is illogical (absurd/anomalous), and the other one is the result of an extensive interpretations of the norm, done *in mala partem* (regarding the accused). Surprisingly, in such cases (or at least, in some of them), the criminal law practice and authors in Romania usually accept the extensive *in mala partem* interpretation of criminal law norms as a natural solution, not seeming to notice and explain the formal disparity between this course of action and the general interpretation rule previously indicated.

1 Introduction

We may consider the criminal law interpretation rule expressed through the Latin aphorism "*poenalia sunt strictissimae interpretationis* (*et applicationis*)" or "*poenalia restringenda sunt*" as representing a genuine axiom, a statement with a long and constant tradition in the theoretical reference space as well as in the practice of

M. Dunea (✉)
Faculty of Law, 'Alexandru Ioan Cuza' University of Iaşi, Iasi, Romania
e-mail: mihai.dunea@uaic.ro

I. Maria Costea (ed.), *Legal Interpretation in Motion*, Ius Gentium: Comparative Perspectives on Law and Justice 144,
https://doi.org/10.1007/978-3-032-32948-6_4

criminal law, not only at national legislation level, but also in international law. According to this rule, the extensive interpretation of criminal law provisions is (in principle) prohibited; the idea is that the interpretation process of criminal law norms requires, usually, a textualist approach (Greenberg 2021), namely the accreditation of a meaning situated as close as possible to the explicit text stated by the legislator.

This conception is of a humanistic nature; it is based on the recognition of the fact that criminal law is a particularly powerful instrument for maintaining social order, very intrusive in the lives of individuals, situated within the reach of the state. Therefore, all situations that can lead to its potential arbitrary use must be limited/restricted within a framework as much legal as possible, so as not to deprive the isolated individual (confronted with the full power and authority of the state) of effective guarantees regarding his person (Edwards 2021).

Basically, criminal law dispositions being capable of harming, to the highest possible degree, the fundamental rights and freedoms of any individual, it is necessary to establish a strict and formalist framework that does not allow their use outside reasonable and strong limits of interpretation and application. In other words, in a state governed by the rule of law, the power exercised by the state, through criminal law (and its interpretation), must be restricted, so as not to become abusive.

In this context, the idea of imposing a strict (restrictive) interpretation of criminal law norms and applying them only according to this interpretation appears to be something natural, of common sense. What better method would there be to ensure the protection of the individual against the state entity—which has the power and right to apply (under certain conditions) the norms of criminal law—than the guarantee that these legal provisions will not be extended, in their application, beyond what the legislative text actually expresses?

In essence, according to this ideal theoretical vision, the recipient of the criminal law has the obligation (and is offered the abstract possibility) to inform himself about all the provisions of the criminal law; afterwards, he has to adapt his conduct in consideration of these norms; if he violates them, the judicial bodies can only make a strict interpretation and application of those dispositions, so that there is no possibility that some aspects that were not initially clearly and effectively brought to the attention of the recipient, can be subsequently taken into account (through an extensive interpretation), in the process of holding him criminally liable. In a biblical phrase: "reap what you sow"[1] (no more, no less). If the criminal law conveys

[1] The Bible—Galatians 6:7-9 *[New International Version]*: "Do not be deceived: God cannot be mocked. A man reaps what he sows. Whoever sows to please their flesh, from the flesh will reap destruction; whoever sows to please the Spirit, from the Spirit will reap eternal life. Let us not become weary in doing good, for at the proper time we will reap a harvest if we do not give up."—at: https://www.bible.com/bible/111/GAL.6.7-9.

everything it needs to convey and cannot be extended to hypotheses that are not effectively, clearly and explicitly regulated by written text, then its recipient has all the knowledge necessary to adapt his conduct to the legal imperatives, and any possible deviation from the behavioral line drawn by the legislator can be attributed to the perpetrator without discussion, and he will be sanctioned as such (according to the penalty he was previously warned about). Any person should thus be protected from the arbitrariness of public power, which cannot intervene outside a predetermined, strict and clearly outlined framework, previously brought to the attention of all legal subjects!

2 Coverage Area

Starting from the considerations stated above, it is easy to understand the reason for establishing this rule, of interpreting the law as strictly as possible, by referring to those criminal norms which, through their application, have the potential to lead directly to a limitation of the person's essential rights and freedoms, namely (mainly): the incrimination norms. By this reference (to the norms of incrimination), we have in mind those provisions of the criminal law through which the legislator provides (describes and prohibits under specific sanctions) the acts/conducts considered to represent crimes (forms of manifestation considered dangerous to a sufficiently high degree to be prohibited as a legal illicit to the highest possible degree: criminal illicit, i.e. criminal offense—and not just as a violation of a less important legal norm, such as a contravention—an act prohibited by administrative law provisions, or a disciplinary offense—an act regulated by labor law, or a simple illicit act causing civil damages—an act combated by private law norms, etc.). Therefore, without a doubt, the aforementioned interpretative rule concerns the special criminal law norms, those that include these criminalization provisions.

On the other hand, it must be recognized that not all criminal norms are of this type/produce this effect through their effective application. On the contrary, some provisions of the criminal law aim to restrict the extent to which certain rights and freedoms of one person can be infringed through criminal law means, limiting the application of other criminal norms or making it conditional on the fulfillment of specific and restrictive requirements. Often, this effect is exerted by various general criminal norms, for example those concerning the existence of causes with extinction effects on fundamental criminal institutions (such as the norms regulating justificatory causes,[2] causes of non-imputability,[3] causes of impunity,[4] causes of removal of criminal liability[5] or removal or modification of punishment etc.).

As a result, the question arises whether it is necessary to retain and apply the rule "*poenalia sunt strictissimae interpretationis*" also with regard to these provisions (?). Couldn't these be interpreted, as a rule, even extensively, for the benefit of persons accused of committing crimes? In other words, the following meditation theme is configured: *cui/quid prodest*?[6] If the stated rule was established as a mechanism to defend the individual against the power of the state (who has the right to hold someone criminally liable), can the necessity of its observance also be supported in situations where there would be no person to invoke a possible prejudice caused by its disregard?

If extensive interpretation would sometimes lead to more advantageous solutions for the recipient of the criminal law, so that no one would have the interest to protest against such a practice (especially in the case of general criminal law norms), should compliance with the rule prohibiting this interpretative procedure still be required as a must?

[2] For example (related to Romanian criminal law): *self-defense* (*legitimate defense*); *state of necessity*; *exercise of a right* or *fulfillment of an obligation*; *consent* of the injured person. See the provisions of Articles 18–22 of the Romanian Criminal Code. An officially translated version of the Romanian Criminal Code in force can be consulted online, on the website of the Romanian Ministry of Justice https://www.just.ro/wp-content/uploads/2021/11/Noul-cod-penal-EN.doc.

[3] For example (related to Romanian criminal law): *physical constraint*; *moral constraint*; *non-accountable excessiveness* of legitimate defense or of state of necessity; *minority*—under certain limits (the commission of the incriminated act by a underage perpetrator); *irresponsibility* (mental incompetence); complete and involuntary *intoxication*; certain types/forms of *error*; *fortuitous case*. See the provisions of Articles 23–31 of the Romanian Criminal Code.

[4] For example (related to Romanian criminal law): *withdrawal* (desisting) or *precluding consummation of offense* (preventing the result from occurring) in the event of an attempt, or *preventing the commission of a crime* by a participant. See the provisions of Articles 34 and 51 of the Romanian Criminal Code.

[5] For example (related to Romanian criminal law): *amnesty*; *statute of limitations for criminal liability* (for most crimes—those subject to prescription); *absence* or *withdrawal of the prior complaint* (for some crimes—those in which the law expressly requires the existence of a prior complaint in order to be able to initiate criminal action); *reconciliation* between the perpetrator and the injured person (for some crimes—those for which the possibility of reconciliation is expressly provided by law); *mediation regarding the criminal side of the case* (for some crimes—those in which the possibility of reconciliation or the need for a prior complaint is expressly provided for by law). See the provisions of Articles 152–159 of the Romanian Criminal Code, respectively the provisions of the Law on Mediation (Law No. 192 of 2006, art. 67–70). For more on criminal mediation in Romanian criminal law, see also Dunea and Mărculescu-Michinici (2019).

[6] *Cui prodest*?, also known as *cui bono*?, is a Latin expression that basically means: "to whom it benefits?"/"Good for whom?"/"Who benefits?"—https://lawsisto.com/legalmaxims. *Quid prodest*? is a related Latin expression that basically means: "what good does it do?"/"what is the use?".

3 Connections with Fundamental Principles of Criminal Law

It is easily observable the interpenetration of the essence of the rule "*poenalia sunt strictissimae interpretationis*" with the fundamental principle of criminal law consisting in the legality (lawfulness) of criminalization and of criminal law sanctions: *Nullum crimen, nulla poena sine lege*![7]

The theoretical concept is known according to which the fundamental principle of the legality[8] of criminalization involves a series of aspects/corollaries that give it an effective character (the guarantees that fill it with substance and give it a real content), namely: *lex scripta, lex certa, lex praevia, lex stricta*![9] In a nutshell:

- *lex scripta* concerns the sphere of criminal law sources, requiring that these be written legal provisions, of a certain legislative rank;[10]
- *lex certa* imposes a certain standard, on the legislator, in criminal law regulation; thus, theoretically and ideally, criminal law should be clear to its recipients, foreseeable and predictable (so that they can easily adapt their conduct to the

[7] In the current Romanian Criminal Code, this basic principle/these two basic principles in criminal matters is/are expressly regulated by the legislator, in Articles 1 and 2, as follows:

Art. 1—*Lawfulness of criminalization*: "(1) Criminal law stipulates the actions that constitute offenses [crimes]. (2) No person can have criminal liability for an action that was not covered by criminal law at the date of its commission".

Art. 2—*Lawfulness of of criminal penalty*: "(1) Criminal law establishes applicable penalties and educational measures that can be ruled against persons who committed offenses, as well as security measures that can be ruled against persons who committed actions covered by criminal law. (2) No penalty, educational or security measure can be ruled that was not stipulated in criminal law at the date when the violation was committed. (3) No penalty can be ruled and enforced outside the law's general limits".

[8] Also see: Myftari and Guço (2021), pp 20–28.

[9] In Romanian criminal law doctrine, the subject is extensively treated by most authors, such as: Streteanu and Nițu (2014), pp. 37 et seq.; Mărculescu-Michinici and Dunea (2017), pp. 58 et seq. Also see: Truu (2022), pp. 98–110.

[10] In Romanian criminal law, only some of the normative acts, expressly called "laws", issued by the proper national legislative forum (the Parliament), can be sources of criminal law; these are classified according to the quorum required for their adoption in three hierarchical categories, namely (in ascending order): *ordinary* laws, *organic* laws and *constitutional* laws; as a rule, only organic laws (*a fortiori*—also constitutional ones) can be sources of criminal law, but not simple ordinary laws [art. 73 para. 3 let. h) and i) of the Constitution]. In situations of maximum urgency, when the usual legislative process, which is very slow, cannot ensure a prompt response imperative for the essential values of the state, the Government also has the possibility to regulate in legislative areas reserved for organic laws (including in criminal matters), through emergency ordinances (which must subsequently be subject to approval by organic laws) [art. 115 para. 5 and 6 of the Constitution]. Therefore, no normative act of lower rank than organic law (such as ordinary laws) or emergency Government ordinance (such as simple Government ordinances)—such as Government decisions, ministerial orders, as well as normative acts at the local level (decisions of local or county councils, etc.) may include criminal law provisions. For more on the subject, see also: Dunea (2016).

legislator's requirements, and can reasonably identify those behaviors that are permitted and those prohibited under criminal sanctions);

- *lex praevia* requires the precedence of the criminal legal provision in relation to the moment at which a certain person adopts a dangerous conduct (criminal law is not retroactive;[11] no matter how serious the act may be, it cannot be considered a crime and penalized if at the time of its commission it was not already expressly prohibited by criminal law);
- *lex stricta* requires, in principle, the restrictive interpretation of the criminal norm, so that it does not unreasonably extend its scope of application to hypotheses not expressly foreseen and—thus—potentially not considered by the addressee when deciding to adopt a certain course of action.

As can be easily observed, the analyzed rule of interpretation ("*poenalia restringenda sunt*"/"*poenalia sunt strictissimae interpretationis*") is closely related to (and gives content to) the corollary of the fundamental principle of the legality of criminalization represented in particular by the concept of *lex stricta*.

4 Analogy (and Analogy Types) in the Criminal Law

At the same time, in a natural continuity, the analyzed rule is also linked to the existing prohibitions in criminal law regarding analogy. Thus, criminalization by analogy[12] is prohibited, as a practice that violates the principle of legality of criminalization and (implicitly) the rule of strict interpretation and application of the provisions of the criminal law. This fundamental rule is, in contemporary times,

---

[11] Only if it benefits the perpetrator the criminal law may have a retroactive application (see art. 5 and 6 of the Romanian Criminal Code).

[12] By "incrimination by analogy" we understand the procedure by which a type of conduct that is not expressly described, prohibited and sanctioned by the criminal law as a crime, but which is dangerous and whose commission is recorded at a given moment in objective reality, could be assessed as criminal (leading to the criminal liability of the perpetrator who manifests it), by analogy with a more or less similar type of act, which is however expressly provided for by the criminal law as a crime. For example, an express case of incrimination by analogy was provided for in the Romanian Penal Code of 1936, following an amendment to it, operated in 1948 (at the time of the consolidation of state power by the communists, with Soviet support). Thus, by Law no. 5/Jan. 19th 1948 (published in the Official Gazette no. 15 of Jan. 19th 1948), art. 1 of the Romanian Criminal Code of 1936 (entered into force on Jan. 1st 1937) was amended to have the following content: "*(1) No one may be punished for an act which, at the time it was committed, was not provided for by law as a crime, nor sentenced to other punishments or subjected to other security measures than those provided for by law. (2) Socially dangerous acts, which have a clear similarity to any of the acts provided for by the criminal law, are considered to be implicitly provided for and punished by the legal provision that provides for and punishes the similar act. (3) Socially dangerous, within the meaning of the preceding paragraph, are those acts which by their nature, or by the manner of their commission, affect or endanger the security of the State or the social order. (4) In the case provided for in paragraphs 2 and 3, criminal action may only be initiated by the Prosecutor General*".

also supported by the provisions contained in Article 7 of the European Convention on Human Rights.[13]

In addition, ensuring the logical continuity of the rule of prohibition of analogy in criminal matters, there is a doctrinal consensus regarding the prohibition, in principle, of analogical (extensive) interpretation[14] also, with predilection when this would lead to an unfavorable solution for the person accused of committing a crime (the prohibition of interpretative analogy carried out *in mala partem* is generally accepted as a rule).

On the other hand (referring also to the previously stated aspects), it is worth noting that the specialized literature tends to generally admit the possibility of analogical interpretation of the criminal norm made *in bona partem* (in cases where this procedure would impose legal solutions in accordance with the interest of the person accused of committing a crime). Or, formally, such an interpretation, when it is extensive (which it usually is), would represent (technically speaking) a disregard for the rule of mandatory strict interpretation of the criminal law.

In summary, analogy, in criminal law, can be linked either to incrimination or to the interpretation of the norm, and in the latter case, a distinction can be made, depending on the result, between analogical interpretation in favor of the perpetrator and analogical interpretation to his detriment; while the first two are, in principle, prohibited, the third tends to be generally admitted (on the other hand, more generally, the doctrine indicates several types of analogy that exist in law - namely: principle-based, rule-based, and factual - Brożek, 2018). However, in our opinion, it is worth noting that the prohibition of analogical interpretation *in mala partem* (which directly harms the *lex stricta* component of the principle of legality of incrimination) is not as absolute and sacrosanct as the prohibition of incrimination by analogy (which directly harms the *lex scripta* component of the principle *nullum crimen, nulla poena sine lege*).

[13] Art. 7. No punishment without law: "*1. No one shall be held guilty of any criminal offence on account of any act or omission which did not constitute a criminal offence under national or international law at the time when it was committed. Nor shall a heavier penalty be imposed than the one that was applicable at the time the criminal offence was committed.*"

[14] For a point of view that separates the two techniques of interpretation (*extensive interpretation* and *analogical reasoning*), based on some relevant nuances, see (among other sources): Canale and Tuzet (2018), p. 65. Also, see: Zajtay (1980), pp. 324–332; "The Use of Analogy in Criminal Law" (1947), pp. 613–629; Langenbucher (1998), pp. 481–521; Golding (2018), pp. 123–136; Macagno and Walton (2009), pp. 154–182.

5 The Limits of Derogation from the Prohibition of Extensive Interpretation of Criminal Law Norms in the Case of Analogical Interpretation

The aforementioned circumstance, namely that the (extensive) analogical interpretation *in bona partem* tends to be admitted as a genuine exception to the general rule *poenalia sunt strictissimae interpretationis* (although it is often not necessarily presented as such in doctrine!), both in the specialized literature and in judicial practice, may have important consequences. Their connection and their apparent incongruity with the axiomatic principle formulated and accepted as a rule in matters of criminal law interpretation (*poenalia restringenda sunt*) does not always seem to be fully explained and clarified.

Often, these two maxims (*criminal law must be strictly interpreted and applied, respectively the fact that there is permission for analogical/extensive interpretation of criminal law to the advantage of the accused*) coexist in legal language and in the practice of applying the law, without noticing at its true value the tension (latent or explicit, as the case may be) that is created between them (because the statement of the second maxim tends not to correspond to the absolute affirmation of the first one). In this context, it appears useful and desirable to note the existence of the derogatory nature of the permission of the extensive analogical interpretation of the criminal law in favor of the accused compared to the rule of mandatory restrictive interpretation of the criminal law, respectively to research and clearly outline, in a theoretical (scientific) manner, the framework and mechanisms that characterize the relationship between the aforementioned rule and the exception to it.

Of course, when the exception takes the form of a hypothesis in which rigid compliance with the rule would be to the detriment of the person for whose protection the principle was established, the explanation of the admissibility of the derogation logically follows from observing the purpose for which the principle under analysis (the *poenalia sunt strictissimae interpretationis* rule) was created/stated by the lawmaker. Since it will be admitted that the reason for the formulation and recognition of this interpretative rule is to protect the individual from state power (guarantee against the possible arbitrary use of public authority, in a clearly disproportionate confrontation of forces), it will be possible to admit as logical (and therefore—natural) the incidental derogation in those cases in which the inflexible application of the rule no longer serves the purpose for which it was established, even producing an effect contrary to this purpose.

The question that arises, however, is whether such an exception can be admitted (and if so, to what extent, under what conditions?), also, in some other situations… (respectively—if the answer is positive: what could those situations be?)…

All the more we appreciate that a theoretical clarification (premise and for illuminating criminal practice) would be required of the problems generated by the issue of this relationship between the rule (criminal law is of strict interpretation/criminal law must be interpreted restrictively) and exception (permission of extensive, including analogical, interpretation of the criminal norm, in certain cases) in those hypotheses in which it can be observed that doctrine and practice tend to sometimes admit (even unconsciously) derogations from the very prohibition of analogical/extensive interpretation, *in mala partem*, of the criminal law.

Resuming an idea previously stated (adopted by us also on other occasions—Mărculescu-Michinici and Dunea 2017, p. 61), starting from the observation and disclosure of these cases, it can be stated that the prohibition of (extensive) interpretation by analogy *in mala partem* of the criminal law is not as strong as the prohibition of admitting incrimination by analogy! The problem we see in this context and which we wish to bring to attention is the relative/approximate nature of this statement, the fact that the mechanism by which the exceptional permission of analogical interpretation *in mala partem* operates (rarely explicitly admitted, but not as rarely implicitly recognized!) and the reasonable limits of such an exceptional permission are not yet sufficiently and clearly explored, revealed, explained and conceptualized (theorized) in the criminal law doctrine, which gives rise to the risk of emergence and consolidation of an inappropriate and non-unitary practice.

As far as we are concerned, we consider that the overcoming (transgression) of the prohibition of extensive interpretation of the criminal norm, especially when the procedure would not be in the interest of the accused, is conferred by the configuration of an absurd/aberrant/illogical interpretative alternative, or one contrary to other principles (including interpretation rules) existing in criminal law,[15] as the only possible alternative to embracing the extensive interpretation (even the one made *in mala partem*). In other words: if, in terms of interpreting a criminal norm, in order to apply it, a choice is required between a solution achieved through the extensive interpretation of that norm (including when this would be to the detriment of the accused/perpetrator), respectively an absurd/illogical solution (or one which, by extension, would lead, in principle, to the inapplicability of the norm in question), then the option should be made, without hesitation, towards the alternative that does not respect the *poenalia sunt strictissimae interpretationis* rule, but which

[15] Thus, we consider the premise that "when the word "statute" is used (…) it is assumed that the statute is rational, and that the reason of the law (…) is intended. Thus, "statute" stands for reasonable, correct law"—Nauke (1986), p. 535, p. 537. Also, in the same source: "(…) the legislative process is treated as if it were inspired by reason. It is trusted to create well thought-out, unequivocably formulated statutes. (…) criminal law is not subject to the winds of politics: it is not at the beck and call of changing perceptions of societal needs. On the contrary, it limits the tendency to respond to every shift in perceived social needs with new criminal law. In essence, criminal law is a stable element in a dynamic process of social development" (Nauke 1986, p. 544). When this axiom is refuted, however, in the objective normative reality, the need for an interpretation in the spirit of legal principles begins to be felt, beyond the regrettable imperfection of its letter. Now, such an interpretation, in the spirit of the law, often appears to be extensive and perhaps even carried out *in mala partem*, but not infrequently it tends to be the only logical option compared to a rigid and simply aberrant alternative.

allows a logical, rational and coherent application of the criminal law, in relation to the principles and rules according to which it essentially functions (Dickson 2016).

As indicated, moreover, even from some early stages of the doctrine in criminal matters (with reference, at least, to the Romanian specialized literature on the subject): "The rule *poenalia restringenda sunt* is therefore not absolute, and it is possible, by way of interpretation, to extend a provision even in the case when it is not favorable to the defendant, if the spirit of the law authorizes the extension" (Tanoviceanu 1924, p. 246).

6 Arguments in Support of the (Exceptional) Admission of the Analogical/Extensive Interpretation of the Criminal Law Even to the Detriment of the Perpetrator (When the Alternative Would Be Absurd)

In order to adopt such a solution to the problem of principle that we are analyzing in this framework, we also rely on the existence of various (other) principles/rules/arguments (including of legal interpretation) functional in the field of law (in general—and implicitly in criminal law),[16] such as:

- the interpretation legal argument *a pari* (based on the identity of situations/hypotheses), in its connection with the interpretative rule according to which where there is identity of reason, there should also be identity of legal solution (*ubi eadem ratio, ibi idem jus/ubi eadem est ratio, eadem solutio esse debet*);
- the (interpretive) principle according to which where the reason (logic/spirit) of the law stops, its application/the legal solution prefigured by it, should also stop (*ubi cessat ratio, ibi cessat lex/ubi cessat ratio legis, cessat ipsa lex*);
- the logical argument of reduction to the absurd (*reductio ad absurdum*) in relation to the objective (and thereby imperative) rule according to which the law cannot oblige to the impossible (*ad impossibilia nemo tenetur/ad impossibillium, nulla obligatio/impossibilium nulla obligatio est*);
- the general rule of interpretation according to which the law must be interpreted in the sense in which it produces an effect, and not in the sense of its inapplicability/in the sense in which it would not produce effects (*actus interpretandus est potius ut valeat quam ut pereat*).

[16] Also see: Vilchez (2024), pp. 212–231.

7 Some Examples from Romanian Legislation in Which the Extensive Interpretation (Even *in mala partem*) of Some Criminal Norms Is Justified as a Matter of Logic

According to art. 396 of the Romanian Criminal Procedure Code,[17] there are five distinct types of possible solutions to the criminal action in the trial phase (five types of decisions that the criminal court can pronounce), namely: *conviction; waiver of the application* of the punishment; *postponement of the application* of the punishment; *acquittal*; and *termination* of the criminal trial. Therefore, the reference in a legal text to the specific notion of "conviction" has the role of excluding, in principle, the possibility of considering any of the other types of solutions/decisions of the criminal court.

However, cases can be indicated (by way of example) that can either be visibly appreciated as representing legislative "loopholes", or that can give rise to discussions regarding the intention or lack of intention of the legislator to consider only the hypothesis of convictions, *stricto sensu*, to the exclusion of any other types of solutions/criminal decisions (which is not always logical and/or fair).

For example, regarding the *mitior lex* principle, in the matter of the timely application of the criminal law after the pronouncement of a final judgment (regulated in art. 6 of the Romanian Penal Code), the legal text refers to the hypothesis of the emergence of a criminal law that provides for a lighter sanction, intervened after a final conviction. A strict interpretation (in accordance with the principle *poenalia sunt strictissimae interpretationis*) leads to the conclusion that the text/institution is inapplicable in all other cases, namely those in which the final decision would not be one of conviction, but of another type, namely of postponement of the application of the penalty. However, we believe that the inapplicability of this article can be discussed, when the final decision is one of postponing the application of the sentence, in relation to the provisions contained in the Romanian Criminal Code, regarding the safety/security measures. Thus, security measures, representing sanctions prescribed by criminal law that are not (in Romanian criminal law) consequences of engaging the criminal liability of the perpetrator (but post-crime preventive measures), can be ordered (as a rule) even when the committed act does not constitute a crime (being sufficient that it is an incriminated act[18]). Therefore, it

[17] An officially translated version of the Romanian Criminal Procedure Code in force can be consulted online, on the website of the Romanian Ministry of Justice, at the following internet address (03.08.2025): https://www.just.ro/wp-content/uploads/2021/11/Noul-cod-procedura-penala-EN.doc.

[18] According to art. 107 paragraph 2 of the Romanian Criminal Code, it is provided that: "Security measures are taken against a person who committed an unjustified conduct stipulated by criminal law"; on the other hand, according to art. 15 paragraph 2, which provides the legal definition of the crime, it is stipulated that it constitutes a whole made up of several component parts, which must necessarily be met cumulatively, namely: "An offense [a crime] is a conduct stipulated by criminal law that has been committed under guilt, without justification and for the commission of which a person can be charged". From the comparison of the two aforementioned legal texts, it can be

is possible to apply such criminal law sanctions also through a decision that is not necessarily a conviction, such as the case of a decision to postpone the application of the penalty.

Another example refers to cases where the criminal law expressly refers to the commission of a crime, although it sometimes actually contemplates less than that. Thus, in Romanian criminal law, a distinction is made between the concept of "crime" (as a whole) and the notion of "act/conduct provided for by the criminal law" ("incriminated act/conduct"), which constitutes only a component part of that whole (of what a crime represents). According to art. 15 par. 2 of the Romanian Criminal Code, in order for a particular behavior to be legally classified as a crime, it is necessary to cumulatively verify the following essential requirements: it must be prohibited by criminal law; it must be committed with the form of guilt specifically provided for by criminal law; it must be unjustified (contrary to the legal order—there must be no justifiable causes underlying it); it must be imputable to the perpetrator (he/she must have criminal capacity—there must be no causes of non-imputability that would benefit the perpetrator).

Thus, we arrive at the axiom according to which: any crime is (among other things) an act provided for by criminal law, but not every act provided for by criminal law constitutes a crime. However, sometimes the criminal law refers to one of the concepts although it actually has in mind the other, which implies an extensive interpretation (often carried out *in mala partem*) in order to determine the correct meaning to be taken into account for the application of the criminal norms.

For example, according to art. 3 of the Romanian Penal Code (the initial text on the application of criminal law in time), it is stipulated that "The criminal law applies to crimes committed during the time it is in force". In a strict interpretation, it would appear that the criminal law can only be applied in the event of the commission of a criminal act formally qualified as a crime, which is inaccurate. In order not to overload this material with technical aspects specific, in particular, to the criminal regulation in Romania, we will be grateful to refer to the same hypothesis that we referred to in the previous example, namely: the possibility of applying Romanian criminal law to a simple unjustified act provided for by the criminal law, for the application of safety/security measures (art. 107 paragraph 2 Romanian Criminal Code), even if this does not constitute a crime!

Or, in this sense, Article 3 of the Criminal Code must be interpreted extensively, analogously, *in mala partem*, which no one logically disputes. Provisions similar to

observed that in art. 107 paragraph 2 of the Romanian Criminal Code, reference is made only to some components of the crime, compared to those indicated in art. 15 paragraph 2, namely: "a conduct stipulated by criminal law", and "without justification" ("unjustified"). Therefore, even if the activity committed by the perpetrator cannot be formally qualified as a crime, in order to generate criminal liability and the application of a punishment (because it does not cumulatively meet all the conditions of the legal definition of the crime), it is still possible to apply safety/security measures, if what was committed meets at least the conditions of being a criminalized conduct and, in addition, an unjustified one. However, this finding can also be made through a court decision of a different type than that of conviction, for example through one of postponing the application of the sentence.

those in Article 3 of the Romanian Criminal Code (in the aspect considered herein) can also be found throughout criminal legislation, and in other normative texts (for example, art. 5 of the Romanian Criminal Code; art. 7; art. 8–13).

The above are just a few examples; many more others can be provided.

8 Instead of Conclusions

In essence, it can be stated, therefore, that although the issue of the rule of interpretation analyzed here (and its potential exceptions) constitutes an aspect directly related to the *lex stricta* consequence arising from the fundamental principle of criminal law consisting in the legality of incrimination, the debate on this subject is largely occasioned (also) by the *lex certa* consequence arising from the same fundamental principle (more precisely: by the inadequate respect, on certain occasions, of this imperative in the activity of legal and criminal regulation, by the legislative power). Thus, it can be observed that if the legislator scrupulously and responsibly fulfilled his obligation to draft clear, complete and certain legal norms in terms of the content of the regulation, with a scope and content that would not raise doubts/would not generate discussions or controversies (thus increasing the ambiguity for the recipients of the criminal law), then the activity of interpreting criminal norms would be extremely limited, and in the process of its implementation, the hypotheses in which the need for an extensive interpretation would be felt would be reduced to the objective minimum possible.

In the absence of such a performance (which, unfortunately, cannot often be attributed to the contemporary criminal legislator), the task of interpreting norms, in the process of understanding/explaining/deciphering and applying the legal (criminal) rule, increases exponentially. Along with this, the need to carry out extensive interpretations of certain provisions, respectively to apply in this interpretative key the provisions they contain, also increases substantially.

Practically, as the legislator becomes more efficient, more technical, more specialized in the process of elaborating criminal law norms (if such an evolution should take place), truly strengthening the *lex certa* corollary of the principle of the legality of incrimination, the more significant will also become the *lex stricta* consequence related to the same principle, strengthening the rule *poenalia sunt strictissimae interpretationis* and reducing the hypotheses in which exceptions to this rule are required.

Until possible improvements in legislative expression, however, it is worth remembering and meditating on the relative nature of the rules of interpretation that underline, rigidly and inflexibly, the strict character that the interpretative process of criminal norms should present. Although this is, without question, the rule in the matter, it no longer appears as absolute as it is usually presented to be. Exceptions are and must be admitted from it, even in the hypotheses of a result to the detriment of the accused after an extensive interpretation, when the alternative is an aberrant solution (illogical or one that blocks the application of the norm in an unjustified way). As already expressed by the doctrine, the idea is that "the jurist must therefore take the law seriously, making sure he does not expose it to haphazard political change. Consequently, he must interpret statutes very narrowly", but also "according to the statute's innate legal reason" and necessarily "according to a reasonable sense of the text. That which does not correspond to the historical juristic sense of the text does not fall within the statute" (Nauke 1986, p. 537). We should never stray from the basic legal principles, among which one of the best known and most firmly embedded in the collective consciousness of humanity is, of course—as the Romans said so well: "*jus est ars boni et aequi*". For this reason, interpreting legal norms with the constant pursuit of respecting logic, common sense and the spirit of the regulation as a guiding compass is a necessity that must be carried out, if necessary, even against the inappropriate expressions of an amateur legislator (but, after all: *errare humanum est*), including (in our opinion) with the risk of sometimes achieving an analogical and/or extensive interpretation *in mala partem*, if this is included in the reasonable margin of carrying out a logical interpretation of the law, in good faith, in the spirit of the law and respecting the basic principles of law.

References

Brożek B (2018) Is analogy a form of legal reasoning? In: Kaptein H, van der Velden B (eds) Analogy and exemplary reasoning in legal discourse. Amsterdam University Press Publishing House, pp 49–64. https://www.jstor.org/stable/j.ctv62hfhb.6

Canale D, Tuzet G (2018) Analogical reasoning and extensive interpretation. In: Kaptein H, van der Velden B (eds) Analogy and exemplary reasoning in legal discourse. Amsterdam University Press Publishing House, pp 65–86. https://www.jstor.org/stable/j.ctv62hfhb.7

Dickson J (2016) Interpretation and coherence in legal reasoning. In: Zalta EN (ed) The Stanford encyclopedia of philosophy (winter 2016 edition). https://plato.stanford.edu/archives/win2016/entries/legal-reas-interpret/

Dunea M (2016) About the formal sources of the current Romanian criminal law. https://revista.universuljuridic.ro/about-the-formal-sources-of-the-current-romanian-criminal-law/

Dunea M, Mărculescu-Michinici M-I (2019) Considerations on an aspect of the restorative justice concept: the conclusion of a mediation agreement in criminal trials in the Romanian legislation. Sci Ann "Alexandru Ioan Cuza" University of Iaşi Tome XII/No. 2. https://anale.fssp.uaic.ro/index.php/asas/issue/view/49

Edwards J (2021) Theories of criminal law. In: Zalta EN (ed) The Stanford encyclopedia of philosophy (fall 2021 edition). https://plato.stanford.edu/archives/fall2021/entries/criminal-law/

Golding M (2018) Argument by analogy in the law. In: Kaptein H, van der Velden B (eds) Analogy and exemplary reasoning in legal discourse. Amsterdam University Press Publishing House, pp 123–136. https://www.jstor.org/stable/j.ctv62hfhb.11

Greenberg M (2021) Legal interpretation. In: Zalta EN (ed) The Stanford encyclopedia of philosophy (fall 2021 edition). https://plato.stanford.edu/entries/legal-interpretation/index.html#ref-16

Langenbucher K (1998) Argument by Analogy in European Law. Camb Law J 57(3):481–521. https://www.jstor.org/stable/4508491

Macagno F, Walton D (2009) Argument from analogy in law, the classical tradition, and recent theories. Philos Rhet 42(2):154–182. https://www.jstor.org/stable/25655348

Mărculescu-Michinici M-I, Dunea M (2017) Criminal law. General part (theoretical course), vol I. Hamangiu Publishing House, Bucharest

Myftari K, Guço S (2021) Prohibition of the application of criminal law by analogy within the principle of legal certainty. J Res Humanit Soc Sci 9(5):20–28. https://www.questjournals.org/jrhss/papers/vol9-issue5/Ser-1/D09052028.pdf
Nauke W (1986) Interpretation and analogy in criminal law. BYU Law Rev 535. https://digitalcommons.law.byu.edu/lawreview/vol1986/iss3/2
Streteanu F, Nițu D (2014) Criminal law. General part (university course), vol 1. Universul Juridic Publishing House, Bucharest
Tanoviceanu I (1924) Treatise on criminal law and procedure, second edition, revised and completed by Vintilă Dongoroz. Curierul Judiciar Publishing House, Bucharest
*** (1947) The Use of Analogy in Criminal Law. Columbia Law Rev 47(4):613–629. https://doi.org/10.2307/1118053
Truu M (2022) The European Court of Human Rights and the principle of foreseeability (Lex Certa and Stricta): how to determine whether an offence is clearly defined in criminal law. Jurid Int Law Rev 31:98–110. https://www.juridicainternational.eu/article_full.php?uri=2022_31_the_european_court_of_human_rights_and_the_principle_of_foreseeability_lex_certa_and_stricta
Vilchez B.B. (2024) Imputation and judicial decision in criminal matters: the crisis of criminal guarantism in the light of "in mala partem" analogy in homotransphobia. Humanit Rights Glob Netw J 6(2):212–231. https://www.humanitiesandrights.com/journal/index.php/har/article/view/141/109
Zajtay I (1980) Reasoning by analogy as a method of law interpretation. Comp Int Law J South Afr 13(3):324–332. https://www.jstor.org/stable/23245212

Tort Law, Droit des Délits: An Impossible Equivalence

Carmen-Ecaterina Ciobâcă

Abstract The chapter focuses on the terminological and conceptual discrepancies between common law and civil law cultures in terms of tort terminology. The etymology, semantics, and history of the concept are examined, then a comparative approach is carried out to emphasize the basic principles and the key tort terminology in the Anglo-Saxon legal tradition and in the continental tradition, respectively. The French and Romanian legal technolect is similar in terms of tortious liability; nevertheless, more work needs to be done for the harmonization of tort law at European level. The last section of the chapter is dedicated to the multiple challenges of translating tort terminology from English into French.

1 Introduction

Our chapter aims to emphasize the complexity of tort law as a legal field, the various approaches related to this topic in common law, French law, Romanian law, and European law, and the translation difficulties associated with the terminology specific to tort law. Even if the term "tort" stems from French general language and does not have a particular legal denotation, referring to the concept of "error" or "fault", it has acquired a specialized meaning in the English legal terminology, namely the liability associated with reprehensible behavior, becoming the key term of a specific branch of law.

To emphasize the translation challenges associated with tort terminology, a comparative approach between the Anglo-Saxon legal culture and the civil legal culture is needed. Thus, in the first part of the chapter we present a general definition of tort and the principles on which tort law is based, the etymology of the term, as well as a brief history of the concept. The second part of the study is dedicated to a comparison between the semantics of tort in common law and civil law, respectively. The

C.-E. Ciobâcă (✉)
Faculty of Law, 'Alexandru Ioan Cuza' University of Iaşi, Iaşi, Romania
e-mail: carmen.ciobaca@uaic.ro

I. Maria Costea (ed.), *Legal Interpretation in Motion*, Ius Gentium: Comparative Perspectives on Law and Justice 144,
https://doi.org/10.1007/978-3-032-32948-6_5

key terminology of the field will be dealt with; a special focus is placed on the equivalence of terms in various legal cultures. Then we examine the avatars of the concept of "tort" in European law, French law, and Romanian law, to be able to approach the issue of translation in the last part of our study.

2 "Tort" as a Legal Concept: Etymology, Semantics, and Brief History

The concept of "tort", borrowed in English from Latin via the French language, is a legal term in the Anglo-Saxon system, an entire area of law being founded on it. Having the general meaning of "a wrongful act other than a breach of contract for which relief may be obtained in the form of damages or an injunction" according to the Merriam-Webster dictionary, it stems from the Latin "tortus" (meaning "crooked" or "twisted"). In Medieval Latin we encounter the term "tortum", translated as "injustice" or "wrong", while in Old French the concept of "tort" is employed to designate a "misdeed" or "wrongful action". Nevertheless, in modern French the noun has lost its legal significance, becoming commonplace: it indicates an error or a fault in the general sense and is used in phrases such as "avoir tort" ("being wrong").

"Tort" is an interesting example of the way in which various cultures internalize words differently: if in the French language the concept does not have any legal connotations, in English it is a key legal term and the foundation of an important area of law, designating "a legal wrong for which the law provides a remedy" (Harpwood 2009, p. 1). Defining the law of torts, on the contrary, is a challenge even within the Anglo-Saxon culture:

Academics have attempted to define the law of tort, but a glance at all the leading textbooks on the subject will quickly reveal that it is extremely difficult to arrive at a satisfactory, all-embracing definition. [...] In order to understand what tort law involves, it is necessary to distinguish tort from other branches of the law, and in so doing to discover how the aims of tort differ from the aims of other areas of law such as contract law or criminal law (Harpwood 2009, p. 1).

Based on a general principle, tort liability refers to actions or lack of actions that harm the personal rights or the legitimate interests of other members of the community, the tortfeasor being compelled to repair the prejudice either by awarding damages or in kind. In Canada, for example, the amendments to the Civil Code concerning the issue of liability set up the obligation not to inflict damages to third parties and provide four types of liability: liability for oneself, liability in relation to third parties, liability for damages caused by things and, eventually, liability involving the payment of damages in one of the three cases already mentioned (Baudoin 1989, p. 601).

Even if it has multiple avatars, tort is also a fundamental concept in civil law, where it is based on the duty of repair in case of a non-contractual breach. In other words, the harm caused to another person or to his/her property through careless or unintentional acts is subject to compensatory damages. Thus, civil law understands "tort" as an extra-contractual breach (an injury that occurs irrespective of contract), a frequent example being represented by unintentional harm to the property of another person (French law defines this situation as a "quasi-délit").

Thus, when we take into consideration various legal cultures, we notice that definitions of "tort law" might differ. As Vivienne Harpwood emphasizes, one basic step in order to understand this area of law is to differentiate it from contract law, and criminal law, among others.

In what concerns the distinction between tort law and criminal law, the task may be challenging, because several torts are also criminal acts in the Anglo-Saxon legal culture ("assault" is one such example). Also, the notion of "délit" pertains to criminal law in the French legal culture and should not be confounded with the concept of "tort" in common law: the standard equivalent of "tort" in French is "la responsabilité délictuelle" or "le délit civil". The Romanian law has borrowed the French technolect and employs the phrase "răspundere delictuală", pertaining to civil law and not to criminal law. Furthermore, in both French and Romanian law we encounter the distinction between "responsabilité délictuelle" ("răspundere delictuală") and "responsabilité quasi-délictuelle" ("răspundere cvasi-delictuală"), respectively, based on the presence or absence of intention when the tortious act was performed. All in all, tort law is a broader area in common law than in civil law, as it is not clearly delimited from criminal law or contractual law.

In civil legal cultures, on the contrary, the distinction between tort law and contractual law is well-established. Both areas of law are based on the principle of compensation in case of damage deriving from a breach. In contract law, a breach of contract is envisaged, whereas tort law focuses on specific injuries affecting the rights or legitimate interests of another person, which compel the breaching party to award compensation (monetary relief or reparation in kind) (Dogaru and Drăghici 2010, p. 245). In the Romanian legal culture, some authors assert that tort law is in some sort of way similar to criminal law, as it is based on the principle of compensation for the harm done, having the aim of insulating citizens from the adverse effects of a wrongful act (Romoşan 2008, p. 28). Anyhow, within the civil legal culture, there is a clear hierarchy of rights that may be affected by reprehensible behavior: attempts on another's life, on his/her bodily integrity and on other rights considered "non-proprietary" or "personal" ("droits extra-patrimoniaux" in French, "drepturi nepatrimoniale" in Romanian) are dealt with by criminal law, whereas violations of purely patrimonial interests (such as unintended deteriorations of property) pertain to tort law, thus to civil law (Kadner Graziano 2008, p. 229).

In what concerns the history of the concept of "tort", it is worth mentioning that it is encountered for the first time in Roman law, more specifically in Lex Aquilia and Corpus Iuris Civile. This is explained by the fact that Roman law was long considered an "ius commune", in other words "the communal law of a large part of the world [...], when 'all the world was Rome' and Roman law was used [...] in all the provinces of the empire extending over the greater part of Western Europe and North Africa" (Borkowski and du Plessis 2005, p. 355). Nevertheless, one of the first avatars of tort liability is to be found in older legislative acts, such as the Code of Hammurabi.

Roman law had a huge impact on the general theory of obligations, a highly technical field. Its fundamental principles, as established by Roman law, were often borrowed without exception by modern civil law systems and by the Anglo-Saxon system (Villiers 1977, p. 429). The concept of "fault", which represents the foundation of tort liability, stems from Roman law, more specifically from the law of obligations and the classification of torts according to the Lex Aquilia. The latter is considered in fact the old version of the modern theory of tort liability, which is referred to even today as the "Aquilian liability" (Ouedraogo 2008, pp. 132–133). The general rule applicable in relation to tort liability was the "culpa" ("fault"): according to it, liability could be invoked, from an objective perspective, when an action or the lack of action led to a damage or a loss ("iniuria"), provided that, from a subjective point of view, involuntary fault was also present, materialized under the form of negligence or omission (Ouedraogo 2008, p. 138).

In Roman Law, the basic principle on which the notion of civil wrong is founded is reflected by the Latin phrase "damno, dolore, incommodo, calamitate, injuria". This phrase establishes the duty of care in relation with others, understood as the behavior specific to a reasonably prudent person (Zimmermann 1990, p. 1004). Thus, the standard of diligence is a Roman legacy, deriving from the concept of "bonus pater familias" ("good family father"). The existence of a tortious action could only be determined in relation to the breach of the duty of care, the latter corresponding to the behavior of a diligent and prudent person (Boila 2009, p. 313).

In the Roman legal culture, torts fell into three classes: liability corresponding to actions or lack of actions leading to violations of a right or to breaches of a duty; liability related to the failure of exercising due care in a specific context; and liability in case of a moral or legal wrong. As we may notice, tort has a broader meaning in Roman law than in current civil law cultures. The comprehensive meaning of tort has been preserved in common law, where this key notion overlaps with criminal law and is not clearly separated from contract law.

In conclusion, the etymological and historical analysis of the concept of "tort" shows the complexity of this legal notion, which is explained by the fact that the term evolved differently in various legal cultures. Even if the main principle on which it is founded refers to the duty to award compensations for a specific damage or harm, tort has a broader scope in common law than in civil law, as it is not explicitly separated from criminal and contract law. In civil law, on the contrary, tort refers rather to unintentionally reprehensible behavior that leads to injuries. Paradoxically, it seems that the Anglo-Saxon system has preserved in general the main principles belonging to Roman law on which tort law is founded, such as the notions of breach ("iniuria") and fault ("culpa"), while the semantics of "tort" is narrower in civil law cultures. Strictly in terms of etymology, the term "tort" has acquired and maintained a legal meaning in common law, while in French, the language from which it originates, it pertains to the common language, referring in general to an error or to the fact of being wrong.

3 The Concept of "Tort" in Common Law and in Civil Law: Basic Principles, Similarities and Discrepancies, Key Terminology

This section of the chapter focuses on the incongruencies between common law and civil law related to the concept of tort. We highlight the basic principles defining each legal system, as well as the criteria employed to ascertain tort in the Anglo-Saxon World and in the civil world, respectively. In the last sub-section, we enumerate several key terms encountered in tort law (such as "fault", "negligence", "damage", "damages") and we discuss the way in which each system has internalized such terms through translation.

3.1 Common Law Versus Civil Law: An Overview

Common law and civil law are the main legal systems that exist in the world. Due to their distinct historical evolution, they share few similarities; in fact, if we consider the main legal source on which each of them is based, we discover that they are, in some way, dichotomous. In civil law, written statutes represent the main reference, while case law is an indirect and secondary source of law. Common law, on the contrary, is based on legal precedent and the legislation has only an ancillary nature (Poirier and Debruche 2005, p. 394). As the perspective adopted by one legal tradition is the reverse of the other, Anglo-Saxon law usually considers a causality criterion based on the principle of precedence, while in civil law causality is established according to legal norms, case law only affirming and developing it (Katsivela 2020, p. 164). In other words, in common law "remedies precede rights", whereas in civil law written statutes prevail over legal precedence (Gémar 2018, p. 561).

Jean-Claude Gémar states that, in fact, common law and civil law are not so different from one another, as they have entered the new era of the *tertium quid* and have acquired a hybrid nature due to the presence of mutual legal transplants, imitations and borrowings (Gémar 2018, p. 962). The presence of the concept of "tort" in European law is one such example: in documents drafted in English, the term appears as such, but it does not necessarily have the connotation it possesses in common law, corresponding rather to what the French legal culture designates by the phrase "responsabilité délictuelle". In Saussure's terms, the signifier has been preserved, while the signified was altered. Gémar emphasizes that most civil law systems were influenced by the Anglo-Saxon system; French law represents an exception, as it has long resisted such interferences (Gémar 2018, pp. 962–963). What is more, France has exported traits of its legal system all over the world, one of the most borrowed items being the Civil code (Gémar 2018, p. 963). As for Canada, the historical confrontation between the English and the French language, on one hand, and between common law and the civil law tradition, on the other, has led to the emergence of a new field, "legilinguistics", with its multiple sub-fields (Gémar 2018, p. 965).

In what concerns tort law or, in civil terms, the "law of delicts", the presence of mutual influences is also noticeable. Thus, even if tort is established in common law based on the legal theory of precedence and in civil law according to provisions in the Civil code, continental lawyers tend more and more to resort to leading cases and to ascertain tort in accordance with the legal precedent (Kadner Graziano 2008, pp. 225–226). Traditionally, the Anglo-Saxon system comprises a unique manner of recognizing tortious acts, marked by its historical evolution, each tort being considered independently and not within a general theory of obligations. As we have emphasized, tort law is broader in common law than in civil law, as it may also refer to specific breaches of contracts or even to criminal acts ("assault" (personal injury), "criminal mischief" (damage to property) or "homicide" (wrongful death) are both crimes and civil torts). Historically, the current terminology employed in common law stems from the various suing procedures, a fact that is obvious in tort law. In this respect, René David gives as an example distinct civil torts, such as "deceit, nuisance, trespass, conversion, libel, and slander", some of which correspond to ancient writs (David 1996, p. 263).

Civil law is also heterogenous in what concerns the law of torts, even if "tort" has a narrower scope. On the European continent, there are numerous discrepancies between the various tort law systems, one of the most noticeable being detected between French law and German law (Kadner Graziano 2008, pp. 226–227). This may also explain the challenge of harmonizing tort law at European level, an aspect dealt with in the fourth section of the chapter.

Therefore, tort law is far from being a unitary field even within the civil law culture. As for the discrepancies between Anglo-Saxon tort law and continental tort law, they seem intractable.

3.2 *Tort: Basic Principles in Common Law and in Civil Law*

Tort is assessed differently in common law and civil law, respectively, because its ascertainment is based on different basic principles. In continental legal tradition, damage is the immediate, logical and direct consequence of fault (therefore, there is a clear cause-and-effect relationship between the damage incurred and the damages to be awarded by the tortfeasor). In common law, on the contrary, the reasonable foreseeability principle prevails: it is the foundation of the duty of care, of the standard of diligence and of causal proximity. In addition, direct causality is evoked in the Civil code and reasserted in case law in continental legal traditions, whereas in the Anglo-Saxon system the two elements of the tort of negligence, namely factual causality and causal proximity, are fixed through case law (Katsivela 2020, pp. 167–168).

The reasonable foreseeability principle, pervasive in common law, is different from direct causality in civil law: according to it, damages are not necessarily the direct consequence of the injury, and a tort may exist if the harm done could have been foreseen by the tortfeasor, aspect that should be proven in court. For instance, if a company delivers a software program that works only on PCs and not on Macintosh computers, and the beneficiary loses a loyal client because of such fault, he/she may recover consequential damages in court provided that he/she is able to prove that the harm could have been foreseen by the software provider. Thus, specific types of remedies available in the Anglo-Saxon legal tradition, such as special or consequential damages, depend on foreseeability.

The distinction between direct causality in civil law and reasonable foreseeability in common law can be summarized as follows: direct causality in continental law may also include reasonable foreseeability, whereas the Anglo-Saxon tradition rejects the cause-and-effect relationship and only adopts the reasonable foreseeability criterion. There are, undoubtedly, conceptual similarities between the two principles (reasonable foreseeability and direct causality, respectively); nevertheless, reasonable foreseeability needs to be proven in court in common law, while in civil law this demonstration does not represent a distinct stage of court proceedings (Katsivela 2020, pp. 170–172).

Another gap between the two main legal systems is represented by the distinction, specific to common law, between independent insufficient causes, on one hand, and independent sufficient causes, on the other. An independent insufficient cause is one that cannot lead *per se* to an injury, but is nevertheless essential to the occurrence of said injury. Tortious factors (e.g.: the tort of negligence) and non-tortious factors (e.g.: a disease or a medical issue leading to the occurrence of harm) pertain to independent insufficient causes. On the contrary, when several causes that may lead to an injury concur or occur successively, they are defined as independent sufficient causes (Katsivela 2020, p. 173).

In civil law, on the contrary, there is no distinction between independent insufficient causes and independent sufficient causes. If several torts are ascertained simultaneously, direct causality is applied with priority, together with the reasonable foreseeability criterion, when necessary (Katsivela 2020, p. 174). One can thus notice that the two legal cultures approach the notion of tort differently in terms of the leading principles based on which tortious acts are recognized in court.

3.3 Tort Law: Key Terminology

The language of law employs terms that usually have a precise meaning, in order to avoid confusion and misinterpretation. Unlike some authors who believe that law has an "overt structure", comprising sometimes unclear or vague terms, such as the adjective "reasonable" and the corresponding noun "reasonableness" (Côté 1999, pp. 353–354), we consider that such lexemes are, in fact, rather infrequent.

On the other hand, the semantics of specialized terms belonging to the legal language is the result of the distinct evolution of cultures across the world: therefore, a concept may have dissimilar connotations in various legal systems. The fact that "legal terminology of different legal systems is, for the most part, conceptually incongruent" (Šarčević 1989, p. 278) is the main challenge for any legal translator. Jean-Claude Gémar shares the same opinion, stating that the greatest impediment to uniform interpretation and enforcement of law is the incongruity of legal cultures. This is explained by the fact that each system possesses its own vocabulary and underlying concepts, its own taxonomies, sources of law, methodologies, and legal principles. Uniform interpretation is thus impossible (Gémar 1995, p. 150).

Tort law is no exception in this respect, as it represents a highly technical legal sub-field. Its terminology comprises specialized concepts specific to each legal culture. That is why the law of torts may be one of the most difficult sub-fields in terms of translation: even if there are shared concepts, their signified is usually dissimilar, as legal cultures are not founded on the same legal principles. To illustrate this discrepancy, we emphasize in what follows the basic terms pertaining to tort terminology in common law, in French law, and in Romanian law, and the semantic incongruencies between them.

We may even start with the notion of "tort", borrowed in English from Latin via French, which has acquired a specialized legal meaning in common law, while in French it pertains to the general language. As we have underlined, tort is understood in the Anglo-Saxon culture as a legal wrong that makes the object of compensation; specific contractual breaches or even crimes may enter this category. In continental legal cultures, on the contrary, tort is limited to extra-contractual wrongs, thus strictly pertaining to civil law. It is translated as "responsabilité délictuelle" in French and as "răspundere delictuală" in Romanian.

In countries marked by bijuralism, such as Canada, mutual influences and legal transplants are frequent and the process of interpretation of legal concepts is certainly more complex than in areas where a single legal system comes into play. Regarding the interpretation of the notion of "tort", Michael Beaupré evokes one interesting example pertaining to Canadian case law. In *Mart Steel Corp. versus R.*, the Federal Court in Montreal took into consideration the translation into French of the Crown Liability Act, in which "tort" was rendered by "délit civil", understood as civil wrong. Thus, to dismiss the charge according to which the Court was liable in case of a tort perpetrated by its servants, the Counsel for the Crown stated that "by using the word *tort*, the Crown Liability Act was intended to have no application in the province of Quebec, where the concept of *tort* is foreign." Nevertheless, this claim was rejected, as the Court considered the phrase "délit civil" employed in the French version of the statute, construed according to Quebec legislation (Beaupré 1986, p. 133). We may conclude that, to warrant uniform interpretation and favor unitary enforcement in jurisdictions characterized by bijuralism and conceptual incoherence, translators should find compensatory techniques whenever possible.

"Tort" is not the only term borrowed from French into the English legal technolect. Another key concept in tort law is "fault". It derives from the French word "faute", which belongs to the general language, designating an error or a guilt. In French, the noun "faute" may also have a subsidiary legal meaning, referring to civil or administrative liability, but also to criminal liability. In civil law, for instance, the term describes an omission or an act of negligence, such as the breach of personal duties (e.g.: the phrase "faute contractuelle" indicates a violation of contract). In criminal law, it designates a crime that involves the violation of a moral duty. The French adjective "fautif, -ve" has a distinct legal meaning, implying the idea of liability, either civil or criminal (it is employed in phrases such as "comportement fautif"/ "culpable behavior").

In common law cultures, on the contrary, "fault" is a legal term, referring to various forms of liability in different sub-fields of law (tort law and criminal law included). It is understood as "an attitude of will, a psychological relationship which exists between the specific injury to the right of another and the material author of such injury" (Pisillo-Mazzeschi 1992, p. 11). As tort itself, the fault principle in common law depends on foreseeability.

In the more general sense, the fault principle rests upon proof of intention (*dol, dolus*) or negligence (*faute, culpa*). The term faute (or *culpa*) is used to describe types of blameworthiness based upon reasonable foreseeability, or foresight without desire of consequences (recklessness, *culpa lata*). Although culpa is not a general condition of liability, it may play an important role in certain contexts. (Brownlie 1983, pp. 44–45).

According to this author, fault may be explained either by intentional harm or by negligence, the latter being another key term in tort law. The concept of "negligence", borrowed from French, is equally present in common law and in civil law, referring to the violation of standard of conduct specific to a reasonably prudent person. In fact, the duty of care, as well as negligent or reckless acts, are ascertained *in abstracto*, based on the considerations that define the conduct of a "bonus pater familias". Nevertheless, "negligence" is one of those notions that share the same signifier in the two legal cultures, but possesses a slightly different signified. In continental legal culture, it generally refers to injuries caused by the breach of a duty of care through action or inaction, whereas in the Anglo-Saxon system it may have two different meanings. On one hand, negligence may be defined as a psychological detail that is associated with specific torts, characterized by a lack of intention. Thus, negligence is not a tort *per se*, but a criterion based on which tort is ascertained. On the other hand, negligence may be construed in common law as an independent tort, deriving from the violation of a specific duty. In other words, it may designate a failure to exercise the duty of care that leads to the occurrence of harm (Zannas 1952, p. 43). Nevertheless, the tort of negligence is based on a more recent legal theory that emerged in common law in the nineteenth century.

The terms "damage" and "damages" are also problematic when translated from one legal culture to another. "Damage" is synonym to "harm", "loss" or "injury", being rendered as "dommage", "atteinte" or "préjudice" in French and as "pagubă" or "prejudiciu" in Romanian. We notice that French and Romanian legal technolect are very close in this respect. In European law, "damage" refers to harm that affects an interest protected by law, leading to material or immaterial loss. According to article 9 in the Council Directive 85/374/EEC of July 25th, 1985 on the approximation of the laws, regulations and administrative provisions of the Member States concerning liability for defective products, "damage" is defined as:

(a) damage caused by death or by personal injuries; (b) damage to, or destruction of, any item or property other than the defective product itself, with a lower threshold of 500 ECU, provided that the item of property: (i) is of a type ordinarily intended for private use or consumption, and (ii) was used by the injured person mainly for his own private use or consumption. (eur-lex.europa.eu)

The conceptual equivalent of "damage" used in the French version of this directive is "dommage", whereas the Romanian version mentions the term "prejudiciu".

As for the concept of "damages", understood as "compensations", "remedies", "relief" or "reparation" to be awarded in case of damage, it has a broader meaning in common law. An entire legal sub-field is dedicated to this notion. The various remedies available in the Anglo-Saxon system, either contractual or extra-contractual in nature, do not have an equivalent in civil law: expectation damages, special or consequential damages, restitution damages, and reliance damages are just a few examples. The equivalent of "damages" in the French legal culture is represented by the phrase "dommages et intérêts", also borrowed by the Romanian terminology ("daune-interese"). Nevertheless, the concept has a narrower meaning in continental law, as it generally designates monetary compensation awarded to a person who suffered moral prejudice and/or harm to his/her property.

A particular category of damages available in common law also implying the notion of tort is represented by the "punitive/exemplary/aggravated damages". More specifically, they are defined as extra-contractual damages awarded by the Court to the injured party if the breaching party has manifested reprehensible behavior, such as tortious acts. Thus, "the intention of the court is to punish the wrongdoer by an additional award on top of the award of compensatory damages, and perhaps to deter others who might be tempted to act in the same way as the defendant" (Harpwood 2009, p. 424). Even if the very existence of punitive damages contradicts the idea that civil liability has a compensatory nature, such damages awarded under Canadian law represent, according to Jean-Louis Baudoin, a technique of social control: the tort of discrimination is such an example (Baudoin 1989, p. 608). According to the Canadian Civil code, exemplary damages may be awarded only in case of gross negligence or willful misconduct. Anyhow, no punitive damages may be awarded if the harm has already been reprimanded based on criminal law. Also, it is worth mentioning that exemplary damages have no correspondent in continental law, despite some voices claiming that the introduction in the Civil code of some form of "punishment" for reprehensible behavior would be useful (Pierre 2014, p. 25). In French and Romanian law, for instance, decisions having a punitive nature fall exclusively within the competence of criminal courts.

An important element to be considered in tort law is the presence or absence of intention when performing a harmful act. In this respect, common law distinguishes between unintentional torts, based on negligence (such as car accidents caused by reckless driving, workplace accidents, medical malpractice) and intentional torts that are carried out deliberately, with ill intent (such as assault, battery, trespassing, slander, libel, false imprisonment). We notice that most intentional torts in common law are also crimes. Civil law, on the contrary, comprises the concept of "quasi-delict" ("quasi-délit" in French, "cvasi-delict" in Romanian), deriving from the

Latin principle "obligatio quasi ex delicto" and corresponding to the liability arising from a wrongdoing performed against another person or against his/her property. The notion of "cvasi-delict" is defined in art. 999 of the Romanian Civil code as "an illicit act, performed without intention, through carelessness or negligence". Thus, even if this concept corresponds roughly to the tort of negligence in common law, it is translated literally as "quasi-delict" in European law to avoid any confusion or misinterpretation. For instance, in the Opinion of Advocate General Richard de la Tour delivered on April 22nd, 2021 (eur-lex.europa.eu), we encounter the following phrase: "jurisdiction in matters relating to *tort*, *delict* or *quasi-delict*".

In this sub-section we emphasized the discrepancies between common law and civil law in terms of tort terminology. The analysis of concepts such as "tort", "fault", "negligence", "damage", "damages" pertaining to the Anglo-Saxon system and "faute", "fautif", "quasi-délit" belonging to the civil legal tradition shows that legal incongruencies are systemic and sometimes turn out to be insurmountable.

4 Comparative Approach: Tort as Reflected in French Law, Romanian Law, and European Law

The current section of the chapter is consecrated to a comparative approach that aims to identify certain similarities and discrepancies between two legal traditions pertaining to civil law, namely the French and the Romanian legal system. We also discuss the concept of tort as reflected in European law and emphasize the importance of the harmonization effort in specific areas, such as the issue of liability in case of cross-border traffic accidents.

4.1 Tort in French Law

French law clearly illustrates the way civil law internalizes the notion of "tort". Understood as "responsabilité délictuelle" ("tortious liability"), this concept belongs to the broader class of "responsabilité civile" ("civil liability"), namely the legal principle according to which a person who caused harm is compelled to provide reparation. In continental legal cultures, civil liability comprises two classes, namely contractual and extra-contractual liability. Tortious liability corresponds, in fact, to the extra-contractual liability, being also named "Aquilian liability" to emphasize its Roman legacy. Unlike tort in common law, which depends on reasonable foreseeability, tortious liability in French law is based on a causality criterion, more specifically on the relationship between the tortious act ("la faute") and the injury suffered ("le dommage", "le préjudice"). Thus, if tort in the Anglo-Saxon system may overlap with contractual or with criminal liability, the French concept of "responsabilité délictuelle" exclusively pertains to civil law and does not interfere with criminal liability or with contractual liability.

Tortious or extra-contractual liability is dealt with in articles 1240–1254 of the French Civil code. It relies on the definition of "délit civil" ("civil tort"), as distinguished from criminal tort ("délit pénal"), the latter representing one of the three classes of crimes ("infractions") provided by the French Criminal code ("délits" are more serious than "contraventions" and less serious than "crimes"). As one may notice, the key terminology employed not only in the field of tortious liability ("la responsabilité délictuelle"), but also in French criminal law is culture-bound and seems untranslatable. Thus, the gap between common law and continental law is obviously significant.

Tortious liability is established in article 1382 of the French Civil code, which stipulates as follows: "Tout fait quelconque de l'homme, qui cause à autrui un dommage, oblige celui par la faute duquel il est arrivé à le réparer." ("Any act whatever of man that causes damage to another obliges him by whose fault it occurred to make reparation.") Also, article 1241 stipulates that "Chacun est responsable du dommage qu'il a causé non seulement par son fait, mais encore par sa négligence ou par son imprudence." ("Everyone is liable for the damage he/she causes not only by his/her acts, but also by his/her negligence or imprudence.") Article 1370 is more specific, as it distinguishes between obligations deriving from the statute ("engagements résultant de l'autorité seule de la loi") and obligations deriving from a personal action ("engagements qui naissent d'un fait personnel à celui qui se trouve obligé"). According to this article, the latter class of obligations stems from "quasi-contrats", "délits" and "quasi-délits". In other words, article 1370 states that "an obligation can arise as the consequence of a delict or a quasi-delict, which is different from the obligation which arises from personal commitment made in contractual relationships" (Sage 1996, p. 293).

Articles 1382–1386 in the French Civil code resume this idea, providing that tortious liability comprises both intentional and unintentional acts that lead to injury and, implicitly, to the obligation of awarding relief for the damage done. Based on this provision, there are two categories of tortious actions fixed in the French legislation that involve the liability of the tortfeasor: the "délits" (intentional torts) and the "quasi-délits" (unintentional or non-deliberate torts). The notion of "quasi-délit" partially corresponds to the delict of negligence in common law.

Also, articles 1382–1386 in the French Civil code do not establish a clear distinction between damages affecting absolute or fundamental rights (which are non-derogable) and purely patrimonial damages (Kadner Graziano 2008, p. 226). Nevertheless, specific damages are described in this part of the Code, namely: injury caused by personal action or by negligence/imprudence (article 1383), injury caused by people for whom one is responsible or by things which he/she has in his/her keeping (article 1384), injury caused by an animal that pertains to said person (article 1385), injury caused by the degradation of one's building deriving from a lack of maintenance or from a construction defect (article 1386).

The conclusion is that, unlike tort in common law, which has a broader meaning and may also interfere with contract law or criminal law, tortious or extra-contractual liability in the French system is strictly limited to the civil field. Both deliberate and non-deliberate tortious acts are envisaged and are subject to reparation, which may be pecuniary or in kind. In addition, moral damages may be awarded in specific cases.

4.2 *Tort in Romanian Law*

Romanian law was largely influenced by the French legal system; that is why the concept of "tort" is approached in a quasi-identical way in the two legal cultures. In Romania, tort liability is part of civil law and, based on it, one is compelled to repair the damage caused to another person by his/her deed.

Expected with enthusiasm, but also with skepticism, the New Romanian Civil code, meant to regulate fundamental aspects of human existence within the society, was enforced on October 1st, 2011. The revision process had the purpose of adapting this fundamental legal instrument to new social realities. Modern terminology was also employed to describe legal phenomena.

As in French legislation, there is a distinction established by Romanian law between contractual liability and extra-contractual or tortious liability, respectively. The former arises in a contractual framework, while the latter derives from an illicit deed (civil offense) causing injury, more specifically from the violation of a personal right or of an interest pertaining to another person in the absence of a contract, which involves the obligation to award damages to the injured person. Even if there is no clear definition of the notion of "damages" in the Romanian Civil code, it may be derived from article 1530, which stipulates the creditor's right to compensation for the damage caused by the debtor as a direct and necessary consequence of default in the performance. Damages in kind, meant to put the non-breaching party in the *status quo ante*, are mentioned in article 1386 of the Romanian Civil code, in addition to pecuniary damages, resorted to when the repair of the damage is impossible or when the non-breaching party is not interested in the repair in kind. Damages are described in the Romanian doctrine as "monetary indemnities that the debtor is compelled to award to repair the damage suffered by the creditor because of the willful non-compliance with the obligations undertaken by the former" (Pop et al. 2012, p. 303).

Tortious liability ("răspunderea delictuală") makes the object of article 1349 of the Romanian Civil code, which stipulates as follows:

(1) Every person is compelled to observe the rules of conduct imposed by statute or by a local custom; one should not harm, through his/her actions or inactions, the legitimate rights or interests of others; (2) The one who violates this duty in a deliberate manner is liable for any damage caused, being compelled to repair it entirely; (3) In situations expressly provided by law, one may be liable to repair the damage caused by the act of another, by things or animals in his/her keeping and by the deterioration of his/her own building; (4) The liability for damages caused by defective products is set forth by special law. (our translation)

The liability for personal deeds is fixed in article 998 of the New Romanian Civil code, being expressed as follows: "Orice faptă a omului care cauzează altuia prejudiciu obligă pe acela din a cărui greşeală s-a ocazionat a-l repara." ("Any deed that causes damage to another person compels the breaching party to repair the damage done.") Also, article 999 stipulates that "Omul nu este responsabil numai de prejudiciul ce a cauzat prin fapta sa, dar şi de acela ce a cauzat prin neglijenţa sau prin imprudenţa sa." ("One is not liable only for damages caused by his/her deed, but also for damages caused by his/her own negligence or imprudence.") Thus, one may notice that article 998 in the Romanian Civil code reproduces the content of article 1382 in the French Civil code and that article 999 in the Romanian Civil code is an exact copy of article 1383 in the French Civil code. Following the pattern of articles 1384–1386 in the French Civil code, the Romanian Civil code sets forth in articles 1000–1002 the liability for other's deeds, the liability for damages caused by animals which one has in his/her keeping and the liability for damages deriving from the deterioration of his/her own building due to lack of maintenance or to a construction default. Also, joint and several liability, corresponding to the situation in which the damage is caused by a tortious act performed by two or more persons, is defined in article 1003 of the Romanian Civil code. The content of this article is inspired by the Italian Civil code.

Taking as an example the French civil code, Romanian legislation distinguishes between torts ("delicte"), namely deeds committed with intent that led to damages, and "quasi-torts" ("cvasi-delicte"), defined as unintentional deeds committed by negligence or recklessness. In fact, an entire section of the Romanian Civil code, comprising articles 998 to 1003, is entitled "Despre delicte şi cvasi-delicte" ("On torts and quasi-torts").

The Romanian law is very similar to French legislation in terms of tortious liability as it has borrowed the French taxonomies and conceptual schemes. In what concerns the terminology employed, we may speak about legal transplants, as the terms were translated literally into Romanian ("răspundere delictuală", "delict", "cvasi-delict" are some illustrative examples in this respect).

4.3 Tort in European Law: The Harmonization Effort

To emphasize the challenge of harmonizing tort terminology, we dedicate the current sub-section to some notable efforts regarding the adoption of a unitary approach concerning tortious activity at the level of the European Union. Some issues, such as tortious liability in the case of cross-border traffic accidents, continue to be problematic.

As Bernhard A. Koch emphasizes,

> [...] tort law is a dynamic area of the law, not only adapting to new challenges posed by real-life settings but also adjusting the assessment of who should bear both old and new risks and of what is deemed 'just' compensation for the ensuing losses. If I had to summarise the developments of these past 21 years in one word, it would have to be 'more': more and new varieties of losses have been recognised as compensable, more claimants were held eligible to claim compensation, and the overall pay-outs clearly increased as well. Tort law throughout Europe has thereby become more victim-friendly, which is not meant as a judgement, but merely as a description of the overall trend. (Koch 2021, 739)

Nevertheless, uniform legislation concerning tortious liability is very rare, and there are few harmonized rules referring to this area at the European level, as this domain strictly falls within the competence of national legislators. The legal norms in force in various European states differ considerably in this respect. On the other hand, tort law does not constitute a specific matter at the EU level; the issue of remedies for breach or damage may be found in various legal sub-fields and is submitted to the causality principle. In other words, liability is involved when conduct characterized by negligence or fault leads to damage, provided that the damage is certain and there is a cause-and-effect relationship between said conduct and said damage.

In what concerns the challenges of the harmonization process, Jaap Spier, the founder of the European Group on Tort Law, emphasizes that there is a huge gap in terms of tortious liability between common law cultures and continental cultures (Kadner Graziano 2008, p. 220). In fact, tort law lacks a unified approach at international and European levels. European legislators only provided harmonized rules on specific issues, such as environmental damage (Directive 2004/35/EC) or liability for defective or non-compliant goods (Directive 85/374/EEC). Considering these irreconcilable discrepancies between the Member States, only a soft harmonization approach would be possible in the field of European tortious liability.

The aim of the harmonization process would be to provide more victim-friendly legislation throughout Europe through the assessment of various damages caused by tortious deeds. In fact, this effort took the form of two main initiatives at European level, namely the publication of the "Principles on European Tort Law" (PETL) (European Group on Tort Law 2005a) by the European Group on Tort Law (ECTIL, also called the "Tilburg Group"), and the drafting of the "Principles of European Law on Non-Contractual Liability Arising out of Damage Caused to Another" (PEL Liab Dam) by the Study Group on a European Civil Code, which is no longer active. The document titled Principles of European Tort Law (European Group on Tort Law 2005a), on the contrary, is currently under revision, but it already had an impact on various legislative initiatives and rulings of supreme courts of law (Koch 2021, p. 717). Besides these Principles, other fundamental publications dedicated to tort law at European level are *Tort Law of the European Community*, edited by Helmut Koziol and Reiner Schulze (Koziol and Schulze 2008), as well as the *European Tort Law Yearbook*, published between 2001 and 2009.

The work of the European Group on Tort Law is a pioneering one, as tort law is a legal area that has become very diverse since the end of the nineteenth century and national systems seem to have become increasingly distant from one another in this respect. For the first time in modern history of law, a group of researchers have managed to elaborate some European tort principles despite the gap existing between the Anglo-Saxon law of torts and continental legal cultures and irrespective of all discrepancies between the legal systems of the Member States. The Principles also reinforce the structure of tortious liability, starting with the causality criterion: there should be a cause-and-effect relationship between faulty conduct and the corresponding damages, fault being defined as the deliberate or involuntary breach of a specific standard of conduct.

The importance of the Principles is unequivocal, as they may serve as a *tertium comparationis* for future debates and deliberations concerning tort law in Europe (Kadner Graziano 2008, pp. 224–225). For instance, they were already considered within national reform projects, such as in case of the revision of the Austrian civil responsibility legislation, which abundantly refers to the Tort Principles (Kadner Graziano 2008, p. 224).

There are nevertheless some drawbacks of the Principles: the major one is represented by the fact that the source text was drafted in English and largely employs the terminology specific to common law. The Principles are also available on EGTL's website into French, Spanish, Catalan, Czech, German, Greek, Italian, Japanese, Korean, Polish, Portuguese, Russian, Slovenian, Turkish, and Chinese; the translations into French, Spanish, and Chinese, and their accompanying commentaries, were published as volumes. Nevertheless, as we emphasize in the last section of our chapter, a strictly source-oriented approach is present in translation, since the original terminology and style, which are not familiar to European lawyers, are maintained. Thus, a terminological and stylistic revision of PETL might be necessary. Another drawback is represented by the fact that some notions, such as the burden of proof, construed as a procedural matter, are not clearly defined (Kadner Graziano, 2008, p. 243).

Despite these shortcomings, the Tort Principles represent an important legal instrument and a tertium comparationis that may be used by lawyers within any soft harmonization effort at European level and not only, provided that the established rules are unbiased and clear, maintain a quality standard and are based on principles that are familiar to the Member States or at least are the result of a negotiation.

For the moment, even if it were a much-needed legal instrument, a unified code dealing with extra-contractual or tortious liability is far from becoming a reality, as national legal systems vary considerably. For instance, there is indirect harmonization regarding liability in case of cross-border traffic accidents because European legislators do not have specific competence on this issue, despite the existence of article 81 in the Lisbon Treaty (the former article 65 in the Rome Treaty), which would be construed as a main source for the harmonization of civil rules across the EU. In this context, the Principles of European Tort Law (European Group on Tort Law 2005a) may constitute a starting point for any unification approach envisaged by European legislators.

5 The Challenge of Translation

We have mentioned in the previous section of the chapter that there are specific issues regarding the translation of the Principles of European Tort Law (European Group on Tort Law 2005a). In fact, tort terminology is difficult to translate in general because of the gaps existing between the various legal cultures.

Law as a field is culture-bound and puts the translator in a situation of "dépaysement linguistique" ("linguistic estrangement") (Moreteau 2009, p. 709). Thus, translation becomes "a cross-cultural event" (Snell-Hornby 1988, p. 43) meant to facilitate communication from one language to another. Nevertheless, even if translation is a necessary product in the modern globalized world, it is regarded as an ancillary activity by lawyers, who consider the target text inferior to the original, incomplete or marked by the translator's subjectivity (Lavoie 2023, p. 122). According to some translation scholars also, translation is never complete, because the source message cannot be entirely reproduced in the target language and the cultural connotations are rendered with difficulty (Didier 1990, p. 246). The source-oriented method largely used in legal translation is also criticized: "translators approach legal text as if it were a biblical text, bearing a secret sacred message revealed to the reader by a close, literalist transcription into the target language" (Kasirer 2001, p. 340). Frederick Sussmann shares the same opinion: "To return to the pitfalls of translating into French a statute drafted in English, we may note generally that very often the insecure translator, no doubt for safety's sake, has clung to too literal a translation of the original version." (Sussmann 1969, p. 19) All in all, legal translation is, according to many scholars, the result of a compromise:

Any attempt to achieve a bilingual statute-book through the translation of legislation initially drafted in one language into another cannot fully succeed. The inevitable limits of discursivity are such that translators will be compelled to sacrifice meaning for textual exactitude, and this sometimes even at the expense of clarity. (Macdonald 1997, p. 159).

The status of the legal translator is also under debate, as his/her work does not involve any creativity, unlike the translation of literature, for example. The legal translator is seen as "a non-actor for law, whose task is limited to transcribing a legal text from one language to another without participating in the production of new ideas", "a faceless player in the transmission of legal ideas", "a simple mediator" (Kasirer 2001, p. 333). Torn between the imperative of faithfulness and the need to convey meaning from one culture to another, the legal translator does his/her best using the means at his/her disposal.

An exception is represented by Canada, where translation is recognized as having the same value as the original legal text based on the rule of equal authority. This principle is consecrated in article 133 of the Canadian Constitution and has been set forth in article 8 of the Official Languages Act (OLA). It reads as follows: "Dans l'interprétation d'un texte législatif, les versions des deux langues officielles font pareillement autorité." Thus, English and French versions of the same law are equally considered. In addition, as there are voices claiming that translation is an approximative and deforming process, co-drafting is also largely used in Canada.

A legal translation is deemed successful when its function in the target culture is accurately considered and when appropriate methods are employed. According to the functionalist approach, the translator is compelled to adapt his/her strategies according to the purpose (*skopos*) that the text will have in the target language and culture. In other words, legal translation is not merely linguistic, but it depends on pragmatic circumstances, including communicative and cultural factors (Salinas 2010, p. 301).

Legal translations are performed for utilitarian or informative purposes, and the approach adopted by translators might differ in each case. If a court decision or an agreement is meant to produce the same legal effect in the target culture, a higher degree of faithfulness and accuracy is needed to render such texts in a foreign language than in the case of the translation of a piece of legislation used by scholars within comparative law research. This is also relevant for tort terminology, as legal cultures approach this legal field differently.

In what concerns the methods to be employed in legal translation, they are based on a comparative approach, a jurilinguistic analysis of the source text, as well as the research of legal equivalence. According to Jean-Claude Gémar, legal translation is essentially an exercise of comparative law (Gémar 2018, pp. 960, 961, 964) and the comparative approach ensures legal equivalence:

Translating law into a different legal culture cannot be accomplished without comparing laws, whose knowledge is essential to achieving legal equivalence. The way the target text is written should match its culture. Translating law is the moment when languages, cultures, and laws meet. To materialize, this encounter has to be based on an *ad hoc* knowledge of the laws at stake (Gémar 2018, p. 959).

In addition, a jurilinguistic examination of the original text shows that not only the signified of a notion is challenging in terms of translation, but also its signifier, its singularity, its relevance, and its appropriateness to the target legal culture (Gémar 2018, p. 975). That is why, for instance, the concept of "tort" is generally rendered as "tortious liability" ("responsabilité délictuelle" in French; "răspundere delictuală" in Romanian) in continental legal terminologies. Thus, extensive research is imperative, especially when the legal discourse contains culture-bound terms. Research work should not be limited to specialized dictionaries or parallel corpora, but should be extended to thorough reading of the main legal sources: the statute, the case law and the doctrine (Salinas 2010, p. 301).

Legal equivalence is ensured according to the function that the translated text will play in the target language by using translation strategies that may be identified at the textual level. Jean-Claude Gémar establishes three main approaches resorted to in legal translation: the source-oriented method, based on a literal rendering of the initial message; the target-oriented perspective, which focuses on meaning and is based on adaptation; and the functional translation, in search of legal equivalence of concepts (Gémar 2018, p. 560). The latter approach seems appropriate to the legal discourse, including tort terminology.

Functional translation is based on the research of conceptual equivalence in the target legal culture. According to Susan Šarčević, "a functional equivalent is a term designating a concept or institution of the target legal system having the same function as a particular concept of the source legal system" (Šarčević 2000, p. 241). "Délit civil", for example, is a functional equivalent of the notion of "tort" in common law. In what concerns the appropriateness of such equivalents, they may be acceptable, partially acceptable, or inacceptable, depending on the context. To illustrate this, we provide in what follows a brief analysis of the way tort terminology has been translated from English into French. Our corpus is represented by official translations published on the eur-lex website and by the bilingual version of the Principles of European Tort Law (PETL) (European Group on Tort Law 2005a, European Group on Tort Law 2005b).

Even if the corpus includes official translations performed by trained professionals, our examination has revealed some terminological inconsistencies. The name of the legal field, for instance, has been rendered in French by the broader phrase "responsabilité civile" ("civil liability"), including in the title of PETL:

Source text	Target text
Principles of European *Tort Law* (PETL)	Principes de droit européen de la *responsabilité civile*
[...] existing provisions of criminal law, unfair competition law or *tort law* [...] (eur-lex.europa.eu)	[...] les dispositions existantes du droit pénal, de la législation contre la concurrence déloyale ou du *droit de la responsabilité civile* [...]
It would appear that this criterion is not commonly found in the *tort law* of any of the Member States. (eur-lex.europa.eu)	Il semblerait qu'aucun des États membres ne prévoie communément ce critère dans *le droit de la responsabilité civile*.

This translation choice may be disturbing, as "civil liability" in continental legal cultures also includes contractual obligations. On the contrary, when there is a clear reference to the liability derived from a tortious act, translations in the corpus are more accurate. As the functional equivalent of "tort" in continental cultures is "délit civil", the equivalent employed for "tortious liability" is "responsabilité délictuelle":

Source text	Target text
LDCOM asserts that the State's *tortious liability* was also incurred, notably under company law. (eur-lex.europa.eu)	LDCOM a affirmé que *la responsabilité délictuelle* de l'État était également engagée, et ce notamment au regard du droit des sociétés.
This requirement will hardly ever be met for claims that are based on *tortious liability*. (eur-lex.europa.eu)	Cette condition ne peut presque jamais être remplie pour une demande fondée sur *une responsabilité délictuelle*.

The notion of "strict liability", corresponding to acts that are characterized by negligence or absence of fault, is translated through an explanatory phrase in French, namely "responsabilité sans faute", as distinguished from "responsabilité pour faute", the latter involving the existence of fault. Nevertheless, the two concepts are approached differently in common law (where foreseeability applies) and in civil law (which limits the existence of strict liability to the causality criterion):

Source text	Target text
National laws can provide for further categories of *strict liability* for dangerous activities even if the activity is not abnormally dangerous. (PETL)	Les droits nationaux peuvent prévoir des catégories supplémentaires de *responsabilité sans faute* pour activités dangereuses même si l'activité n'est pas anormalement dangereuse.
Strict liability up to a sufficiently high limit and extended liability in case of fault or neglect. (eur-lex.europa.eu)	*Responsabilité sans faute* plafonnée à un montant suffisamment élevé et responsabilité étendue en cas de faute ou de négligence.

Translators of PETL have repeatedly resorted to explanatory phrases to render concise English concepts. Considering the context, the term "defences", for instance, has been translated as "causes limitatives ou exonératoires de responsabilité". Such explanations are needed because the two languages express legal realities in different manners:

Source text	Target text
Title IV. *Defences* (PETL)	Titre IV. *Les causes limitatives ou exonératoires de responsabilité*
Defences against strict liability (PETL)	*Causes d'exonération en cas de responsabilité sans faute*

We noticed a major incoherence related to the term "damage", which, according to the context, is translated as "dommage" or as "préjudice". Unfortunately, this terminological inconsistency is to be found even within the same paragraph, as in case of the second sentence included in the table below:

Source text	Target text
(1) A person to whom *damage* to another is legally attributed is liable to compensate that *damage*. (PETL)	(1) Toute personne à qui *le dommage* subi par autrui est légalement imputable est tenue de *le* réparer.
(2) *Damage* may be attributed in particular to the person a) whose *conduct constituting fault* has caused it; (PETL)	(2) *Le préjudice* peut être imputé en particulier à toute personne: a) dont *le comportement fautif* a été la cause du *dommage*;
The court may estimate the extent of *damage* where proof of the exact amount would be too difficult or too costly. (PETL)	Le juge peut s'en remettre à une simple estimation de l'étendue du *préjudice* lorsque la preuve du montant exact se révèle trop difficile ou trop coûteuse à établir.

Also, the phrase "recoverable damage" is rendered as "préjudice réparable" (PETL, Chapter 2). In fact, the term "préjudice" is more frequently resorted to in PETL as a functional equivalent for "damage". In Title VI, for instance, there is a distinction between "pecuniary damage" ("préjudice matériel") and non-pecuniary damage ("préjudice extra-patrimonial"). In the French legal culture, the two concepts correspond to violations of the property that may be monetarily compensated ("atteinte aux droits patrimoniaux") and to violations of rights that are intangible ("atteinte aux droits extra-patrimoniaux"), respectively. Thus, we notice an adaptation of concepts to the target legal culture:

Source text	Target text
Pecuniary damage (PETL)	*Le préjudice matériel*
Non-pecuniary damage (PETL)	*Le préjudice extra-patrimonial*

Nevertheless, even if "dommage" et "préjudice" are synonyms, only one term should be preferred and used systematically. The translation of PETL needs revision to provide more terminological consistency.

In what concerns the notion of "remedies", specific to common law, it is also rendered by an explanatory paraphrase in French ("la réparation du dommage"). On the other hand, the term "damages" is consistently translated using the functional equivalent "dommages et intérêts":

Source text	Target text
Title VI. *Remedies* (PETL)	Titre VI. *La réparation du dommage*
Chapter 10. *Damages* (PETL)	Chapitre 10. *Les dommages et intérêts*
Damages are a money payment to compensate the victim, that is to say, to restore him [...] to the position he would have been in if *the wrong complained of* had not been committed. (PETL)	*Les dommages et intérêts* consistent en le paiement d'une somme d'argent visant à compenser le préjudice de la victime, c'est-à-dire, à la replacer [...] dans la position qui aurait été la sienne si *l'atteinte dont elle se plaint* n'avait pas été commise.

We also notice that the phrase "the wrong complained of" above is rendered by "l'atteinte dont elle se plaint", a clumsy literal version, as the verb "se plaindre" does not pertain to legal language. In the context below, the noun "atteinte" is present again as the equivalent of "harm":

Source text	Target text
Damage requires material or immaterial *harm* to a legally protected interest. (PETL)	Le préjudice consiste en *une atteinte* matérielle ou immatérielle à un intérêt juridiquement protégé.

Other key terms in the tort field are adapted in translation to the target language and culture. It is the case of "tortfeasor", rendered by "auteur du dommage" or simply by "auteur":

Source text	Target text
Liability can be excluded or reduced to such extent as is considered just having regard [...] to any other matters which would be relevant to establish or reduce liability of the victim if he were *the tortfeasor*. (PETL)	La responsabilité peut être exclue ou réduite dans des proportions considérées comme justes eu égard à [...] tout autre élément qui permettrait d'établir ou réduire la responsabilité de la victime si elle avait été *l'auteur du dommage*.
Solidary and several liability: relation between victim and multiple *tortfeasors* (PETL)	Responsabilité solidaire et conjointe: relation entre la victime et des *auteurs* multiples

Also, the common law term "wrongdoing" is translated as "la mauvaise action", an inappropriate solution, as the French expression does not pertain to specialized language:

Source text	Target text
Liability is solidary where: a) a person knowingly participates in or instigates or encourages *wrongdoing* by others which causes damage to the victim; (PETL)	La responsabilité est solidaire lorsque: a) une personne participe sciemment ou suscite ou encourage *la mauvaise action* d'autres personnes qui cause un dommage à la victime;

The phrase "consequential loss", rather specific to common law, is rendered by its explicative equivalent "préjudice indirect". As this concept is not specific to the French legal culture, it adds a touch of strangeness to the target text:

Source text	Target text
No *consequential losses* shall be taken into account for that purpose. (eur-lex.europa.eu)	Aucun *préjudice indirect* n'est pris en compte à cet effet.
Damages may also be awarded for loss of use of the thing, including *consequential losses* such as loss of business. (PETL)	Des dommages et intérêts pourront également être alloués en cas de perte relative à l'usage de la chose, incluant *les dommages indirects* tels que les pertes relatives à une activité professionnelle.

Basic common law notions, such as "foreseeability" ("la prévisibilité"), are adapted to the target language:

Source text	Target text
[...] *the foreseeability* of the damage to *a reasonable person* at the time of the activity [...] (PETL)	[...] *la prévisibilité* du dommage par *une personne raisonnable* au moment de l'activité [...]

We also notice that the phrase "a reasonable person" above has been rendered literally.

PETL have a hybrid nature, as they also include key concepts in the continental legal tradition that are strange to common law, such as "causation" ("lien de causalité"):

Source text	Target text
Causation (PETL)	*Le lien de causalité*
[...] in view of the conclusions reached regarding subsidies, injury, *causation* and Community interest [...] (eur-lex.europa.eu)	[...] sur la base des conclusions établies concernant les subventions, le préjudice, *le lien de causalité* et l'intérêt de la Communauté [...]

The concept of "fault", deriving from French, is rendered by its literal counterpart "faute":

Source text	Target text
A person is *liable on the basis of fault* for intentional or negligent violation of the required standard of conduct. (PETL)	Toute personne qui viole, intentionnellement ou par négligence, le standard de conduite requis, engage sa *responsabilité pour faute*.
[...] *civil liability based on fault* [...] (eur-lex.europa.eu)	[...] *responsabilité civile reposant sur une faute* [...]

An interesting example is represented by the term "defect", defined by the drafters of PETL as a deviation from expected standards in a professional or industrial context. The French term "défaillance", on the contrary, has a more precise meaning, referring to failure or even breakdown:

Source text	Target text
A person pursuing a lasting enterprise for economic or professional purposes [...] is liable for any harm caused by a *defect* of such enterprise [...] (PETL)	Toute personne poursuivant une activité durable dans un but économique ou professionnel [...] est responsable pour toute atteinte causée par *la défaillance* d'une telle entreprise [...]
"*Defect*" is any deviation from standards that are reasonably to be expected from the enterprise or from its products or services. (PETL)	La « *défaillance* » s'entend de toute déviance par rapport aux standards qui peuvent raisonnablement être attendus de la part d'une entreprise ou de ses produits ou services.

The brief examination of the corpus showed that tort terminology is not easily rendered in continental legal cultures because of the conceptual gaps already emphasized. In addition, languages describe legal realities differently and the translator faces sometimes impossible choices. The French version of the Principles of European Tort Law (European Group on Tort Law 2005b), as well as the bilingual versions available on eur-lex propose a hybrid tort terminology, based on concepts pertaining either to common law or to civil law. In addition, there are multiple lexical inconsistencies that are disturbing for any lawyer or legal professional interested in tort law. From this perspective, more efforts need to be undertaken in view of harmonizing tort law at the European level.

6 Conclusions

The comparative analysis that we carried out shows that tort is a culture-bound concept, specific to common law, and its rendering in civil law cultures is problematic. First, its semantics in the Anglo-Saxon system is broader than the connotation it has in continental cultures, as it is not clearly separated from contractual law and it may also refer to specific crimes. In addition, tort is ascertained in common law based on the foreseeability rule, whereas in civil law cultures causality is considered.

The functional equivalent of "tort" in continental cultures would be "civil delict" ("délit civil" in French, "delict civil" in Romanian). It involves the idea of tortious or extra-contractual liability ("responsabilité délictuelle"/"răspundere delictuală"), thus limited to the civil field. Nevertheless, one has to understand the semantics of legal concepts in the source legal culture in order to apprehend their complexity.

If the gap between common law and civil law in terms of tort terminology seems insurmountable, there are also discrepancies between different continental cultures. In what concerns the harmonization process, tort legislation varies largely across the EU. Even if the effort of the European Group on Tort Law is notable, more work needs to be done, as PETL includes hybrid terminology and conceptual inconsistencies that may be confusing. Having uniform tort legislation at the European level is, for the moment, just a faraway dream.

References

Baudoin JL (1989) La responsabilité civile délictuelle. Les Cahiers de droit 30(3):599–609

Beaupré M (1986) Interpreting bilingual legislation. Carswell, Toronto

Boila LR (2009) Răspunderea juridică subiectivă. C. H. Beck Publishing House, Bucharest

Borkowski A, du Plessis P (2005) Textbook on Roman law, 3rd edn. Oxford University Press, Oxford

Brownlie I (1983) System of the law of nations. Part I: state responsibility. Clarendon, Oxford

Côté PA (1999) Interprétation des lois, 3rd edn. Thémis, Montreal

David R (1996) Les grands systèmes du droit contemporain, 10th edn. Dalloz, Paris

Didier E (1990) Langues et langages du droit. Étude comparative des modes d'expression de la Common Law et du Droit Civil, en français et en anglais. Wilson and Lafleur, Montréal

Dogaru I, Drăghici P (2010) Drept civil. Teoria generală a obligațiilor. C.H. Beck Publishing House, Bucharest

European Group on Tort Law (2005a) Principles of European tort law (PETL). Text and commentary. Springer, Vienna/New York

European Group on Tort Law (2005b) Principles of European Tort Law (PETL), French version. http://www.egtl.org/docs/PETLFrench.pdf

Gémar J (1995) Traduire ou l'art d'interpréter, vol II. Presses de l'Université de Québec, Sainte-Foy

Gémar JC (2018) L'analyse comparée en traduction juridique, ses enjeux, sa nécessité. Int J Semiot Law 31(4):957–975

Harpwood V (2009) Modern Tort Law, 9th edn. Routledge-Cavendish, Taylor and Francis Group, London and New York

Kadner Graziano TM (2008) Les principes du droit européen de la responsabilité délictuelle (Principles of European Tort Law) – Forces et faiblesses. In Winiger B (ed.) (2008) La responsabilité civile de demain/Europäisches Haftungrecht morgen, 219–247, Schulthess, Zurich

Kasirer N (2001) François Gény's libre recherche scientifique as a guide for legal translation. Louisiana Law Rev 61(2):331–352

Katsivela M (2020) La notion de causalité et le délit de négligence (common law)/responsabilité extracontractuelle du fait personnel (droit civil) au Canada: une étude de droit comparé. Revue générale de droit 50(1):151–177

Koch AB (2021) The dynamics of tort law in Europe—two decades of accumulated experience. Eur Tort Law Yearb 11(1):711–740

Koziol H, Schulze R (eds) (2008) Tort law of the European Community. Springer, Vienna/New York

Lavoie J (2023) Le bilinguisme législatif et la place de la traduction. TTR 16(1):121–139

Légifrance. Le service public de la diffusion du droit. https://www.legifrance.gouv.fr/

Macdonald RA (1997) Legal Bilingualism. Revue de droit de McGill 42:119–168

Moreteau O (2009) Les frontières de la langue et du droit: vers une méthodologie de la traduction juridique. Revue internationale de droit comparé 61(4):695–713

Ouedraogo A (2008) L'évolution du concept de faute dans la théorie de la responsabilité internationale des États. Revue québécoise de droit international/Quebec Journal of International Law/ Revista quebequense de derecho internacional 21(2):129–165

Pierre P (2014) Les dommages et intérêts punitifs ou restitutoires (en droit français et européen). Revue juridique de l'Ouest 2:23–35

Pisillo-Mazzeschi R (1992) The due diligence rule and the nature of international responsibility of states. German Yearb Int Law 35:9–5

Poirier D, Debruche AF (2005) Introduction générale à la common law, 3rd edn. Yvon Blais et Bruylant, Cowansville (QC) et Bruxelles

Pop L, Popa IF, Vidu SI (2012) Tratat elementar de drept civil. Obligațiile. Universul Juridic Publishing House, Bucharest
Romoșan ID (2008) Vinovăția în dreptul civil roman. All Beck, Bucharest
Sage YL (1996) French law of delict: the role of fault and the principles governing losses and remedies. Victoria Univ Law Rev (VUWLawRw) 26(2):293–311
Salinas CB (2010) Les clauses d'exonération de responsabilité: stratégies de traduction. Meta 55(2):287–308
Šarčević S (1989) Conceptual dictionaries for translation in the field of law. Int J Lexicogr 2(4):277–293
Šarčević S (2000) New approach to legal translation. Kluwer Law International, The Hague
Snell-Hornby M (1988) Translation studies: an integrated approach. Benjamins, Amsterdam
Sussmann FB (1969) Bilingualism and the law in Canada. Travaux du sixième colloque international de droit comparé. Éditions de l'Université d'Ottawa, Ottawa, pp. 9–38
Villiers R (1977) Rome et le droit privé. Albin Michel, Paris
Zannas PA (1952) La responsabilité internationale des États pour les actes de négligence. Gangin et Laubsher, Montreux
Zimmermann R (1990) The law of obligations: Roman foundations of the civilian tradition. JutaandCo, Cape Town

Procedure and Methods of Interpretation

The Principle of Cooperation as Reflected in Romanian Civil Procedural Law

Nicolae-Horia Țiț

Abstract Although not expressly regulated in the Romanian Code of Civil Procedure, the principle of cooperation is present in Romanian civil procedural law through several mechanisms and obligations established for the court, the parties and their lawyers. The chapter analyzes, starting from the principles existing in the European Model Rules of Civil Procedure elaborated by the European Law Institute and UNIDROIT, the cooperation mechanisms present in Romanian civil procedural law and comments on the way in which they can be implemented in practice.

1 Introduction

Civil proceedings represent a complex activity designed to resolve a legal dispute arising between private persons, with a view to restoring legal order. In light of this purpose, the rules governing civil proceedings must ensure, on the one hand, a fair balance between the rights of the parties, so that they may effectively present their case before the court, both in terms of claims and defences, and, on the other hand, the general interest of safeguarding the stability of civil relations, through the prompt and efficient resolution of disputes. The person entrusted with guaranteeing the effectiveness of these purposes is the judge, whose primary task is to ensure that procedural rules governing the exercise of the parties' rights are observed and to deliver a lawful and well-reasoned solution to the dispute. The judge's role is therefore central, the law conferring upon him or her a series of prerogatives and responsibilities which make it possible to control proceedings and apply the law to the concrete circumstances of the case. These prerogatives place the judge in the position of "manager" of the proceedings, while the exercise of such "powers" ensures the legality of the proceedings. At the same time, the judge is under the duty of impartiality and must respect the principle of equality of arms, exercising his or her

N.-H. Țiț (✉)
Faculty of Law, 'Alexandru Ioan Cuza' University of Iași, Iași, Romania
e-mail: horia.tit@uaic.ro

I. Maria Costea (ed.), *Legal Interpretation in Motion*, Ius Gentium: Comparative Perspectives on Law and Justice 144,
https://doi.org/10.1007/978-3-032-32948-6_6

prerogatives in such a way as to secure each party's right to be heard and to serve the objective of fact-finding. Modern civil proceedings are to be viewed as a comprehensive activity based on cooperation between the parties, their legal representatives and the court, aimed at ensuring the fair, prompt, and efficient resolution of disputes (van Rhee 2022; Uzelac 2025; Chainais et al. 2020; Strickler and Alexey 2021).

This dimension of judicial activity is set out in legal doctrine as a constituent of the principle of cooperation: civil litigation is understood as an activity in which parties and judicial authorities cooperate in order to resolve individual disputes brought before the judicial courts by those concerned. The principle of cooperation ensures a balance between the prerogatives conferred by law upon the judge (mainly subsumed under the principle of its function in fact-finding, and likewise under the principle of legality) and the principle of party autonomy (which determines the scope of procedural rights and obligations, as well as the good-faith exercise of such rights and the avoidance of procedural abuse). Its overarching purpose is to guarantee the delivery of justice that is both fair and efficient: on the one hand, through the well-grounded, lawful, and prompt settlement of disputes; on the other, through the effective functioning of the judicial mechanism, in view of the resources committed by the parties and the State to the proper administration of justice. It follows that the links with the principle of proportionality are both evident and inherent, the objective being to give full effect to all the guarantees of the right to a fair trial, in each of its dimensions (van Rhee, 2022; Uzelac, 2025).

Despite its importance, the principle of cooperation has not been expressly codified in the New Romanian Code of Civil Procedure[1] (hereinafter referred to as the "Romanian Code of Civil Procedure" or "RCCP"). Although the Romanian Code of Civil Procedure, in its Preliminary Title, contains a chapter dedicated to the fundamental principles of civil proceedings, the term "cooperation" does not appear in any of those provisions nor in subsequent articles. Likewise, the principle of cooperation has not enjoyed particular attention in Romanian doctrine or case-law, which have remained anchored rather in classical concepts such as the principle of party autonomy, the active role of the judiciary, the principle of adversarial proceedings, and the right to a fair trial.

While the principle of cooperation is not, terminologically, framed in Romanian civil procedural law, it is nevertheless embodied in the rules of procedure laid down in the RCCP and in special legislation. Procedural mechanisms as currently shaped tend towards the idea of cooperation between parties and courts, constituting the real basis for resolving disputes in a sound and lawful manner. The following analysis will therefore examine how the principle of cooperation is reflected in Romanian civil procedural law, with reference to the ELI/UNIDROIT European Model Rules of Civil Procedure (European Law Institute (ELI), International Institute for the

---

[1] The New Romanian Code of Civil Procedure was adopted under Law No. 134/2010 and republished in the Official Gazette No. 545 of 3 August 2012, following the amendments brought by Law No. 76/2012 aimed at implementing Law No. 134/2010. Following its entry into force, it has undergone several successive amendments.

Unification of Private Law (UNIDROIT), 2021), in particular Rules 2, 3, and 4, which deal with the general duty of cooperation, the role of the parties and their lawyers, and the role of the court.

2 General Duty of Cooperation

According to Rule 2 of the ELI/UNIDROIT European Model Rules of Civil Procedure (European Law Institute (ELI), International Institute for the Unification of Private Law (UNIDROIT), 2021), parties, their lawyers and the court must co-operate to promote the fair, efficient and speedy resolution of the dispute. The rule of cooperation is therefore the foundation of the entire procedural activity, upon which the entire structure of litigation is built (Uzelac 2025).

Cooperation concerns, on the one hand, the role of the court and of the judge, as well as the duties incumbent upon them in organising and managing the proceedings, and, on the other hand, the role of the parties and their representatives, in bringing the case before the court and determining the limits of the procedural framework, presenting the facts and adducing evidence, and seeking amicable settlement of the dispute, etc. (van Rhee 2022; van Rhee 2018).

At the same time, cooperation requires that procedural rights be exercised in good faith, so as to avoid delaying the resolution of the dispute or engaging the parties or the State in unnecessary or disproportionate costs in relation to the value and importance of the litigation.

Cooperation between the parties and the court assumes that any procedural means must undergo a complete procedural cycle, moving from the parties to the court and returning from the court to the parties. The mechanisms of cooperation must be effective, ensuring that the parties acquire a proper understanding of judicial procedure and allowing the court to clarify the issues in dispute clearly and promptly. Cooperation is premised on balancing the roles conferred upon the parties and the court, in order to ensure the prompt and efficient resolution of the dispute (Uzelac 2025; Jeuland 2014).

Although, as mentioned, the Romanian Code of Civil Procedure does not expressly regulate the principle of cooperation, there are sufficient provisions which reflect its substance. For example, it is established that proceedings may be initiated only at the request of the interested party [article 91 para. (1), article 192 para. (1)–(2) of the RCCP; Rule 21 para. (1) of the ELI/UNIDROIT European Model Rules of Civil Procedure]; civil proceedings are initiated by submitting a statement of claim to the court [article 192 para (2) of the RCCP], which must comply with the formal requirements laid down by the law [article 193 of the RCCP]. However, the mere filing of a claim does not in itself trigger judicial proceedings; prior to the statement of claim being officially notified to the defendant for the purpose of preparing his defence, it undergoes a preliminary regularisation procedure [article 200 of the RCCP] which, in principle, entails two stages: the review of the claim by the judge and informing the claimant of the deficiencies observed, with the possibility to rectify them within 10 days of such notification; the annulment of the claim, through an order rendered without summoning the parties, if such deficiencies are not remedied. The claimant may request the re-examination of the annulment order by another panel of the same court, which shall adjudicate the request only after the claimant has been duly summoned.

The regularisation procedure forms an essential mechanism of cooperation, as it serves to prevent the annulment of the claim for procedural reasons before the claimant has been given the possibility to remedy the shortcomings indicated by the court, by means of a personalised notification specifying exactly which elements of the claim are missing or incomplete. At the same time, this mechanism ensures the proportionality of the sanction of annulment, since such sanction is not applied without the claimant being aware of its causes and without having previously been given the opportunity to remedy them. The right of access to a court is not affected, as annulment of the claim on procedural grounds does not prevent the bringing of a new claim before the court for the resolution of the dispute, the sanction of annulment being the result of a purely formal review of the claim, without examination of its merits. Moreover, if the new claim is filed within 6 months from the annulment of the first claim, the claimant still benefits from the interruptive effect of the first claim on the limitation period of the substantive right of action, irrespective of the annulment of the initial claim. It is also highly relevant that, through the regularisation procedure, the judge ensures that the claimant provides a complete and accurate presentation of the dispute brought before the court, in particular with regard to the claims and the factual situation, thus securing for the defendant the right to an effective defence. As indicated, the claim is not notified to the defendant until this verification stage is completed. Even though, at this pre-trial stage, the judge does not carry out a substantive examination of the merits of the case, he or she must nevertheless read the claim with a view to the future need of examining it in depth. In other words, although at this stage the court does not exercise proper jurisdictional prerogatives, it carries out the necessary checks to ensure, on the one hand, that the defendant is fully apprised of the claimant's claims, arguments, and evidence, and, on the other hand, that in the next stage the court may analyse the facts submitted and deliver a solution in accordance with the law.

What may be criticised, from the perspective of efficiency and proportionality, in relation to the verification and regularisation procedure, is the fact that the 10-day deadline is absolute and cannot be varied by the court, either by shortening it (in urgent cases) or by extending it (where the claimant requests such extension for good reasons). From this perspective, the judge should be able to adjust the time-limit for remedying the shortcomings of the claim to the claimant's specific situation or to the nature of the verifications or steps required (for instance, in some cases the claimant may need to contact other authorities or institutions, which may not respond in due time).

In order to maintain the proportionality of the sanction of annulment and in line with the principle of cooperation, the amendment of the Romanian Code of Civil Procedure by Law no. 310/2018 introduced the rule that a claim cannot be annulled for lack of data or information which the claimant does not possess and for the obtaining of which the assistance of the court is required. Thus, where the statement of claim contains shortcomings which can only be remedied with the assistance of the court, the latter must not annul it, but must instead undertake the necessary steps to obtain the information from public institutions, authorities, or third parties.

At the same time, the verification and regularisation procedure may lead to an increase in the judge's non-jurisdictional workload, especially with regard to the verification and calculation of court fees. For this reason, the current legislative solution should be adjusted so that certain tasks specific to this pre-trial stage are performed not by the judge but by the court clerk or another officer of the court (such as a judicial assistant), in particular with respect to the determination of court fees (Committee of Ministers to the Member States of the Council of Europe 1986).

Another procedural mechanism which illustrates the general duty of cooperation is the determination of the procedural framework, the legal characterisation of the acts and facts subject to adjudication, and the adducing of evidence. As regards the first issue, as a rule, the framework of the proceedings is established by the parties through their claims and defences [article 9 para. (2) of the RCCP], and the court is bound to respect the scope of the proceedings, as defined by the claims and defences submitted [article 22 para. (6), article 397 para. (1) of the RCCP]. However, in cases expressly provided by law, the court shall, ex officio, order the participation of third parties in the proceedings (for example, in litigation concerning road traffic accidents, the insurers of the drivers involved must be joined to the case of the court's own motion); in other instances, where the court, having regard to the specific circumstances of the case under examination, deems the joinder of third parties necessary, it shall submit this issue to the adversarial discussion of the parties. If neither party requests the joinder of such third parties, and the court finds that the resolution of the dispute cannot be achieved without the participation of the said third party, the claim shall be dismissed without an examination on the merits [article 78 para. (2) of the RCCP]. This is, therefore, a mechanism of cooperation through which the court can indicate to the parties the possible requirement of completing the procedural framework with third parties; however, as a general rule, the judge is not empowered to introduce them *motu proprio*, but merely to decline hearing of the case if the parties refuse to adjust the procedural framework accordingly.

As regards the establishment of the factual elements of the case and their legal characterisation, the mechanisms regulated by the Romanian Code of Civil Procedure essentially follow the traditional rule *da mihi factum, dabo tibi ius*, originating in French procedural law (Chainais et al. 2020; Croze 2011; Uzelac 2017). The parties are required, in their submissions—namely, the statement of claim and the defence—to present correctly and comprehensively the facts of the dispute and put forward their own position regarding the arguments of the opposing party. As a rule, this duty is fulfilled during the written stage of proceedings, prior to the scheduling of the first hearing, so that the judge may already have an overview of the disputed issues. Of course, the judge may request further clarifications from the parties, including raising additional factual issues not mentioned in the submissions [article 22 para. (2) of the RCCP; Rule 24 para. (1) of the ELI/UNIDROIT European Model Rules of Civil Procedure], but may not modify the essential factual elements which form the basis of the claim. In other words, the court may request clarifications but cannot establish *ex officio* the factual grounds of the parties' claims or defences.

As regards the legal characterisation, the situation is fundamentally different: the court is not, as a rule, bound by the legal qualification advanced by the parties, and the judge may modify it, provided that the matter is subjected to the adversarial debate of the parties. Naturally, the parties may advance before the judge a particular legal qualification; nevertheless, generally, the judge is not bound thereby, but must adopt the correct legal characterisation, also with regard to the application of foreign law [article 22 para. (4) of the RCCP; Rule 26 para. (1)–(2) of the ELI/UNIDROIT European Model Rules of Civil Procedure]. Furthermore, the court is precluded from annulling a claim on account of the absence of a legal characterisation by the party; accordingly, access to the court may be ensured by a simple indication of the claims and the facts, without the need for a legal qualification. In such cases, the judge is required to establish the proper legal characterisation of the acts and facts for the adjudication of the claims. Similarly, in respect of defences, the defendant is not required to rely on specific legal grounds, being sufficient to present his or her own account of the facts. In all situations, the legal characterisation or recharacterisation of the acts and facts submitted for adjudication requires adversarial debate [Art. 22 para. (4) of the RCCP]; the court must therefore inform the parties of the qualification envisaged and provide them with the opportunity to submit their arguments, in writing or orally.

Legal characterisation cannot be made by the court for the first time in the judgment itself, without having first been the subject of adversarial debate [article 14 para. (6) of the RCCP]. In accordance with the principle of cooperation, the court must clearly inform the parties which factual and legal issues it seeks to clarify, in such a way as to enable them effectively to respond. In principle, the court should notify the parties, before the hearing, of the issues it wishes to clarify, so that they may prepare their submissions, which may even be filed in writing before the hearing.

However, where the dispute concerns rights over which the parties may freely dispose of, they may, by express agreement, determine the legal characterisation of the acts and facts submitted for adjudication. In such cases, the judge is required to adhere to the legal qualification indicated by the parties yet may change it if that qualification would infringe upon the rights or legitimate interests of third parties [article 22 para. (5) of the RCCP; Rule 26 para. (3) of the ELI/UNIDROIT European Model Rules of Civil Procedure]. Even in this situation, however, reclassification must be discussed with the parties in adversarial proceedings. Therefore, while non-contestation of factual allegations may relieve a party from the burden of proof [article 255 para. (2) of the RCCP], legal classification cannot bind the judge unless it is the result of an express agreement of the parties concerning rights at their disposal and provided it does not prejudice third parties.

Accordingly, the mechanism of cooperation emphasises the duty of the parties to present the facts and the duty of the court to provide the correct legal characterisation of the facts and acts submitted to it. Consistently with this mechanism, the burden of adducing evidence rests primarily with the parties (art. 249 of the RCCP), so that their submissions are not left as bare assertions. This rule is accompanied by procedural guarantees intended to instil discipline in litigation: as a general principle, evidence must be adduced during the written stage of the proceedings, by the claimant in the statement of claim and by the defendant in the statement of defence [article 254 para. (1) of the RCCP]. However, in certain cases expressly provided by law, the parties may adduce new evidence during the taking of evidence, provided the principle of equality of arms is observed: whenever one party is allowed to adduce evidence at this stage, the other party must also be allowed to counter it.

As a specific expression of the principle of cooperation, the court may request clarifications from the parties or may raise with them the necessity of taking additional evidence [article 22 para. (2), Article 254 para. (5) of the RCCP; Rule 25 para. (3) of the ELI/UNIDROIT European Model Rules of Civil Procedure]. The court may also, of its own motion, order the taking of evidence, even in the face of the parties' opposition; such prerogative must be exercised prudently and only in exceptional circumstances [Rule 25 para. (3) of the ELI/UNIDROIT European Model Rules of Civil Procedure], so as not to undermine the principle of equality. The evidence adduced by the parties must be administered first; where, following this, the judge still has uncertainties as to the factual background, the judge must inform the parties, allow them to submit additional evidence to clarify the facts, or subject to adversarial discussion the necessity of administering a given evidentiary measure. Where the parties fail to react, and only where clarification of the matter on which the judge remains uncertain is essential to the fair resolution of the dispute, may the court, of its own motion, order the taking of evidence, even in the face of the parties' opposition; the parties shall then bear, at the court's order, the obligation to advance the costs of administering the evidence, generally incumbent upon the claimant, whose refusal entails suspension of the proceedings under art. 242 of the Romanian Code of Civil Procedure.

The general duty of cooperation between the court and the parties is also found in other procedural rules, such as: the court's duty to ensure that any matters of fact or law, including those raised ex officio, are submitted to the adversarial debate of the parties, and the prohibition against a judgment being based on factual or legal issues which have not been previously submitted to the adversarial debate of the parties [article 14 para. (5)–(6) of the RCCP]; debates may only be closed only after all factual and legal aspects of the case have been clarified [article 394 para. (1) of the RCCP]; however, if the judge does not deem the case sufficiently clarified, he or she may order the reopening of the proceedings for further explanations or additional evidence, with mandatory summoning of the parties [article 400 of the RCCP]; the parties must also be informed of the estimated duration of the evidentiary phase, which may be reconsidered, where appropriate, after hearing the parties (article 238 of the RCCP); furthermore, the judge shall endeavour to secure an amicable settlement between the parties, which may include ordering their personal appearance, even if represented, or inviting them to attend an information session on the benefits of mediation before an authorised mediator [article 227 para. (1)–(2) of the RCCP].

3 The Role of the Parties and Their Lawyers

Rule 3 of the ELI/UNIDROIT European Model Rules of Civil Procedure regulates the role of the parties and their lawyers in giving effect to the principle of cooperation. It sets out five categories of obligations concerning: the amicable settlement of the dispute, the proper conduct of judicial proceedings, the presentation of facts and the adducing of evidence, assisting the judge in establishing the facts and in applying the law, as well as the obligation to act in good faith and to avoid abuse of procedural rights in relation to the court and to the other parties (Uzelac 2017, 2025).

3.1 The Duty to Pursue an Amicable Resolution of the Dispute

The primary obligation among these five concerns the duty of the parties to an amicable settlement of the dispute. This obligation is further detailed in Rule 9 of the of the ELI/UNIDROIT European Model Rules of Civil Procedure, according to which the parties are under an obligation to cooperate with a view to reaching an amicable settlement of the dispute, both before and after proceedings are brought before the court (van Rhee 2022; Uzelac 2017). Lawyers have an essential role here, being under a professional duty to inform the parties of the existence of alternative dispute resolution methods and to assist and encourage them to use appropriate methods where relevant. These duties are not expressly regulated in Romanian civil procedural legislation. The Romanian Code of Civil Procedure refers to the obligation incumbent on the judge to advise the parties to seek an amicable settlement of the dispute through mediation [article 21 para. (1) of the RCCP, and to attempt their reconciliation throughout the proceedings by providing the necessary guidance [article 21 para. (2) of the RCCP]; these duties are further specified in article 227 of the Romanian Code of Civil Procedure and Law no. 192/2006. However, Romanian civil procedural legislation does not impose a corresponding duty on the parties to attempt an amicable settlement, particularly since the Constitutional Court, by Decision no. 266/2014 (published in the Official Gazette, Part I, No. 464 of 25 June 2014), struck down as unconstitutional the legislative provision requiring parties, before commencing certain disputes, to attend an information session on the advantages of mediation.

It is regrettable that the special legislation on mediation has remained unrevised after the Constitutional Court's ruling invalidating the 2012 legislative measure [which required parties to attend, free of charge, an information session on the benefits of mediation prior to filing a claim, under the sanction of inadmissibility in specific disputes, such as those relating to consumer protection, family law, possession, boundaries or neighbourhood relations, professional liability and malpractice, individual employment disputes, and patrimonial disputes up to 50,000 lei (aprox. EUR 10,000)]. The inadmissibility sanction, overly harsh and undermining the guarantees of effective access to justice, ought to have been replaced by less intrusive sanctions or incentives, consistent with the express wording of article 5 para. (2) of Directive 2008/52/EC.

Accordingly, as the legislation was not amended following this decision of the Constitutional Court, there is at present no legal requirement obliging parties to resort to mediation, or even to receive information on its advantages, in any category of disputes. The choice to use mediation or other alternative dispute resolution (hereinafter referred to as "ADR") methods rests entirely with the parties; the court may only invite them to such an information session or recommend mediation, but never coerce them [article 227 para. (2)–(3) of the RCCP; article 5 para. (1) of the Directive 2008/52/EC; Rule 10 para. (3) of the ELI/UNIDROIT European Model Rules of Civil Procedure]. However, if parties accept to attend such an information session but then fail to appear, the court may impose a fine, though the maximum amount (approx. EUR 200) is insignificant.

Romanian legislation also does not authorise judges to act as mediators or to assist the parties in drafting settlement agreements [Rule 10 para. (3) of the ELI/UNIDROIT European Model Rules of Civil Procedure]. Judges may only recommend mediation, invite the parties to participate in an information session on mediation and its benefits [article 227 para. (2)–(3) of the RCCP], or personally undertake the procedure of informing such parties about the advantages of mediation. [article 227 para. (2)–(3) of the RCCP], [article 2 para. (13) of Law no. 192/2006 on Mediation and the Organisation of the Profession of Mediator]. Nor do civil procedural rules or the legislation on the legal profession clearly impose a professional duty on lawyers to inform their clients of ADR mechanisms, or to assist them in identifying the appropriate alternative method according to the nature of the dispute [Rule 9 para. (2) of the ELI/UNIDROIT European Model Rules of Civil Procedure]. Some provisions to this effect are nonetheless contained in article 2 para.(6) of Law No. 192/2006 on Mediation and the Organisation of the Profession of Mediator, which requires the lawyer to recommend to the parties, or to the party he or she represents, the amicable settlement of the dispute or conflict through mediation, in accordance with the special law. Moreover, article 2 para. (13) of the same act provides that lawyers may carry out the information procedure concerning the advantages of mediation. There remains, however, no clear regulation sanctioning lawyers for the abusive use of judicial proceedings, notwithstanding the existence of simpler amicable remedies that might have ensured a swifter and more effective resolution of the dispute (see Principle 2 (2–3) of the Annex to Recommendation R (84)5 of the Committee of Ministers of the Council of Europe).

In the event that the parties resolve their dispute amicably, by mediation or by another alternative means of resolution, the court shall endorse their settlement through a judgment of expedient nature, which can be challenged solely by appeal, and exclusively on procedural grounds [articles 438–441 of the RCCP].

3.2 *The Duty to Contribute to the Proper Conduct of Judicial Proceedings*

The second core duty of the parties and their lawyers is to cooperate in securing the proper conduct of judicial proceedings. This obligation is laid down in general terms by article 10 of the Romanian Code of Civil Procedure, which requires the parties to perform procedural acts in accordance with the conditions, sequence and time-limits established by law or by the judge, as well as to contribute to the proceedings being conducted without undue delay, with a view to their proper conclusion. These obligations are closely linked, as will be shown below, to the general duty of good faith. The procedural means by which the parties contribute to the conduct of judicial proceedings are varied, including: the direct service of claims, defences or other pleadings where represented by lawyers or legal advisers (article 169 of the RCCP); the rule of deemed knowledge of the hearing date, under which parties who appear personally or through a representative at a hearing, or who have signed for service of a summons for a given hearing, will not be summoned again for subsequent hearings before the same court, being under a duty to follow the further progress of the case and comply with the court's orders (article 229 para. (1) of the RCCP); the obligation of a party to produce evidence in its possession where so ordered by the judge, ex officio or at the request of the other party (articles. 10 para. (2), 293 of the RCCP); ensuring the attendance of witnesses at the hearing at which they are to be examined, without any need for further summons (article 312 para. (2) of the RCCP); the personal appearance of a party before the court, when so ordered (article 13 para. (4) of the RCCP), for example in order to attempt an amicable settlement (article 227 para. (1) of the RCCP) or for answering interrogatories (article 352 para. (1) of the RCCP); the taking of evidence through lawyers and legal advisers (articles 366–388 of the RCCP), although this latter procedure is unfortunately rarely used in practice.

3.3 *The Duty to Submit the Facts of the Case and the Relevant Evidence in Support Thereof*

The third duty incumbent upon the parties and their lawyers concerns the presentation of the facts of the case and of the relevant evidence for their determination. Presenting the facts of the case is a fundamental duty of the parties, intrinsically connected to both the principle of party autonomy and the principle of adversarial proceedings. Seising the court implies laying out the procedural framework in full, that is, alongside the statement of claims or defences, a detailed presentation of the facts, so that the court may identify the issues in dispute and determine whether evidence is required. Accordingly, the parties are obliged to present the factual circumstances on which their claims or defences rest fully and truthfully, without distortion or omission of facts known to them [article 14 para. (3) of the RCCP]. This duty reflects their role in shaping the procedural framework, the object and limits of the trial; it is for the parties to bring the dispute before the court, and in that context, providing a detailed account of the facts is an essential obligation.

This obligation is expressly reflected both in the provisions on the content of the statement of claim and in those on the statement of defence [article 194 letter (d), article 205 para. (2) letter (c) of the RCCP]. In particular, omission of the factual grounds in the statement of claim may lead to its annulment [article 196 para. (1), article 200 para. (4) of the RCCP]. Parties are further required to set out their own position in response to the opposing party's allegations on relevant facts [article 14 para. (3) of the RCCP], since failure to contest may amount to recognition, thereby dispensing with the need for proof [article 255 para. (2) of the RCCP]. While the court may request clarifications or invite discussion on additional factual elements [article 22 para. (2) of the RCCP], it cannot change the essential facts underlying the claims or defences. The court is bound by the facts as presented by the parties, which it may only clarify, supplement, or complement with implicit facts, always respecting the adversarial principle (as reflected in Rule 24 of the ELI/UNIDROIT Model Rules).

With regard to evidence, the burden of proposing it rests primarily on the parties, who are required to substantiate their allegations before the court (article 249 of the RCCP). Their duty goes beyond simply listing the means of proof: they must indicate with precision what each item of evidence is intended to establish, so that the court can determine its relevance and usefulness in clarifying the facts [article 255 para. (1) of the RCCP]. If the evidence adduced proves insufficient, the court must raise with the parties the need for supplementation and may even initiate the taking of additional evidence [article 254 para. (5) of the RCCP]. Where it is indispensable to ascertain the truth, the court may order the taking of evidence despite the parties' opposition [articles 22 para. (2), 254 para. (5) of the RCCP], though this prerogative should be exercised prudently and only in exceptional cases. These duties reflect the approach embodied in Rule 25 of the ELI/UNIDROIT Model European Rules of Civil Procedure.

3.4 The Duty to Assist the Court in Establishing the Facts and in Applying the Law

The fourth duty of the parties and their lawyers, reflecting the principle of cooperation, is their involvement in the establishment of facts and in the application of the law by the judge. This represents one of the key mechanisms of cooperation (Uzelac, 2017). As regards the establishment of facts, beyond presenting truthfully and fully their own account of the relevant circumstances, parties are required to provide the court with all relevant evidence and to facilitate the judge's access to information considered relevant. Thus, a party in possession of a relevant document must, as a rule, submit it, even when requested by the other party; otherwise, the court may regard the opposing party's allegations as proven (article 295 of the RCCP). Parties must also cooperate with court-appointed experts by providing all necessary explanations and clarifications; if a party obstructs the expert's task, the court may deem the opposing party's assertions proven, in conjunction with the other evidence in the case (article 335 para. (3) of the RCCP). During interrogatory, parties must disclose to the court personal facts capable of resolving the dispute (article 351 of the RCCP), and unjustified refusal to appear or to reply may be treated as an admission in full or as prima facie evidence for the opposing party (article 358 of the RCCP).

Regarding the application of the law, as stated above, the parties are not bound but are free to indicate the legal characterisation of the dispute. Both claimant and defendant may, in their pleadings, set out the legal basis of their claims or defences, though this is not a condition of admissibility. During the proceedings they may also put forward arguments as to the legal qualification, without thereby altering the framework of the case. The court, however, bears the general duty to give or, if necessary, to restore the correct legal characterisation. The parties must in every instance be given the chance to express their views on this issue; the judge cannot alter or reclassify the legal basis directly in the judgment [article 22 para. (5), article 14 para. (6) of the RCCP; Rule 26 para. (2) of the ELI/UNIDROIT Model European Rules of Civil Procedure]. Nonetheless, the parties may agree upon the legal characterisation of the matter where it relates to rights at their disposal and does not prejudice the rights or legitimate interests of third persons [article 22 para. (5) of the RCCP; Rule 26 para (3) of the ELI/UNIDROIT Model European Rules of Civil Procedure].

3.5 The Duty to Act in Good Faith and to Avoid Abuse of Process

A fifth and particularly significant obligation derived from the principle of cooperation is that of exercising procedural rights in good faith and refraining from abusive use of such rights. The Romanian Code of Civil Procedure, in article 12, articulates this duty in a dual dimension: on the one hand, it requires parties to exercise their rights in line with the purpose for which the law recognises them and with due regard to the rights of the opposing party; on the other hand, it attaches liability where rights are exercised abusively. The sanctions available to the court range from judicial fines to the award of damages—both material and moral—to the affected party (articles 187–191 of the RCCP). Beyond sanctions, the system also incorporates preventive mechanisms against abuse, such as rules of inadmissibility, whereby procedural steps undertaken in bad faith are deprived of effect. Thus, for instance, a second motion for challenging the same judge on an identical ground already rejected is inadmissible (article 47 para. (3) of the RCCP), as is a subsequent request for change of venue based on circumstances that already existed and were known to the party when the earlier request was lodged (article 146 para. (1) of the RCCP).

To discourage abuse of procedural remedies, Romanian law has instituted mechanisms limiting the dilatory effect of motions for challenging the judge and changing of venue. Thus, under article 49 para. (2) of the Romanian Code of Civil Procedure, challenging the judge does not suspend the proceedings; the judge concerned is merely barred from delivering the final decision but remains competent to conduct all other procedural steps. If the challenge is subsequently allowed, the acts already performed may be either preserved or annulled, depending on the circumstances. Similarly, a motion for changing the venue does not suspend the proceedings by operation of law; any stay of proceedings may only be ordered by the court competent to rule on the request for changing the venue [article 143 para. (1) of the RCCP], while if the case continues and the venue is later changed, the judgment rendered is automatically annulled [article 145 para. (2) of the RCCP]. Furthermore, in order to guarantee compensation for the damage caused by the abusive exercise of procedural rights, in certain cases the law requires the prior payment of a bond or security (for example, as regards requests for suspension of enforcement proceedings or suspension of proceedings pending the decision on the motion for change of venue).

4 Role of the Court

The court's main obligation is to actively and effectively conduct the proceedings and to ensure that the parties benefit from equal treatment and comply with their procedural duties (Rule 4 of the ELI/UNIDROIT Model Rules of Civil Procedure). Although the Romanian Code of Civil Procedure does not expressly regulate this obligation nor synthesize, in a general provision, the judge's duties regarding the conduct of the proceedings, numerous prerogatives are nevertheless conferred upon the judge in this respect. The judge is bound to decide upon any claim falling within the jurisdiction of the courts and may not refuse to resolve a dispute on the grounds that the law does not provide or is unclear or incomplete [article 5 para. (1)–(2) of the RCCP]. The judge's role as "director" of the proceedings is essential, with many concrete applications: the judge sets the first hearing date after verifying and regularising the statement of claim and orders the parties' summons [article 201 para. (3)–(4) of the RCCP]; schedules the timetable of hearings throughout the trial [article 241 para. (1)–(2) of the RCCP]; verifies the proper service of summons for each hearing and, where necessary, adjourns proceedings to ensure lawful summons or knowledge of the proceedings [article 153 para. (1)–(2), article 219, article 241 para (3) of the RCCP]; at the first hearing with the parties duly summoned, the judge is obliged ex officio to verify jurisdiction, regardless of whether any objection has been raised [article 131 of the RCCP]; the judge may order measures to ensure procedural efficiency and expedition, such as measures for the evidentiary proceedings (summoning or ensuring the attendance of witnesses, production of documents, etc.), precautionary measures if requested, or for securing of evidence [article 203, article 241 para. (4) of the RCCP]; the judge must recommend that the parties resolve their dispute through mediation and attempt reconciliation throughout the proceedings [article 21, article 227 para. (1) of the RCCP]; the judge presides over hearings and may impose measures, including sanctions, to preserve solemnity or order in the courtroom [article 217 of the RCCP]; the judge determines which evidence adduced by the parties is to be admitted and in what order [article 255 para. (1), article 260 para. (1) of the RCCP], being able to reconsider previously admitted evidence if no longer necessary [article 259 of the RCCP]; the judge evaluates whether the adduced evidence is sufficient and, if additional evidence is necessary, raises this issue with the parties [article 254 para. (5) of the RCCP]; finally, the judge raises for discussion any factual or legal matters necessary to resolve the case, within the procedural framework defined by the parties, and decides when and under what conditions the evidentiary phase and the hearing of submissions may be brought to an end, in accordance with the guarantees of fair trial [articles 22 para. (2), article 244 para. (1), article 392, article 394 of the RCCP].

In a traditional approach, the Romanian Code of Civil Procedure entrusts judges with extensive powers, both to safeguard the lawfulness and fairness of proceedings and to secure the delivery of a lawful and well-reasoned judgment in disputes brought before them. The conduct of proceedings must be ensured actively and effectively by the court; judges are required, on the one hand, to examine in detail the facts of the dispute and to determine the relevant factual basis in light of the evidence so as to provide the correct legal qualification, and, on the other, to guarantee compliance with procedural standards and enforce procedural discipline. These dual dimensions of the judicial function -substantive and procedural—are interrelated and guarantee the equilibrium necessary to secure equality of arms and fair treatment under Article 6 ECHR.

For example, regarding the submission of evidence, the general rule requires parties to indicate, during the written phase of the proceedings, the means of proof they intend to rely on in substantiating their allegations, either through the statement of claim or the defence, subject to forfeiture [article 254 para. (1) of the RCCP]. Accordingly, as a principle, parties may seek the taking of only such evidence as indicated in the written stage, the supplementation of evidence during trial being allowed solely in circumstances expressly prescribed by law. Where the court authorises the taking of evidence at the request of one party, it is incumbent upon the judge to secure the opposing party's right to counterproof with respect to the disputed fact [article 254 para. (3) of the RCCP], in conformity with the principle of equality of arms. The court does not necessarily administer all proposed evidence but first conducts an inquiry into their admissibility, considering the twin criteria of legality and relevance. This assessment serves to identify genuinely necessary evidence to the resolution of the dispute and to ensure an efficient organisation of the evidentiary stage. Moreover, the judge retains a managerial prerogative to establish the order in which the evidence is taken [article 260 para. (1) of the RCCP]."

As emphasised, the judge's exercise of functions relating to the management of proceedings must be carried out in a manner that safeguards the equality of arms. The principle of equality of the parties, codified in article 8 of the Romanian Code of Civil Procedure, requires that parties be guaranteed the equal and non-discriminatory exercise of their procedural rights. Procedural rules must be applied consistently by the court so as to ensure that each party can present its arguments and evidence and participate effectively, either directly or through representation, in the proceedings. Equality of arms should thus be understood as a structural guarantee of the fair trial, ensuring that both parties may exercise their procedural means as they deem appropriate; failure to observe a time-limit or exceeding it entails the legal consequences prescribed, including those affecting the substantive outcome, where so provided by law.

By way of example, in order to secure the defendant's right to a fair trial and to equality of arms, the court must, before fixing the first hearing, during the written phase, ensure the communication of the claim to the defendant, who is entitled to file a defence within the statutory period of 25 days, a time-limit that may be shortened in urgent cases [article 201 para. (1), (5) of RCCP]. The failure to respond within the prescribed period results in the loss of the right to raise certain procedural objections of a private nature and to submit evidence, which may lead to a disadvantageous judgment. The judge is bound to enforce this consequence and cannot admit evidence submitted outside the statutory time-limit. The requirement of equality of arms excludes any judicial favouritism, demanding instead that the court apply procedural norms uniformly and without discrimination, including with respect to procedural sanctions. However, should the court, in light of the specific circumstances, deem that a party is unable to defend its position, it may appoint a special curator from among the lawyers designated by the Bar, defining the scope and duration of such representation [article 80 para. (4), article 58 of the RCCP]. In particular cases, such appointments are mandatory, such as when the defendant has been summoned through public notice [article 167 para. (3) of the RCCP].

An essential element in the fulfilment of the court's duty to conduct the proceedings concerns the guarantee of its impartiality, ensured through procedural mechanisms designed to prevent situations of incompatibility in which the judge might find himself. Equality of arms requires judicial impartiality and the Romanian Code of Civil Procedure expressly regulates both cases of incompatibility and the procedure of withdrawal and challenge (articles 42–54 of the RCCP). Moreover, where there are reasons capable of affecting the impartiality of the entire court, the interested party may request the change of venue, respectively, that the case be transferred to another court of equal rank (Articles 140–147 of the RCCP).

Regarding the judge's role in ensuring procedural discipline, the Romanian Code of Civil Procedure contains several provisions enabling the court to monitor the parties' compliance with their procedural duties and to apply sanctions where non-compliances occur, taking into account their seriousness. For example, pursuant to Article 242 of the Romanian Civil Procedure Code, where the claimant fails to fulfil a duty incumbent upon him during the course of proceedings, thereby preventing the continuation of the trial, the court may suspend the proceedings, which shall only be resumed at the claimant's request and only after the fulfilment of the respective obligation and the payment of a judicial stamp duty amounting to 50% of the initial fee; where the administration of evidence depends on the advance of costs, the court may decline to admit such evidence in the absence of payment and decide the case without it (article 262 para. (3) of the RCCP). Similarly, the failure of a party to produce relevant documents when ordered may allow the court to draw adverse inferences and to consider established the assertions of the opposing party (article 295 of the RCCP).

5 Conclusions

Even though the Romanian Code of Civil Procedure does not explicitly codify the principle of cooperation, it is nonetheless widely embedded across its provisions. The architecture of civil proceedings requires active collaboration between the court, the parties and their lawyers, both in pursuit of procedural efficiency and expedition of the proceedings and to establish the truth, culminating in a lawful and well-reasoned judgment. The judge, tasked with managing proceedings and supervising their proper conduct, is primarily responsible for ensuring respect for procedural requirements, jurisdiction and the regularity of the trial. The judicial function also includes the duty of correctly determining the legal characterisation of both procedural acts and the substantive legal relationship brought before the court, thereby safeguarding the legality of the process [article 7 para. (2), article 22 para. (1), article 22 para. (4), article 152 of the RCCP]. On their part, the litigants and their lawyers are bound to respect procedural requirements and time-limits as set by law or the judge [article 10 of the RCCP], to set out the factual framework and their claims and defences accurately and in full [article 14 para. (2)–(3) of the RCCP], to adduce relevant evidence [article 10 para. (1) of the RCCP], to provide the court with the evidence in their possession [article 10 para. (2) of the RCCP], and, more generally, to contribute to the orderly and timely conclusion of the proceedings [article 10 para. (1) of the RCCP].

In light of these considerations, the express recognition of the principle of cooperation among the fundamental principles of civil procedure would underline its importance and steer judicial practice towards a more efficient application of procedural norms.

References

Chainais C, Ferrand F, Mayer L, Guinchard S (2020) Procédure civile, Droit commun et spécial du procès civil, MARD et arbitrage, 35th edn. Dalloz, Paris

Croze H (2011) Procedure civile, 3rd edn.. LexisNexis, Paris

European Law Institute (ELI), International Institute for the Unification of Private Law (UNIDROIT) (2021) ELI-UNIDROIT model European rules of civil procedure. From Transnational Principles to European Rules of Civil Procedure. Oxford University Press.

Jeuland E (2014) Droit processuel général, 3rd edn. LGDJ, Paris

Strickler Y, Alexey V (2021) Procédure civile, 10e édition. Bruylant, Brussels

Uzelac A (2017) Towards European rules of civil procedure: rethinking procedural obligations. Hungarian Journal of Legal Studies 58(1):3–18
Uzelac A (2025) Principles of civil procedure under ELI-UNIDROIT rules: convergence through a uniform approach to procedural obligations? Uniform Law Review 30:18–32
van Rhee CH (2018) Case management in Europe: modern approach to civil litigation. International Journal of Procedural Law 8(1):65–84
van Rhee CH (2022) Case management and co-operation in the model European rules of civil procedure. Journal of International and Comparative Law 9(2):1–16

The Implications of Teleological Interpretation in Forensic Science

Ancuța Elena Franț

Abstract Interpretation of legal norms is of crucial importance in law, because it adapts laws to real-life and helps in overcoming the rigidity of law, making laws easier to apply. At a first glance, it might seem that in Forensic Science there is little need to interpret the law, because Forensics is based on natural science. Despite this, interpretation of legal norms is sometimes needed in Forensics. The interpretation of law in Forensic Science can be extremely important for allowing certain evidence to be admitted in front of the court. As regards the teleological interpretation, this type of legal interpretation takes into account the purpose of the legal act. In Forensics, for example, teleological interpretation can be useful in understanding evidence preservation laws, taking into account the need to ensure the scope of preventing wrongful convictions and ensuring all conditions for a fair trial. In Romania, during communism, teleological interpretation in Forensics was present, but it was done in accordance with the goal of maintaining social order and the ideological purity of the leading party. Currently, Romania pays high attention to respecting human rights, without losing sight of the importance of the truth; teleological interpretation is indispensable in Forensic Science and, as long as the legal framework and human rights are respected, forensic investigators have all the means at their disposal to discover the truth, as revealed by the evidence.

A. E. Franț (✉)
Faculty of Law, 'Alexandru Ioan Cuza' University of Iași, Iași, Romania
e-mail: ancuta.frant@uaic.ro

I. Maria Costea (ed.), *Legal Interpretation in Motion*, Ius Gentium: Comparative Perspectives on Law and Justice 144,
https://doi.org/10.1007/978-3-032-32948-6_7

1 The Necessity of Law Interpretation

Interpretation of legal norms is of crucial importance in law, and, before we look at different ways to interpret the law, we should first understand why interpretation of the law is necessary. Essentially, we must interpret the law because, no matter how well the laws are written, they cannot encompass the whole reality. In other words, human society is much more complex than the concepts referred to by the laws. This is mainly because there are countless forms in which real-life situations can occur, while laws, no matter how elaborate, are still limited, as they cannot take into account the vastness of details which define humans' lives and human society. Of course, some situations are very similar with others, and they are regulated by the same laws; still, in situations which are very similar there are differences, some of them being subtle, others being pronounced differences, all of these particularities creating the uniqueness of every real-life situation.

As we try to deepen our understanding of the reasons behind the need for law interpretation, a series of elements are highlighted: the need to understand the true intent of the legislator; the need to find a solution for situations when law does not refer to a specific issue; the need to solve a conflict between two or many legal norms; the obscurity or equivocation of the language in which laws are written; the need to prevent a possible incorrect result which can result from a rigid application of the law; the need to adapt old laws to new realities, especially as the society and technology are quickly evolving. In the following lines we will make a short analysis of the elements presented above (Ignătescu 2013).

The need to understand the true intent of the legislator is often required, as laws are written in a general language and the legislator takes into account multiple reasons, with some of them being difficult to perceive. One of the reasons is that, often, even if a legal provision refers to a specific aspect, it is connected to other legal norms, which can refer to different aspects. This is because, for the legislator, all norms should reflect a certain vision or a certain policy, in order to create a coherent legal system. But, when we take into account just one legal provision, it is possible that we do not see the whole picture and we do not immediately understand the purpose of that specific provision of the law. This is why interpretation can help to fit that provision into the broader frame of the legal system.

The need to find a solution for situations when law does not refer to a specific issue occurs every time a real situation does not find a perfect correspondent in the law's provision. And this is often needed, because, as we have said before, law cannot take into account all situations which can occur in reality. Laws are finite, while real-life is, actually, infinite in what regards the number of possibilities of events to happen.

The need to solve a conflict between two or many legal norms can appear if a situation falls within the competence of two or several norms, for example, when a case seems to contain elements which are of criminal law and also of tort law, if a new law has been adopted or when the laws of several countries could be applicable. For such cases, specific rules have been adopted, for example, the rule that stipulates the priority of the special law over the general law, and the rule that provides the priority of the newer law.

The obscurity or equivocation of the language in which laws are written is a common issue, grounded in the fact that many words are polysemantic, having multiple meanings. This means that law interpreters must choose the meaning which is the most suitable, taking into account the specificity of the case and the overall significance of the legal act which contains that word. For example, the word "reasonable", from the syntagm "reasonable term", frequently used in Criminal procedure law, has created an intense debate over its exact meaning.

The need to prevent a possible incorrect result which can result from a rigid application of the law stems from the fact that law contains general and abstract provisions, which cannot take into account all the specific implications of a particular case. Thus, a strict interpretation can lead to unfair situations. For example, in the case of Riggs vs. Palmer,[1] a New York civil court case from 1889, the court decided that the grandson who murdered his grandfather in order to benefit from his will could not profit from the will, although there were no laws to prevent the murderer from obtaining his grandfather's wealth. The majority of the judges in this case held that the legislators cannot foresee all situations which can occur and, if the legislators could imagine that a grandson could murder his grandfather in order to obtain his assets, they would have addressed such a situation, excluding the grandson from the heirs. This interpretation was based on the general principles of law.

The need to adapt old laws to new realities is an important reason for interpreting the law, especially as the society and technology are quickly evolving. It is obvious that a law adopted decades (or even hundreds) of years ago possibly is no longer appropriate for present-day realities. When new laws are slow to emerge, interpretation of old laws is absolutely necessary. For example, if there is no law regulating the effects of Artificial Intelligence (AI) on privacy, judges must interpret the existing laws, in order to ensure proper protection.

Overall, we can conclude that interpretation of law is the process which adapts laws to real-life and helps in overcoming the rigidity of law, making laws easier to apply.

2 A Brief Historical View on Law Interpretation

In our quest to understand the role of the teleological interpretation in Forensic Science, we think we could benefit from a historical view on the interpretation of legal norms. Mainly, we want to find out if interpretation was always necessary or if it is a modern matter in the field of law.

In order to fulfil our analysis, we turn our attention to one of the most ancient laws ever known, namely the Code of Hammurabi, the legal text from Babylon,

[1] Available at https://www.nycourts.gov/reporter/archives/riggs_palmer.htm.

dated 1755 - 1750 B.C. The Code of Hammurabi represents a collection of 282 laws carved into a *stela*, which regulate areas of law such as family, property, crime, contracts, commerce, and also civil rights (for example, the right to a fair trial). The intensive analysis which was made on this code allows us to state that the Code of Hammurabi needed to be interpreted in order to be justly applied (Nagarajan 2011). Although the Hammurabi Code is very detailed, still, it uses general terms and could not cover every imaginable real situation. Where the code used ambiguous terms or where it lacked direct reference, interpretation was needed. A specific aspect of the Code of Hammurabi is that it provided different punishments for different social classes; it results that judges must have encountered situations where they should have interpreted the correct social status and the right meaning of law, in accord with the position in the social hierarchy of the defendant. Also, just like in the present-day court cases, judges must have been in the situation to establish the form of guilt (for example, intention, recklessness or negligence) or the credibility of the witnesses, which are also forms of interpretation in the field of law. It results that, even in ancient times, judges needed to use interpretation in applying the law.

Also, in Ancient Rome jurists have paid much attention to the interpretation of the law, creating elaborate methods for interpreting legal provisions. This was especially needed because the roman legal system gradually became a very complex one. In order to clarify the complex normative acts, the roman specialists in law resorted to different solutions. For example, they wrote comment books containing explanations of the laws and structures the different categories of the ambiguities which could be found in laws (Stein 1995).

Specific issues can arise in the common law system, where judges must apply not only laws, but also past judicial decisions. This means that judges must interpret the provisions of law and also the way that laws have been applied before, establishing if the past judicial decisions are still applicable in the cases which they must pronounce a court decision. In what regards the interpretation of law, common law judges face the same challenges as judges in civil law, but in what concerns the interpretations of judicial decisions, there are some particular aspects which must be taken into account. For example, if different courts have pronounced different judicial decisions in similar cases, judges have to decide which precedent judicial decision best suits the case. It is also possible that judicial precedents are no longer in line with current realities. Also, there is the possibility that, for certain areas, there are no precedents, especially if a new topic is involved, for example AI; in such cases, judges must adopt decisions which are new in the field, thus creating new precedents. However, even if these problems seem difficult, judges in common law system are prepared to overcome them, in order to ensure the needed adaptability of the common law system (Baldacci 2022).

In conclusion, we can say that interpretation of law has a very important role in ensuring the viability of a legal system, providing flexibility and also resilience.

3 Interpretation of Law in Forensic Science. Overview. Special Features of the Romanian Legal System

At a first glance, it might seem that in Forensic Science there is little need to interpret the law, because Forensics is based on natural science, which is independent from the legal systems made by humans. As we have stated before (Franț 2023) Forensics relies on domains like Physics, Chemistry, Biology, Mathematics, where the laws of nature or pure logic are applied. In these domains, results are usually very clear and beyond doubt, because they are grounded on solid research and generally accepted research, actually forming the core of human knowledge. For example, when calculation of a bullet trajectory is correctly made, there is nothing to comment, or to interpret. Also, the result of a DNA analysis, when all procedures are followed, should be beyond doubt.

Despite this, interpretation of legal norms is sometimes needed in Forensics. This is mainly because applying Forensic Science in real cases depends on procedural law, and, as any of the laws within a legal system, procedural law needs to be interpreted. We must highlight that the specificity of the procedural law requires that, in this field, interpretation is as little as possible, in order to ensure that there are no controversies in the enforcement of the law. However, the vastity of situations which can occur in real life surpasses the rigid frame of the laws, leading to cases where interpretation of the law is mandatory.

The interpretation of the law in Forensic Science can be extremely important for allowing certain evidence to be admitted in front of the court. Basically, law interpretation in Forensics is needed in order to ensure that scientific methods are complying with the legal standards and that they are admissible in the court. If evidence does not meet the needed requirements, it cannot be used in a trial. The importance of the interpretation in Forensics resides in that, if the interpretation is wrongfully performed, this can result either in eliminating viable evidence, either in admitting doubtful evidence. In both cases, the result of the trial, in what refers to its accordance with the truth, is severely endangered.

In what regards the methods of interpretation in Forensic Science, the forensic experts and the jurists can use a range of methods which are established for being used due to their proved value in judicial practice. Usually, these methods of interpretation are drawn from general methods of interpretation used in the field of law, but they are adapted to the field of Forensic Science. The methods that are generally used in law interpretation in Forensics and are found within this category include literal interpretation, comparative interpretation, historical interpretation, judicial interpretation, systematic interpretation, teleological interpretation. The specificity of Forensic Science sometimes requires a specific interpretation, which is not usually used in other fields of law, for example the scientific-legal interpretation. In the following lines, we will highlight some aspects regarding the specific way these methods apply in Forensic Science. Also, we must point out the fact that other methods of interpretation may be used, if necessary, in order to obtain the best results, given a certain situation.

Literal interpretation, also known as grammatical interpretation, is one of the most widely spread methods to interpret the law. Essentially, it means that the words within a law must be interpreted in their plain meaning, without seeking other significance. Despite its simplicity, this method is controversial (Flanagan 2010). In Forensics, it is used in the interpretation of some terms, for example "probable cause". The literal interpretation of this term is important in properly understanding forensic reports, in order to prevent to misunderstand the word "probable" as "certain". Another case when literal interpretation is required is the use of the term "reasonable doubt", where "reasonable" must be understood as something which exists in normal conditions. This interpretation is very important for the proper application of procedures, including those which lead to decision-making. However, in many cases, literal interpretation is not enough, because words may have multiple meanings.

Comparative interpretation refers to comparing the norm which is unclear with similar norms in other countries, including the way these similar norms are interpreted in those countries. It is a very useful method, which uses the experience of other countries in dealing with similar legal issues (Dammann 2002). The utility of this method in Forensics is clearly highlighted when we think of new scientific methods, that haven't yet been applied in a certain country, but which have been used in another country. However, it is important to verify that the systems to be compared are compatible, meaning they do not have substantial differences. Still, despite the differences that may be very important (for example, the difference of the judicial systems in common law versus civil law), in Forensics there is mainly about using scientific methods, which are the same, no matter what legal system is in force. It results that, in Forensic Science, more than in other fields, comparative interpretation is prone to give good results. In order to sustain our point of view, we can use as an example the use of the polygraph in Romanian judicial system, versus the use of the polygraph in the United States of America's judicial system. In Romania, the Government Ordinance No. 75/2000 refers to the forensic expertise in identifying simulated behavior (through the use of the polygraph) in the same law article which refers to all categories of forensic expertise which are acknowledged as such in Romania. This implies that the polygraph expertise can be accepted as a means of proof both during the criminal prosecution and during the judicial trial. In the USA, by contrary, the polygraph cannot be used as a means of proof in front of a court, because the polygraph technique does not comply with the standards accepted in the USA, namely the Daubert and Frye standards (Fournier 2016; Cheng and Yoon 2005). The two judicial systems (the Romanian and the USA system) have fundamental procedural differences (for example, in Romania the expert is not a witness, as in the USA system), but this does not mean that these differences exist in what regards the way that science is perceived. As we have pointed out before, in Romania, the law refers to the polygraph using the same general terms as those used for other categories of expertise (for example, genetic expertise), considering it a type of forensic expertise; the Romanian law does not go further, meaning that it does not make a difference between the probative value of different types of expertise. But, in taking their decisions, the judges must take into account the state of the art in the scientific field, and, even though the law does not differentiate, the judges must appreciate the specificity and the limitations of every means of proof. It results that, even if in Romania the Daubert and Frye standards do not apply, the reasoning which forms the basis of these two USA standards is still applied in Romanian legal system. In the absence of an express specification of the law, it is possible that the present-day attitude towards the polygraph expertise of Romanian courts was shaped also through comparative interpretation, applying in Romania the reasoning that underlies the way the polygraph expertise in used in the USA courts. As regards comparative interpretation, we must add that this kind of interpretation can be very useful in cases with international elements.

Historical interpretation offers a good understanding of the intent of the legislators, taking into account the general context existent at the moment when a law has been adopted. It allows us to perceive the problems existing in the society, which generated the need for adopting that specific law (Rodin 2021). Historical interpretation also can highlight the mistakes that have been made in the past, showing us that we must go in another direction than that considered by the lawmakers at a past moment. Analyzing the preparatory work for a certain law can be very useful in defining the context existing when the issue of adopting a certain law arose. In Forensic Science, historical interpretation can be of great value when the problem of applying a new forensic technique arises. In the lack of a reference point towards the implications of the new techniques, we should search for the ways that the legal system reacted when new technologies have been implemented in the past. Also, historical interpretation teaches us to find out similarities between the reasons that sustain certain legal amendments in the present and the reasons which justified legal changes in the past. When the legal system deals with new concepts and scientific methods (as is the case of Forensics), historical interpretation can help us find similarities between the new scientific achievements and the existing legislation, thus ensuring that the new techniques can be applied, at least until the legal system is changed, in order to contain express references to the novelties in a specific field. For example, this is the case in Romania in what regards the digital domain, which is evolving much faster than the legal system can evolve. This being the case, digital forensics in Romania must sometimes rely on procedural norms which have not been made for the digital domain, but are applied through legal interpretation, including historical interpretation.

Judicial interpretation is mainly applicable in judicial systems that rely on the judicial precedent, like the common law system. The meaning of judicial interpretation is that courts must take into account the way that other courts, in the past, have interpreted certain legal provisions. As examples which are important for Forensics, we can refer to the rulings in the cases Frye v. United States and Daubert v. Merrell Dow Pharmaceuticals. In the case of Frye v. United States (1923),[2] the United States Court of Appeals, District of Columbia, stated that expert testimony must be based on scientific methods that are generally accepted as reliable in the relevant scientific

[2] Available at: https://nys-fjc.ca2.uscourts.gov/programs/10-4-18%20Frye%20v%20US.pdf.

community. As a result of this case, the Frye standard (also called the general acceptance test) was created. In the light of this standard, when someone brings a new scientific method in front of the court, the court must make all research needed, in order to decide if the method is generally accepted as reliable. In the Daubert v. Merrell Dow Pharmaceuticals (1993),[3] the United States Supreme Court established the standards for admitting expert testimony in federal courts. Essentially, this standard means that, in order to be admitted, expert testimony must be relevant and reliable. Relevance refers to the fact that the expert testimony must help the judge or the jury to understand the evidence or a fact issue, and reliability means that the method or the reasoning used must be scientifically valid. In the view of the Daubert standard, judges act as "gatekeepers", and, in fulfilling their duty, they may consider the following aspects: Can the theory or technique be tested? Has it been published and reviewed by other experts? Is there a known or potential error rate? Are there standards controlling the technique's operation? Is it widely accepted in the relevant scientific community? These aspects can be synthesized as follows: testability, peer review standard, error rate standard, general acceptance. It is important to mention that these aspects are not limiting the judges, who can also take into account other aspects.

The Daubert standard applies in all US federal courts, but not in all US state courts. For example, the Daubert standard applies in Alabama, Florida (since 2019), Georgia, Massachusetts, Oklahoma, Texas, Wisconsin. In some US state courts, Frye standard is used, for example in Illinois, Pennsylvania, New York, North Dakota, Washington. Also, some state courts use a hybrid form, or a state-specific standard, as in Hawai'i, Indiana, Montana, New Jersey, New Mexico, Oregon, Tennessee, Virginia.[4]

If we were to make a comparison between the two standards, essentially, the Frye standard admits scientific evidence only if it is generally accepted by the experts in certain scientific field, while the Daubert takes into account a broader range of validity elements. While it may seem that the Daubert is more rigorous than Frye, it actually can be more flexible, especially because the judge (who usually is not a scientific expert in Forensics) must decide upon the validity of a scientific method.

We have paid close attention to the two US standards in evidence admissibility because, although they are applied only on the US territory, they are very important for Forensics all over the world, as they have influenced the general view regarding the conditions that a scientific procedure must fulfill, in order to be admitted as a source of evidence in the court (Groscup et al. 2002). However, the standards for evidence admission in the US have been continuously debated. Some scholars consider that the Daubert standard is superior to the Frye standard, and believe that expanding its application is beneficial for the US judicial system (Rutner and Bach 2015). There is also the opinion that the Daubert and the Frye standards basically

[3] Available at: https://supreme.justia.com/cases/federal/us/509/579/.

[4] Available at: https://ncji.org/wp-content/uploads/2024/01/Evidence-Standards-by-State-7.12.23.pdf.

have the same requirements, with little difference (Jensen 2003). Also, some researchers believe that the two standards are not enough in order to ensure that true scientific knowledge is admissible in the courts, and that many non-scientific methods are still used in US courts, leading to wrongfully convictions (Hilbert 2019).

An interesting aspect to be discussed in relation to judicial interpretation is that even in the countries that are not part of the common law certain forms of judicial interpretation do exist. For example, in Romania, which is among the countries that are part of the civil law system, there are some courts whose rulings have binding power over other courts. This is the case of the Romanian High Court of Cassation and Justice, which can pronounce preliminary rulings for resolving legal issues and rulings in an Appeal in the interest of the law, which are mandatory for all courts. Also, the Constitutional Court of Romania rules on the conformity of laws with the Constitution, its decisions being binding on all courts.

Systematic interpretation (also called systemic construction or systemic interpretation) is very important, because it ensures the unity of a legal system, making sure that its different components are consistent with its leading principles (Padjen 2020). However, for a systematic interpretation, it is necessary that the legal system where it operates to be logic and well-organized. Some authors (Padjen 2020) point out that, in the present-day, a re-systematization of the legal systems is needed, and only after such re-systematization is done, we can perform an efficient systematic interpretation. Indeed, systematic interpretation needs solid benchmarks to refer to. When a legal system contains evident contradictions, a systematic interpretation is difficult, if not impossible. In such a context, a true systematic interpretation could only be done by referring to the basic principles of that legal system (like the constitutional principles), of course, if they make a coherent system. In the absence of any reliable benchmarks (even of the constitutional ones), a true systematic interpretation cannot be performed. Some authors debate whether it would be better to establish general rules of interpretation, but a number of problems would arise, especially related to the loss of adaptability in interpretation (Konca 2021). Leaving aside the possible problems, we must value the utility of the systematic interpretation, which has the power to fill in the gaps existing in a certain law, by referring to legal principles and related laws (Salehijam 2018). Even more, systematic interpretation can be done by using laws that are not related (at least not closely related) to the law that must be interpreted, especially if there are no similar regulations on the same subject or on similar domains. Of course, using related laws for systematic interpretation is easier, because related laws share common concepts and terminology. But relying on laws that are not related for systemic interpretation can also be successfully done, if this approach is helpful in revealing useful information, for example general principles of law (like the free access to justice, equality in front of the law, the right to a fair trial), citizens' rights and duties, and the significance of some legal concepts. In Forensics, the systematic interpretation is very important, because it helps alleviate the difference between the scientific knowledge (which is the basis for forensic evidence) and legal procedures (which are general frames, built on different principles than forensic technical methods). Overall, in Forensic Science, systematic interpretation ensures that forensic methods are applied not only in accordance with scientific rules, but also in accordance with the general legal frame (for example, in accordance with the principle of equality of arms or the presumption of innocence principle). Systematic interpretation can be difficult, and, in Romania, there were several occasions where these difficulties were shown. This assertion can be explained by the fact that there have been inconsistencies in the decisions of the Romanian Constitutional Court and the High Court of Cassation and Justice of Romania. Basically, the High Court of Cassation and Justice tried to apply the law in a pragmatic way, from the practical perspective of justice, while the Constitutional Court intervened in a more formalistic manner, strictly regarding the constitutional texts. For example, as regards the prescription of criminal liability, in 2018, the High Court of Cassation and Justice issued an Interpretative Decision on the interruption of the prescription period in certain criminal cases. In 2022, the Romanian Constitutional Court, through Decision no. 297/2018 and subsequently no. 358/2022, established that certain texts on the interruption of the prescription period are unconstitutional, which caused the automatic cancellation of some files. The High Court of Cassation and Justice, at first, applied these decisions at a hesitant pace, which created a period of legal uncertainty (Oncescu 2022). Also, As regards the Panels of 5 judges of the High Court of Cassation and Justice (2014–2018), the Romanian Constitutional Court decided, by Decision no. 685/2018,[5] that the way in which the panels of 5 judges of the High Court of Cassation were constituted was unconstitutional, because it did not comply with the law (in particular, the lack of a draw). The High Court of Cassation and Justice had previously considered that their organization was legal and that no change was required. As a result, the Romanian Constitutional Court ordered the resumption of the trials affected by these panels (especially corruption cases), which led to the annulment of some final sentences. The cases mentioned before underly the idea that, for a systematic interpretation to have the desired effect, first the legal system must be well structured, having solid and clear principles. This is important in all domains, and even more so in Forensics, if we want to transpose the rigor of the scientific approach, which is vital in Forensic Science, into the judicial rulings.

Teleological interpretation (also called the purposive interpretation) is very important, but we will only make a brief reference here, because we will develop this topic in a separate section. We want to point out that this type of legal interpretation takes into account the purpose or the final goal of the legal act. Teleological interpretation can be really challenging, as it can be difficult to determine the intent of the legislators, which is not always expressly stipulated in the law. In Forensics, for example, purposive interpretation can be useful in understanding evidence preservation laws, taking into account the need to ensure the scope of preventing wrongful convictions and ensuring all conditions for a fair trial.

Scientific-legal interpretation is not usually used for the interpretation of legal norms, but is often used in Forensics, in the effort to make scientific knowledge comply with the legal frame. This interpretation is especially useful when there

[5] Available at: https://legislatie.just.ro/Public/DetaliiDocument/208176.

arises a problem concerning a new forensic technique, for which there are no specific legal provisions. In such a context, scientific-legal interpretation can help the judicial authorities to understand whether a forensic procedure is valid or not and to establish the thresholds needed in order to ensure that a scientific method or reasoning can be used as evidence.

The elements presented above support the idea that interpretation is extremely important for a proper application of Forensic Science in judicial trials, ensuring that scientific methods are properly understood and applied in order to achieve correct judicial decisions.

4 The Importance of Teleological Interpretation in Forensic Science

All types of law interpretation are important, as each of them can be crucial in a specific case, depending on the circumstances. In what regards highly technical elements, literal interpretation or systematic interpretation can be extremely important, for example in following laboratory protocols, chain of custody or in courtroom testimony, or whenever precision is essential. Still, teleological interpretation stands out, because it is orientated towards the final aim of a judicial trial, which is discovering the truth and the punishment of the guilty persons. Having in mind the purpose of the whole procedure can help the judicial bodies to stay on track and be equidistant towards all the persons who are considered by the investigation. Teleological interpretation helps a forensic expert to understand that the forensic work does not consist only in an automatic application of the scientific methods, but also in understanding that the scientific procedures must be used in order to reveal the truth, thus leading to a judicial ruling. Knowing the important practical effect of their work, forensic experts must be very careful in making conclusions, as any small deviation from scientific rigor can lead to a wrong decision. These are the reasons why we have chosen to analyze in more detail the teleological interpretation in Forensic Science.

From an etymological point of view, the word "teleology" comes from two Greek roots, namely "telos", which means "end", "purpose", "aim" or "goal", and "logy" (from "logos"), which means "study", "reason", "explanation" or "discourse" (Partridge 1977). It results that "teleology" (from which "teleological" is derived), means the "study of purposes". The word "teleology" was coined by the German philosopher Baron Christian von Wolff (1679–1754), in the Latin form, "teleologia" (Harper n.d.).

The concept of "teleology" is very important in Philosophy. Its roots can be traced back in the writings of ancient philosophers Plato and Aristotle. In Plato's work Phaedo, the character Socrates makes the assertion that the true explanation for physical phenomenon is teleological. In Aristotle's concept of the Four Causes, the Final Cause, which is the purpose for which a thing exists, plays an important role in explaining why things exist or happen the way they do, along with Material Cause (meaning what something is made of), Formal Cause (the form or the shape which essentially makes a thing what it is) and Efficient Cause (the process or the factor which brings into being a certain thing). Teleological argument is considered by many philosophers very important in proving the existence of God, based on the perceived purposefulness of nature. For example, the Stoics, Saint Thomas Aquinas and Isaac Newton, to name only a few, believed that the complex structure of nature is a proof that an intelligent creator exists (Ratzsch and Koperski 2023).

As in the general meaning of the teleological interpretation, in Forensic Science, the purposive interpretation is based on the idea that there must be a reason why a certain legal norm exists and that there must be a purpose in applying it in the correct way, with the term "correct" being understood in a universal and abstract manner, not only as what the literal words of the law are saying. The coordination of the forensic investigation with a final purpose (which is often not explicitly presented in the law) therefore becomes the reason for teleological interpretation in Forensics.

The theoretical framework presented above provides a foundation for the subsequent analysis, ensuring that methodological choices are grounded in established principles of teleological interpretation in Forensic Science. By explicitly linking theory to practice, it highlights how these principles guide the evaluation and assessment of evidence in a judicial context, especially in criminal cases.

5 Teleological Interpretation in Forensics in Communist Romania

In Romania, during communism (roughly 1947–1989), while under a Soviet-influenced regime, Forensic Science was heavily influenced by the political and ideological context. Teleological interpretation was certainly present, but it was shaped by the specific needs of the state apparatus.

The purpose of forensic investigations was not only to discover the truth, but also to protect the socialist regime. Thus, forensic evidence was often interpreted in accordance with the goal of maintaining social order, ideological purity, and supporting the official narrative. As a consequence of this point of view, if evidence could be interpreted in two or many ways, the one that supported socialist values or the interests of the Communist Party would be favored.

In accordance with the official policy, forensic experts sometimes had to interpret evidence in a way that proved that crimes were remnants of bourgeois mentality, results of a foreign influence (meaning the influence of Western capitalism), or acts of anti-socialism behavior, thus giving a political meaning to otherwise ordinary crimes. A theft or violent crime could be framed not just as a personal act, but as an ideological failure, with forensic evidence pointing to political explanations.

In cases against political dissidents, Forensics was used not to neutrally assess evidence, but to validate preordained conclusions. Forensic reports were sometimes written to clearly demonstrate that the accused were enemies of socialism, often ignoring or defying scientific standards.

This situation was actually paradoxical, because, in communist Romania, great emphasis was placed on high-quality scientific knowledge. Romanian forensic scientists were trained in rigorous scientific methods, which came naturally, as Romania had a strong interwar tradition in Forensics and Medicine. Unfortunately, during communism, scientific objectivity was often compromised when it clashed with political objectives, and the aim of reinforcing socialist ideals could override strict scientific neutrality. This created a striking disparity between the official forensic manuals (which emphasized the need to apply scientific rigor), and what happened in practice, where actions were often subordinated to political necessity.

It is important to mention that Romanian forensic practice was modeled after Soviet practices, where Pavlovian theories and Marxist-Leninist interpretations of behavior heavily influenced how forensic evidence was perceived. The Soviet model itself was highly teleological, as truth served the socialist ideology. We must mention the fact that the Soviet system also promoted rigorous scientific training, and the scientific quality of Soviet experts was often the highest (Kojevnikov 2008). The problem was that this valuable scientific knowledge was often put in the service of the ideology, instead of serving the objective truth.

In order to better understand what teleological interpretation in Forensics meant in communist Romania, we will shortly analyze two real cases: the Ioanid Gang Robbery (1959) and the Pitești Experiment (1949–1952).

In the case of the Ioanid Gang Robbery, a group of high-ranking Communist Party members (mostly of Jewish origin) were accused of robbing the National Bank of Romania. The trial became highly publicized, and the accused, who were quickly arrested, confessed their crime under pressure, and were ultimately sentenced to death. The robbery was said to reveal that even trusted communists could betray the system. The way that evidence was used in this case is an example of teleological interpretation in Forensic Science, the purpose being to defend the Party's ideology. Forensic evidence (fingerprints, ballistics, timeline reconstruction) was selectively used, in order to confirm the ideological explanation that the defendants had planned the robbery out of bourgeois greed. Doubts or inconsistencies were ignored, because the purpose was not to find the objective truth, but to show that inside the Communist Party there were traitors and to warn others who might have wanted to become traitors, too (Bouleanu 2016).

The Pitești Experiment (also called "the re-education experiment") was an infamous communist program meant to "re-educate" political prisoners (who were mostly students), through systematic torture. The goal was to break the prisoner's personality completely and rebuild it according to communist ideology. This is considered one of the most brutal experiments in psychological and physical destruction in the Eastern Bloc. Many prisoners died because of torture (consisting of beatings, starvation, experimental psychological abuse and so on). However, the forensic doctors working for the state issued autopsy reports in which they falsified the truth. Causes of death were falsely listed as natural causes (like pneumonia or heart attack), suicide (even if the body showed clear signs of torture), or accidents (for example, falling down stairs). This result was ensured by several methods. The autopsies were supervised by members of the secret police (named "Securitate"), and the forensic doctors were expressly instructed what to mention and what not to mention in the autopsy reports. Doctors were taught to use euphemisms, for example, *contusion* instead of *beating trauma* or *internal swelling* instead of *organ rupture*. There was a list of words which were forbidden to be written in an autopsy report, for example *torture*, *violence*, or *battery*. External marks should have been explained as postmortem effects or consequences of previous illnesses. Actually, there were templates for autopsy reports, which provided only the causes of death accepted by the political regime. If a doctor refused to cooperate, he or she risked severe consequences, not only for him or her person, but also for their families. However, a few doctors chose to secretly keep private notes on real causes of death, risking their lives; these private notes became important evidence after the Revolution of 1989. In this case, the teleological interpretation of forensic rules meant that the evidence must be interpreted in accord with the idea that it was a noble goal to defeat the enemies of the regime, regardless of the methods used, including through forensic evidence manipulation (Demetriade 2017; Banu and Pleşa 2008).[6]

6 Teleological Interpretation in Forensic DNA Analysis. Specific Aspects of Romanian Legislation

In fighting criminality, judicial bodies must have proper methods, in order to ensure that those who break the law are punished. The technological development in recent years has brought in many procedures that have a high precision in identifying a person, thus being very useful in revealing the identity of a perpetrator. However, some of these methods bring into discussion the right to privacy, as many of them have the potential to violate this right, if they are not properly used. A wide range of forensic evidence can raise the issue of a potential conflict between the judicial bodies' interest to solve a case and the right to privacy, for example, digital evidence (extracted from computers, smartphones, emails, social media, cloud storage), biometric evidence (like fingerprints, DNA, facial recognition data, voice recognition data), financial records (like bank accounts, cryptocurrency wallets, bank transactions history). In all these cases, forensic investigators must be careful not to infringe an individual's rights, like the right to privacy. In order to fulfill this goal, the judicial bodies must follow the law, which generally provides the obligation to get warrants, to limit the access to personal data, to anonymize data, and to keep evidence secure.

[6] See also the Reports of National Council for the Study of Security Archives (Consiliul Naţional pentru Studierea Arhivelor Securităţii—CNSAS), available at http://www.cnsas.ro/reeducarea.html.

However, in achieving the scope of protecting the right to privacy, the authorities must not lose sight of the aim of a forensic investigation, which is to find the truth in a certain case. If the right to privacy would be invoked in an absolute way, this would mean that authorities could never obtain evidence in order to punish the perpetrators. For example, if a person could arbitrarily refuse to be fingerprinted, this would lead to the impossibility to solve a case, or at least would make the investigation very difficult, because it would be hard to find out if the fingerprints found at the crime scene match or do not match those of that specific person. This is why the legislator has the difficult mission to ensure a balance between the right to privacy and the authorities' interest (which is ultimately the society's interest) to identify and punish those who break the law.

In analyzing the impetus to protect the right to privacy in forensic investigations, a special attention must be paid to DNA analysis, because, while being a potential source for crucial forensic information, it is also one of the highest expressions of human uniqueness. Actually, the DNA is a symbol of the specificity of every single person, so a very important reason must exist in order to justify the processing of DNA data.

6.1 Teleological Interpretation in DNA Data Storage in Romania

The Romanian legislation protects DNA data, within the frame created by the European Union's General Data Protection Regulation—GDPR (Regulation (EU) 2016/679). Law no. 190/2018[7] (on measures for the implementation of GDPR), provides that the processing of genetic, biometric or health data for the purpose of automated decision-making or profiling is permitted with the explicit consent of the data subject or if the processing is carried out on the basis of express legal provisions, with the establishment of appropriate measures to protect the rights, freedoms and legitimate interests of the data subject. Furthermore, as regards genetic data, Law no. 76/2008[8] on the organization and operation of the National Judicial Genetic Data System (S.N.D.G.J.) provides, in article 1 (3), that biological samples may be taken and processed for certain purposes, namely: excluding persons from the circle of suspects and identifying the perpetrators of certain crimes (expressly included in the law's annex); establishing the identity of persons who are victims of natural disasters, mass accidents and acts of terrorism; exchanging information with other states and combating cross-border crime; identifying participants in the commission of the crimes included in the law's annex; preventing and combating acts of a sexual nature, exploitation of persons or minors; preventing and combating acts in the field of drug trafficking. The annex of the Law no. 76/2008 refers to serious crimes

[7] Published in the Official Gazette No. 651 of July 26, 2018.

[8] Published in the Official Gazette No. 289 of April 14, 2008.

concerning life, bodily integrity and health, freedom of sexual life, human and drug trafficking, terrorism and other highly serious offenses.

Regarding the persons whose genetic profiles are stored in the S.N.D.G.J., Law no. 76/2008 provides, in article 4 (1), that these persons can be: suspects (persons about whom there is data and information that they could be perpetrators, instigators or accomplices of the crimes included in the annex); persons definitively convicted for committing the crimes included in the annex to the prison sentence, as well as persons for whom the court has pronounced the postponement of the application of the sentence or the waiver of the application of the sentence; persons registered according to the law in the National Automated Register of persons who have committed sexual crimes, crimes of exploitation of persons or crimes against minors; persons registered according to the law in the National Automated Register of persons who have committed crimes in the field of drug trafficking. This article also provides that the S.N.D.G.J can store biological traces taken during the on-site investigation and biological samples from bodies with unknown identity, missing persons or persons deceased as a result of natural disasters, mass accidents, murder or acts of terrorism. Also, regarding the above categories, the law provides that the S.N.D.G.J stores personal data and case data, along with genetic profiles.

An important issue on the interpretation of law existed in reference to storing information regarding the persons definitively convicted for committing the crimes included in the annex of Law no. 76/2008 to the prison sentence, as well as persons for whom the court has pronounced the postponement of the application of the sentence or the waiver of the application of the sentence. The problem was generated by the fact that the law contains contradictory provisions. In article 3, law refers to offences for which "biological samples *may be taken*…", while, in article 7, it states that "the collection of biological samples (…) *is ordered* by the court, by the sentencing decision or by the decision to postpone the application of the sentence or to waive the application of the sentence." In the law specialized literature, it was appreciated that the legislator wanted to avoid a formulation that would be reminiscent of the legislative style used in authoritarian regimes, but it was not consistent with this intention throughout the whole text of the law (Nestor 2024). It resulted that, within the same law, there are two phrases with opposite meanings, implying that, at the same time, the court "may" and "must" order the taking of biological samples, in order to store DNA data. Of course, on the ground of logical interpretation, these two phrases of the law cannot apply at the same time. This problem was solved by the High Court of Cassation and Justice of Romania, which, in 2022, in a decision regarding an Appeal in the interest of the law (RIL no. 20/2022[9]), stated that the collection of biological samples from persons definitively convicted or against whom the application of the sentence has been postponed or the application of the sentence has been waived, for the commission of the crimes included in the annex to Law no. 76/2008, is optional and not mandatory, the courts having the power to assess whether or not genetic fingerprints should be entered into the

[9] Published in the Official Gazette No. 1103 of November 16, 2022.

National System of Judicial Genetic Data (S.N.D.G.J.). The interpretation given by the High Court of Cassation and Justice, which is binding on all Romanian courts, is welcome, as it puts an end to the non-unitary practice in this area. However, at the same time, it leaves another issue unresolved, namely that of the *criteria* that the court could use to decide whether or not to require the collection of biological samples and the storage of genetic data.

The express provision of criteria would be useful in order to ensure compliance with European Court of Human Rights (ECtHR) jurisprudence regarding restrictions to the exercise of rights. The ECtHR allows for restrictions, but only if the restriction is prescribed by the national law (the law being accessible and predictable), it pursues a legitimate aim (for example, crime prevention or public safety), and is necessary in a democratic society (with "necessary" meaning to respond to a pressing social need). To verify compliance with these criteria, the proportionality of the restriction to the aim pursued is taken into account, as well as the relevance and sufficiency of the reasons invoked by the authorities for that restriction (Trykhlib 2020). In this case, the main problems are that the proportionality test is difficult to perform, and the law is not predictable, in the absence of expressly-mentioned criteria.

Some authors consider that the courts could use, by analogy, the criteria expressly-provided by the law in other situations, for example for the individualization of punishment (provided by article 74 of the Criminal Code[10]) or those provided for analyzing the existence of the public interest in ruling a solution to waive criminal prosecution (provided by article 318 (2) of the Criminal Procedure Code[11]). But, in the absence of an express indication within the law to apply these criteria by analogy, there is the risk of violating the right to a fair trial (Nestor 2024).

Until the legislature amends the law, we believe that the use of the teleological interpretation is very useful for the courts for making the right judgement. In this question with profound forensic implications, we think that the teleological interpretation must be performed on two grounds: the explicit purpose of the law and the implicit general purpose of Forensic Science.

As regards the explicit purpose of the law, we mention that Law no. 76/2008 provides, in article 1, that the establishment of the National System of Judicial Genetic Data (S.N.D.G.J.), has the purpose of prevention and combating certain categories of crimes that seriously violate the fundamental rights and freedoms of the person, in particular the right to life and to physical and mental integrity, as well as for the identification of bodies with unknown identity, missing persons or persons who have died as a result of natural disasters, mass accidents, murder or acts of terrorism. In the light of this purpose, we believe that courts must have a proactive attitude, without undue indulgence. This means that the decisions that genetic data must not be stored should be carefully taken, only when the judges reach the conclusion that there is no rational reason to believe that DNA data storage will be needed

[10] Law No. 286/2009, published in the Official Gazette No. 510 of July 24, 2009.

[11] Law No. 135/2010, published in the Official Gazette No. 486 of July 15, 2010.

to fulfill the purpose of the law. For example, in the ECtHR case of Aycaguer v. France (2017), the applicant was sentenced to 2 months imprisonment (suspended) for having struck gendarmes with an umbrella during a farmers' trade union demonstration, and the ECtHR ruled that the deed had a low gravity, which does not justify the enforcement of a procedure meant to collect and store genetic data.[12] A conclusion that can be drawn is that the courts should not order genetic data storage on cases where the consequences of the crime have not been severe and there are no other circumstances to justify such a measure.

However, in Romania, due to the fact that the law expressly provides the crimes for whose commission the DNA data storage is considered, and due to the severity of these crimes, we believe that, in practice, there will be fewer cases where the courts will decide that biological samples must *not* be taken. Because the legislator has mentioned only certain situations when DNA data storage is considered for convicted persons, excluding others, measures have already been taken in order to protect individuals from an abusive infringement of their right to privacy.

As regards the implicit general purpose of Forensic Science, which is to identify the perpetrators and to punish them according to their guilt, as well as to prevent crimes, we think that the teleological interpretation determines the judges not to show unjustified leniency, and to order DNA data storage whenever there are strong clues that such a decision would help forensic investigators. In favor of this conclusion, we mention that, in Romania, although the general crime rates are lower than in other countries, there has been an increasing number of murders with unknown perpetrator, from 405 cases in 2014 to 811 cases in 2023 (Nestor 2024).[13] In this context, we believe that authorities, including judicial courts, must show high level of interest in taking the right measures in order to identify the criminals and to prevent crime.

6.2 *Teleological Interpretation in the Use of DNA for Familial Searching in Romania*

One of the purposes for which genetic analysis can be used is for familial searching, which means identifying potential relatives of an unknown DNA profile in a database (Stanciu et al. 2024; Niedzwiecki et al. 2016). It is important to mention that familial DNA searching raises a lot of ethical issues. Some of these issues are related to privacy concerns, because people who submit their DNA for non-forensic aims (for example, to find their ancestry) might not be aware that their data could be used for forensic purposes, and can involve family members in forensic investigations.

[12] The case of Aycaguer v. France, 8806/12, Judgment 22.6.2017, https://hudoc.echr.coe.int/eng#{%22itemid%22:[%22002-11703%22]}.

[13] The statistics can be found on the official site of the Public Ministry of Romania, https://www.mpublic.ro/ro/content/raport-de-activitate.

Another problem is referring to informed consent, because, if people give their consent for their DNA analysis, they accept the consequences regarding their own person, not for their relatives, in absence of an explicit mention. Also, if law enforcement databases are skewed toward certain ethnic, racial or socioeconomic groups (which they often are), familial searching could reinforce systemic biases, leading to unbalanced search within communities. In some countries, a big problem is that people who are identified through familial searching might become subjects to criminal investigations even if there is no other evidence to support their involvement in criminal activities; for example, in the USA, such implications can raise the problem of an infringement to the Fourth Amendment. There is also concern that familial DNA searching can become a common one, being used not only for severe crimes, but also for minor offences or even for investigations in other fields than criminal law, leading to a generalized genetic surveillance. Indeed, we can reasonably think that familial searching can lead to exposure of family secrets, for example, children born out of wedlock, children who are adopted, or undisclosed biological relationships (Berkman et al. 2018). A major source for concern is the fact that, although genetic analysis has a high degree of accuracy, DNA matches between relatives aren't perfect, meaning that the judicial bodies could make mistakes and consider innocent people to be the real perpetrators (Mateen et al. 2021). All these issues have been raised in some countries, where familial DNA searching has led to strong debates (Formici 2021). However, beyond any possible discussions and criticism, we must underline that this method can be extremely useful in the so-called "cold cases" (usually in reference to a severe crime), which are cases that haven't been solved and in which the authorities don't have enough evidence to continue the criminal investigation.

In Romania, for the aim of DNA profiling, the CODIS system (Combined DNA Index System) is used. The institution which uses CODIS for forensic purposes is the National System of Judicial Genetic Data, which is managed by the National Forensic Institute. This system uses several DNA searching methods, namely direct searching, pedigree searching and familial searching. *Direct searching* is based on the *one-to-many* rule, and seeks for a direct match, which could lead to the identification of a certain person. *Pedigree (or indirect) searching*, is based on the *many-to-many* rule, and it generates lists of candidate DNA profiles, being very useful, for example, in finding missing persons. *Familial DNA searching* is a hybrid method, which uses elements from both direct and pedigree searching, and usually leads to lists of candidates, further forensic investigations being needed, in order to identify a specific person (Stanciu et al. 2024).

In what regards the potential ethical issues of the Familial DNA searching, in Romania, this method has not been a significant subject of public criticism. The method, which is relatively new in Romania, has been used in a number of cases. In 2019, in Romania, there was the first solving of a case using familial DNA searching, which was a murder case (Stanciu et al. 2021).

The reason behind the seemingly wide acceptance of this method in Romania may be the fact that DNA searching in Romania (including familial DNA searching) has been implemented with caution and within a strict legal framework. As we have already pointed out in this chapter, in Romania, there are strict regulations on the use of genetic data, which prohibit the use of DNA data for other purposes than those explicitly stated and in other conditions than those expressly provided by the law.

We believe that this acceptance of familial DNA searching in Romania is not only the result of a legislation that efficiently protects privacy, but also a consequence of a wide understanding of the need to apply the teleological interpretation in Forensics. In other words, people agree that the overall purpose of Forensic Science, which is to identify the perpetrators and, furthermore, to prevent crimes, is of utmost importance, so it is worth to interpret the law in order to apply all needed forensic methods, as long as they are legal and all cautions have been taken to protect human rights, including the right to privacy.

7 Conclusions

Our research leads us to the conclusion that, in Romania, the teleological interpretation in Forensic Science is generally applied in the meaning accepted by the majority of democratic states, but there are also certain specific aspects. These particularities are determined by historical aspects, but also by a fairly deep understanding of the importance of protecting human rights. As regards the historical influence, Romania still bears the marks left by the communist system, which in criminal investigations sometimes interpreted evidence in favor of ideology, not in favor of objective truth. This led to a deep appreciation of the importance of truth for society, although in communism this must have been an intimate, hidden thought. After the Romanian Revolution of 1989, this appreciation for the truth came out to the light, and the desire to know the truth no longer had to be hidden. As a proof for this statement, we mention the Romanian people's interest for the declassification of the archives of former secret police ("Securitatea"). This attitude can lead to the tendency to seek the truth at any cost, even at the cost of violating human rights. Fortunately, this is not the case, because, currently, Romania has a strict legal framework which efficiently protects human rights, including the right to privacy, which can be often endangered in forensic investigations. The legislation can be further improved, but, overall, it allows forensic procedures to be performed only in certain conditions, with the declared aim to protect human rights, among other objectives. This system seems to work, because, for example, some procedures that arise strong ethical debates in other countries (like familial DNA searching) did not spark debates in Romania. This context makes us conclude that, in Romania, teleological interpretation in Forensic Science is very important, and, as long as the legal framework and human rights are respected, forensic investigators have all the means at their disposal to discover the truth, as revealed by the evidence.

References

Baldacci CJ (2022) The common law of interpretation. Va Law Rev 108(5):1243–1288

Banu F, Pleşa L (2008) Simpozionul Internaţional „Experimentul Piteşti—Reeducarea prin tortură, Ediţia a VIII-a, Piteşti, 3–5 octombrie 2008, Caietele CNSAS. Revistă semestrială editată de Consiliul Naţional pentru Studierea Arhivelor Securităţii, Year I, no. 2/2008, CNSAS Publishing House, Bucureşti, pp. 394–396

Berkman BE, Miller WK, Grady C (2018) Is it ethical to use genealogy data to solve crimes? Ann Intern Med 169(5):333–334. https://doi.org/10.7326/M18-1348

Bouleanu E. (2016) Misterul „afacerii Ioanid", marele jaf comunist: cum a dispărut o sumă enormă din Banca Naţională şi ce s-a ascuns de fapt în spatele incidentului" ('The mystery of the "Ioanid affair", the great communist robbery: how an enormous sum disappeared from the National Bank and what was actually hidden behind the incident"). Historia, Published online at 19.05.2016. https://adevarul.ro/stiri-locale/alexandria/misterul-afacerii-ioanid-marele-jaf-comunist-1709151.html

Cheng EK, Yoon A (2005) Does Frye or Daubert matter? A study of scientific admissibility standards. Va Law Rev (97):471–513 https://scholarship.law.vanderbilt.edu/faculty-publications/161

Dammann J (2002) The role of comparative law in statutory and constitutional interpretation. St. Thomas Law Rev (14): 513–560, https://ssrn.com/abstract=818204

Demetriade M (2017) Istoricul Serviciului de Contrainformaţii Penitenciare (1949–1967). Caietele CNSAS. Revistă semestrială editată de Consiliul Naţional pentru Studierea Arhivelor Securităţii, Year VIII, no. 2 (16)/2015, CNSAS Publishing House, Bucureşti, pp. 7–180

Flanagan B (2010) Revisiting the contribution of literal meaning to legal meaning. Oxf J Legal Stud 30(2) (summer 2010), 255–271, Oxford University Press. https://www.jstor.org/stable/40660488

Formici G (2021) From 'familial searching' to 'forensic genetic genealogy': new frontiers – and challenges – of DNA analysis in criminal investigations". BIOLAW JOURNAL - ISSN 2284-4503 – 1/2021, 305–328. https://doi.org/10.15168/2284-4503-788

Fournier LR (2016) The Daubert guidelines: usefulness, utilization, and suggestions for improving quality control. J Appl Res Mem Cogn 5(3):308–313. https://doi.org/10.1016/j.jarmac.2016.06.012

Franţ AE (2023) Criminalistica, la intersecţia dintre legile naturii şi legile făcute de oameni" ("Forensics, at the crossroad between laws of nature and laws made by humans"). Dialogi Juridici – Volumul Patrulaterului Facultăţilor de Drept Iaşi – Chişinău – Bălţi – Cahul, Tudorel Toader (coordonator), Pulishing House of "Alexandru Ioan Cuza" University of Iaşi

Groscup JL, Penrod SD, Studebaker CA, Huss MT, O'Neil KM (2002) The effects of Daubert on the admissibility of expert testimony in state and federal criminal cases. Psychol Public Policy Law, 8(4), 339–372. doi:https://doi.org/10.1037/1076-8971.8.4.339

Harper D (n.d.) Etymology of teleology. Online Etymology Dictionary. https://www.etymonline.com/word/teleology

Hilbert J (2019) The disappointing history of science in the courtroom: Frye, Daubert, and the Ongoing Crisisof "Junk Science" in Criminal Trials". Oklhoma Law Rev 759, 71(3):759–821

Ignătescu C (2013) Considerations regarding the interpretation of legal norm. The USV Annals of Economics and Public Administration 13(2[18]):245–248

Jensen PJ (2003) Frye versus Daubert: practically the same?. Minnesota Law Rev 773, 87, 1579–1620, https://scholarship.law.umn.edu/mlr/773

Kojevnikov A (2008) The Phenomenon of Soviet Science. Osiris 23(1), Intelligentsia Science: The Russian Century, 1860–1960, 115–135. https://doi.org/10.1086/591871

Konca P (2021) Creating law of interpretation: a risky or fundamental step?". Revus, 45. https://doi.org/10.4000/revus.7500

Mateen RM, Sabar MH, Hussain S, Parveen R, Hussain M (2021) Familial DNA analysis and criminal investigation: usage, downsides and privacy concerns. Forensic Sci Int 318:110576, ISSN 0379-0738. https://doi.org/10.1016/j.forsciint.2020.110576

Nagarajan KV (2011) The code of Hammurabi: an economic interpretation. Int J Bus Soc Sci 2(8):108–117

Nestor RA (2024) Utilizarea datelor stocate în Sistemul Naţional de Date Genetice Judiciare – restrângere necesară adusă vieţii private sau protecţie dincolo de limitele convenţionale?" ("Use of data stored in the National Judicial Genetic Data System – necessary restriction of privacy or protection beyond conventional limits?"). Juridice. Essentials, https://www.juridice.ro/essentials/, published online 12.06.2024

Niedzwiecki E, Debus-Sherrill S, Field MB (2016) Understanding familial DNA searching: coming to a consensus on terminology. National Institute of Justice, US

Oncescu C (2022) Prescripţia răspunderii penale, Decizia nr. 358/2022 pronunţată de Curtea Constituţională şi modalitatea de aplicare a legii penale mai favorabile" ("The statute of limitations for criminal liability, Decision No. 358/2022 issued by the Constitutional Court and the method of applying the more favorable criminal law"), published online 14.06.2022, https://www.juridice.ro/

Padjen IL (2020) Systematic interpretation and the re-systematization of law: the problem, co-requisites, a solution. Int J Semiot Law 33:189–213. https://doi.org/10.1007/s11196-019-09672-x

Partridge E (1977) Origins: a short etymological dictionary of modern English. Routledge, London

Ratzsch D, Koperski J (2023) Teleological arguments for God's existence. The Stanford Encyclopedia of Philosophy (Summer 2023 Edition), Edward N. Zalta and Uri Nodelman (eds). https://plato.stanford.edu/archives/sum2023/entries/teleological-arguments/>

Reports of National Council for the Study of Security Archives (Consiliul Naţional pentru Studierea Arhivelor Securităţii – CNSAS), http://www.cnsas.ro/reeducarea.html

Rodin S (2021) Time, history and legal interpretation. Maastricht J Eur Comp Law 28(4):433–436. https://doi.org/10.1177/1023263X211039980

Rutner EW, Bach LB (2015) Florida's "Brave New World": the transition from Frye to Daubert will transform the playing-field for litigants in medical causation cases". Barry Law Rev 20(2):Article 4, 173–191. https://lawpublications.barry.edu/barrylrev/vol20/iss2/4

Salehijam M (2018) The value of systematic content analysis in legal research. Tilburg Law Rev 23(1–2):34–42. https://doi.org/10.5334/tilr.5

Stanciu F, Dragomir E, Bratu T (2021) Solving the first murder case in Romania using familial searching. Romanian J Legal Med 29(3):295–298. https://doi.org/10.4323/rjlm.2021.295

Stanciu F, Cuţăr V, Vladu S, Stoian IM, Rădulescu A, Cotolea A, Păunache MA, Cucoş A (2024) Unlocking forensic potential: CODIS implementation and DNA data exchange in Romania. Genomica 1(1):3–9. https://doi.org/10.5281/zenodo.11069588

Stein P (1995) Interpretation and legal reasoning in Roman law. Chicago-Kent Law Rev 70(4):Article 7, 1539–1556

Trykhlib K (2020) The Principle of Proportionality in the Jurisprudence of the European Court of Human Rights. Conference: EU 2020 – lessons from the past and solutions for the future, Eu and Comparative Law Issues and Challenges Series (Eclic) – issue 4, 128–154. https://doi.org/10.25234/eclic/11899

Fundamental Rights and Interpretative Practice

Charter of Fundamental Rights of the European Union: A Prolific Inspiration for Romanian Legislation

Alina Mirabela Gentimir

Abstract Currently, the national standard of protection of human rights provided in legislation or interpreted by the judiciary system is influenced considerably by European standard represented by the European Convention on Human Rights and the Charter of Fundamental Rights of the European Union in conjunction with the case law of European Court of Human Rights and Court of Justice of the European Union. Particularities are noted, recently, regarding the right to a fair trial, a real chameleon right, and related to the principle *ne bis in idem*. Beyond these new jurisprudential developments remains the constant challenge concerning the common standard of protection of human rights the European level, especially in the circumstances of a still non-accession of the European Union to the European Convention on Human Rights.

1 Introduction

Inherent to all persons on the basis of their humanity, human rights affirm their fundamental character serving "as international benchmarks designed to shield people from severe abuses in political, legal, and social spheres" (Gordon 2024).

The legal dimension of human rights is expressed primarily in human rights treaties that are binding under public international law (Krennerich 2024). European Convention on Human Rights is the oldest legally binding treaty on human rights and is considered the most effective international convention on the protection of human rights (Koula 2024) has inspired for decades both regional and national legislation, shifting the focus from the persons to the States as the primary bearers of obligations. Thus, precisely through the international human rights treaties such as European Convention, within the framework of international organizations, States mutually undertake to respect, protect and guarantee the human rights of all the

A. M. Gentimir (✉)
Faculty of Law, 'Alexandru Ioan Cuza' University of Iaşi, Iaşi, Romania
e-mail: gentimir@uaic.ro

I. Maria Costea (ed.), *Legal Interpretation in Motion*, Ius Gentium: Comparative Perspectives on Law and Justice 144,
https://doi.org/10.1007/978-3-032-32948-6_8

persons who live in their sovereign territory or are subject to their jurisdiction, taking into account their "extraterritorial" human rights obligations. Incorporation of human rights into national legislation as fundamental rights binds the State authorities and directly affect the relationship between the State and individuals and indirectly also between private individuals (Krennerich 2024).

Dynamics of international and national dimensions of human rights intertwine and emphasise the necessity of the cooperation of States, at both the vertical and horizontal levels. Vertical cooperation refers the distinct feature of rejecting reciprocity as the basis of obligation, shifting their focus towards the international public policy nature of collective interests, the breach of a human rights treaty by a State not empowering other parties to default on their obligations (Klipfel 2024).

Concerning horizontal cooperation, in the conditions of absence of "effective means of coercion and enforcement comparable to national law" of the binding legal judgements pronounced by regional human rights courts, appears more important that international human rights conventions to be "adopted or transformed into national law, preferably in the form of fundamental rights in national constitutions" and subsequent legislation, the rights being enforced in national court (Krennerich 2024).

Fundamental rights are even "particularized in domestic legislation and explained by the legislator in the travaux préparatoires", might reveal "the discrepancies between the Constitutional rights and the Convention rights" and might create space for the national system precedence, despite the necessity of the compliance with European standards (Granmar 2024) required by the accession of the State to the European Union. Nevertheless, in case of a norm conflict the primacy of one system over the other depends on what supranational court decides the case (Granmar 2024).

Thus, the system of European Convention has been doubled since 2000 by the system of Charter of Fundamental Right of the European Union. Concretely, gradually the supremacy of EU law and the effects of legislative acts transposing the rights and freedoms enshrined in the provisions of the EU Charter into national law, is transforming the domestic legal system. In case secondary legislation is not given the intended effect, provisions in the EU Charter may take upon direct effect independently in the national legal systems in parity with provisions in the ECHR. (Granmar 2024). Even the roots of these instruments generate a special atmosphere, their interpretative methods, as well as the typologies of States obligations (van Daalen 2025) emphasis relevant particularities of these instruments.

In comparison with European Convention that is a well-known legal instrument, Charter of Fundamental Rights still has the status of Cinderella of human rights instruments. Oscillating between traditional rights and progressive rights, the Charter of Fundamental Rights challenges both European Union institutions and organs and member States, as well human rights holders. Having an original structure established taking into account the fundamental values of the European Union, creates the space of a harmonious dialogue of civil right with political rights and with economic rights and with social and cultural rights.

Given the prominence of the right to fair trial—provided in article 47 of the Charter—and principle of *ne bis in idem*—regulated in article 50 of the Charter—in the case law of European Court of Human Rights and Court of Justice of the European Union, in current paper will be presented, shortly, their implications in Romanian Criminal Procedure Code in tight connection with the legislation for judiciary cooperation in criminal matters. As well, as key legal provision, it will be analyzed article 52 of the Charter of Fundamental Rights, as a bridge which balances the protection of human rights imposed to European level.

2 Is the Right to a Fair Trial Still the One?

The relevance of the right to a fair trial for judicial system and human rights holders has been underlined for decades of case law of national and regional courts. Its direct connections with principle of rule of law put it in the peak of human rights pyramid.

Concerning its regulation, while European Convention contains the two types of guarantees—general guarantees for all kinds of trials and specific guarantees for criminal trials—in the same article—article 6 –, EU Charter and Romanian criminal procedural legislations pick out a different structural approach. EU Charter contains in the same article—article 47—both fundamental procedural guarantees: right to an effective remedy and right to a fair trial. Romanian Criminal Procedure Code provides the general and specific guarantees in several articles, qualifying these rights as rules of Romanian criminal trial. The first guarantee regulated in the Code—article 4—is a specific one for criminal trials: presumption of innocence and is different in its statement of content than both European catalogues "(1) Every person is presumed innocent until proven guilty by a final criminal judgment. (2) After all evidence has been taken, any doubt in forming the conviction of the judicial bodies shall be interpreted in favor of the suspect or defendant." Article which makes references to the tribunal is article 3 of Romanian Criminal Procedure Code; it is an indirect modality to guarantee the three exigences related to the tribunal—provided by law, independent, impartial –, mentioning the principle of separation of judicial powers. The third article—article 8—provides as general rule of Romanian criminal trial the general guarantees of equity and reasonable time of the criminal trial. The right to the defence, as special guarantee constitutes the rule stipulated in article 10 of the Romanian Criminal Procedure Code, having the same approach that the Charter: recognizing the defense as a right belonging to all the parties of criminal trial and a subsequent defence rights related to the information about accusations, preparation of the defence, which are provided in European Convention and in Explanations of the Charter. Beside these defence rights are included another guarantee as the right to remain silent and two obligations for judicial authorities and defence lawyer: to ensure exercise of an effective defence during the entire trial; the defence to be created with good-will. Last article of Romanian Criminal Procedure Code which establishes an important rule for criminal trial—article 12—is a specific defence guarantee: right to an interpreter.

Understanding the importance of the legal provisions, it is essential to keep updated on the evolution of interpretation of these provisions. Having in mind the effects of the European case law over the national authorities, would be suitable to be presented recent jurisprudential developments of the interpretation of the right to a fair trial stipulated in the EU Charter: preliminary rulings, European arrest warrant, right to be present in the trial, right to be informed about accusation.

2.1 Preliminary Ruling

The Charter of fundamental rights is relevant in preliminary rulings procedure, having article 267 TFEU as pivot read in the light of article 47 paragraph 2 of the Charter and article 6 of the European Convention (Callewaert 2024a). The premise situation for this legal aggregation appears when the national legislation doesn't provide a judicial remedy against a decision of a national court on point of law, parties may introduce a request for a preliminary ruling made by Court of Justice of the European Union. Taking into consideration that the system of preliminary ruling doesn't belong only to the European Union judicial framework, European Court of Human Rights having in its competence this procedure as well, it would be relevant to be underlined that in the case law of the both European jurisdictions is settled that the national court which dismisses the request of a party for a preliminary ruling have to give reasons for its dismissal (CJEU, *Cilfit*, 1998, 16; ECtHR, Georgiou, 2023, paras. 23–25). This common approach has the role to increase the role of parties to the proceedings in the system of preliminary rulings, going beyond the dialogue between national and European courts (Callewaert 2024a). This similarity doesn't exclude the existence of differences between European jurisdictions. While Strasbourg jurisdiction is focused on substantive law arguments centered on the right to fair trial seen as a expression of the rule of law and guarantee against arbitrariness and is not requiring the same level of reasoning (ECtHR, *Baydar*, 2018, para. 42) in all circumstances, Luxembourg jurisdiction is more concerned by the preservation of the effectiveness of the system of preliminary rulings (Callewaert 2024a; CJEU, *Kubara*, 2024, paras. 45–46). In this dynamic of convergences and divergences, from the point of view of substantive provisions of human rights prevails the obligation for national courts, obligation not provided by national legislation, but by European caselaw.

2.2 European Arrest Warrant

In cases of European arrest warrant, article 47 paragraph 2 of the Charter is applied with direct connection to article 6 of the Charter, as well with the right to freedom of movement and residence and, essentially, with principle of equality and principle of mutual trust. Nevertheless, national decision on the arrest and information on the possibilities of challenging that decision are not included in the object of an obligation for judicial authorities issuing a European arrest warrant whether are not fulfilled two cumulative conditions: the person is in the member State executing the European arrest warrant and the person has not been surrendered to the competent authorities of the member State issuing the arrest warrant. But the essential argument for this approach is that issuing judicial authority has the obligation to interpret its national law in conformity with EU law, taken into consideration the application of the principle of the primacy of EU law. Subsequently, in this manner is enabled to be ensured an outcome compatible with the aim pursued by secondary EU law (Framework Decision 2002/584) which precludes national law to include any obligation to the judicial authorities issuing European arrest warrant before the surrender of the person to them (CJEU, *IR*, 2022, para. 41).

2.3 The Right to Be Present at the Trial

In order to reinforce procedural guarantees, paragraph 2 of the article 47 of Charter may be applied together with another paragraph—paragraph 3 of the same article –with strong connection with article 48 of the Charter, too, taking into account that both articles constitute the content of the article 6 of European Convention, each of them providing general and specific dimensions of procedural guarantees. The perfect example for this strong interdependence is represented by the cases on the right to be present at the trial in criminal proceedings which represents an essential element of the right to a fair trial (CJEU, *HN*, 2022, para. 54). In fact, precisely the interpretation of the two mentioned paragraphs of the article 47 and article 48 must ensure a level of protection which does not disregard the level of protection guaranteed by article 6 of the European Convention (ECtHR, *Hermi*, 2006, para. 58). Thus, the presence of an accused has a crucial importance in the interest of a fair and just criminal trial. For this reason, the obligation of the national authorities to guarantee the right of the accused person to be present in the courtroom is one of the essential requirements of the article 6 of the European Convention. however, the right to be present in the courtroom has a relative nature taken into consideration that neither the letter nor the spirit of article 6 of European Convention don't preclude the possibility to waive to this right, in different manners—expressly or tacitly—but respecting the exigencies of free will, non-equivocation, minimum safeguards (ECtHR, *Vilches Corodnado*, 2018, para. 36). Nevertheless, Eu secondary law (Directive (EU) 2016/343) can contain transform the right to be present in court in an obligation for defendant to be present in court, taken into consideration that is not precluded that national legislation to impose such an obligation to suspects and accused. As well, is precluded the national legislation which permits a trial to be held in the absence of the suspect or accused. There are provided two conditions: the suspect or accused is outside that member State and the competent authorities of that member State imposed an entry ban to the suspect or accused who is unable to enter on its territory.

2.4 The Right to Information About Accusation

Article 47 of the Charter, in almost the same normative conjunction—with article 48 of the Charter and article 6 of European Convention to which are added article 5 of European Convention—defines the bases of the legal framework for secondary EU law (Directive 2012/13) related to the common standards to be applied in the field of information about rights and of information about accusation to be given to persons suspected or accused of having committed criminal offences. Challenges appear in cases in which there are procedural defects in the indictment (CJEU, *ZX*, 2021, para. 24), considered to be substantial and impeding the proper conduct of the criminal proceedings. If these defects are established at the pre-trial hearing, the court proceedings should be suspended and the case should be referred back to the prosecutor with the instruction to remedy them and to draw a new indictment? If the defects of indictment are signalized at subsequent hearings, once the evidence gathering is complete, but before the court has given judgment on the substance of the charges, is possible to be remedied or not? The amendment of charges—errors and omissions—must be accompanied by the necessary safeguards to ensure that the accused is able to defend himself/herself—prosecutor inform the defence *ex officio* and give the opportunity to prepare for those amendments. In accordance with article 47 of the Charter and article 6 paragraph 3 of the Directive 2012/13, national legislation must provide a sufficiently effective mechanism to remedy defects in the indictment which prejudice the right of the accused to be provided with detailed information about the charges, following the pre-trial hearing in a criminal case (CJEU, *Korolev*, 2018, 2020). In fact, the right to be informed about the charges constitutes the space of interconnection between fairness of the procedure, effectiveness of the defense (CJEU, *Moro*, 2019, para. 43) and effectiveness of a remedy (CJEU, *Staatsanwaltschaft Offenburg*, 2020, para. 71). Regarding the authority competent to remedy the defects of indictment, whether it is the court itself or the case has to be referred to the prosecutor, in the Directive 2012/13 is provided precluding judges to regularize the indictment, right to defense and right to a fair trial being necessarily being protected (CJEU, *Korolev,* 2018, para. 94). As concerning the moment at which the benefit of the procedural rights must be ensured it is established as final limit the acts before the criminal court begins to examine the charges on the merits and the commencement of the proceedings (CJEU, *Korolev*, 2020, para.39). Nevertheless, legal classification of the alleged acts may suffer changes. In this case, it is imposed a condition related to the effectiveness of information of the accused and his lawyer which may be satisfied only if they have the opportunity to respond effectively before the stage of deliberation (CJEU, *ZX*, 2020, para. 29). Article 47 of the Charter in conjunction with article 6 paragraph 3 of the Directive 2012/13 must be interpreted as precluding national legislation which does not provide for a procedural mechanism for remedying errors and omissions in the indictment which prejudice the right of the accused person to be provided with detailed information concerning the charges following the pre-trial hearing in a criminal case (CJEU, *ZX*, 2020, para. 32). EU law does not specify the national authority responsible for ensuring that accused persons benefit from the rights enshrined in Article 6(3) of Directive 2012/13, nor the procedure to be followed for that purpose (CJEU, *ZX*, 2020, para. 34). But appears relevant the procedural autonomy of the Member States in compliance with the principle of equivalence, which requires that national rules are not less favorable than those governing similar domestic situations, and the principle of effectiveness, which requires that national procedural rules do not make it excessively difficult or impossible in practice to exercise the rights conferred by EU law (CJEU, *ZX*, 2020, para. 39). in order to ensure the effectiveness of all the provisions of EU law, the principle of the primacy of that law requires the national courts to interpret, as far as possible, their domestic law in a manner consistent with EU law (CJEU, *Popławski*, 2019, para. 57). So, whenever the point in time when the information is provided the accused person and his or her lawyer must have, inter alia, with due regard for the adversarial principle and the principle of equality of arms, sufficient time to become acquainted with that information, and must be placed in a position to prepare the defence effectively, submit any observations and, when necessary, to make any application, such as an application for further investigation, that they are entitled to make under national law (CJEU, *Moro,* 2019, para. 53). It is only where it is unable to interpret national law in compliance with the requirements of EU law, that the national court, which is called upon within the exercise of its jurisdiction to apply provisions of EU law, is under a duty to give full effect to those provisions, if necessary refusing of its own motion to apply any conflicting provision of national legislation, even if adopted subsequently, and it is not necessary for that court to request or await the prior setting aside of such provision by legislative or other constitutional means (CJEU, *Popławski,* 2019, para. 58). Where it is impossible to give a consistent interpretation, any national court, hearing a case within its jurisdiction, has, as an organ of a Member State, the obligation to disapply any provision of national law which is contrary to a provision of EU law with direct effect in the case pending before it, thanks to the direct effect of EU law (CJEU, *Popławski,* 2019, para. 61). In conclusion, Article 47 of the Charter must be interpreted as requiring the referring court to give an interpretation of the national rules on the amendment of the indictment, as far as possible in a manner consistent with that law, so as to enable the prosecutor to remedy errors and omissions in the content of the indictment at the trial, while at the same time actively and genuinely safeguarding the rights of the defence of the accused person. Only if the referring court considers that such an interpretation is not possible should it disregard the national provision prohibiting the suspension of court proceedings and refer the case back to the public prosecutor in order for the latter to draw up a new indictment (CJEU, *ZX*, 2021, para.45).

3 Ne Bis in Idem Loses Is No Longer a Character of Absolute Right?

Principle *ne bis in idem* is a fundamental principle of EU law (CJEU, *Generalstaatsanwaltschaft Münnhen*, 2022, para.64), which derives from the constitutional traditions common to the Member States (CJEU, *Generalstaatsanwaltschaft Münnhen*, 2022, para. 65). In Romanian Criminal Procedure Code is provided as general rule of a criminal trial—article 6: "No person may be prosecuted or tried for committing a crime when a final criminal judgment has previously been rendered against that person regarding the same act, even under another legal framework". As well, this principle is mentioned in the Law no. 302 from 2004, a special Law for international judicial cooperation—article 8. Romanian legislator uses the technique of mentioning what is not included in the object of international judicial cooperation: same acts are object of two trials; these two trials are conducted in two States; in one trial already is issued a final decision in which has been ordered the acquittal or termination of the criminal trial or the punishment imposed in the case, by a final decision of conviction, has been executed or has been the subject of a pardon or amnesty, in its entirety or on the unexecuted part or if the renunciation of the application of the punishment or the postponement of the application of the punishment has been ordered and the term provided for in art. 82 paragraph (3) of the Criminal Code, respectively the supervision term provided for in art. 84 of the Criminal Code, has expired without their revocation or annulment. As well, are mentioned two situations in which the conditions presented above not apply: if assistance is requested for the purpose of reviewing the final decision, for one of the reasons that justify the promotion of one of the extraordinary appeals provided for in the Romanian Criminal Procedure Code; if an international treaty to which Romania is a party contains more favorable provisions in terms of the non bis in idem principle.

Romanian jurisprudence establishes that Romanian courts interpret and apply the national provisions related to the principle analyzed by reference to the corresponding international conventional provisions (Bradu and Preda 2022). In the field of criminal procedure, the issue of a possible duplication of procedures arises when the first set of procedures has ended as a result of ordering a solution to dismiss, acquit or terminate the criminal trial, respectively when a case provided for in art. 16 para. (1) of the CPP is an incident. In Romanian law, the notion of "final criminal judgment" within the meaning of art. 6 CPP is assessed by reference to its autonomous meaning configured in the case law of the European Court of Human Rights and the Court of Justice of the European Union, in order to guarantee compliance with art. 11, art. 20 and art. 148 of the Constitution (Tudorache 2023).

The European standard related to the principle of ne bis in idem establishes that the content of the principle includes specific references, such as "A person whose trial has been finally disposed of in a State may not be prosecuted in another State for the same acts provided that, if a penalty has been imposed, it has been enforced, is actually in the process of being enforced or can no longer be enforced under the laws of the sentencing State"(CJEU, *MR*, 2023, para. 4).

The application of the principle ne bis in idem includes the fulfilment of two conditions: firstly, there must be a prior final decision (the 'bis' condition) and, secondly, that the prior decision and the subsequent proceedings or decisions must concern the same facts (the 'idem' condition) (CJEU, *bpost*, 22, para. 28; CJEU, *MR*, 2023, para. 33).

The 'idem' condition refers to the prohibition for the same person from being tried or punished in criminal proceedings more than once for the same offence) (CJEU, *bpost*, 22, para. 31; CJEU, *MR*, 2023, para. 34). It is imposed the existence of a set of concrete circumstances which are inextricably linked together and which have resulted in the final acquittal or conviction of the person concerned. Therefore, it is prohibited the imposition, with respect to identical facts, of several criminal penalties as a result of different proceedings brought for those purposes (CJEU, *Generalstaatsanwaltschaft Münnhen*, 2022, para. 128; CJEU, *MR*, 2023, para. 35).

The 'idem' condition requires that the material facts be identical. The principle ne bis in idem is not intended to be applied where the facts at issue are not identical, but merely similar purposes (CJEU, *Generalstaatsanwaltschaft Münnhen*, 2022, para. 129; CJEU, *MR*, 2023, para. 37).

The identity of the material refers to a set of concrete circumstances of the events which are, in essence, the same. As well, the events have to satisfy other exigencies related to the perpetrator—to be the same—and to interconnection in time and space (CJEU, *Generalstaatsanwaltschaft Münnhen*, 2022, para. 130; CJEU, *MR*, 2023, para. 38).

Whether a State intends to derogate from the principle *ne bis in*, it limits the fundamental right guaranteed by Article 50 of the Charter (Escobar Veas 2023). Such a limitation—acts to which the foreign judgment relates constitute an offence against national security or other equally essential interests of a State—is in accordance with human rights standards only whether it justify the conditions stipulated in Article 52 paragraph 1 of the Charter (CJEU, *MR*, 2023, para. 48). The first condition imposed to any limitation on the exercise of the rights and freedoms is to be provided for by law (CJEU, *Spasic*, 2014, para. 57; CJEU, *MR*, 2023, para. 50) which accomplish requirements of clarity and precision and define the scope of the limitation (CJEU, BV, 2022, para. 31; CJEU, *MR*, 2023, para. 50), and to respect the essence of those rights and freedoms. The second exigency refers to the principles of proportionality and necessity, "limitations on those rights and freedoms may be made only if they are necessary and genuinely meet objectives of general interest recognised by the European Union or the need to protect the rights and freedoms of others" (CJEU, *MR*, 2023, para.59).

Even the scope of the protection conferred by Article 50 of the Charter cannot vary from one Member State to another (CJEU, *bpost*, 22, para. 34), a limitation of the principle *ne bis in idem* in cases related, for example, to transnational organized crime respects the essence of Article 50 of the Charter whether "that limitation does no more than allow for further proceedings and penalties in respect of the same acts in pursuit of a distinct objective" (CJEU, *bpost*, 2022, para. 43; CJEU, *MR*, 2023, para.52).

The objective of safeguarding national security, as an objective of general interest (CJEU, *MR*, 2023, para.58), implies "the primary interest in protecting the essential functions of the State and the fundamental interests of society, by the prevention and punishment of activities capable of seriously destabilizing the fundamental constitutional, political, economic or social structures of a country and, in particular, of directly threatening society, the population or the State itself" (CJEU, *SpaceNet and Telekom Deutschland*, 2022, para. 92; CJEU, *MR*, 2023, para. 55).

Applying this ratio to the same example of participated in a criminal organisation which had a cross-border dimension and a sophisticated modus operandi and whose activities caused thousands of victims to suffer financial damage, the injured parties residing in different States (CJEU, *MR*, 2023, para. 40) requires a closer cooperation between the Member States of the European Union in order to counter the dangers and proliferation of criminal organisations and to respond effectively to citizens' expectations and Member States' own demands (CJEU, *MR*, 2023, para.7).

Despite the gravity of such offences, the principle of proportionality must be respected. So, limitations imposed by acts of EU law, by default national law, on rights and freedoms have to cover suitability and necessity and to grant double type of interests fulfilling the condition of legitimacy—public interests or private interests. The essence of the principle of proportionality is ensuring a proper balance of the objective of general interest with the private interests of the person in question in order to avoid "the disadvantages caused by that measure to be not disproportionate to the aims pursued", respectively "measuring the seriousness of the interference which such a limitation entails and by verifying that the importance of the objective of general interest pursued by that limitation is proportionate to that seriousness" (CJEU, *Orde van Vlaamse Balies and Others*, 2022, para.41). As well, the principle of proportionality may imply existence of alternatives modalities of intrusion, being required the use of the modality which is the least harmful. CJEU, *MR*, 2023, para. 59).

Particularly taken into consideration the nature and the particular gravity of such harm, it can be affirmed that the importance of that general interest objective seems to be more important than combating crime in general, even serious crime. For being in conformity with article 52 paragraph 1 of the Charter, such an objective is, consequently, able of justifying measures implying interferences with fundamental rights which would not be authorised for the purpose of prosecuting and punishing criminal offences generally (CJEU, *Commissioner of An Garda Síochána and Others*, 2022, para. 57; CJEU, *MR*, 2023, para. 61).

For concluding, regarding the application of the article 50 of the Charter in conjunction with Schengen Convention, may be added that the particular case of transnational organized crime "must be interpreted as not precluding the courts of a Member State to settle down that, so far as concerns the offence of forming a criminal organisation, that Member State is not bound by the provisions where the criminal organisation in which the person prosecuted participated has engaged exclusively in financial crime, in so far as the prosecution of that person is, in the light of the actions of that organisation, intended to punish harm to the security or other equally essential interests of that Member State" (CJEU, *MR,* 2023, para. 84).

As well, article 50 of the Charter in conjunction with Schengen Convention, "must be interpreted as precluding the extradition, by the authorities of a Member State, of a third-country national to another third country, where, first, that national has been convicted by final judgment in another Member State for the same acts as those referred to in the extradition request, and has been subject to the sentence imposed in that State, and, second, the extradition request is based on a bilateral extradition treaty limiting the scope of the principle ne bis in idem to judgments handed down in the requested Member State" (CJEU, *Generalstaatsanwaltschaft Münnhen*, 2022, para. 137).

4 Article 52 Paragraph 3 of the Charter or Minimum Protection European Standard

European standard of protection of human rights is determined to be the minimum protection standard. The common European standard is guaranteed by the article 52 paragraph 3 of the Charter of fundamental rights: rights provided in the catalog of the Charter have the same meaning and the same scope as those guaranteed by the European Convention (Explanations relating to the Charter of fundamental rights).

The interest for this particular standard of protection appears in the cases in which member States are obliged to apply EU law and to respect the autonomy of EU law (CJEU, *W.Z.; Orde van Vlaamse Balies and Others,* 2022), but they are exposed to breach European Convention. Establishing a common standard will be convenient for both European organizations and States authorities.

4.1 Gender Issues

The recognition by a member State of the change of first name and gender identity lawfully acquired in another member State States (CJEU, *Mirin,* 2024; ECtHR, *X. and Y. v. Romania*, 2021), as the recognition in a member State of a homosexual partnership lawfully established in another member States (CJEU, *Coman,* 2018), constitutes the object of a case based on the interplay of Strasbourg and Luxembourg case law related to the articles 20 and 21 paragraph 1 of TFEU read in the light of articles 7 and 45 of the Charter, respectively article 8 of European Convention (CJEU, *Alchaster*, 2024). Particularly, the same European standards of protection contributed essentially for the draw the obligation for States to provide a clear and foreseeable procedure in case of legal recognition of gender identity. The key legal apposition which creates pressure on national authorities to change the legislation on these controversial issues in Eastern Europe is represented by the right to free movement, the essential difference ratione materiae between Strasbourg and Luxembourg case law, whose application is conditionate by the use of it by human rights holders (Callewaert 2024b).

4.2 Freedom of Press

The freedom of the press with references to political speech and speech on matters of public interest offers the opportunity to see the complementarity between the paragraphs 1 and 3 of article 52 of the Charter applied together with article 11 of the Charter. In the general context of the principle of mutual trust, the refusal to enforce a judgment delivered by a court of another member State by invoking a public policy clause is accepted only in cases of the" manifest breach of a rule of law regarded as essential in the EU legal order or of a right recognized as being fundamental within that legal order and therefore in the legal order of that member State", such as manifest breach of the freedom of the press (CJEU, *Real Madrid Club de Futbol,* 2024).

4.3 Plea-Bargening

Criminal procedur e relating to plea-bargaining (CJEU, *PT*, 2024), even in the absence of an EU law obligations to legislate on the settlement of criminal cases, they didn't come within the scope of the EU Charter, because this did not constitute "implementation of Union law" for purposes of article 52 paragraph 1 of the Charter (Petursson 2025) in combination with secondary EU law (Decision 2004/757), keep the attention of EU court according to article 19 paragraph 1 TEU—value of the rule of law, respectively impartiality of the courts (ad hoc court to rule on an agreement for settlement of the case entered into by a defendant and the public prosecutor) and rights of the defense(judicial approval of an agreement is subject to the consent of all the other defendants). In this case the standard of minimum protection provided by article 52 paragraph 3 of the Charter makes references to interplay of the article 47 paragraph 2 of the Charter and article 6 paragraph 1 of the European Convention related to the principle of effective judicial protection as general principle of EU law (Callewaert 2025a), "field covered by Union law" being inside "the fields covered by the Convention" (ECHR, *Bosphorus v. Ireland*, 2005).

4.4 Trialed in Absentia

The protection of the absent accused created the opportunity for analysis article 52 paragraph 3 of the Charter along with non-regression clause (Directive 2016/343) in order to assure the similar level of protection between EU and Council of Europe. The methodology of this analysis emphasizes, unfortunelly, the difference of approaches (Callewaert 2025b), Strasbourg court preferring objective criteria—non-appearance at trial of the defendant properly informed may offer indications about the intention of the accused to waive his/her right or to escape justice, while EU law promoting objectivation (CJEU, *IR*, 2022) and autonomization of some Strasbourg criteria, ignoring individualized operation concerning individual intention and circumstances beyond the control of the accused, like health problems, force majeure (ECtHR, *Sejdovic,* 2006, para. 86; ECHR, *Somogyi,* 2004, para. 72). In order to avoid divergence of application of minimum standard of human rights protection till the European Union will access to European Convention, it is proposed, even CJEU does not have jurisdiction to assess the compatibility of EU legislation with the Convention (CJEU, *Akerberg Fransson*, 2013, para. 44) particularly according to a very extensive interpretation of the article 52 paragraph 3 of the Charter, Court of Luxembourg to be allowed to at least indirectly verify to what extent EU law complies with minimum Convention protection level (CJEU, *VB II*, 2025). Nevertheless, to the European level it creates the obligation for national authorities to apply EU in compliance with the Convention in order to avoid a conviction in front of Strasbourg Court (ECtHR, *M.B.,* 2024).

5 Conclusions

The recognition of international human rights by national authorities proposes a supra-national human rights construct that requires to the national member to integrate international human rights principles into domestic legislation and case law, generally, and into criminalization decisions, particularly (Malby 2024).

European human rights set forth minimal standards, focusing on the prevention of the atrocious rather than the pursuit of the ideal (Gordon 2024). For this reason, "political elites in new democracies have stronger incentives to commit to human rights treaties and international organizations as a means to defend newly gained democratic rights and freedoms against future illiberal attempts by non-democratic actors. Having a democratic cabinet free of former autocratic elites explains more accurately increases in human rights commitment in new democracies" (Olar 2025).

Concretely, it is necessary for securing of rights encompassing negative and positive obligations which are imposed to the states as duty-bearers (Holder and Dearing 2024). A lot of discussions are focused on existence and limits of the "special nature" of human rights obligations which necessarily implies the disappearance, or simply the overcoming, of any form of reciprocity (Klipfel 2024).

The case law of European courts demonstrates the full engagement of national authorities in ensuring the efficient exercise of human rights included in European human rights catalogues. As other national authorities, Romanian judiciary body are focused on their obligations which are correlatives to the rights, generally, and procedural rights, specifically.

References

Bradu C, Preda C (2022) Ne bis in idem, double jeopardy or the right not to be punished twice for the same act. https://www.juridice.ro/687358/ne-bis-in-idem-double-jeopardy-sau-dreptul-de-a-nu-fi-sanctionat-de-doua-ori-pentru-aceeasi-fapta.html

Callewaert J (2024a) An upgrading of the parties to the proceedings in the system of preliminary rulings: judgment of the CJEU in KUBERA, https://johan-callewaert.eu/an-upgrading-of-the-parties-to-the-proceedings-in-the-system-of-preliminary-rulings-judgment-of-the-cjeu-in-kubera/

Callewaert J (2024b) Benchmark function of the Convention stressed by CJEU in Mirin and Real Madrid Club de Futbol. https://johan-callewaert.eu/benchmark-function-of-the-convention-stressed-by-the-cjeu-in-mirin-and-real-madrid-club-de-futbol

Callewaert J (2025a) The fields covered by Union law: not outside the fields covered by the Convention: Judgment of the CJEU in the case of PT. https://johan-callewaert.eu/the-fields-covered-by-union-law-not-outside-the-fields-covered-by-the-convention-judgment-of-the-cjeu-in-the-case-o

Callewaert J (2025b) Convention protection of the absent accused lowered under EU law: judgment of the CJEU in the case of VB II. https://johan-callewaert.eu/a-different-understanding-of-the-waiver-of-the-right-to-attend-trial-judgment-of-the-cjeu-in-the-case-of-vb-ii/

Escobar Veas JI (2023) Reconceptualising the Ne Bis in Idem. In: Ne bis in idem and multiple sanctioning systems. Legal studies in international, European and comparative criminal law, vol 8. Springer, Cham. https://doi.org/10.1007/978-3-031-16556-6_9

Gordon J S (2024) On human rights. Morality and Justice. Palgrave Macmillan, Cham. https://doi.org/10.1007/978-3-031-65980-5_7

Granmar CG (2024) Sweden, fundamental rights and the EU charter. In: Heger A, Malkmus M (eds) On the relation between the EU charter of fundamental rights and National Fundamental Rights. Springer, Cham. https://doi.org/10.1007/978-3-031-52685-5_10

Holder RL, Dearing A (2024) Human dignity, rights and victim participation in criminal justice. Int Criminol 4:108–119. https://doi.org/10.1007/s43576-024-00119-3

https://johan-callewaert.eu/an-upgrading-of-the-parties-to-the-proceedings-in-the-system-of-preliminary-rulings-judgment-of-the-cjeu-in-kubera/

Klipfel C (2024) Reciprocity and human rights. In: Kałduński M (ed) Reciprocity in international law. Global issues. Palgrave Macmillan, Cham. https://doi.org/10.1007/978-3-031-66746-6_9

Koula AC (2024) Human rights violations committed against human rights defenders through the use of legal system: a trend in Europe and beyond. Hum Rights Rev 25:99–122. https://doi.org/10.1007/s12142-024-00717-8

Krennerich M (2024) Human rights and human rights politics. In: Human rights politics. Interdisciplinary studies in human rights, vol 12. Springer, Cham. https://doi.org/10.1007/978-3-031-57026-1_1

Malby S (2024) Public wrongs and human rights: an orderly approach? Crim Law Philosophy, 19:236–286. https://doi.org/10.1007/s11572-024-09746-3

Olar RG (2025) Locking in democracy? Transitions, returning autocratic elites, and human rights treaty commitment. Rev Int Organ. 21:263–280 https://doi.org/10.1007/s11558-024-09582-z

Petursson GT (2025) A new framework for limitation of fundamental rights in EU law? In: Engel A, Groussot X, Petursson GT (eds) New directions in digitalisation. European Union and its neighbours in a globalized world, vol 13. Springer, Cham. https://doi.org/10.1007/978-3-031-65381-0_12

Tudorache I (2023) Application of the rule non bis in idem to the national level. https://www.juridice.ro/714943/aplicarea-regulii-ne-bis-in-idem-la-nivel-national.html

van Daalen O (2025) Human rights in context. From encryption to quantum computing. Information technology and law series, vol 38. T.M.C. Asser Press, The Hague. https://doi.org/10.1007/978-94-6265-635-2_4

Evolutionary Interpretation of the Concept of Family: Adapting Legal Norms to New Families

Lucia Irinescu

Abstract Family and family relations are becoming an integral part of globalization. The family is no longer based on marriage, but on filiation, thus confirming the fact that family life exists and develops on the basis of the multitude of forms of social coexistence. The Romanian legislator has the possibility of repairing the existing shortcomings by recognizing regimes parallel to marriage and meeting the requirements of the European Court of Human Rights. On the other hand, in the area of filiation, a balanced regulation will have to be found, balancing the right to have recourse to medically assisted human reproduction techniques with the child's right to identity. In national legal systems, there has recently been a contractualization of family law institutions. In practice, new concepts are developing which are moving further and further away from the traditional ones and are centered on the protection of individual rights. In this context, looking inevitably towards our system of law, we naturally ask how long we will be able to keep up with the tide of change in family relations.

1 Introduction

In the context of the changes that have taken place in Western society in recent decades, the idea of a new civilization has emerged in the public sphere and more and more voices are presenting the problem of a "family decline" or "family crisis". This chapter distinguishes between the current legal framework governing family relations (lex lata) and potential directions for future legal development (de lege ferenda). While the analysis first examines the existing legal regulation of family relations under Romanian and European law, the final sections explore possible legislative evolutions required to adapt family law to emerging social realities.

L. Irinescu (✉)
Faculty of Law, 'Alexandru Ioan Cuza' University of Iaşi, Iaşi, Romania
e-mail: lucia.irinescu@uaic.ro

I. Maria Costea (ed.), *Legal Interpretation in Motion*, Ius Gentium: Comparative Perspectives on Law and Justice 144,
https://doi.org/10.1007/978-3-032-32948-6_9

The reasons behind these concerns are the decline in the number of marriages in recent years, the rise in divorce rates and the emergence of new forms of social cohabitation. The German sociologist Ulrich Beck pointed out that changes in the family are the result of long-term trends in modern societies to grant greater autonomy to individuals, leading to a liberation from traditional responsibilities and personal empowerment. As a result, the family as the standard model of living together has been replaced by a multitude of lifestyles, and traditional family ties have been replaced by so-called "pure relationships" built on emotional communication (Beck 1995).

The precise definition of the concept of family presents some difficulties, generated by the fact that the family is the subject of research in several sciences, such as psychology, sociology, medicine and law.

Sociologically, the family is a field of sociology which studies the family as a dynamic structure in relation to the overall social environment. Sociologically, the family consists of a set of affective and communicative relationships formed through marriage, filiation or adoption. From a sociological point of view, the family unit is found in all forms of social life. Even in advanced societies such as modern Western societies, the importance of the family in social life remains considerable. From the sociological perspective, the family has several dimensions: biological (procreation takes place within it); psychological, affective and interactional; social (a community of life is created between spouses, parents and children); moral and educational (it creates an environment with educational values for children). Traditional sociological literature analyzes two types of family: the family of origin (the family into which we are born), and the family of procreation (the family we create through marriage) (Turliuc 2004).

Historically speaking, marriage in the Middle Ages was not based on love; marriage served the economic and political needs of an extended family group. In the mid-seventeenth century, the notion of free choice and marriage of love begins to be promoted as a cultural ideal. From that point on, the family becomes an optional and fragile institution and its future structure is strongly influenced. In the nineteenth century, it became popular that the husband was the provider and the wife the homemaker. This changed with the end of the Second World War. Economic changes and pop culture gave rise to trends never seen before. Couples married young and had many children. In the late 1970s divorce rates rose and the average age of first marriage also increased.

From a demographic perspective, whereas young people used to stay in the parental home even after marriage, with the extended family running the household, today things are very different. Young people want to live on their own, as this change cultivates a sense of responsibility and gives them more privacy.

Etymologically, the term 'family' comes from the Latin familia(e), which meant all the members of a household or a gentry. In ancient Roman law, family meant a large group of free and enslaved persons living in the same domus and under the power of the same *pater familias*. This family included: the wife married cum manu; sons with their wives; daughters and granddaughters until married cum manu. Later, the patriarchal family was extended to include adopted persons and legitimized children. Family law recognizes the agnatic family in Roman law, based on blood relationship.

Traditionally, the family is made up of people united by marriage and filiation. Although the concepts of family and marriage are closely connected, today we are increasingly seeing more and more alarm signals about the decline of marriages, the redefinition of the family in terms of same-sex marriages or same-sex or opposite-sex partnerships. It is undeniable that family relationships present numerous particularities in everyday life, which makes it necessary to regulate the family according to the elements of originality that exist in fact.

At the European level, the legislative harmonization of family relations became an important objective with the creation of the European Commission on Family Law (1 September 2001), which aimed to develop a set of European principles of family law that would become models for the harmonization of family law in Europe. Thus, this harmonization was to be achieved through comparative research aimed at harmonizing family law in European countries, by questioning the current state of these regulations, by searching for a common denominator for certain legal problems, by comparing the different solutions proposed by family law in different European jurisdictions and by questioning the (potential) future role of Member States in the process of harmonization of family law.

In this context, the Commission has developed four categories of basic principles, namely:

- European family law principles on divorce and maintenance of ties between former spouses;
- principles of European family law relating to matrimonial property;
- principles of European family law relating to parental authority;
- principles of European family law relating to property, maintenance and inheritance rights in the case of unmarried couples.

Although these principles are not binding, it can be said that family relations have acquired a new dimension with their elaboration and publication. For example, some States have modeled their provisions on the rights of the child (Portugal, Norway) and parental responsibility (Czech Republic) on the principles developed by the Commission. At the same time, we should not forget the role of the Convention and the European Court of Human Rights, which have influenced and continue to influence European national family laws in very many cases and, in most of them, have shaped these laws and created minimum standards in almost all areas of family law. Although substantive family law has been transformed under the pressure of globalization and human rights, the European Union's policies have focused only on the development of sectoral legislation governing family relations with international elements. A European private international family law has thus been created in certain matters, namely divorce, parental authority and legal maintenance obligations.

This chapter distinguishes between the analysis of the current legal framework governing family relations (lex lata) and possible future developments of family law (de lege ferenda).

2 Family Functions in Contemporary Society

The family remains one of the most important social institutions, but its role and functions have evolved under the influence of economic, cultural and technological change. In contemporary society, the family fulfills several essential functions:

The biological or perpetuating function of the human species is fundamental, as it ensures the perpetuation of the human species. The family thus plays an important role in population dynamics and is strongly influenced by the socio-economic framework. In order to fulfill this function, the family is based on marriage by free consent between spouses, who must be able to procreate. In demographic terms, fertility is an index calculated on the basis of the number of children born alive and the number of women in the population.

The economic function of the family is the expression of the property relations between spouses, between parents.

The family also has an educational function as it creates an environment with strong educational values for children Parents have the right and the duty to bring up their child, caring for his physical, mental and intellectual health and development, for his education, teaching and vocational training, according to their own convictions, abilities and needs; they are duty-bound to give the child the guidance and advice necessary for the proper exercise of the rights which the law recognizes to him. The aim of education is not only to acquire the basics of learning (literacy, expression, numeracy), but also to develop the child's full potential as a whole, including the cultivation of respect for human rights, the development of a sense of identity and belonging, and the child's socialization and interaction with the environment.

3 The Legal Concept of Family Life in International and European Law

The concept of family life has no general legal definition and no clear legal content. The right to found a family and the right to respect for and protection of family life are considered to be fundamental human rights and freedoms.

Article 12 of the Universal Declaration of Human Rights states for the first time that "No one shall be subjected to arbitrary interference with his privacy, family, home or correspondence, nor to attacks upon his honor and reputation. Everyone has the right to the protection of the law against such interference or attacks". This text was also taken over by Article 17 of the International Covenant on Civil and Political Rights.

Subsequently, Article 8 of the European Convention for the Protection of Human Rights and Fundamental Freedoms, under the marginal heading "Right to respect for private and family life", stipulates:

1. Everyone has the right to respect for his private and family life, his home and his correspondence.
2. There shall be no interference by a public authority with the exercise of this right except such as is in accordance with the law and is necessary in a democratic society in the interests of national security, public safety or the economic well-being of the country, for the prevention of disorder or crime, for the protection of health and morals, or for the protection of the rights and freedoms of others.

The right to privacy includes the right to personal privacy, the right to social privacy and the right to a healthy environment. The right to family life is recognized to everyone, regardless of whether they have established a legitimate family based on marriage or a de facto relationship.

At the same time, Article 12, ECHR entitled "Right to marry", states: Men and women of marriageable age have the right to marry and to found a family, according to the national laws governing the exercise of this right.

Under these articles, States have positive and negative obligations. The positive obligations involve the adoption of measures to ensure respect for private life, even in the sphere of relations between persons, and the negative obligations of abstention, not to interfere with the right to privacy.

In Romanian domestic law, Article 26(1) of the Constitution, under the marginal heading 'Intimate, family and private life', provides that 'The public authorities shall respect and protect intimate, family and private life.

In the case law of the European Court of Human Rights, the meaning of the expression "family life" has evolved continuously. Judges in Strasbourg have analyzed the incidence of Article 8 of the Convention in a number of areas, including relations between two persons of the same sex, the right to procreate, the right to adopt a child, the right to identity, the relationship between parents and their minor children, child protection measures, and the right of persons in custody to marital relations. The family remains, however, one of the institutions on which all States seek to uphold principles rooted in thousands and hundreds of years of evolution. In this connection, the Court has recognized that the application of the Convention must not lead to uniformity but, by virtue of the margin of appreciation accorded to the States, they are free to take an active part in preserving the defining social and cultural values.

One of the most intense debates remains that surrounding the institution of marriage. There are those who argue that establishing and maintaining a balance between the individual's natural aspiration for personal freedom, including in his or her personal life (intimate, family and private), and the interests of society and the State, which are to ensure general respect for imperative models of social conduct that ensure harmony in inter-social relations, is a sensitive issue. The restriction of the individual's free will with regard to his or her private and family life within certain legal structures has led and will increasingly lead to legal abuses.

For example, the European Court of Human Rights noted many years ago, in *Goodwin v. United Kingdom* decision in 2002, that the institution of marriage is being strongly shaken by developments in society, with advances in medicine and science bringing about fundamental changes in the field of transsexuality, to the point where the determination of a person's sex cannot be made on purely biological grounds. This after the Court pointed out in *Rees v. the United Kingdom* decision in 1986 that the same Article 12 of the Convention does not recognize the right of persons born with the same biological sex to marry, even after undergoing a sex change operation. Thus, since the Goodwin case, the right to found a family and the right to marry have been seen as two distinct rights, in the sense that family life can exist outside marriage.

Today, at European Union level, the legal reasoning that there must be an alternative to civil marriage and/or access to civil marriage for same-sex couples is increasingly being enforced. On July 2, 2009, the Constitutional Court of Slovenia ruled in *Blažič & Kern v. Slovenia* decision that registered same-sex partners must be granted the same inheritance rights as opposite-sex spouses. On July 7, 2009, the Federal Constitutional Court of Germany ruled that registered same-sex partners and opposite-sex spouses must be granted the same inheritance rights, and since September 22, 2011, the Constitutional Court of Austria has handed down five decisions finding that registered (same-sex) partners must enjoy the same rights as married (opposite-sex) couples.

An interesting and noteworthy perspective is outlined by the New Mexico Supreme Court in *Griego v. Oliver* decision in 2013: 'We conclude that the purpose of New Mexico's marriage laws is to bring stability and order to the legal bond of stable couples by defining the rights and responsibilities that partners have to each other, to their children if they choose to raise children together, and to their property. The prohibition of same-sex marriage is not essentially linked to the governmental interests promoted. Therefore, prohibiting individuals from marrying and depriving them of the rights, responsibilities, and protections of civil marriage solely because of their sexual orientation violates the equal protection principle of the New Mexico Constitution (NeJaime 2014).

In *Oliari and Others v. Italy* decision in 2015, the claimants argued that it was particularly relevant that they had no other option available to them to obtain legal recognition of their union.

It is in the general interest of a society, therefore, to assimilate and grant equal rights to all people, regardless of their sexual orientation, religious orientation, etc. As long as civil marriage is recognized, it is wrong to conflate legal rules with religious dogmas.

The Court of Justice of the European Union also plays an important role in standardizing family law. In the *Maruko v. Versorgungsanstalt der deutschen Bühnen* decision, the surviving partner of a registered (same-sex) partnership was not entitled to a survivor's pension in Germany, as the law only granted these benefits to spouses (marriage was not available to same-sex couples at that time). The Court held that, in so far as the couples were in comparable situations, this amounted to direct discrimination within the meaning of Council Directive 2000/78/EC of 27 November 2000 establishing a general framework for equal treatment in employment and occupation. Although Member States were in principle free to legislate on adult relationships (and in particular marriage), they were obliged to do so without discrimination.

In *Coman, Hamilton v. Asociatia Accept v. Inspectoratul General pentru Imigrări and Ministry of Internal Affairs of Romania* decison in 2018, the European Court answered some preliminary questions referred by the Constitutional Court of Romania, including: "Does 'spouse' in Article 2(2)(a) of Directive 2004/38 (...) include the same-sex spouse, from a non-EU Member State, of a European citizen to whom the citizen has lawfully married under the law of a Member State other than the host Member State?" The Court replied and stated that "the obligation of a Member State to recognize a same-sex marriage contracted in another Member State under the law of that State solely for the purpose of granting a derived right of residence to a national of a non-member State does not affect the institution of marriage in that first Member State, which is defined by national law and falls (...) within the competence of the Member States. It does not require that Member State to provide in its national law for the institution of same-sex marriage. It is limited to an obligation to recognize such marriages, concluded in another Member State in accordance with the law of that State, solely for the purpose of exercising the rights conferred on such persons by Union law. (...) Thus, such an obligation of recognition, solely for the purpose of granting a derivative right of residence to a third-country national, does not affect the national identity or threaten the public policy of the Member State concerned.

Later, the Constitutional Court of Romania stated that "the relationship of a same-sex couple falls within the notion of "private life" and the notion of "family life", as does the relationship established in a heterosexual couple, which determines the protection of the fundamental right to private and family life, guaranteed by Article 7 of the Charter of Fundamental Rights of the European Union, Article 8 of the European Convention for the Protection of Human Rights and Fundamental Freedoms and Article 26 of the Romanian Constitution. Enjoying the right to private and family life, persons of the same sex who form stable couples have the right to express their personality within these relationships and to benefit, at the time and by the means provided for by law, from legal and judicial recognition of the corresponding rights and duties".

4 The Legal Definition of Family in Romanian Law

The family is a dynamic entity, in which members are bound to each other by a legal or factual bond, continuously shaping their relationships and building a group existence (Irinescu 2024a, b).

In Article 16 of the Universal Declaration of Human Rights[], the family is defined as "(...) the natural and fundamental group unit of society (...)". According to Articles 8 and 12 of the European Convention on Human Rights, the right to private and family life constitutes a fundamental human right. The right to found a family includes the right to procreate and the right to adopt. "(...) The constitutional protection of the family against any attempt to erode marriage, as a freely consented union between a man and a woman, for the purpose of founding a family and procreation, is thus an essential measure for the protection of the Romanian people, its identity and unity in the great European family", said the Constitutional Court, which was asked to rule on the constitutionality of Article 48 of the Constitution. By replacing the phrase "between spouses" with "between a man and a woman", only a clarification is made with regard to the exercise of the fundamental right to marriage, in the sense of expressly establishing that it is concluded between partners of different biological sex, which is, moreover, the very original meaning of the text.

By the same decision in 2016, the Romanian Constitutional Court gave a favorable opinion to one of the biggest initiatives of civil society, namely to define marriage in the Constitution as a union between a man and a woman. This step is part of a European and international effort to redefine the concept of family. In recent years, several European countries, such as Belgium, Denmark, Finland, France, Germany, Iceland, Ireland, Luxembourg, Malta, Norway, Portugal, Spain, Sweden, the Netherlands, the United Kingdom (except Northern Ireland) and the United Kingdom (except Northern Ireland) have legalized same-sex marriages. Civil unions and registered partnerships are also considered equivalent or comparable to marriage in some EU countries.

In Romanian legislation we identify several types of family as being regulated: natural family, extended family, substitute family, adoptive family, single-parent family. From the perspective of positive law (*lex lata*), Romanian legislation defines the family primarily through the institution of marriage and filiation, while also recognizing several derivative legal categories such as the extended family, the adoptive family or the single-parent family.

The legislator has chosen to define the notion of family in different fields, especially in the field of child protection and special assistance, as follows:

According to Art. 258 para. (1) of the Romanian Civil Code: "(1) The family is based on marriage freely entered into by the spouses (...). (4) For the purposes of this Code, 'spouses' means the man and woman united by marriage" (n.n.). According to Article 259 of the Civil Code: "(1) Marriage is a union freely entered into between a man and a woman, entered into in accordance with the law. (2) A man and a woman have the right to marry in order to found a family.

According to Article 4 of Law no. 272/2004 on the protection and promotion of the rights of the child, the family includes the parents and their children, the extended family is composed of the child's relatives up to the third degree included, with whom the child or his/her family has maintained personal relations and direct contacts, and substitute family means persons other than those belonging to the extended family, including relatives up to the third degree, with whom the child or his/her family has maintained personal relations and direct contacts, as well as the person, family or foster-parent who is responsible for the upbringing and care of the child, in accordance with the law. The family may also be a single-parent family when it consists of a single person (parent, guardian, person to whom the child has been entrusted or placed in foster care) and the dependent child/children up to the age of

18 or up to the age of 26 for those attending a form of education—day courses, organized according to the law, and who live and live together.

According to Article 3 lit. b) of Law no. 156/2023 on the organization of the activity of prevention of child separation from the family: by family means married parents or unmarried parents and the child/children raised/brought up and cared for/cared for by them, as well as the single parent and the child/children raised/brought up and cared for/cared for by him/her, living together.

According to Article 2 of Law no. 273/2004 on the adoption procedure, the family means the parents and their dependent children, the adoptive family means the husband and wife who have adopted or wish to adopt, under the conditions of the law.

According to Art. (1) letter b) of Law no. 196/2016 on the minimum inclusion income, a family is constituted by persons in one of the following situations: 1. husband and wife, married under the law, living together; 2. husband and wife with their unmarried, dependent children up to the age of 18, or up to the age of 26 for those attending a form of education—day courses, organized according to the law, with common domicile or residence registered in their identity documents and living together; 3. unmarried man and woman living and residing together, if this situation is confirmed by the on-site verification; 4. unmarried man and woman living and residing together, with their unmarried children and/or the children of each of them, up to the age of 18, or up to the age of 26 if they are in full-time education organized by law, living together, if this is confirmed at the on-the-spot verification; 5. parent(s) living with his/her/their dependent unmarried child(ren) over 18 years of age and certified as having a severe or severe handicap/disability.

According to Art. 17 of Law no. 114/1996 on housing, states that the family means husband, wife, children and parents of spouses, who live and manage the household together.

5 Contemporary Challenges to the Legal Regulation of Family Relations

Despite a traditionally and religiously rooted view of marriage, Western countries, influenced mainly by the transformations that the institution of marriage is undergoing, have adapted their legislation to protect the right to private and family life. As emphasized above, the modern concept of the family is much broader today than in recent decades. Sociologists try to define marriage in an inclusive way, covering all variations of legal unions between two persons. Sociologists are interested in the relationship between the institution of marriage and the institution of the family because, historically, it is marriages that create a family, and families are the most basic social unit on which society is built.

In the context of the EU-wide debate on same-sex and transgender marriage, many countries have chosen to amend their laws to legalize same-sex marriage. In this context, the European Court of Human Rights has played and continues to play a particularly important role. In Romania, the Constitutional Court ruled on the citizens' legislative initiative entitled "Law on the Revision of the Constitution of Romania" to amend Art. 48 para. (1) of the Constitution by Decision No 580/2016.

According to the constitutional text, "The family is based on marriage of free consent between spouses, on their equality and on the right and duty of parents to ensure the upbringing, education and training of their children". The Court found that the initiative to amend the Constitution to replace the term "spouses" with "man and woman" is well-founded, thus formalizing, as has been pointed out in the doctrine, "a doctrinal thesis expressed at the beginning of the 20th century and perpetuated until the adoption of the current Civil Code".

To summarize, it can be seen that social, cultural and legal changes have had and will have a significant impact on family relationships in general and marriage in particular. The most recent directions and changes concern:

1. same-sex marriage: the legalization of same-sex marriage has become one of the most striking legislative trends in recent decades. Many countries have passed laws allowing same-sex marriage, giving same-sex couples the same rights and responsibilities as heterosexual couples. Other countries have introduced civil partnerships or consensual unions as alternatives to marriage, offering some of the rights and benefits associated with marriage, but without the same legal obligations;
2. changes in the regulation of the minimum age for marriage: as can easily be seen, marriageable age was the first condition for marriage that has seen a significant rise throughout history. In many countries, there has been pressure to increase the minimum age at which a person can marry. This is part of a global effort to combat underage marriage and to protect children's rights, especially in countries and cultures where girls are forced to marry at young ages;
3. in the area of divorce, there is a legislative trend towards simplifying the divorce process, excluding fault and allowing couples to separate more quickly and without invoking serious grounds. In our opinion, one of the reasons for the decline in the rate of marriages being finalized is the lengthy divorce proceedings, which in the end prove to be emotionally traumatic for both spouses and children. Also, greater emphasis is being placed on the protection of children in divorce cases, with mandatory mediation in many countries and joint custody set as standard in many jurisdictions. The best interests of the child must be paramount, and parents must be the first to understand that they do not become a bone of contention in the event of marital breakdown;
4. sex and gender transition and access to marriage for transgender people bring further challenges to marriage. As a result of the case law of the European Court of Human Rights, laws have been adopted in some countries that allow for gender reassignment without the need for surgery, making it easier for transgender people to marry and have their relationships legally recognized. These changes reflect an ongoing effort to harmonize legislation with human rights and gender

equality, helping to broaden the concept of marriage to include transgender people without discrimination;

5. protection against domestic violence: paradoxically, in many Western countries, but also in our own country, domestic violence has become a large phenomenon recently. Many countries have tried to combat domestic violence by introducing in their legislation measures to protect victims during and after marriage, including protection orders and victim protection and rehabilitation programs for abusers. Others have begun to extend protection orders to civil partnerships or cohabiting partnerships;
6. artificial intelligence (AI) is beginning to have a growing impact on many aspects of modern life, including the institution of marriage. For example, dating apps and social networks have transformed the way people meet and form relationships. Compatibility algorithms as well as personal data analytics are being used to connect people who might be compatible, fundamentally changing the dynamics of relationships. During the COVID-19 pandemic, some states (USA, India, United Arab Emirates) allowed marriages to be performed online. In the future, these practices could become more common, especially for couples living in different geographical locations or in situations where face-to-face meetings are difficult.
7. blockchain and smart contract technology could enable the signing and management of digital prenuptial agreements, which could be automated and executed without third-party intervention. Technology can streamline the divorce process by providing digital solutions for managing documents and agreements. Online platforms already exist to facilitate amicable divorces without the need for physical presence in court. Sharing privacy details on online platforms can create situations that fall under criminal and/or civil laws.
8. autonomy of decision in family law matters is beginning to grow. Contractual freedom, based on the individual's free will to draw his or her own rules in the family universe, is leading to the emergence of new family models that are different from the traditional ones. Although the contractual nature of marriage has long been denied, recent doctrine has highlighted current trends towards the privatization of marriage, in the context of a weakening of the effects of the legal provisions determining the legal status of the spouses. Within marriage, the will of the parties is manifested at the time of its formation, during its duration (with regard to patrimonial and non-patrimonial elements) and at the time of divorce.
9. with artificial intelligence and other advanced technologies, the design process could become much more personalized and automated. For example, AI could help monitor fertility, select the healthiest embryos or provide personalized reproductive health recommendations. The technology for 3D printing of reproductive organs and tissues has advanced considerably and could in the future allow the creation of artificial reproductive organs or tissues. This could make it possible to create innovative solutions for people who lack the biological ability to conceive or carry a pregnancy (Irinescu 2019);

10. child conception is a process that has evolved at a fast pace, now reaching the point where legislators are being overtaken by assisted reproductive technologies, which continue to develop and offer increasingly efficient and personalized solutions. Same-sex couples can use surrogacy, ova or sperm donation and other assisted reproductive technologies to conceive children. Egg and sperm cryonics is already a technology used to preserve genetic material for conception at a later date, even post-mortem (Hageanu 2023);
11. technologies that edit the human genome will allow parents to choose and edit the genes of embryos before birth. This could prevent certain genetic diseases and allow parents to influence traits such as height, eye color or intelligence - a concept known as designer babies (Seppe et al. 2019). Although this type of technology currently presents many ethical and legal dilemmas, in the future it could become an important part of the conception process, especially for preventing hereditary diseases (Carbone 2020).
12. The development of artificial uteri would allow the complete growth of a fetus outside the human body and could eliminate the need for traditional pregnancy, offering solutions for women who cannot carry a pregnancy for medical reasons.
13. reproduction from somatic cells (without eggs or sperm) to create embryos, currently under research, could dramatically change the landscape of reproduction, offering solutions for infertile people or couples who cannot conceive traditionally. This could mean that in the future it may be possible to create eggs or sperm from ordinary body cells, allowing conception without the need for traditional eggs and sperm (Wardle 2006).

6 Changing Families

6.1 Marriage: The Foundation of the Family in Contemporary Society

Marriage is one of the oldest and most fundamental social institutions, playing an essential role in the organization of relationships between individuals and in the structure of society. Over time, it has evolved in response to cultural, religious, economic and legal factors, but it has remained a central foundation of the family and social continuity.

Marriage is a legally, socially and, in many cases, religiously recognized union between two persons for the purpose of family formation, mutual protection and emotional and material support. Although the forms of marriage differ from one culture to another, the main purpose remains the creation of a stable framework for relationships between the partners and the raising of children (Avram 2022). Its evolution reflects cultural and economic changes, but its fundamental functions - social, affective, reproductive and economic - continue to be essential for the stability and development of communities. In this context, adaptation of public rules and policies is necessary to respond to the needs of a changing society.

Marriage has a social and legal function, an affective and psychological function, a reproductive, an educational function and an economic one. Marriage confers social status and establishes rights and obligations between the spouses as well as towards their children. It provides a legal framework for regulating property relations and inheritance. Marriage also provides an emotionally supportive environment, contributing to the psychological stability and balance of the partners and promotes solidarity and long-term commitment. Marriage is the traditional framework for the birth and growth of children, providing generational stability and continuity and Ensures the transmission of values, norms and culture to new generations. Also, marriage creates economic units that foster cooperation and sharing of resources and contributes to the financial security of partners and children (Nicolescu 2023).

Every natural person has the right to marry. From a human rights perspective, the right to marry is based on fundamental principles of equality, freedom of choice and non-discrimination. From this perspective, the right to marry implies the free and equal access of all persons to marry and found a family, without discrimination based on sex, race, ethnicity, religion, nationality or sexual orientation. Over time, this right has been extended to include and protect various categories of people, especially those vulnerable to discrimination, such as women, minors and LGBTQ+ people. However, debates around legally recognizing all forms of marriage and ensuring equal access for all continue to be a challenge in some parts of the world.

The right to marry is an internationally recognized fundamental right, but it is not absolute. There are various legal limitations that are imposed by states for social, religious or cultural reasons or to protect certain vulnerable groups. These restrictions are usually justified to ensure public order, morality or to protect the rights of others. The main legal limitations on the right to marry include:

i. imposing a minimum age for marriage in order to protect minors from forced or early marriage and to ensure that those entering a marriage have the maturity to understand its implications;
ii. same-sex marriage. For example, same-sex marriage is prohibited in Romania;
iii. polygamy (marrying more than one person at the same time) is forbidden in most countries, especially those following Western legal traditions or adhering to secular principles;
iv. biological kinship (incest) between spouses is another criterion limiting the right to marry. Most legal systems prohibit marriages between people who are biologically related in the direct line (e.g. parents and children) or in the collateral line (brothers and sisters); marriages of convenience concluded in the context of migration, between a national and a foreigner in order to obtain the nationality of a State;
v. previous marital status: a person cannot enter into a new marriage if they are already married;

vi. mental capacity: if a person does not have the mental capacity to understand the nature and consequences of the marriage, then the marriage may be considered void. This is a measure designed to protect vulnerable people who cannot make informed decisions.
vii. marriages of convenience concluded in the context of migration, between a national and a foreigner in order to obtain the nationality of a State;
viii. respecting certain formalities: in some countries, the law distinguishes between religious marriages and civil marriages, allowing only civil marriages to be legally recognized. In others, both types of marriage are recognized, but civil marriage may be necessary to guarantee the couple's legal rights.

One sensitive issue is the right of transgender people to marry. With regard to transgenderism, the European Court of Human Rights has emphasized in numerous cases that "transsexuality continues to present complex scientific, legal, moral and social issues, on which there is no general common approach among the Contracting States". The judgments have concerned the recognition of the identity of transgender persons who have undergone a sex reassignment operation, the conditions of access to such an operation or the recognition of the identity of transgender persons who have not undergone sex reassignment treatment or who should not have undergone such treatment.

The Court has also ruled on other legal implications of transsexualism, such as the exercise of parental rights, medical costs under health insurance, pension rights, etc.. The Court ruled, in A. P. Garçon and Nicot v. France decision in 2017, that making recognition of the sexual identity of transgender persons conditional on their undergoing an operation or sterilization treatment which they did not wish to undergo made the full exercise of the right to respect for private life conditional on the waiver of the full exercise of the right to respect for physical integrity.

The Romanian law allows the change of sexual identity, with the legal effects, according to Law no. 119/1996 on civil status documents. In those circumstances, it recognizes as valid and qualifies as marriage the union between a person who has undergone a medical intervention for gender change and a person of the opposite sex to the sex resulting from that intervention. The factual situation must be converted into a legal situation for the legal effects to be produced. Following Romania's condemnation at the European Court of Human Rights in X and Y. v. Romania decision in 2021, the Romanian legislator is obliged to adopt a clear regulation on the procedure of sex change in our country. Until that time, the courts may hold that the requirement to perform sex reassignment surgery violates Article 8 of the Convention, while the requirement of a psychiatric examination to prove the reality of transsexualism syndrome or the requirement of a medical examination remains applicable.

However, another issue that requires urgent regulation is situations where the sex conversion operation is not actually carried out, but the person's gender is changed and the person wishes to enter into marriage. In the case of transgender persons for whom the sex change has not been carried out surgically, we consider that it is currently possible for them to marry persons of the same physical sex, circumventing national provisions prohibiting such marriages. Given that the legal conditions for the conclusion of marriage are to be verified exclusively on the basis of entries in civil status records, it is incumbent on the civil registrar to investigate very carefully whether there have been any changes in the sex of the future spouses.

There is also no established legal solution if a change of sex is obtained during the existing marriage. In our opinion, as we have already pointed out, the only existing solution at the present time would be for the marriage to be void (Jugastru 2015).

Recently, the Court of Justice of the European Union ruled in Mirin v. Romania decision that "the refusal of the competent authorities of a Member State to recognize and enter in the civil-status registers and in particular in the birth certificate of a national of that Member State a change of surname and gender identity legally acquired by him in another Member State, on the basis of national legislation which does not permit such recognition and registration, with the consequence that the person concerned is obliged to initiate a new procedure, of a judicial nature, for a change of gender identity in that first Member State, which disregards that change already lawfully obtained in that other Member State, is liable to restrict the exercise of the right to move and reside freely within the territory of the Member States".

The importance of this ruling extends beyond the individual situation of the claimant and emphasizes the broader problem faced by trans people, who do not enjoy the same legal gender recognition in all EU Member States, preventing them from freely travelling, living, working or studying in another country. The judgment in the Mirin case confirms the principle that rights legally acquired in one Member State must remain valid throughout the European Union. On the other hand, this will create problems with regard to the right to private and family life, as this solution places the applicant in a situation where he is treated as a man for matters concerning cross-border activities, but as a woman in matters of marriage and parentage in his own State, as these matters fall within the competence of the Member States.

6.2 *Legal Recognition of Same-Sex Families in European Human Rights Law*

Same-sex families are an increasingly visible and recognized social reality in many parts of the world. Over the last decades, legal and cultural changes have led to a wider acceptance of same-sex marriages and adoptions by same-sex couples. Although their legal recognition and social acceptance have progressed significantly, challenges remain in ensuring full equality. Legal developments, education and cultural changes will play a key role in integrating and protecting these families in the future.

Homosexual families include diverse structures, including:

- married couples or same-sex civil partnerships;
- families with children, either biological or adopted;
- families formed through medically assisted reproduction (IVF, surrogacy, sperm or egg donors).

These families function in a similar way to heterosexual families, with mutual emotional and economic support and the raising of children in a stable environment at their core.

In recent decades, many countries have legally recognized same-sex marriages, starting with the Netherlands in 2001. The European Court of Human Rights and the US Supreme Court have issued decisions that have influenced the recognition of marriage equality. In Europe, the evolution of civil partnership legislation and same-sex marriages reflects a significant change in societal attitudes towards the diversity of family relationships. Thus, even in a human rights context, civil partnerships reflect an important change in the way European states are adapting their legislation to meet the needs of a society.

In many countries, same-sex couples can adopt children, either together or through social-parent adoption and the access to assisted reproductive technologies has been extended to lesbian and gay couples. Studies show that there are no significant differences between children raised by homosexual parents and those raised by heterosexual parents in terms of emotional health, academic performance and social integration because the essential factor for the child's development is not the sexual orientation of the parents, but the stability and quality of the relationships in the family. However, in some states, same-sex families still face discrimination and lack of equal rights, and homophobia and religious conservatism remain barriers to full recognition of these families.

The European legislator emphasized in the preamble of Regulation (EU) 2016/1104 that "The way in which forms of union other than marriage are provided for in the legislation of the Member States differs from one State to another and a distinction should be made between couples whose union is institutionally recognized by registration of partnerships with a public authority and couples cohabiting de facto. Even if certain Member States regulate de facto unions, they should be dissociated from registered partnerships, whose official nature makes it possible to take account of their specific nature and to define the provisions applicable to them in a Union instrument (...)."

The judgments of the European Court of Human Rights and the European Court of Justice have also had and continue to have a major impact on the domestic legislation of Member States, which have a positive obligation to adopt a legal framework providing an adequate form of protection for same-sex couples.

In Schalk and Kopf v. Austria decision, concerning a same-sex "couple" consisting of two men, neither of whom had any children, who wished to marry or enter into a civil union, the European Court ruled that "it is artificial to continue to consider that a homosexual couple, unlike a heterosexual couple, would not enjoy.

a 'family life' within the meaning of Article 8" and that "consequently, the relationship between the applicants, a homosexual couple cohabiting de facto on a stable basis, falls within the notion of "family life", in the same way as a heterosexual couple in the same situation".

In Fedotova and Others v. Russia case, the European Court had to rule on the question of whether the Convention creates a positive obligation for States to provide same-sex couples with a form of legal recognition (marriage or equivalent).

The Court refused to accept Russia's arguments based on support for the traditional family and emphasized that there was no basis for considering that granting legal recognition and protection to same-sex couples in a stable and committed relationship could, in itself, prejudice traditionally constituted families or compromise their future or integrity. Moreover, the Court also rejected the argument that the majority of Russians disapprove of homosexuality in the context of cases concerning freedom of expression, assembly or association of sexual minorities. The Court concluded that the defendant State exceeded its margin of appreciation and failed to fulfill its positive obligation to guarantee the applicants' right to respect for their private and family life.

The judgments of the European Court, culminating in Fedotova, clearly indicate a repositioning of the Court in the direction of raising European requirements in this area and limiting the margin of discretion of States; the content of international public policy is reconfigured, and it cannot be used as a tool for refusing to recognize same-sex marriages concluded abroad (Popescu and Oprea 2023).

In Romania, there have been several legislative initiatives to regulate cohabitation, but none of them has been enshrined in law. In these drafts, civil partnership was defined as "the freely consented union between two persons of different or the same sex"; "the freely consented union between two natural persons for the purpose of organizing their common life, which shall be recognized and protected as family life"; "the association between two natural persons for the purpose of organizing and protecting their common life as family life"(Mihăilă 2019).

In this context, Buhuceanu and 21 same-sex couples complained to the European Court that they have no means to legally protect their relationship and that it is impossible for them to enter together into any kind of legally recognized union in Romania and that they are therefore discriminated against because of their sexual orientation and disadvantaged because of the lack of legal recognition of their relationship (Jugastru 2023a, b, c). The Court held that there was no provision in Romanian law recognizing same-sex marriage or any other form of partnership, and the Government had not demonstrated how the Constitutional Court, the national courts or any other Romanian authorities could, in the absence of any form of legal regulation, give judgments in favour of the applicants as long as none of those authorities could amend the law or create new rights for the applicants. The Court also rejected the Romanian State's arguments that the majority of Romanians do not approve of same-sex unions, concluding that the allegedly negative or even hostile attitude of part of the heterosexual majority could not be invoked against the applicants' interest in having their relationships adequately recognized and protected by law. There has therefore been a violation of Article 8 of the Convention The Court found, in particular, that Romania was under an obligation to ensure adequate recognition and protection of same-sex relationships, although it had a margin of discretion as to the form and protection afforded. The ECHR thus condemned Romania for the first time for failing to provide a legal framework for the recognition and protection of the right to respect for private and family life of same-sex couples. As in the Fedotova decision, the Court pointed out that the allegedly negative or even hostile attitude on the part of the majority of heterosexual couples could not be put against the interests of the applicants and categorically rejected the arguments of the defendant state (Jugastru 2023a, b, c).

However, recent developments indicate that registered partnerships for same-sex couples are ultimately more of a transitional phenomenon. As of April 2025, 38 countries allow same-sex marriage. With regard to children, despite the recognition as a couple, frequently same-sex partnerships were not—or at least at first not—treated equally to heterosexuals. Same-sex couples are increasingly being granted access to assisted reproduction. Nevertheless, they frequently encounter significant obstacles when seeking to establish legal parentage of the child conceived by means of assisted reproductive technology. Male couples have to resort to surrogacy, which may still more often than not be prohibited in their home country. The recognition of legal parentage after a surrogacy carried out abroad is then in many cases fraught with considerable difficulties (Dethloff et al. 2023).

6.3 Cohabiting Families and the Limits of Legal Recognition

The family is one of society's fundamental institutions, but its form has evolved significantly over time. Whereas in the past marriage was considered the only legitimate structure for starting a family, cohabitation has now become an increasingly common option. More and more couples are choosing to live together without formalizing their relationship in a marriage certificate, either for personal, economic or legal reasons. But this form of union presents many questions about legal recognition, property protection and parental rights.

Concubinage is defined as a stable cohabiting relationship between two people who are not married but who share responsibilities and sometimes material goods. It is common among both heterosexual and homosexual couples, especially in countries where same-sex marriage is not recognized. In many societies, cohabitation is accepted as a legitimate alternative to marriage, giving partners the freedom to organize their lives without the constraints of a formal marital contract. This flexibility is one of the main reasons why many people choose this form of cohabitation, seeing it as more suited to their lifestyle.

Cultural and economic changes in recent decades have contributed to the growing popularity of cohabitation. In an age where personal independence and autonomy are increasingly valued, the idea of a rigid legal commitment may seem outdated to some partners. Also, the reduced influence of religion on private life and a more relaxed perception of social norms have meant that marriage is no longer seen as a prerequisite for starting a family. In addition, there are also economic factors influencing this choice—avoiding the costs of eventual marriage or divorce, simpler asset management and flexibility in managing joint finances are important to many couples (Irinescu 2024a, b).

However, while cohabitation offers advantages in terms of freedom for the partners, it also comes with a number of challenges, particularly in terms of legal recognition and legal protection. In many countries, cohabitation does not confer the same rights as marriage, which can lead to difficulties in the event of separation or in situations such as inheritance or child custody. For example, if one partner dies without a clear will, the other partner may have difficulty in claiming rights to joint property. Also, in the case of separation, the division of property can be complicated, especially if there is no cohabitation agreement setting out the rights of each partner (Bénabent 2022).

Another major problem linked to cohabitation is that of parental rights. In many legal systems, only the biological parent automatically has rights over the child, which can create difficulties if the relationship ends. In the absence of a marriage or explicit legal recognition, the partner who is not the biological parent may face obstacles in terms of custody or even the right to make important decisions for the child. This presents issues of protection of the best interests of the child, especially in situations where the cohabitation has been of long duration and the child has been raised by both partners (Fenouillet 2022).

Cohabitation is also not viewed in the same way in all societies. In some cultures it is fully accepted, while in others it continues to be viewed with skepticism or even stigmatized. This cultural variation also influences the legal recognition of cohabitation. In some countries cohabiting unmarried partners may enjoy rights similar to those of married couples, while in others they have no legal status at all, being considered merely cohabitants with no special rights or obligations. These differences create inequalities in the protection afforded to partners and their children, which presents the question of the need for more uniform regulation at international level.

In conclusion, cohabiting families are an increasingly common reality in today's society and are preferred by many couples because of the flexibility they offer. However, the lack of adequate legal protection can pose serious problems in the event of separation or death of one of the partners. Although cohabitation is increasingly accepted, legislation needs to be adapted to provide a clear and fair framework for these families so that partners and their children have adequate rights and protection. From a *lege ferenda* perspective, Romanian legislation could consider introducing a clearer legal framework for cohabiting couples.

References

Avram M (2022) Civil law. Family, 3rd edn. Hamangiu Publishing House, Bucharest

Beck U (1995) Risk society: towards a new modernity. Sage Publication, London

Bénabent A (2022) Droit de la famille, 6th edn. LGDJ, Paris

Carbone J (2020) CRISPR and the future of fertility innovation. SMU Sci Technol Law Rev 23(1):31–64

Dethloff N, Kaesling K, Leven F (2023) From marriage to family. In: Nina D, Kaesling K (eds) Between sexuality, gender and reproduction. On the pluralisation of family forms. Intersentia, Cambridge, pp 1–22

Fenouillet D (2022) Droit de la famille, 5th edn. Dalloz, Paris

Hageanu C (2023) Family law, 3rd edn. Hamangiu Publishing House, Bucharest

Irinescu L (2019) The child, a present or a rights? Family Law Magazine 1-2:208–218

Irinescu L (2024a) Civil partnership—a future institution in modern Romanian law? Family Law Magazine 2:149–174
Irinescu L (2024b) Family law. Hamangiu Publishing House, Bucharest
Jugastru C (2015) Marriage contracting in private international law, developments and trends. Romanian Rev Private Law 5:62–111
Jugastru C (2023a) Buhuceanu and others against Romania. Lines of consolidation and dilemmas. Family Law Magazine 2:337–354
Jugastru C (2023b) The Law Applicable to Civil Partnership in the Romanian Law. De Lege Ferenda Proposals (I), Dreptul, 8:58–80
Jugastru C (2023c) The Law Applicable to Civil Partnership in the Romanian Law. De Lege Ferenda Proposals (II), Dreptul, 9:9–34
Mihăilă C (2019) Registered partnership. Between reality and legislative and social desiderate. Family Law Magazine 1-2:286–304
NeJaime D (2014) Before marriage: the unexplored history of nonmarital recognition and its relationship to marriage. Calif Law Rev 102(1):87–172
Nicolescu C (2023) Family law, 2rd edn. Solomon Publishing House, Bucharest
Popescu DA, Oprea EA (2023) Privat international law. Hamangiu Publishing House, Bucharest
Seppe S, Guido P, Wybo D, De De Wert G, Mertes H (2019) In vitro gametogenesis and the creation of 'designer babies'. Camb Q Healthc Ethics 28(3):499–508
Turliuc M (2004) Couple and family psychology. Performantica Publishing House, Iasi
Wardle LD (2006) Global perspective on procreation and parentage by assisted reproduction. Capital Univ Law Rev 35(2):413–478

Interpretive and Jurisprudential Values of Religious Freedom in Comparative Vision. Confluences Between Criminal Law and Fundamental Rules

Andra Iftimiei

Abstract Religious freedom is perhaps one of the most sensitive subjects. Situated on the border between feeling and expressing, the confluence of this freedom with the norms of criminal law through the mirror of the fundamental law leads to interpretative valences that we propose to analyse. The chapter proposes an incursion into the triple dimension of religious freedom, through the interpretation of the European Court of Human Rights, the guarantees in fundamental laws, but also through the means of protection in criminal law. The binder of the three dimensions is given by the comparative method, namely the analysis of legislation and jurisprudential elements from several member states of the European Union.

1 Introduction

Methodological clarification: In order to improve analytical clarity, the chapter distinguishes between descriptive analysis (presentation of legal norms, case law and comparative frameworks) and normative analysis (evaluation of the principles and limits governing religious freedom).

One of the most difficult questions to ask, in general, regardless of the research topic, is to define the concept to be analyzed: what is it? What is religious freedom? The multiple normative and jurisprudential frameworks to which we can refer are designed to give us an overview: international documents protecting fundamental rights and freedoms, fundamental laws, criminal and even non-criminal laws.

The analysis we propose is both pluri- and interdisciplinary. The main criterion for the selection of the decisions analyzed is chronological. We propose an analysis

A. Iftimiei (✉)
Faculty of Law, 'Alexandru Ioan Cuza' University of Iaşi, Iaşi, Romania
e-mail: andra.iftimiei@uaic.ro

I. Maria Costea (ed.), *Legal Interpretation in Motion*, Ius Gentium: Comparative Perspectives on Law and Justice 144,
https://doi.org/10.1007/978-3-032-32948-6_10

of recent case law in order to reflect the way in which the various courts understand religious freedom in the light of contemporary reality. Does freedom of religion today have the same valence as in other historical periods? Are we today at a crossroads? Are we, as jurists, (re)interpreting the limits of religious freedom? Is freedom of religion a vector of unification and harmonization, including at the normative and jurisprudential levels?

The intersection of law and religious freedom is a very consistent effort of analysis and interpretation, as two different "worlds" are mirrored: a world based on faith, on intrinsic values and a world based on prevention and repression; a world built on love and a world that is confined within well-defined rules.

We intend that the research hypotheses that we formulate are based on research hypotheses already confirmed/confirmed, so that a possible interpretative evolution of the notion of religious freedom can be faithfully highlighted.

The research hypotheses we propose are the following:

Can state authorities take measures to restrict religious freedom, both internally and externally?

Religious freedom and the freedom to manifest religious freedom must be seen in different legal structures and dimensions, especially at the level of terminological interpretation.

The research methods used are subsumed under specific legal sciences, namely: comparative method and case-law analysis.

The comparative method was chosen on the grounds that an overview of the interpretative value of freedom of religion can be obtained by referring to the normative frameworks in force in the states chosen as representatives. In the light of the criterion of representativeness of the legal orders chosen for the comparative normative analysis, we emphasize that the Member States of the European Union enjoy similar legal orders, thus fulfilling one of the main purposes of the comparative method, namely the choice of states with similar normative provisions.

In addition to the comparative method, the method of jurisprudential analysis is chosen and used, which is necessary in order to highlight the way in which the national courts have understood to interpret the modes of manifestation of religious freedom in relation to positive law, as it is of interest whether the national courts' optics has evolved or regressed in relation to the case law of the European Court of Human Rights.

Beyond all this, we believe that the simple intersection of the two research methods chosen, within the same chapter, represents a successful technique of evolutionary interpretation of such a profound concept with vast implications, including in guaranteeing the principles on which a rule of law is built, regardless of the legal order analyzed.

Preliminary Issues

"For the modern world, religion, as a form of life, is confused with Christianity", and "desacralization characterizes the total experience of the non-religious man in modern societies".

Mircea Eliade in the work Sacred and Profane (Eliade 1992) introduces us to the principles necessary to understand the externalized behavior of homo religious, a work that is defining for defining the experiences of the religious man in comparison with the experience of the man without religious feelings.

The presence of Mircea Eliade's work in our research is no coincidence; it is necessary, regardless of the era in which we live or the era to which we refer, to be aware of the existence of "two ways of being in the world": the sacred and the profane seen in the light of two existential situations assumed by man throughout history.

From the sacred to the profane and from the profane to the sacred there has always been a fine line, history showing us that man can, at any time, fall into the mistakes of the past. This chapter does not propose a descriptive analysis of religious manifestations and transformations throughout history, but rather highlights the specific features of religious experiences.

Our research brings to the fore three very powerful concepts: religion, freedom and law. Their analysis in an interdisciplinary key leads to a distinct, new and original interpretative picture. All three concepts converge towards a guiding interpretation towards the idea of peace: external and internal. It is important to see religion as one; if the philosopher Kant marveled at the expression "diversity of religions" (Kant 2008), he did so only from the point of view of a desirable heterogeneity for understanding the guiding precepts of religious manifestations. "There are different books of religion (Quran, Vedas etc.), but only one religion, valid for all men and in all times. They can be nothing but vehicles of religion" (Kant 2008).

The notions of right and freedom are distinct, and it is wrong to equate the two. The distinction is definitely one of nuance: while freedom is conceived of as "a power to act or not to act" (Bîrsan 2005, p. 8), the notion of human rights must be seen as having a broader meaning, anchored in the concept of natural law, according to which man has a set of rights inherent in his very nature (Bîrsan 2005, p. 8).

Therefore, freedom is circumscribed within a space of self-determination of the individual's activity.

According to the legal norms in force in Romania, "freedom of religion includes the right of every person to have or to adopt a religion, to manifest it individually or collectively, in public or in private, through practices and rituals specific to the religion, including religious education, as well as the freedom to maintain or change their religious faith." (Law no. 489/2006 on religious freedom and the general regime of cults).

In the light of all these preliminary clarifications, we emphasize the fact that religious freedom must always be seen as a concept with a double valence: the internal aspect, expression of the internal forum, and the external aspect, expression of the external exercise of internal beliefs.

2 Interpretation of the Concept of Religious Freedom in the Case Law of the European Court of Human Rights

Descriptive section: The following analysis presents the relevant jurisprudence of the European Court of Human Rights concerning religious freedom. The aim is to describe how the Court interprets Article 9 of the Convention in concrete cases.

Human rights have become a binding anchor in any modern discourse. The gradual enshrinement of human rights in European and international normative provisions has led to the construction of a model, and in the contemporary era internationalization, but above all the Europeanization of human rights has rapidly become a reality.

The European Court of Human Rights has consistently paid particular attention to freedom of religion; the European court has not attempted a definition of religion, but has always referred to the notion in its "non-restrictive sense" (Renucci 2012, p. 234). The freedom to manifest religious beliefs and convictions is in fact the subject of multiple forms of protection. The purpose of the recent case analysis is to highlight recent interpretations, i.e. recent forms of manifestation of religious freedom.

The main issues referred to the European Court of Human Rights for rulings concerned issues such as[1]: ritual slaughter of animals (Cha'are Shalom Ve Tsedek v. France case of June 27, 2000); missionary activities (Case Ossewaarde v. Russia of March 7, 2023); change of religion and religious beliefs (Neagu v. Romania, see below); collection of personal information in the context of door-to-door preaching (Jehovah's Witnesses v. Finland case of May 9, 2023); challenging constitutional provisions banning the construction of minarets (Ouardiri v. Switzerland case of June 28, 2011); dissemination of hostile and pejorative information about certain religious movements (Case Tonchev and Others v. Bulgaria of December 13, 2022); forced dissolution of religious organizations and prosecution of members of such organizations (Case Taganrog LRO and Others v. Russia of June 07, 2022); education of children and religious convictions of parents (Case Papageorgiu and Others v. Greece of October 31, 2019); religious holidays (Case Francesco Sessa v. Italy of April 3, 2012); freedom of worship in the community (Case of Abdullah Yalçın (no. 2) v. Turkey of June 14, 2022); places of worship (Case Pantelidu v. Greece of September 17, 2019); obligation to take the religious oath (Case Shortall and others v. Ireland of October 19, 2021); obligation to disclose religious beliefs (Case Dimitras and Others v. Greece of June 3, 2013); proselytism (Case Larissis and Others v. Greece of February 24, 1998); recognition, organization and management of schools and religious communities (Case of Ilyin and Others v. Ukraine of November 17, 2022); refusal to provide a religious public service (Case Izzettin

[1] For details see https://www.echr.coe.int/documents/d/echr/fs_freedom_religion_fra.

Dogan and Others v. Turkey of April 26, 2016); religious rites (Korostelev v. Russia case of May 12, 2020); religious insignia and vestments[2]; conscientious objectors.[3]

As protected by Article 9 of the Convention, freedom of thought, conscience and religion is one of the cornerstones of a "democratic society" within the meaning of the Convention. This freedom, in its religious dimension, is one of the essential elements of the identity of believers and their outlook on life, but it is also a precious asset for atheists, agnostics, skeptics and the indifferent. At stake is pluralism—achieved at great cost over the centuries—which cannot be dissociated from such a society. This freedom implies, among other things, the freedom to join or not to join a religion and the freedom to practice or not to practice it (European Court of Human Rights, Neagu v. Romania, available at https://ier.gov.ro/wp-content/uploads/2022/06/Neagu-impotriva-Romaniei.pdf). Although freedom of religion is primarily an internal matter, it also implies the freedom to manifest one's religion individually and privately or collectively, in public and in the circle of those who share the faith in question (European Court of Human Rights, Neagu v. Romania, available at https://ier.gov.ro/wp-content/uploads/2022/06/Neagu-impotriva-Romaniei.pdf).

In order to highlight how the guarantee of freedom of religion raises issues of interpretation, including at the level of the review of conventionality, we have identified three decisions of the European Court of Human Rights, which help to define the limits of this freedom.

In Neagu v. Romania (European Court of Human Rights, case no. 21969/15), the applicant challenged the prison authorities' refusal to provide him with meals in accordance with their religious precepts following a change of religion.[4] The Court held that the national authorities had unbalanced the interests between the prison, the other prisoners and the prisoners concerned. The Court held that the applicant's request in the Neagu case for a religious diet would not have disrupted the functioning of the prison and would not have affected the meals of the other prisoners. The Court found a breach of the national authorities' positive obligations under Article 9 of the Convention.

In fact, on April 22, 2009, the applicant was remanded in custody. At that time, he declared himself an Orthodox Christian. He was subsequently sentenced to a term of imprisonment and from 2009 until 2017 he was detained in various penitentiaries in Romania. He explained to the Court that, during the first three years of his imprisonment, he had established links with Muslim prisoners and that, after having discussed at length with them, he decided to convert to Islam. On September 27, 2012, while he was deprived of his liberty in Galati Penitentiary, he informed the management of the penitentiary that he had converted and asked to have meals without pork, which was refused. Subsequently, the complainant was transferred to Brăila Penitentiary, where he requested several times to receive meals without pork.

[2] For details see https://www.echr.coe.int/documents/d/echr/FS_Religious_Symbols_ENG.

[3] For details see https://www.echr.coe.int/documents/d/echr/FS_Conscientious_objection_ENG.

[4] In the same sense, see Saran v. Romania, case no. 65993/16.

All his requests were rejected on the grounds that he had not presented a certificate issued by the representatives of the cult in question attesting to his conversion. He then lodged a complaint with the judge supervising deprivation of liberty, who worked in this institution. The judge rejected the complaint on the ground that the applicant had declared himself to be an Orthodox Christian when he entered the place of detention and subsequently did not produce any document attesting to his conversion.

Another case selected for analysis in this study is Hamidović v. Bosnia and Herzegovina (European Court of Human Rights, case 57,792/15).

In fact, the complainant, who was a member of a local militant group for the Wahhabi/Salafi branch of Islam, had been called to testify at the criminal trial of other members of the group accused of committing terrorist offenses. He duly appeared at the trial as summoned but refused to remove his skullcap when asked to testify, claiming that it was his religious obligation to wear it at all times. After being given time for reflection and warned of the consequences of continued disobedience, he was found guilty of contemptuous attitude to the court and ordered to pay a fine, which was later converted to thirty days' deprivation of liberty when he refused payment.

The punishment imposed on the plaintiff for wearing a headscarf in the courtroom constituted a restriction on the manifestation of his religion. The restriction was based on the inherent power of the judge in the case to regulate the conduct of proceedings in the State Court, noting that the applicant had been informed of the applicable rule and the consequences of non-compliance. The restriction also pursued a legitimate aim, as the Court had previously held that secularism was a belief protected by Article 9 of the Convention and that a link could be established between the aim of maintaining secular and democratic values and the legitimate aim of "protecting the rights and freedoms of others".

The applicant's case concerned a witness in a criminal trial and constituted a completely different matter, which had to be distinguished from cases concerning the wearing of religious symbols and clothing in the workplace, particularly by public officials exercising official authority. Since Article 9 did not protect every act motivated or inspired by a religion or belief and did not always guarantee the right to behave in public in a manner dictated by one's religion or belief, and since there could be cases where it was justified to order the removal of a religious symbol in the case of a witness, the authorities were required not to neglect the special characteristics of different religions. The freedom to manifest your religion was a fundamental right: not only because a healthy democratic society must tolerate and support pluralism and diversity, but also because of the importance for a person who has made religion a central tenet of his or her life to be able to communicate that belief to others.

The Court found no reason to doubt that the plaintiff's action was inspired by his sincerely held religious conviction that the permanent wearing of the scapula was a religious obligation, with no secret agenda to persiflage the trial, incite others to reject secular and democratic values or cause a disturbance. Unlike other members of his religious group, the complainant appeared before the court after being summoned and rose from his seat when spoken to, thus complying with the laws and courts of the country. There was no indication that he was unwilling to testify or that he displayed a disrespectful attitude. In these circumstances, punishing him for contempt of court on the sole ground of his refusal to remove his hood was not necessary in a democratic society and the national authorities exceeded their wide margin of discretion.

Finally, the third selected case is Pindo Mulla v. Spain (European Court of Human Rights, Case No. 15541/20), which concerns blood transfusions administered to an applicant, a Jehovah's Witness, during emergency surgery. The Court found that the judicial authorization granted for these transfusions was the result of a decision-making process which omitted essential information about the patient's wishes concerning her religious beliefs, which were duly recorded on several occasions. The Court concluded that there had been a violation of Article 8 of the Convention, interpreted in the light of Article 9, because the medical personnel had not sufficiently respected the applicant's autonomy, which she wished to exercise in order to respect an essential tenet of her religion.

The above-mentioned decision was controversial even within the panel of the European Court of Human Rights, so that throughout the reasoning we find concurring opinions (all of them in the sense of the existence of a violation of Article 9 in relation to Article 8 of the Convention), but also a separate opinion.

The Court recognized in the judgment that the actions taken by the physicians were motivated by an overriding concern to provide effective treatment for a patient under their care in accordance with the most fundamental standard of the medical profession, namely the preservation of life and the protection of health. The Court did not question their assessments as to the seriousness of the applicant's condition at the time, the urgency of administering the necessary treatment and the medical options available in the circumstances. It should be added that, in view of the urgency of the risk to the applicant's life, the judge did not have time to examine the case in more detail.

In making these observations, we do not intend to call into question the conclusion that the decision-making process as a whole was flawed; however, in the circumstances, the blood transfusions cannot be equated with 'rape', contrary to the applicant's contention. There was no evidence of bad faith on the part of the medical staff or the duty judge. Given that no appeal was used to establish the relevant facts at national level, any other conclusion would be pure speculation. It is important to note that the harm alleged in this case, namely the administration of blood transfusions, was a direct consequence of the applicant's underlying pathology.

Furthermore, we are obliged to find that the applicant's life was saved that day. She survived thanks to a medical intervention which, according to the medical assessment made by the doctors, was necessary to save her life—which is a fundamental value protected by the positive obligations flowing from Article 2 of the Convention, as well as an absolute precondition for the exercise of any other right or freedom enshrined in the Convention, including freedom of religion. Although the applicant stated that she would have confirmed her refusal if the question had been put to her at the time of the events, when asked at the public hearing whether she would have been prepared to die without a blood transfusion, her representative replied that she wanted and still wanted to live. Furthermore, in her pre-hearing submissions, the applicant argued that her freedom to live in accordance with her religious beliefs was at stake (paragraph 49). It is difficult to see how she could have remained alive had she not been given blood transfusions. While we are aware of the dilemma faced by the applicant, we do not consider that it resulted from any of the shortcomings in the decision-making process which led the Court to find a violation.

In conclusion, we note that at the level of treaty scrutiny, more attention is being paid to how religious freedom interferes with other fundamental rights and freedoms. Although in a separate opinion, the question of prioritization of the guarantees established by the European Convention on Human Rights has been raised. Which comes first: the right to life, guaranteed in Article 2, or freedom of religion, guaranteed in Article 9?

3 Normative Values of the Notion of Religious Freedom: Fundamental Value. Comparative View

Descriptive–comparative section: This part describes constitutional guarantees of religious freedom in selected European states. The objective is to outline the different normative frameworks before evaluating their implications.

Freedom of religion—freedom of conscience—freedom of thought; these are the three main components that each constituent legislator had in mind when they laid down constitutional guarantees in the texts of the fundamental laws. The terminological triad is of real interest from an interpretative perspective, since each of these expressions is used to guarantee a different facet of religious freedom.

The purpose of the comparative analysis that follows is to crystallize the three concepts seen in the interpretative light of the fundamental rules in countries such as France, Romania, Germany, Switzerland and Italy.

3.1 *France*[5]

Originally conceived as a fundamental principle recognized by the laws of the Republic (Decision No. 77–87 DC of 23 November 1977), freedom of conscience is now linked to Article 10 of the Declaration of the Rights of Man and of the Citizen of 1789.[6] Moreover, this substitution of the constitutional basis of freedom of conscience has no impact on the constitutional value and scope of this freedom.

[5] https://www.conseil-constitutionnel.fr/la-constitution/la-liberte-de-conscience.

[6] See French Constitutional Council decisions No 2013–353 QPC of October 18, 2013 and 2017–695 QPC of March 29, 2018.

In constitutional jurisprudence, freedom of conscience has two dimensions:

- religious dimension when it is associated with the principle of secularism, which requires in particular that the Republic guarantees the free exercise of religious denominations (Decision No. 2012–297 QPC of February 21, 2013). For example, in its Decision No. 2017–695 QPC of March 29, 2018, the Council had the opportunity to examine the constitutionality of the provision of Law No. 2017–1510 of October 30, 2017 on strengthening internal security and the fight against terrorism which allows the prefect, in order to prevent the commission of acts of terrorism, to temporarily close places of worship under certain conditions. In this case, the Council considered that the legislator ensured a reconciliation that was not manifestly unbalanced between, on the one hand, the constitutional objective of preventing violations of public order and, on the other hand, freedom of conscience and the free exercise of religious beliefs.
- a "secular" dimension. For example, the Constitutional Council has ruled that, by providing that the head of a public health unit retains the right not to carry out a voluntary termination of pregnancy himself, the legislator has protected "his freedom, which is a matter of his personal conscience" (Decision no. 2001–446 DC of June 27, 2001). On the other hand, by not allowing civil registrars to evade the duties entrusted to them by law for the celebration of marriages of same-sex couples, the legislature did not violate the freedom of conscience (decision no. 2013–353 QPC cited above). This is because "the act performed is a legal act which does not involve the conscience of its author in conditions comparable to the diagnostic or therapeutic act of a doctor".

3.2 *Romania*

Article 29 para. (1) of the Constitution provides that "freedom of thought and opinion and freedom of religious beliefs may not be restricted in any form. No one shall be compelled to adopt an opinion or to adhere to a religious belief contrary to his convictions". The content of the constitutional text reveals the absolute nature of the rights it enshrines, prohibiting any form of limitation of those rights.

The case law of the Constitutional Court of Romania has highlighted a double interpretative dimension of religious freedom, namely an internal and an external dimension.[7]

The internal dimension of the beliefs, convictions or opinions that a human being may hold is reflected in the prohibition of any form or method "by which a person may be subjected to coercion in order to alter his or her conception of the world

[7] Decision of the Constitutional Court of Romania no. 49 of February 15, 2022 on the exception of unconstitutionality of the provisions of Art. 5 para. (3) lit. a), Article 45 and Article 65 lit. j), k) and l) of Law no. 55/2020 on some measures to prevent and combat the effects of the COVID-19 pandemic, published in the Official Gazette no. 755 of July 27, 2022.

around him or to prevent him or her from thinking and forming his or her own opinions freely".[8]

The external dimension of freedom of conscience, going beyond the internal sphere of a person's psyche, inevitably involves acts and deeds that may have an impact on the surrounding world, including on the rights and freedoms of other persons. Therefore, the constitutional provisions of Article 57, according to which "Romanian citizens, foreign citizens and stateless persons must exercise their constitutional rights and freedoms in good faith, without infringing the rights and freedoms of others", become relevant in his case.[9]

Thus, "while these rights are absolute in their internal, intimate aspect, their relative nature is recognized from the perspective of their external component" (Decision of the Constitutional Court of Romania no. 845 of June 3, 2009, published in the Official Journal of Romania no. 524 of July 10, 2009). The consequence of this is that the exercise of freedom of conscience, in its external dimension, is compatible with restrictions under the conditions laid down in Article 53 of the Constitution.

3.3 *Switzerland*[10]

The guarantee of freedom of conscience and belief in the Swiss Federal Constitution (Article 15) and in international agreements is closely linked to the prohibition of discrimination on grounds of religious, philosophical or political beliefs (Article 8(2) of the Federal Constitution).[11]

Religious freedom encompasses not only the traditional forms of faith of Western religious communities, but all religions.

For Muslim religious communities, freedom of religion is constitutionally limited by the ban on the construction of minarets (Article 72(3) of the Federal Constitution[12]). The ban on the construction of minarets was voted on following the popular initiative to revise the Constitution in 2008. The vote was close: out of 53.76% voters present at the vote, 57.5% voted in favor and 42.5% voted against.[13]

The corollary of the right of every individual and group to exercise their religion is the obligation of public authorities to respect religious neutrality and to refrain from preventing the exercise of religious beliefs without compelling justification.

---

[8] *Idem.*

[9] *Idem.*

[10] For details see https://www.isdh.ch/fr/infoportal/les-droits-humains-en-un-coup-doeil/liberte-de-religion.

[11] For more details, see https://www.fedlex.admin.ch/eli/cc/1999/404/fr#fn-d7e2525.

[12] Article 72 of the Federal Constitution of Switzerland, with the marginal title *Church and State*, states in para. (3): "The construction of minarets is prohibited" (https://www.fedlex.admin.ch/eli/cc/1999/404/fr#fn-d7e2525).

[13] Statistical information available and retrieved from https://www.bk.admin.ch/ch/f/pore/va/20091129/index.html.

As summarized by the Federal Supreme Court in a judgment, "... the secular character of the State can be summed up as an obligation of neutrality which requires it to refrain, in its public acts, from any denominational or religious considerations of such a nature as to compromise the freedom of citizens in a pluralist society. In so doing, it seeks to preserve the religious freedom of citizens and to maintain religious peace in a spirit of tolerance".[14] Religious freedom does not stop at the subjective right to exercise one's religion and the State's obligation of neutrality. Article 8 of the FC also prohibits any discrimination based on origin or religious, philosophical or political beliefs.

However, there is a growing desire to restrict certain religious manifestations in the public space that are perceived as extreme or dangerous to the coexistence or neutrality of the state. These include the constitutional ban on minarets and the ban on hiding one's face, approved by the Swiss people in 2009 and 2021 respectively.[15]

At the cantonal level, the canton of Geneva is the canton that most restricts the display of religious symbols and religious practices in the public space. The Law on Secularism, approved by the people of Geneva in 2019, reaffirms the neutrality of the state and non-discrimination on religious grounds and prohibits elected representatives and state employees who are in contact with the public from wearing religious symbols, including the headscarf.[16]

For the Federal Court, a belief must "have some essential or metaphysical meaning and be related to an overall worldview. It must therefore lead the believer to approach fundamental issues from a perspective influenced by his or her religious convictions. Otherwise, the constitutional guarantee would amount to a general freedom of thought and action without precise limits".[17]

The Federal Court has ruled that the free choice of a vegetarian diet is an ethical and philosophical concept that is only remotely related to religion. Consequently, the right to such a diet is protected by personal freedom and not by religious freedom.[18]

3.4 Germany

The limits of freedom of belief can only be determined by the Constitution, as the Federal Constitutional Court of Germany ruled in 1971.[19]

Article 4 paragraph 1 of the German Basic Law declares freedom of faith, conscience and confession inviolable.

---

[14] For details see https://swissjews.ch/fr/services/savoir/fiches/la-liberte-religieuse-en-suisse/.

[15] *Idem.*

[16] *Idem.*

[17] Bellanger (2002), pp. 2–22.

[18] *Idem.*

[19] The case "Healing through prayer", BVerfGE 32, 98 in the work N.A. (2013), pp. 198–200.

If a conflict arises between freedom of conscience and the criminal protection of the right to life, as in the case of the conviction of a person for the crime of leaving a person without help when his wife opposed a blood transfusion, preferring prayer to ask God for help,[20] the criminal sanction is—regardless of its severity—not an appropriate sanction in any respect.

Another highly publicized and hotly debated issue in Germany concerning religious freedom is the Kruzifix case.[21] The installation of a cross in the classrooms of a compulsory state school, which is not a denominational school, violates Article 4(1) of the German Basic Law.

The installation of a cross is not justified by the positive religious freedom of Christian parents and pupils. The conflict that arises here cannot be resolved according to the majority principle, since it is precisely the fundamental right of freedom of religion that is aimed above all at protecting minorities.[22] To consider the cross as a mere insignia would lead to the idea of secularizing its profound meaning, embodying the salvation of man through the sacrifice of Christ's life, but also the victory over death, being both a symbol of suffering and victory.

The German state is strongly bound by the obligation of religious neutrality; this neutrality, however, is not to be understood as a distancing attitude in the sense of a very strict separation between state and church, but as an open attitude that encourages freedom of faith equally for all denominations.

Article 4 of the Basic Law protects both negative and positive forms of manifestation of freedom of belief in equal measure. For example, the freedom to manifest religious convictions by wearing an Islamic headscarf in school collides with the negative freedom of belief of pupils.[23]

3.5 Italy[24]

The 1948 republican constitution, on the one hand, confirms the Lateran treaties signed by the state with the Catholic Church, naming them explicitly in Article 7; on the other hand, it creates the basis for a system of religious freedom more compatible with the principles of liberty and equality.

At the same time, the new Constitution places particular emphasis on the "institutional" profiles of religious freedoms. Articles 7 and 8, devoted to the relations between the state and religious denominations (confessioni religiose), are included among the fundamental principles, strictly linked to the "material constitution" of

[20] For details, see case above.

[21] Case "The Crucifix", BVerfGE 93, 1 in the work N.A. (2013), pp. 206–213.

[22] *Idem.*

[23] The "Kopftuch" case, BVerfGE 108, 282 in the book N.A. (2013), pp. 223–228.

[24] A. Ferrari, S. Ferrari, "Religion and the Secular State: The Italian Case," available at https://original.religlaw.org/content/blurb/files/Italy.pdf.

the state and therefore commonly considered as unchangeable. On the contrary, Articles 19 and 20 deal with religious freedom as an individual right (not necessarily linked to its institutional). They are placed in the civil relations part of the Constitution.

In Italy, freedom of religion is enshrined as a fundamental value with a double dimension: individual and institutional.

Article 19 guarantees freedom of religion for "everyone", regardless of nationality, guaranteeing not only freedom of religion (e.g. public propaganda, the building of places of worship and religious cemeteries, and the ritual slaughter of animals), but also freedom from religion, with the only limit on rites contrary to public morality, identified in the sexual decency protected by the penal code. Thus, Article Nineteen is considered to protect all positions on matters of conscience, including atheist and agnostic ones, and is also invoked to underpin conscientious objection laws (and claims).

As far as the institutional side of religious freedom is concerned, a strict application of the principle of bilateralism gives rise to two main problems. First, the need for representative institutions of religious denominations at the national level is a requirement that has proved problematic for some religions, such as Islam, for example. Secondly, the excessive amount of discretion that the public authorities have in deciding whether to accept or reject a denomination's proposal to enter into negotiations for an agreement.

If, as far as the Roman Catholic religion is concerned, numerous documents have been signed and approved by the Parliament (for example: Catholic religious education in state schools[25]), as far as religious pluralism of non-Catholic origin is concerned, the Parliament has approved agreements with the Lutheran Church, the Seventh Day Adventist Christian Churches, all of them for example. At the same time, there are religious denominations with which the Italian State has signed agreements, but which have not been approved by Parliament (Ferrari and Ferrari n.d.) (also by way of example: Jehovah's Witnesses or the Italian Buddhist Union).

4 Normative Values of Religious Freedom from a Penal Perspective. Offenses Against Religious Freedom in Comparative Perspective

Descriptive section: The following comparative overview presents criminal law provisions that protect religious freedom in several European jurisdictions.

Religious freedom has been one of the major concerns of criminal lawmakers in the Member States of the European Union. It is clear from a detailed analysis of the criminal law provisions in the Member States' legislations that each of these states

[25] From 1985 to 2004, no less than 8 concordats were signed on Catholic religious education in state schools.

has criminal offenses to protect religious freedom. Therefore, each of these Member States has understood and provided for as part of the criminal offences which infringe religious freedom. All this is fully in line with the vision of the European legislator, i.e. in line with the European dimensions and guidelines of religious freedom.

By way of observation, it should be noted that the scope of freedom of religion is manifold, and the form of protection naturally differs from state to state; while most States have regulated offenses targeting religious freedom, as a term interpreted in extenso, as is the case, for example, in Hungary, Slovakia, Luxembourg, Cyprus or Estonia, there are also particular situations where the national criminal legislator has understood to protect only certain components of religious freedom, as is the case in countries such as Greece, where "religious peace" is protected, Malta, where "religious sentiment" is protected, Germany, where in addition to religious freedom, "ideologies about the world" are also protected, or Slovenia, where only the external expression of religion, namely religious ceremonies, are protected.

The comparative analysis will take into account, on the one hand, normative provisions from states where religious freedom is protected in its entirety, while, on the other hand, we will consider states where the criminal legislator has nuanced the limits of protection of religious freedom.

4.1 Italy

In Italy, offenses against religious freedom are included in Title IV of the Criminal Code, with the marginal title On offenses against religious sentiment and respect for the deceased. The text of the law in force is as follows:

> Art. 403. Offenses against a religious denomination by defamation of persons
>
> (1) Any person who publicly offends a religious denomination by defaming its practitioner shall be punished by a fine of between 1000 and 5000 euros.
>
> A fine of between €2000 and €6000 is imposed on anyone who offends a religious denomination by defaming a priest of that faith.
>
> Art. 404. Offenses against a religious denomination by defamation or destruction of property.
>
> (1) Whoever, in a place of worship or in a public place or a place open to the public, offends a religious denomination, defames by insulting expressions goods which are objects of worship or are consecrated to worship, or are obligatorily intended for the practice of worship, or commits the act during religious services preached in a private place by a priest of the cult, shall be punished by a fine from 1000 to 5000 euros.
>
> Whoever publicly and intentionally destroys, scatters, damages, renders unusable or defiles goods which constitute an object of worship or are consecrated to worship or are obligatorily intended for the exercise of worship, shall be punished by imprisonment for up to 2 years.
>
> Art. 405. Disturbing the religious services of a religious denomination.
>
> Whoever hinders or disturbs the performance of religious services, ceremonies or religious practices of a religious denomination, which take place with the participation of a representative of that denomination or in a place intended for worship or in a public place or a place open to the public, shall be punished by imprisonment for up to 2 years.

> If acts of violence against persons or threats are involved, imprisonment from 1 to 3 years is applicable.

A few observations are necessary: until 2006 the entire text of the law referred to the protection of the "Catholic cult". However, with the entry into force of Law No. 85 of February 24, 2006, the Italian criminal legislator extended the limits of protection of religious freedom to all cults operating on the territory of the Italian State. This step is very important and of profound significance, since in this way full protection has been granted to any person regardless of the religious denomination expressed. The amendment of the penal code in 2006 was motivated by the need to express the secular character of the Italian State. Secularism presupposes the existence of plurality of value systems—the equal dignity of all personal choices of religion and conscience—it presupposes equal protection of religious and non-religious beliefs and requires the neutrality of the state towards both (Ferrari and Ferrari n.d.).

4.2 Romania

In the national criminal legislation, the Criminal Code, in Article 381, provides for the offense of Hindering the exercise of religious freedom. The text of the law stipulates the following:

> (1) Hindering or disturbing the free exercise of the ritual of a religious cult, which is organized and functions according to the law, is punishable by imprisonment from 3 months to 2 years or a fine.
>
> (2) Coercing a person to participate in religious services of a cult or to perform a religious act related to the exercise of a cult shall be punishable by imprisonment for a term of one to three years or a fine.
>
> (3) The same punishment shall be imposed for forcing a person, by violence or threat, to perform an act forbidden by the cult, organized according to the law, to which he belongs.

With the help of grammatical interpretation, we observe that the Romanian criminal legislator has paid particular attention to protecting the freedom of expression of religion, in its external form, and has included in the scope of criminal offense any form of hindering or disturbing the free exercise of the rituals of a religious cult.

The offense of hindering the exercise of religious freedom has a prerequisite, which is very important in the economy of criminal law, namely the existence of a religious cult operating in accordance with the legislative norms in force. The status of a State-recognized cult is acquired by Government decision, at the proposal of the State Secretariat for Religious Denominations, by religious associations which, by their activity and number of members, offer guarantees of durability, stability and public interest (according to Art. 17 para. (1) of the Law on Worship). Recognition of statutes and canonical codes shall be granted to the extent that their content does not prejudice public security, public order, public health and morals or fundamental human rights and freedoms (according to Art. 17 para. (1) of the Law on Worship).

In Romania, the following 18 cults are recognized by law (according to the Annex to the Law on Cults, consulted on April 28, 2025): Romanian Orthodox Church, Serbian Orthodox Diocese of Timişoara, Roman-Catholic Church, Romanian Church United with Rome, Greek-Catholic Church, Archdiocese of the Armenian Church, Russian Old Rite Christian Church of Romania, Reformed Church of Romania, Evangelical Church of the C.A. in Romania, Evangelical Lutheran Church in Romania, Unitarian Church in Transylvania, Union of Christian Baptist Churches in Romania, Christian Church according to the Gospel in Romania—Union of Christian Churches according to the Gospel in Romania, Romanian Evangelical Church, Pentecostal Union—Apostolic Church of God in Romania, Seventh Day Adventist Christian Church in Romania, Federation of Jewish Communities in Romania, Muslim Cult, Jehovah's Witnesses religious organization.

4.3 Greece

Greece has chosen one religion to predominate over the others: the constitutionally dominant religion is the Orthodox. This explanation is necessary in order to justify the increased protection of the Orthodox religion in criminal law, to the detriment of other religions recognized by law. Thus, while all religions can express themselves, one will always remain privileged. In theory, this system is not contrary to religious freedom.

In the Greek Penal Code, the provisions on the protection of religious freedom are set out under the marginal heading Breach of religious peace.[26] The chapter in question consists of the following legal provisions:

Art. 198 - Blasphemy with malice

1. The offense of a person who publicly and maliciously defames God shall be punishable by imprisonment for up to two years.

2. Except in the situation provided for in para. 1, the act of a person who publicly shows, through blasphemy, disrespect for the divinity, shall be punishable by imprisonment of up to six (6) months or a fine of up to three thousand (3000) euros.

Art. 199 - Denigration of religion.

The act of a person who publicly and maliciously insults in any way the Eastern Orthodox Church of Christ or any other religion recognized in Greece is punishable by imprisonment of up to two years.

Art. 200 - Disturbing religious assemblies.

1. The offense of a person who maliciously attempts to hinder or intentionally disturbs a religious assembly accepted by the Greek system of government for the performance of worship or ceremony shall be punishable by imprisonment for up to two years.

2. The offense of a person who, in a church or in any place established for religious assemblies accepted by the Greek system of government, commits undue acts in an abusive manner shall be punished by the same penalty.

---

[26] Text retrieved from https://codexpenal.just.ro/laws/Cod-Penal-Grecia-RO.html.

Of the three articles presented, Article 199 raised the most problems. I draw attention to two distinct situations,[27] summarized as follows:

In 2003, a painting by the Belgian painter Thierry de Cordier was exhibited at the Cultural Olympiad. It depicted Jesus Christ crucified on the cross with a male genital organ next to him. The whole creation was considered scandalous by church representatives, some politicians and a section of public opinion. Despite the fact that the organizers immediately withdrew the artwork following the reactions it provoked, the prosecutor of the Athens Correctional Court ordered the prosecution for the offences under Article 199 of the Greek Penal Code. The indictment labeled the art painting as "perverse" and "a pseudo work of art", insulting everything that Christianity stands for. In the end, the Athens Court of Appeal acquitted the organizer of the exhibition, on the grounds that the painting was a work of art and a balance had to be struck between freedom of expression and religious freedom.

Austrian Gerhard Haderer created the comic book "The Life of Jesus". In Greece, criminal proceedings were brought against the Greek author and publisher for the offense under Article 199 of the Greek Penal Code, denigration of religion. At first instance the author was convicted and the publisher acquitted on the grounds of lack of intent. On appeal to the Athens Court of Appeal, both were acquitted on the same ground of lack of intention to denigrate religion.

We note that, at first sight, freedom of religion is protected with precedence over freedom of expression, but in reality, in the light of the two cases summarized and presented, freedom of religion knows some limits in the face of freedom of expression.

It is also interesting, from the point of view of the interpretation of the concepts involved in the definition of the concept of religious freedom, to note the marginal name of the chapter of the Criminal Code that regulates the rules for the protection of religious freedom, namely Breach of religious peace. The natural question is whether the rules of criminal law can lead to the creation of what is called "religious peace". Peace is based on truth, justice, love and freedom (Godfried 2003). Incorporating the four anchors on which peace is based, in the deeply philosophical understanding of Greek criminal law, freedom of any kind stands behind a peace, so that religious freedom is also the foundation for religious peace.

5 Conclusions

Normative evaluation: Based on the descriptive analysis conducted in the previous sections, the following conclusions assess the principles that should guide the interpretation and limitation of religious freedom.

From the comparative analysis undertaken in the present study, to answer the two research hypotheses formulated in the introduction, we have drawn the following conclusions:

---

[27] For details, see Iliopoulos-Strangas and Georgitsi (2008), pp. 265–310.

The notion of religious freedom is interpreted in a terminological and factual diversity, based on the way society evolves;

The three dimensions of freedom of religion reflect the two interpretative valences derived from the analysis of the normative provisions of the fundamental laws, namely the inner dimension, identified in freedom of conscience and freedom of thought, and the dimension of external manifestations, identified in freedom of religion. In this context, starting from one of the ideas expressed in the chapter, whether it is possible to equate freedom of religion and freedom of religious manifestation, we conclude by emphasizing that freedom of religion is related to the internal side of the individual and is identified with freedom of conscience, while freedom of religious manifestation is connected with the externalization of the experiences of homo religiosus;

In close connection with the two sides of religious freedom, internal and external, we conclude that the internal side can never be subject to any limitation, whether by state authorities or other subjects of law; on the other hand, as regards the external side, it is essential to peaceful coexistence that it knows certain limits, imposed by the need to respect the principle of secularism and the principle of religious neutrality. In most cases, such restrictions have concerned the wearing of religious vestments or symbols, or even the prohibition of the construction of buildings specific to a particular religion;

With regard to the interpretation of religious freedom in relation to other fundamental rights and freedoms, it should be made clear that religious freedom can only exist in its intrinsic aspect as a self-sufficient and independent entity. Whenever religious freedom is externalized in any form, this will implicitly lead to its interpretation in relation to other fundamental rights and freedoms (an example of this is undoubtedly the right to privacy). Religious freedom will not be able to be opposed to the guarantee of the right to life.

References

Bellanger F (2002) La liberté religieuse Fiches juridiques suisses n° 53, pp. 2–22

Bîrsan C (2005) European Convention on Human Rights. Commentary on articles, volume I, Rights and Freedoms, All Beck, Bucharest

Eliade M (1992) The sacred and the profane. Humanitas Publishing House, Bucharest

Ferrari A, Ferrari S (n.d.) Religion and the Secular State: The Italian Case. https://original.religlaw.org/content/blurb/files/Italy.pdf

Godfried (2003) Religions et paix. Revue Nouvelle revue théologique 125(4):529–540

Iliopoulos-Strangas J, Georgitsi E (2008) Greece in Annuaire international de justice constitutionnelle, 23–2007. Constitution et liberté d'expression - Famille et droits fondamentaux, pp. 265–310

Kant I (2008) Towards eternal peace. All Publishing House, Bucharest

N.A. (2013) Selection of decisions of the Federal Constitutional Court of Germany. C. H. Beck Publishing House, Bucharest

Renucci JF (2012) Droit européen des droits de l'homme L. G. D. J, Paris

Private Law and Emerging Regulatory Markets

Legal Tech Companies, Air Passenger Claims and Romania's Litigation Market: A Disruptive Synergy

Carmen Tamara Ungureanu

Abstract Law and technology have come together to form legal tech companies (LTCs), which work in a number of fields, including compensating consumers for damages they are entitled to from air travel. LTCs offer them access to justice in an efficient and financial risk-free manner. Taking Romania as a reference system, first, we will clarify what is meant by LTCs and how they function in the field of air travel compensation. Based on an empirical study conducted on a sample of 10 LTCs acting on the Romanian litigation market, we will outline their business models, noting that consumers' recourse to their services is not without risks. We will then characterize the adhesion contracts proposed by LTCs according to Romanian law, showcasing the rules applicable to the mandate contract and the assignment of rights/receivables. We will, also, analyze the services offered by LTCs from the perspective of third-party litigation funding. The consumer alternative to the LTCs model—RAD's representative actions—will be discussed in the final section. Our endeavor aims to demonstrate the effectiveness of the mechanism employed by LTCs and to emphasize that, given the current circumstances in Romania, private funding—with all the associated risks—is the best option for guaranteeing consumers' access to justice in the air passenger claims sphere.

1 Introduction

Technology influences all areas of law, including the exercise of the rights of injured people in court. Various private actors perceive the judicial system as a market, which they can use to make a profit. In the field of consumer protection, the interaction of technology with law has led to the creation of legal tech companies (LTCs), which act in various spheres, including that of compensation for damages in air

C. T. Ungureanu (✉)
Faculty of Law, 'Alexandru Ioan Cuza' University of Iaşi, Iaşi, Romania
e-mail: carmen.ungureanu@uaic.ro

I. Maria Costea (ed.), *Legal Interpretation in Motion*, Ius Gentium: Comparative Perspectives on Law and Justice 144,
https://doi.org/10.1007/978-3-032-32948-6_11

transport to which consumers are entitled. They provide access to justice in an efficient and financial risk-free manner.

In this chapter, we analyze the activity of LTCs in Romania in the field of compensation owed by airline companies to injured passengers. Passengers are consumers of air transport services, who benefit from protective rules. These rules are included in the EU Air Passenger Rights Regulation, the EU Regulation on small claims procedure, as well as in other regulations of a general protective nature in matters of jurisdiction, applicable law or other special rules applicable to consumers.

LTCs facilitate access to justice for consumers (Schmitz and Zeleznikow 2022), i.e. individuals who conclude contracts with professionals for private purposes unrelated to their professional activity.

Taking Romania as a reference system, first, we clarify what is meant by LTCs and how they function in the field of air travel compensation.

Based on an empirical study conducted on a sample of 10 LTCs acting on the Romanian litigation market, we outline their business models, noting that consumers' recourse to their services is not without risks. For this endeavor, to identify the main actors active in the Romanian air passenger compensation market, a Google search was conducted using the Romanian term *"despăgubire companie aeriană"* (airline compensation). This approach provided a practical overview of the LTC services most accessible to Romanian consumers. Ten LTCs were selected based on their visibility in the search results and the availability of websites containing information in Romanian: AirAdvisor, AirHelp, Airclaim, Compensair, Skycop, Refundio, AirCashBack, Întârziere.ro, ZborulÎntârziat.ro and TroubleFlight. For each LTC, the Terms and Conditions (T&C) were examined, focusing on three elements: (a) the nationality of the LTC, in order to determine whether the contractual relationship with consumers is domestic or international; (b) the applicable law and competent jurisdiction, to highlight potential risks for consumers and the possible need to challenge such clauses as unfair; (c) the business model, with a view to assessing the efficiency and operational approach of LTCs in recovering compensation from airlines.

In addition, the practical involvement of these companies in litigation was assessed by consulting two official online judicial databases: the Romanian courts' portal (*Portal Just*), administered by the Ministry of Justice, and the case law portal of the Superior Council of Magistracy (*ReJust*). *Portal Just* provides information on pending and resolved cases, including hearing lists, while *ReJust* allows access to court decisions. This step made it possible to evaluate the actual presence of the selected LTCs in Romanian judicial practice (d). The analysis therefore covers four aspects: (a) LTC nationality, (b) applicable law and jurisdiction, (c) business model, and (d) presence in Romanian case law.

Next, we characterize the adhesion contracts proposed by LTCs according to Romanian law, showcasing the rules applicable to the mandate contract and the assignment of rights/receivables. We analyze the services offered by LTCs from the perspective of third-party litigation funding, as well. The consumer alternative to the LTCs model—Representative Actions Directive (hereinafter, RAD)—is discussed in the final section. We conclude by stating that LTCs currently provide consumers with simple and fast access to justice, often as their only option. Private funding helps ensure this access, despite its risks. However, the surge in LTC activity is creating new imbalances: courts face heavy caseloads, and airlines are diverting substantial resources to handle claims, with potential financial impact.

2 What Are Legal Tech Companies (LTCs) and How They Work in the Air Passenger Claims Field?

For a comprehensive analysis, we will first clarify the meaning of LTCs and then briefly describe how they function using technology in the sector of air passenger compensation.

2.1 What Are LTCs?

The term "legal tech" has been perceived in many ways. One of the simplest definitions is that Legal Tech is *about the application of software technology in the legal profession* (Damasceno 2019; Hartung et al. 2018). A more complex approach, provided by Ryan Whalen, who did a thorough literature review on the meaning of the term, is that legal tech means *'all devices, capable of being used as a means for interacting with the substance of law or assisting its user to interact with the law, and the skills and techniques by which we use them.' This encompasses all technologies that are capable of being used towards 'legal ends'* (Whalen 2022).

In the legal literature (Szostek 2021) the interference of technology with law was considered to have three phases. The first one is *digitalization*, in which legal documents are digitized, and lawyers gain the ease of consulting various legal sources in electronic format and have access to search engines. The second phase focuses on the *automation* of the decision-making process, using algorithms, machine learning, which propose solutions to legal problems. In the third phase, called *legal engineering*, there is the implementation of the provisions of law into programming codes, such as smart contracts or tokenisation of values.

If we were to include LTCs that facilitate access to justice for air passengers/consumers in one of these phases, they would probably be in the second. As an author (Ruhl 2024) stressed LTCs „*use digital technologies to automate, simplify, and thus improve the enforcement of lower value, especially consumer claims. More specifically, they take easily standardizable, well-structured claims, check their legitimacy (largely) automatically with the help of algorithms and, in close cases, enforce them in return for a contingency fee.*"

Legal tech claims management companies is another name for legal tech companies, which are active, mainly, in the air passenger rights sector. They have also achieved positive results in actions brought by consumers affected by the Volkswagen scandal (Rott 2023).

2.2 How Do LTCs Function in the Sector of Air Passenger Compensation?

Air Passenger Rights Regulation is the main piece of (European) legislation used by LTCs in their activity. The aim of the regulation is to ensure a high level of protection for passengers, as stated in recital 1. It applies to flights departing from the EU or coming to the EU from a third country [art. 3(1)]. It grants redress for passengers when: they are denied boarding against their will; their flight is cancelled; their flight is delayed [art. 1(1)].

According to art. 7, passengers are entitled to receive compensation amounting to: EUR 250 for all flights of 1500 km or less; EUR 400 for all intra-Community flights of more than 1500 km, and for all other flights between 1500 and 3500 km; EUR 600 for all other flights. In determining the distance, the basis is the last destination at which the denial of boarding or cancellation would delay the passenger's arrival after the scheduled time. When passengers are offered re-routing to their final destination on an alternative flight the operating air carrier may reduce the compensation by 50%. The compensation could be a monetary one or, with the signed agreement of the passengers, in travel vouchers and/or other services.

Denied boarding usually occurs when there is an overbooking. In case of a delay the passengers redress depends on the number of hours and the distance: for 2 h or more in the case of flights of 1500 km or less; or for 3 h or more in the case of all intra-Community flights of more than 1500 km and of all other flights between 1500 and 3500 km; or for 4 h or more for the remaining flights (art. 6). Passengers' remedies include compensation, ticket reimbursement, rerouting, and assistance (such as free phone calls, hotel accommodation, food, and refreshments).

So, compensation consists in fixed amounts of money depending on the flight length, and in case of delay, and on the number of hours, no matter what the individual circumstances. This means that the process is highly standardized (de Elizalde 2021). The ECJ confirms it: in the case C-354/18, (Radu-Lucian Rusu, Oana-Maria Rusu v. SC Blue Air — Airline Management Solutions SRL), point (28) it is stated that „With regard to the amounts set by Article 7(1) of Regulation No 261/2004, they are intended to compensate, in a *standardized* and immediate manner (...)". Also, the breach of air transport contract cannot be the subject of interpretation: the EU Regulation describes all the situations the compensation is due to the passengers, so there is an objectivization.

Standardization and objectivization of compensation make this regulation *technologically highly efficient*, as it is an excellent input for IT systems (de Elizalde 2021). LTCs „*are able to autonomously assess the plausibility of the claim, that is, whether the plane arrived late, a passenger was denied boarding, or a flight was cancelled (objectivization). Additionally, the IT systems can calculate compensation without the intervention of experts. With fixed amounts of compensation, it is relatively easy to standardize. These two activities, which were traditionally carried out by lawyers with the support of non-legal experts, have been heavily automated.*" (de Elizalde 2021).

3 LTCs on Romanian Air Passenger Litigation Market

By searching Google for "despăgubire companie aeriană" (meaning *airline compensation*) in Romanian, we were able to obtain a concise overview of the services offered by LTCs in the Romanian litigation market. Ten LTCs have been chosen, which have websites with information in Romanian.

The Terms & Conditions (T&C) for every LTC were then examined, with a particular emphasis on three areas:

(a) the LTC's nationality, which aims to categorize contracts between consumers/passengers and LTCs as either domestic or international;
(b) the applicable law and the competent court for potential disputes between LTCs and consumers; the purpose is to draw attention to the risk that consumers may be exposed to and the need to request that such clauses be declared null and void;
(c) business model, to demonstrate the efficiency of LTCs in collecting compensation from airlines.

Also, we have investigated two online portals—the courts portal, *Portal Just*, which is owned by the Romanian Ministry of Justice, and the case law portal of the Superior Council of Magistracy, *ReJust*—to evaluate the implication of the ten LTCs in court proceedings (d). On *Portal Just* data on resolved or pending cases can be accessed, including lists of court hearings. On *ReJust* the decisions issued by the courts can be consulted.

All LTCs act on the principle of "No win, No fee". So, the consumer does not pay, if compensation is not obtained from the airline company, the LTC bearing all the expenses. In the case of winning, meaning collecting compensation, the LTC keeps a percentage, which varies between 25%–35%,[1] and can reach 50% if the compensation is obtained in court.[2]

3.1 A Survey of LTCs on Romanian Air Passenger Claims

The 10 LTCs analyzed are: AirAdvisor, AirHelp, Airclaim, Compensair, Skycop, Refundio, AirCashBack, Întârziere.ro, ZborulÎntârziat.ro., TroubleFlight.

[1] For instance, AirHelp, available at: https://www.airhelp.com/en-int/our-fees/.

[2] For instance, Refundio, available at: https://www.refundio.eu/check-compensation#pricing.

We will investigate four aspects: LTC's nationality (a), competent jurisdiction and applicable law (b), business model (c) and the LTC's `presence` in the Romanian case law (d).

3.1.1 AirAdvisor

a. AirAdvisor International Inc. is a legal entity registered in accordance with the laws of the state of Delaware, USA, of US nationality, with a subsidiary registered in Poland, Air Advisor Ltd., of Polish nationality.
b. From point 8.3. of its *Terms* it could be understood that the agreement between *AirAdvisor International Inc.* and the consumer is governed by the laws of the State of Delaware, USA and in the event of any dispute it will be resolved in court in accordance with the substantive and procedural law of the state of Delaware, USA. The agreement between *Air Advisor Ltd.* and the consumer/passenger is governed by the law of Poland (unless otherwise expressly provided in the agreement) and the competent court for any dispute is a Polish court.
c. As to the model used, point 1.5 from its Terms[3] reads: „*A moment of submitting an application to Contractor* [AirAdvisor] *is the moment of signing by Member* [consumer] *a document authorizing Contractor to represent Member's interests in matters before third parties stipulated in this document. Such a document may exist in different forms and under different names, including but not limited to a power of attorney, assignment of claim, agreement, etc. (hereinafter referred to as the «Assignment of Claim»). An "Assignment of claim" is also a digital document that is signed by Member with an electronic signature at the end of the process of submitting an application on the Website.*". AirAdvisor provides *services* for collection of compensation for disrupted flights (T&C, section 1).
d. From 2022 to the present, the name "AirAdvisor" shows up in 2491 results on Portal Just, some of which are listings of court hearings and others of cases that have been resolved or are still pending.[4] "AirAdvisor" can be found in 1247 court decisions on ReJust.[5]

3.1.2 AirHelp[6]

a. AirHelp Germany GmbH is a company based in Germany, of German nationality.
b. At point 9.12 from its T&C with the title *Governing Law and Jurisdiction* an applicable law clause is included (but no jurisdiction clause, although the title announces it): the agreement between AirHelp and the consumer, and any dis-

[3] Available at: https://airadvisor.com/en/terms.

[4] Available at: https://portal.just.ro/SitePages/cautare.aspx?k=airadvisor&start1=81.

[5] Available at: https://www.rejust.ro/.

[6] Available at: https://www.airhelp.com/en-gb/terms/.

pute or claim arising out of or in connection with is governed by the laws of Germany, without regard to conflict of laws principle. *This shall not affect mandatory provisions of the legal system that would apply without this choice of law clause, e.g. the mandatory provisions of the customer's country of residence* (the customer is the consumer).

c. In its T&C it is stipulated that the "*Assignment Agreement" means the document, in electronic or other format, requested by AirHelp on a case-by-case basis, whereby* the consumer *and AirHelp agree that AirHelp shall become the owner of the Claim, subject to the terms of the Assignment Agreement, in order to collect and receive payments.* (2.11). *The AirHelp Group provides* services *to help air passengers manage the impact of flight disruption* (point 1.2. from its T&C).

d. AirHelp has a quite long presence in the Romanian litigation market. From 2019 to the present using the name "AirHelp" to search the *Portal Just* yields 5438 results,[7] some of which are listings of court hearings and others of cases that have been resolved or are still pending. On *ReJust* "AirHelp" is mentioned in 6709 rulings from 2019 until the present.[8]

3.1.3 AirClaim[9]

a. Airclaim is a company based in Romania, Constanta. Another LTC with almost an identical name, AireClaim,[10] is based in Portugal, with no activity in Romania, to our knowledge. AirClaim is part of a group of companies as could be inferred from point 9.4 of its T&C (*The rights and obligations related wholly or partly to any claim filed may be transferred without restriction by AirClaim to any entity within the AirClaim group of companies and by AirClaim to third parties.*).

b. The applicable law to the contract is the German law. *However, the client* (the consumer) *always has the right to request the protection due under the legal provisions of the country where the client resides.* ((point 9.2. T&C). No clause on competent jurisdiction was found.

c. In providing services to consumers, AirClaim uses both models, assignment agreement and the contract of mandate. Although not expressly stated, it seems that the choice of model belongs to the consumer, called *client*. In its T&C at point *1.5* the *"Assignment Form"* is defined as *the document by which the client, according to the terms and conditions stipulated in it, transfers ownership of the request to AirClaim.* At point *1.6* the *"Claim Request Agreement*" is defined as *a document provided by AirClaim to the client, which authorizes AirClaim or one of its affiliates or partners to act on behalf of the client. The document can come*

[7] Available at: https://portal.just.ro/SitePages/cautare.aspx?k=airhelp&v1=%2Bmjmpdosardata.

[8] Available at: https://www.rejust.ro/.

[9] Available at: https://airclaim.com/terms-conditions/.

[10] Available at: https://aireclaim.com/terms.

in various forms, including, but not limited to, a Power of Attorney or a Customer Support Agreement.

d. AirClaim served as an assignee in 23 small claims that were resolved between 2020 and 2021.[11] The name "AirClaim" is present in 65 decisions from 2021 to the present on ReJust.[12]

3.1.4 Compensair[13]

a. Compensair Pte.Ltd. is a company registered in Singapore. It has a website with information in Romanian language.
b. For any disputes between the contractual parties the competent jurisdiction is a court from Singapore and the applicable law, included that of the agreement, is the law from Singapore (point 6.3 and 6.4 T&C).
c. Even though the terms aren't specifically classified as such, it may be assumed from the T&C that the consumer-Compensair agreement is an assignment one. But according to a 2024 ruling,[14] Compensair used the mandate contract model, not the assignment agreement model, to act as a conventional representative in that case. The court acknowledged the claim without addressing Compensair's representative status.
d. On Portal Just, 13 files were identified, in which Compensair acts as a plaintiff: 11 files from 2024, as an assignee, and 2 files from 2023, where Compensair was a conventional representative. The national court annulled both these last claims as having been filed by a person for whom no proof of representative capacity was provided.[15]

3.1.5 Skycop[16]

a. Skycop is a company registered in Vilnius, Republic of Lithuania, of Lithuanian nationality.
b. The laws of the Republic of Lithuania apply to the agreement, except if otherwise agreed. The consumer is also entitled to claim protection under mandatory provisions provided by the laws of the country where the consumer resides (point 6.2 T&C). For any dispute, controversy or claim, arising out of or relating

[11] Available at: https://sintact.ro/#/search?sl=RO&q=airclaim&sortBy=dateDESC.

[12] Available at: https://www.rejust.ro/.

[13] Available at: https://www.compensair.com/documents/Compensair/en/TermsConditions_Compensair_en.pdf.

[14] Decision no. RJ ee765gg6g/2024, Brasov court, available at: https://sintact.ro/.

[15] Available at: https://portal.just.ro/SitePages/cautare.aspx?k=Compensair&start1=1.

[16] Available at: https://www.skycop.com/terms-and-conditions/.

to the agreement a court of the Republic of Lithuania is competent, unless mandatory provisions of law specify otherwise (point 6.5 T&C).

c. Skycop has T&C in Romanian and employs an agreement which *combines the assignment agreement and agreement on provision of services; the legal relationship of the assignment and provision of services is referred to as services, unless it is clearly stated otherwise.*
d. On the Portal Just the name "Skycop" shows up in 1136 results (listings of court hearings and cases that have been solved or are still pending),[17] with Skycop as plaintiff (assignee). On the ReJust "Skycop" appears in 54 court decisions.[18]

3.1.6 Refundio[19]

Refundio is part of the Verdikto Group, a company of Czech nationality with no T&C, available on the website in Romanian or on any other of its websites. It is an LTC that offers compensation in advance, on case-by-case basis, depending on the risk that the company assumes. In fact, there is the only LTC that does upfront payments, identified by us, on the Romanian market. We have not found any indications about the model it uses. No case law was found. In only one decision,[20] available on the ReJust, the name 'Refundio' is mentioned as part of and managed by the European company Verdikto Group, who was the plaintiff in that decision.

3.1.7 AirCashBack[21]

a. AirCashBack is a company from Poland, of Polish nationality.
b. The contract is governed by Polish law and the disputes fall under the competence of a Polish common court. The choice of Polish law and court does not have to deprive the consumer of the protection afforded to him/her under the laws that cannot be excluded by agreement between AirCashBack and the consumer, under the law that would be applicable under the relevant regulations in the absence of the choice (point 14.6 Terms of Service).
c. AirCashBack provides services by assisting the consumer in pursuing compensation, based on a mandate contract. As point 4.4 from its Terms of Service reads: '*Upon receipt of a copy of the power of attorney and other necessary information and/or documents needed to take action on behalf of the User, AirCashBack shall take action to settle the User's claim.*`.

[17] https://portal.just.ro/SitePages/cautare.aspx?k=Skycop&v1=%2Bmjmpdosardata&start1=61.

[18] Available at: https://www.rejust.ro/.

[19] Available at: https://www.refundio.ro/formular#pricing.

[20] Decision no. 500/2025, Bucharest First court, cod RJ 86g74g9dd (Available at: https://www.rejust.ro/juris/86g74g9dd).

[21] Available at: https://aircashback.com/en/worth-knowing/terms-and-conditions.

d. On the Portal Just, 4 cases were found,[22] dated from 2022 and 2023, in which AirCashBack acted, either as a conventional representative (one action being annulled due to lack of proof of representative capacity[23]), or as a plaintiff. On the ReJust, 18 decisions were identified, in which the name "AirCashBack" was mentioned: 2 were admitted, 10 annulled due to lack of proof of representative capacity and 6 rejected.

3.1.8 Întârziere.ro[24]

a. Întârziere.ro is the name Eurosell Network SRL uses to provide services to air passengers. It has its seat in Romania and is of Romanian nationality. It has T&C only in Romanian.
b. In the T&C there is no information on applicable law or competent court in case of disputes between the contractual parties.
c. At point 7 of its T&C it is stipulated that in the event that passengers wish to recover any compensation from the airline company using the services provided by intarziere.ro, they understand that they are going to enter into a contract with an entity which acts either as a lawyer or as a *collection agency*; the entity will take all due care and make the best efforts in collecting the compensation, on behalf of the passenger, by all means. After the amount is collected, it will be remitted to the passenger (75% of it). The details (right of representation for contacting the airline, for suing the airline, etc.) will be brought to the passenger's attention together with the legal assistance contract/the mandate contract.

The use of the term "collection agency" could imply that it refers to debt collectors. Although the characterization is not wrong, the rules governing the activity of debt collectors cover situations in which consumers are debtors (Law no. 243/2024, GEO no. 52/2016) and are pursued for the payment of their debts and not creditors, such as the situation of passengers harmed by airline companies. The rules on debt recovery are intended to protect consumers as debtors and do not apply in the opposite situation, when consumers are creditors. In this regard, in an action brought by Eurosell against an airline, the defendant invoked the fact that the plaintiff could not file the claim as a plaintiff, since it is not registered with the ANPC (National Authority for Consumer Protection) as an entity carrying out debt recovery activity. The court established, however, that the provisions of GEO (Government Emergency Ordinance) no. 52/2016 could only be applicable in the event that the plaintiff would act against a consumer, and not against a professional, given that the purpose of the ordinance is to establish *a balance in the contractual relationship between*

[22] Available at: https://portal.just.ro/SitePages/cautare.aspx?k=aircashback&v1=%2Bmjmpdosardata.

[23] Available at: https://portal.just.ro/94/SitePages/Dosar.aspx?id_dosar=9400000000337627&id_inst=94.

[24] Available at: https://intarziere.ro/termeni-si-conditii/.

consumers and entities carrying out debt collection activities, respectively to *ensure the necessary protection for consumers in the event of difficulties in repaying installments, in the event of forced execution, as well as the assignment of the claim to entities carrying out debt collection activities.*[25]

d. In the period 2018–2024, 22 decisions were found on ReJust, with Eurosell as the plaintiff. In all those decisions, Eurosell acted as an assignee[26] and not as a conventional representative, as stipulated in the T&C. On Portal Just, the name "Eurosell" shows up in 341 results,[27] in files from 2019 to the present.

3.1.9 Zborulintarziat.ro[28]

a. Zborulîntârziat.ro is the name used by the company Skyline Express SRL to provide services to air passengers. It is of Romanian nationality. Its website has information only in Romanian.
b. In the T&C there is no information on applicable law or competent court in case of disputes between the contractual parties.
c. The LTC uses the mandate contract as a business model. In the T&C it is stated that once the legal assistance or mandate contract is concluded, the relationship with the passenger is governed by the rules of the Law 51/1995 for the organization and practice of the legal profession and/or art. 2009 and the following of the Romanian Civil Code, regarding the mandate, as the case may be.
d. No Romanian case law was detected with Skyline Express as claimant.

3.1.10 Trouble Flight[29]

a. Trouble Flight is the name Doorify Tech S.R.L., seated in Romania, of Romanian nationality, provides services to air passengers.
b. In its T&C there is no information on applicable law or competent court in case of disputes between the contractual parties.
c. Trouble Flight enters into a mandate contract with the consumer," Power of Attorney", which means the document that lets Trouble Flight represent the consumers in dealings with the airline and other institutions about their claim.
d. Despite the business model assumed in the T&C, in court, Trouble Flight acted as an assignee, not a conventional representative. On Portal Just, the name

[25] Decision no. 8157/2019 Buftea Court, cod RJ 729d74gd available at: https://www.rejust.ro/juris/729d74gd).

[26] Decision no. 16580/202,1 Buftea Court, Decision no. 175/2021, Ilfov Tribunal, sintact.ro.

[27] Available at: https://portal.just.ro/SitePages/cautare.aspx?k=eurosell&v1=%2Dmjmpdosardata.

[28] Available at: https://zborulintarziat.ro/politica-de-confidentialitate/?tab=termeni-si-conditii.

[29] Available at: https://www.troubleflight.com/en/terms-conditions.

"Doorify Tech", shows up in 4682 results,[30] some of which are listings of court hearings, and others are solved or pending cases, from 2022 to the present. In a random check, Doorify Tech acted as a plaintiff, the disputes being qualified as disputes between professionals. On ReJust "Doorify Tech" appears in 118 decisions, as a plaintiff, as well.

On Romanian litigation market is, also, active an intermediation service, offered by FlightClaimer.com,[31] as a third model. In its T&C is stated that FlightClaimer.com is an independent website (owned and operated by Zenfco Limited registered in Hong Kong) which acts as an i*ndependent introducer for flight delay claims management companies*, from which it receives referral fees.

3.2 The Survey's Conclusions

According to the purposes pursued, we found the following:

(a) Among the 10 LTCs examined, 6 are of foreign nationality, originated from both the EU and third countries, such as the USA (Delaware) or Singapore. Among the 4 LTCs of Romanian nationality, one (AirClaim) belongs to a group of companies, likely with a parent company based in Germany, as the governing law is German. Consequently, Romanian consumers engage in international contracts with 6 LTCs, among which 2 (AirAdvisor, an American company, and AirHelp, a German company) are the most prominent and have the highest number of lawsuits filed. Contracts that involve an international aspect, such as the nationality of the LTC, fall under the private international law rules.

(b) Regarding the provisions pertaining to the competent court and the applicable law, the LTCs of foreign nationality and AirClaim of Romanian nationality propose foreign laws applicable to the contracts concluded with consumers. 4 LTCs (3 of Romanian nationality and Refundio) do not have clauses regarding the competent court and the applicable law in their T&C. Airhelp and AirClaim have only one clause regarding the applicable law.

In case of a disagreement between the contractual parties the consumer could sue the LTC. Would she/he be protected? The idea of protecting consumers in international contracts means the assurance that they will not be forced to leave their comfort zone: as a rule, the competent court for resolving consumer disputes is the one at the consumer's domicile (art. 18, Brussels I bis Regulation), and the applicable law, according to art. 6 Rome I Regulation, is the law of the consumer's habitual residence (Calvo Caravaca 2020). The clauses in the T&C, which are adhesion contracts, are, however, abusive clauses. According to art. 3 of Directive 93/13/EEC on

[30] Available at: https://portal.just.ro/SitePages/cautare.aspx?k=doorify%20tech&v1=%2Bmjmpdosardata&start1=121.

[31] Available at: https://ro.flightclaimer.com/terms.

unfair terms in consumer contracts, a contractual term is unfair if it has not been individually negotiated and if, contrary to good faith, it causes a significant imbalance between the rights and obligations of the parties arising under the contract to the detriment of the consumer.

The sanction for unfair clauses is determined by the court, on a case-by-case basis. According to Romanian law (Law no. 193/2000, art. 6), unfair terms do not produce effects on the consumer, and the contract continues to bind the parties, if it can continue to exist after the unfair clauses are removed; the applicable sanction (Gaudemet 2006) is the *absolute partial nullity* (Pop 2009). The consumer should therefore address a claim to a Romanian court that will first declare the absolute nullity of the abusive clauses and then resolve the consumer's claim against LTC, applying Romanian law, from his/her habitual residence.

For example, AirAdvisor provides in its T&C that the applicable law is that of the state of Delaware, USA, and the competent court is also in Delaware, if the passenger has contracted with AirAdvisor International Inc. The consumer has as alternative, AirAdvisor Ltd., which uses Polish law as the applicable law and the courts from Poland. Nevertheless, it seems that Romanian consumers chose in many cases AirAdvisor International Inc..[32] A Romanian court could be competent to solve a dispute related to the assignment agreement, after the abusive clauses are declared null and void.

We did not find any case law on disputes between consumers and LTCs.

(c) As to the business models used by the LTCs, from the analysis of the adhesion contracts proposed by them, we found that two models are employed, with different variations, which are based either on the assignment of rights agreement or the mandate contract; the first model prevails. Moreover, in practice, LTCs that proposed the mandate as a business model, used instead the assignment agreement, because of the procedural difficulties they encountered in courts. We will discuss that in the following section.
(d) Regarding the presence of LTCs in national courts, an intense activity was observed in the past 5 years, with thousands of court decisions being issued in their favor, as assignees of rights. The German company AirHelp is at the top of consumers' preferences, followed by the American company AirAdvisor, the two dominating the air passenger litigation market in Romania.

3.3 *Is the LTCs Business Models Free of any Risks for Consumers?*

Firstly, not all consumers have access to LTCs offerings, especially the elderly, who lack IT literacy or/and digital equipment.

---

[32] For example, Decision no. 3246/2025, Buftea Court, cod RJ 59dd92e58 (available at: https://www.rejust.ro/juris/59dd92e58).

The algorithms and AI used in assessing a claim could exclude it on flawed reasons or, in particular situations, could predict smaller compensation than the entitled one according to the Air Passenger Rights Regulation. Also, the technology used by LTCs lacks transparency, its outcomes are difficult to understand, and all these could lead consumers to wrong ideas on the legal services they receive. As, traditionally, only lawyers provide legal services, the consumers could expect the same protection from the LTCs (Ebers 2021). Additionally, the consumers lack information on how the LTCs work. They just do what they are asked to do, give access to all their personal data, including their bank accounts, and, afterwards, just wait for the money.

The survey has shown that the consumers are exposed to risks, associated with the agreement they enter into with the LTCs. They might not even be aware that they enter a contract, that the T&C *is* a contract, an adhesion one with abusive clauses, like those concerning the competent jurisdiction for the disputes and the applicable law.

In a nutshell, if something goes wrong, the consumers are protected as in every B2C contract, national or international, with all legal issues attached. According to Romanian law, LTCs do not provide legal services. Unlike lawyers for whom the *pactum de quota litis* is prohibited in Romania, which is akin to the common law contingency fees payment system for lawyers, LTCs can employ the "no win- no fee" approach, therefore having a considerable advantage over lawyers (Rott 2023).

4 Characterization of LTCs Adhesion Contracts in Romanian Civil Law

LTCs provide services to air transport consumers, facilitating their access to compensation. The provision of services on the litigation market is traditionally reserved for legal professionals. As we have already stressed out, LTCs are not considered providing legal services on the Romanian litigation market. Nevertheless, for the activity of LTCs to be legal and for the actions undertaken to be successful, LTCs mainly use the institution of assignment of rights. Those who applied the conventional representation model, by concluding a mandate contract with consumers, encountered difficulties in the national courts, which led them to switch to the assignment agreement.

4.1 Issues Related to the Mandate Contract in Court

The conclusion of a mandate contract is possible in the analyzed situation, the consumer being able to empower a conventional representative to act on his/her behalf to collect the compensation to which she/he is entitled. And this representative could be a LTC.

The mandate contract is regulated in art. 2009–2038 Romanian Civil Code. To obtain compensation from the airline company following an amicable way, the representative should not run into any issues regarding its capacity. If it is necessary to initiate legal action, however, conventional representation in court is subject to the rules of civil procedure, which are stricter.

As a rule, the conventional representative is a lawyer. But the law allows the parties in a judicial proceeding to choose another representative, who is not a lawyer. Thus, according to art. 80 and art. 83 Romanian Code of Civil Procedure, the parties may be represented in court by a lawyer or another person, before the first instance, in appeal, as well as in extraordinary remedies of appeal for annulment and revision.

Nevertheless, if the mandate is given to someone other than a lawyer, the conventional representative may not draw conclusions on procedural exceptions and on the case's merits on his/her own; he/she needs a lawyer, because he/she can act only through a lawyer, both during the process investigation stage and during the deliberations stage.

In addition, art. 85 Romanian Code of Civil Procedure imposes the form of an authentic document, as a condition of evidence, for the mandate given by a natural person to the representative who is not a lawyer. This means that consumers and LTCs should go together to a notary to conclude a mandate contract in an authentic form. This procedure runs counter to the fundamentals of how LTCs function by streamlining the steps required to obtain compensation using technology.

Therefore, LTCs that would choose to conclude mandate contracts with consumers should comply with the form of the authentic document and use the services of a lawyer. Failure to comply with the form leads to the impossibility of proving the quality of representative in court, with the sanction of annulment of the application filed, as was the case of AirCashBack and Compensair, noted above. It turns out that the most efficient model is that of the assignment of rights.

4.2 The Assignment Agreement in Romanian Courts

From the brief survey undertaken, it was observed that the national courts did not question the active procedural capacity of the applicant, the assignee of rights. The decisions only mentioned that the applicant concluded an assignment agreement with the passenger, by which the passenger assigned all his/her rights regarding obtaining the compensation due under the Air Passenger Rights Regulation.

According to the Romanian Civil Code, the assignment of rights is an agreement by which the assignor, in the analyzed case, the consumer, transmits to the assignee, i.e. LTC, a right against a third party (the airline company) (art. 1566). When the assignment is for pecuniary interest, the rules of sales apply [art. 1567 (3) Civil Code]. The sale price consists of an amount of money, as provided for in art. 1660 Civil Code. In the assignment agreement the price is the agreed percentage of the compensation (in money) that LTC will take from the airline company.

The basis for the provision of services is, therefore, the assignment of rights. In characterizing the contract, we should not consider the provision of services as a distinct agreement. Such an approach would lead to the question of whether a contract of sales (of the right) or a contract for the provision of services, with distinct legal regimes, was concluded. According to the Civil Code, a service provision agreement falls into the category of enterprise contracts. In art. 1851 (1) Civil Code, the enterprise contract is defined as the agreement by which the entrepreneur undertakes, at his/her own risk, to execute a certain work, material or intellectual, or t*o provide a certain service for the beneficiary, in exchange for a price*.

But LTC would not be able to provide any service to the consumer in the absence of the assignment of the right (or the existence of a mandate). If it were to provide *legal* services, then it would have to comply with the strict rules in the field applicable to lawyers. Without the assignment, LTC would lack the requisite authority to claim compensation either amicably from the airline company or in court, in the event of failure to resolve the issue amicably.

Therefore, the contract between the consumer and LTC is a contract for assignment of rights/receivables with the legal regime of the sales contract. Although the sales is, as a rule, a commutative contract (at the time of its conclusion, the existence of the rights and obligations of the contractual parties being certain, and their extent being determined or determinable—art. 1173(1) Civil Code –) in this case, the contract is aleatory. A contract is aleatory, by its nature or by the will of the parties, when it offers at least one of the parties the chance of a gain and at the same time exposes her/him to the risk of a loss, which depends on a future and uncertain event (art. 1173(2) Civil Code). The random character is not incompatible with the sales contract. The sales of litigious rights is also a random contract, a characterization accepted both in doctrine and in practice (Stănciulescu and Nemeş 2013).

In the contract between the LTC and the consumer, both parties are subject to the risk of losing compensation and the chance of winning it. The consumer risks less. The LTC also risks its own resources, since, in practice, it finances the litigation.

4.3 LTCs Business Model as Litigation Funders

LTCs can be seen as litigation funders facilitating access to justice, and the contracts concluded as funding agreements.

Third-party litigation funding, originating in common law (de Morpurgo 2011), is the practice where individuals or entities with no connection to the dispute, usually specialized companies, pay all or part of the expenses of their clients (plaintiffs or defendants) involved in the lawsuits, in exchange for a percentage of damages obtained by the clients through the court decision or through a settlement (de Morpurgo 2011). If the lawsuit is not successful, the funder receives nothing, losing the investment made. When the financed party wins, the funder receives, according to the funding contract concluded, a percentage, which varies from case to case.

Litigation funders, which could be spin-offs of insurance and reinsurance companies, are particularly financially powerful entities, hedge funds and private equity, some of which are listed on the stock exchange (Tzankova and Kramer 2021), such as Burford Capital.[33] Litigation funders could also be LTCs.

In the Proposal for a Directive on the regulation of third-party litigation funding from 2022 all types of funding are included. The „*'third-party funding agreement' means an agreement in which a litigation funder agrees to fund all or part of the costs of proceedings in exchange for receiving a share of the monetary amount awarded to the claimant or a success fee, so as to reimburse the litigation funder for the funding it provided and, where applicable, cover its remuneration for the service provided, based wholly or partially on the outcome of the proceedings. This definition covers all agreements in which such a reward is agreed, whether offered as an independent service, or achieved through* a purchase or assignment of the claim." [art. 3(h) from the Directive Proposal].

In this vein, the essential element of a funding agreement is the existence of an outcome-based reward for the funder (Augenhofer and Dori 2023) (not the type of contract), including the assignment agreements (used by LTCs).

It is too early to assess how LTCs will evolve if the proposed directive is adopted. In any case, the strict rules imposed on litigation funders could have a negative effect on them, regardless of their type, and consequently could affect access to justice funding.

In broad terms, the proposed directive provides that litigation funders must be authorized in the EU, otherwise the funding agreements will be declared null and void (art. 14). The agreements should encompass certain mandatory elements (art. 12). In addition, a declaration from the litigation funder on the absence of a conflict of interest is required [art. 12, letter (g)]. Any clause in third-party funding agreements granting a litigation funder the power to take or influence decisions in relation to proceedings shall have no legal effect [art. 14 (2)].

According to Article 16 of the proposed directive, disclosure of the third-party funding agreement is mandatory. Claimants or their representatives are required to inform the court or the relevant administrative authority of the existence of a third-party funding agreement and the identity of the litigation funder and to provide a complete and unredacted copy of such agreements relating to the proceedings in question, at an early stage of those proceedings. Defendants must be informed by the court or the administrative authority of the existence of a third-party funding agreement and the identity of the litigation funder.

Absent exceptional circumstances, if a litigation funding agreement were to grant a litigation funder the right to receive a share of any award that would dilute the share available to the claimant and the intended beneficiaries to 60% or less of the total award, including all amounts representing damages, costs, fees and other expenses, such an agreement would have no legal effect [art. 14.4].

---

[33] Available at: https://www.burfordcapital.com/eu/.

The proposed directive has not been well received by litigation funders (ILFA 2023). In particular, the last two conditions imposed, the mandatory disclosure of the funding agreement and the cap of 40%, were considered to be problematic. The European Commission conducted a research, collecting and analyzing data on the legal framework and the practical functioning of the institution of third-party litigation funding in EU Member States and some third countries, with a view to adopting future policies in this area. The outcome is the document, *Mapping Third Party Litigation Funding in the European Union,* released in late March 2025. Unfortunately, *three different approaches are considered in the document, along with their rationale: (1) No regulation, (2) Light-touch regulation, (3) Strong regulation.* So, it seems that third party funding is still groping in the dark for a solution.

The implementation of the Representative Actions Directive (RAD) in the Member States, which has several provisions on third-party funding, and the application of those funding rules in practice, will influence the future European legislation on third party funding (Augenhofer and Dori 2023).

5 The Consumers' Alternative to the LTCs Model: RAD's Collective Actions[34]

LTCs use individual claims in court for compensation based on the Air Passenger Rights Regulation. However, they do not treat each individual action as a lawyer would traditionally do. They specialize in this type of claim, which allows them to use technology (AI, algorithms, etc.) to make the management of a large portfolio possible and suitable for automation (de Elizalde 2021). From this perspective, LTCs practically administer class actions. But, since the legal norms do not allow them to act as a representative of the interests of all damaged consumers and to make profit from it, they choose to use the law in their favor.

They have approached the traditional class actions model, as well, but not in this kind of litigation (Azar-Baud and Biard 2021) and not in Romania.

If we were to consider LTCs as litigation funders, then third-party litigation funding already exists in Romania, although in our legal system this institution was unknown, until the implementation of the RAD in national legislation.

Next, we will briefly discuss the way of transposing the RAD in national legislation in the matter of third-party funding, aiming at identifying the possibility for the consumers to use the mechanism RAD proposes, as an alternative to the LTCs model.

---

[34] A version of this part is included in the author's article in Romanian, *Contracte de finanţare de către terţi a litigiilor colective de consum. Un transplant dezirabil în dreptul român?* (EN-Third-party financing contracts for collective consumer litigation. A desirable transplant into Romanian law?), accepted for publication in Revista Română de Drept Privat no. 1/2025.

5.1 RAD in Romania's Legislation

RAD was transposed by Law no. 414/2023 on representative actions for the protection of the collective interests of consumers (hereinafter, Law 414/2023). According to art. 4 and art. 5 of Law 414/2023, actions for the representation of consumer interests may be brought only by qualified entities. The actions that a qualified entity may bring are either injunction actions or redress actions for compensation (art. 7 of Law 414/2023).

Regarding the funding of collective consumer litigation by third parties, which concerns only actions for redress, the national legislator took over this institution from the RAD in art. 10 of Law 414/2023, attempting an adaptation to the specifics of Romanian law:

> (1) A representative action for obtaining redress measures may be funded by a third party, in accordance with the provisions of Law no. 32/1994 on sponsorship, as subsequently amended and supplemented, only if there are no conflicts of interest.
>
> (2) The funding of a representative action for obtaining redress measures by third parties who have an economic interest in the introduction or in the outcome of that action does not affect the protection of the collective interests of consumers.

Although art. 10(1) RAD, which states (in other words), that it is not mandatory for the Member States to include in their national legislation institutions that they do not know (the directive aiming at a minimum harmonization) would have allowed the Romanian legislator to choose otherwise, it boldly included the institution of third-party litigation funding in Romanian law, in the consumer protection sector.

Analyzing the steps leading up to the adoption of Law 414/2023, one can see that the national legislator was informed about the negative aspects of this institution. For example, the American Chamber of Commerce, in an opinion expressed on February 7, 2023, indicated, among other things, that since Romania is not a jurisdiction with experience in litigation funding, the risk of funding representative actions may materialize in abusive actions, diverting them from the legitimate purpose towards obtaining huge profits for funders at the expense of consumers. In the same opinion the recommendation was to not test this tool (litigation funding) in consumer protection field for the first time in Romanian law.

According to art. 10 of Law 414/2023 (reproduced above) the funding of collective consumer litigation for obtaining redress measures can be done in two ways:

- funding under the Sponsorship Law;
  funding by third parties, who have an economic interest in the introduction or in the outcome of the action.

5.1.1 Funding Under the Sponsorship Law

The Sponsorship Law prescribes two types of funding: sponsorship and patronage.

Sponsorship is the legal act by which two parties agree on the transfer of ownership of material goods or financial means to support non-profit activities carried out by one of the parties, called the beneficiary of the sponsorship [art. 1(1) Sponsorship Law]. Patronage is an act of generosity by which a natural or legal person, called the patron, transfers, without any obligation of direct or indirect consideration, his or her ownership of material goods or financial means to a natural person, as a philanthropic activity of a humanitarian nature, for the carrying out of activities in the fields of: cultural, artistic, medical-sanitary or scientific—fundamental and applied research [art. 1(3) Sponsorship Law].

From these definitions it is clear that only sponsorship can be considered as litigation funding. Patronage concerns areas in which litigation for obtaining redress measures cannot be included.

Sponsorship can be both a *direct* way of funding representative actions, by paying the necessary expenses for a particular legal action, and an *indirect* one, by sponsoring a qualified entity, such as a consumer association, which has active procedural capacity in representative actions (Agulló Agulló 2022).

Recital (52) of the RAD refers to these two types of third-party funding: direct and indirect: „(...) *The direct funding of a specific representative action by a trader operating in the same market as the defendant should be considered to imply a conflict of interest, since the competitor could have an economic interest in the outcome of the representative action which would not be the same as the consumers' interest.*

The indirect funding of a representative action by organisations that are funded through equal contributions by their members or through donations, including traders' donations in the framework of corporate social responsibility initiatives or crowdfunding, should be considered eligible for third-party funding, provided that the third-party funding complies with the requirements of transparency, independence and the absence of conflicts of interest.(...)".

It seems that the European legislator looks at direct *financing* with caution, suspecting it of potential conflicts of interest, but approves *indirect financing*, without a commercial purpose, which comes, above all, from legal acts not for a pecuniary interest.

In European law the institution of third-party funding has acquired new dimensions compared to the traditional meaning. The possibility of direct funding for commercial purposes (for profit), as the institution is understood in its originating system (ELI Principles 2024), has not been eliminated, but indirect funding, through self-funding or through not for pecuniary interest funding, for charitable purposes, has been preferred. It seems that the Romanian legislator understood the idea and transposed it into the first part of article 10 of Law 414/2023, in a quite comprehensive way.

5.1.2 Funding by Third Parties, Who Have an Economic Interest in the Introduction or in the Outcome of the Action

Paragraph 2 of art. 10 of Law 414/2023, which concerns funding by third parties, who have an economic interest in the introduction or in the outcome of the action and which does not affect the protection of the collective interests of consumers, is more difficult to understand, given the legislative vacuum in the matter of third party funding.

First, what does it mean that a third party has an economic interest in the introduction or in the outcome of the action in representation?

If the interpretation were to strictly target the legislator's wording, anchored in the Romanian legislative and doctrinal reality, then the result would be extremely unsatisfactory, both for consumers and for qualified entities or for potential funders. According to this line of reasoning an economic interest in the introduction or outcome of the representative action may be held by one or more competitors, who would seek to eliminate the defendant in the representative action from the market. And this also results from the recitals of the directive, as we have shown above. Some authors (Hornkohl 2021) even state that this was the intention of the European legislator: the protection of the professional—defendant from abusive actions funded by his/her competitors.

The interpretation of third party funding should not be made, however, by referring to the receiving system, i.e. Romanian law, nor to the first receiving system, i.e. European law, where it has not yet been used and does not yet benefit from an interpretation at the jurisprudential level. The answer must be sought in the system of origin, i.e. common law, where the Romanian lawyer can find the meaning of the institution and its interpretation in jurisprudence and doctrine. Therefore, a third party that has an economic interest in the introduction and the outcome of the representation action is, as a rule, an enterprise specialized in investments in litigation. The funder aims to obtain profit from the investment made. The profit consists of a (significant) percentage of the compensation awarded to the consumer.

5.2 *RAD: A Viable Alternative to the LTCs Model?*

Qualified entities have the *effective* possibility to bring actions in the representation of consumer interests *only if they are funded.* Article 20(1) of Law 414/2023 provides that qualified entities must ensure *themselves* that they have the necessary funds for the procedures related to a representative action. They have the status of plaintiff and are exempt from paying stamp duty. They can also receive *public financing*, according to art. 20(3), including in the form of structural support for qualified entities.

The wording used infers that public financing is a possibility, which the Romanian government is unlikely to turn it into reality, at least as regards private qualified entities. The initial draft proposal of RAD had provisions [in (art. 15 (1)] that made the Member States ensure that qualified entities benefit from funding. These did not survive in the final version (Stadler 2021), being replaced by milder rules. In transposing the RAD, the Romanian legislator has assigned the task of financing to qualified entities, which are the ones that must ensure that they have the necessary funds to initiate representation actions.

What or who are the qualified entities in Romanian law?

Law 414/2023 provides for two types of qualified entities. The first one refers to private *entities designated* as qualified entities, such as consumer associations, after having followed a procedure with the fulfillment of certain conditions expressly provided for by law. The second category consists of qualified entities that are *entitled by law* to have this status. According to art. 4(6) of Law 414/2023 the authorities and bodies providing public services with powers in the application of the rules from a list of 66 pieces of legislation (in the annex to the law) are qualified entities, each of these in its own field of competence.

Responsible for the list of qualified entities is the Ministry of Economy, Entrepreneurship and Tourism [art. 5(2) of Law 414/2023], which must communicate the list to the European Commission.

More than a year after the law entered into force, there is no public information on such qualified public (or private) entities, no list can be found on the ministry's website, and on the dedicated website of the European Commission, the only qualified entity in Romania is the National Authority for Consumer Protection (ANPC) and only for collective injunction actions. For actions under the RAD Romania is not on the list. There is also no public information on the steps to follow to obtain the status of qualified entity, either on the ANPC website or on that of the Ministry of Economy, Entrepreneurship and Tourism.

However, in the future, given that a large number of the qualified entities are designated by law, meaning all authorities and bodies providing public services [as specified in art. 4(6) and art. 5 of Law 414/2023], their public financing should not be lacking. We are wondering, anyway, if they will be available to deal with collective consumer actions on top of all the other responsibilities they have.

In foreign legal literature (Stadler 2021), it has been proposed an access to justice fund at the disposal of qualified entities. Although such funds already exist, for example in Canada,[35] this idea has not been echoed in the EU due to the lack of funds (Stadler 2021), although there would be sources, such as fines applied to professionals for violating consumer rights, which are particularly consistent, especially in the field of personal data protection,[36] as well as fines applied for violating commercial competition rules.[37]

In Romania, the issue of financing qualified entities is, for the time being, only a theoretical issue or, for a more optimistic view, work in progress.

If there were qualified entities and they were active in the field of representative actions, would there be interest in using their mechanism of functioning?

Consumers could be compensated based on Law 414/2023, since the Air Passenger Rights Regulation is an integral part of the list annexed to the law (and to

[35] Available at: https://faac.justice.gouv.qc.ca/.

[36] For instance, in September 2024 Meta was ordered to pay a €91 million fine by the Irish Consumer Protection Authority for inadequate protection of users' passwords. Available at: https://www.euronews.com/next/2024/09/27/meta-hit-with-91-million-fine-for-lax-password-safety.

[37] For example, in November 2024, Meta was ordered by the European Commission to pay a fine of approximately 800 million euros for abusive commercial practices in the commercial advertising market. Available at: https://ec.europa.eu/commission/presscorner/detail/el/ip_24_5801.

the RAD). In this way, they would enjoy adequate protection, thanks to the supervised and controlled environment in which the entire procedure must take place. In addition, the amount of compensation they would take could be higher, compared to what they receive from LTCs.

However, the disadvantages seem to outweigh the advantages: the procedure is complicated and lengthy; qualified entities only introduce collective actions; the decision to act belongs exclusively to the qualified entity [art. 13(1) a) Law 414/2023]; lack of funding may lead to the qualified entity refraining from acting or choosing only the representative actions it considers more meritorious; lack of information available to consumers regarding qualified entities and their mode of operation, to name just a few.

LTCs provide simple, fast and almost effortless solutions. They offer flexibility and variety: their services are available 24 h a day, 7 days a week with no geographical restraint. The price is reasonable and transparent (Ebers 2021). In addition, it is a system that has been proven to work. It could be said that it is a *win-win* approach: consumers are compensated, and LTCs make a profit from it.

LTCs, as funders, though, could not provide services that facilitate access to justice through the RAD mechanism, even if they were involved in collective actions. Their model is incompatible with that of the RAD. LTCs have control of all the procedures, either amicable or judicial action, and if they are assignees of rights, they are, in addition, the owners of the claims. The court only verifies the existence of the assignment agreement, after which LTC is treated as a plaintiff and obtains compensation from the airline company, of which it retains a considerable percentage, according to the contract concluded with the consumer.

The cumbersome mechanism of RAD discourages third-party funding, regardless of funders' way of organization. LTCs would be subject to double control: both by the qualified entity and by the court. On the one hand, the qualified entity, which will have the status of plaintiff (LTCs losing any control over the action), will carry out the necessary checks in order to exclude any influence on the part of the funder, which could harm the collective interests of the consumers targeted by the representative action and also to prevent the introduction of any action against a defendant who is a competitor of the funder or against a defendant on whom the funder is dependent [art. 10(3) Law 414/2023]. On the other hand, the courts have the power to assess compliance with these rules, if justified reasons arise. Qualified entities may be required to provide a financial statement listing the sources of funding used to support the representative action, so that the court can verify any potential conflict of interest [art. 10(4) and (5) Law 414/2023]. If a breach of the legal provisions is found, national courts have the power to take all necessary measures, such as ordering the qualified entity to refuse or make changes to the funding in question, and, if necessary, to declare the qualified entity to lack standing in a particular representative action and to dismiss the action [art. 10(6)].

Therefore, representative actions within the meaning of RAD do not seem to be a viable alternative to the system practiced by LTCs, at least not at present, in the unclear situation of qualified entities in Romania.

6 Conclusions

Consumers may be reluctant to exercise their rights to obtain compensation from airline companies under the Air Passenger Rights Regulation. This is justified by the fact that any legal action involves costs, time and uncertainty as to the amount of the costs and the likelihood of success with the action. In addition, they may not have all the information they need. Therefore, they may not take the risk, especially when they find that the benefits they would obtain are lower than the costs. The psychological reluctance of the claimant can be counterbalanced by assuming the risk and costs of the action by a third party, such as LTCs.

LTCs ensure consumers' access to justice, remedying a market failure, namely the lack of public financing for access to justice, the remedy consisting of private funding (Cordina 2021). They act on a *no win-no fee* system, i.e. *win-win*: consumers are compensated, and LTCs make profit.

The majority of LTCs operating on the Romanian litigation market are of foreign nationality, both from the EU and from third countries. The empirical research carried out on a sample of 10 LTCs showed that the model preferred by them is the assignment of rights. Even those who proposed at the beginning the mandate contract model in their T&C, changed their approach to the claims filed in court. The reason could be observed in several court decisions, which were annulled for lack of proof of representative capacity. In Romanian law, the mandate given by a natural person to someone who is not a lawyer must comply with a prescribed form that of an authentic document, under the sanction of the impossibility of its proof.

Considering the services offered by LTCs as third-party litigation funding, as the proposed European directive does, would make their operation problematic.

The alternative for consumers to get compensated from airline companies by using representative actions under the RAD and the corresponding national legislation (Law 414/2023) is not a viable one, at least for the time being. When it comes to large scale small claims, LTCs are indeed effective (Rott 2023). LTCs offer consumers access to justice simply, quickly and effortlessly. For now, it is all they have got. Private funding is the answer to ensuring real access to justice for consumers, with all the potential risks that entails.

It should be added, however, that the recent surge in LTC activity may lead, if it has not already done so, to further imbalances. Courts are overwhelmed by the high volume of claims filed by LTCs, and airlines are allocating significant resources to satisfy these claims, which could significantly affect them financially.

References

Agulló Agulló D (2022) Directive 2020/1828 on representative actions for the protection of the collective interests of consumers: an overview. UNIO EU Law J 8(1):127–142

American Chamber of Commerce, Opinion, (2023), [Online]: https://www.amcham.ro/download?filename=Position%20Paper%20on%20Collective%20Redress&file=committeePaper/uC5oRQf.pdf

Augenhofer S, Dori A (2023) The proposed regulation of third party litigation funding—much ado about nothing? Zeitschrift für das Privatrecht der Europäischen Union 20(5). https://doi.org/10.9785/gpr-2023-200505

Azar-Baud MJ, Biard A (2021) The Dawn of collective redress 3.0 in France? In: Uzelac A, Voet S (eds) Class actions in Europe.Holy grail or a wrong trail? Springer, pp. 73–95 https://doi.org/10.1007/978-3-030-73036-9

Burford Capital. https://www.burfordcapital.com/eu/

Calvo Caravaca AL (2020) Consumer Contracts in the European Court of Justice Case law. Latest Trends. Cuadernos de Derecho Transnacional 12(1): 86–96

Cordina A (2021) Is it all that fishy? A critical review of the concerns surrounding third party litigation funding in Europe. Erasmus Law Rev 14(4):272–280. https://doi.org/10.5553/ELR.000211

de Elizalde F (2021) Legal tech in consumer relations and small-value claims. A survey. In: DiMatteo LA, Janssen A, Ortolani P, de Elizalde F, Cannarsa M, Durovic M (eds) The Cambridge handbook of lawyering in the digital age. Cambridge University Press, pp. 159–179. https://doi.org/10.1017/9781108936040.013

de Morpurgo M (2011) A comparative legal and economic approach to third-party litigation funding. Cardozo J Int Comp Law 19:343–410

Ebers M (2021) Legal tech and EU consumer law. In: DiMatteo LA, Janssen A, Ortolani P, de Elizalde F, Cannarsa M, Durovic M (eds) The Cambridge handbook of lawyering in the digital age. Cambridge University Press, pp. 195–219. https://doi.org/10.1017/9781108936040.015

ELI (2024) Principles Governing the Third Party Funding of Litigation, [Online]: https://www.europeanlawinstitute.eu/fileadmin/user_upload/p_eli/Publications/ELI_Principles_Governing_the_Third_Party_Funding_of_Litigation.pdf, 20.04.2025

European Commission, C/2024/1125 Notification from the Commission concerning Article 4(3) of Directive 2009/22/EC of the European Parliament and of the Council on injunctions for the protection of consumers' interests.

European Commission (2025) DG Justice and Consumers, Mapping Third Party Litigation Funding in the European Union, https://doi.org/10.2838/3795189

Gaudemet S (2006) La clause réputée non écrite. Economica, Paris

Hartung M, Bues M, Halbleib G (2018) Legal tech: a Practitioner's guide. Blooms-bury Publishing Plc. apud. Damasceno E C (2019) Business Models in Legal Tech Companies, Guimarães M R (ed.), University of Porto

Hornkohl L (2021) Up-and downsides of the new EU directive on representative actions for the protection of the collective interests of consumers—comments on key aspects. Journal of European Consumer and Market Law, Issue 5:189–199. https://kluwerlawonline.com/journalarticle/Journal+of+European+Consumer+and+Market+Law/10.5/EuCML2021039

International Legal Finance Association-ILFA (2023) Resourcing the Rule of Law in Europe, https://www.ilfa.com/news

Pop L (2009) Tratat de drept civil. Obligațiile, vol. II. Contractul, Universul Juridic Publishing House, Bucharest

Rott P (2023) The balance in consumer protection between substantive law and enforcement. Eur Rev Private Law 31(4). https://doi.org/10.54648/erpl2023032

Ruhl G (2024) Legal tech companies and access to justice in Germany. Forthcoming in rethinking the Lawyer's monopoly: access to justice and the future of legal services (Freeman Engstrom N & Engstrom D.). https://doi.org/10.2139/ssrn.5043883

Schmitz AJ, Zeleznikow J (2022) Intelligent legal tech to empower self-represented litigants. Columb Sci Technol Law Rev XXIII(1). https://doi.org/10.52214/stlr.v23i1.9391
Stadler A (2021) Are Class Actions Finally (Re)conquering Europe? Some Remarks on Directive 2020/1828. Juridica International 30:14–22. https://doi.org/10.12697/JI.2021.30.03
Stănciulescu L, Nemeş V (2013) Dreptul contractelor civile şi comerciale în reglementarea noului Cod civil. Hamangiu Publishing House, Bucharest
Szostek D (2021) The concept of legal technology (LegalTech) and legal engineering. In: Szostek D, Załucki M (eds) Legal tech. Information technology tools in the administration of justice. Nomos, pp. 19–28. https://doi.org/10.5771/9783748922834
Tzankova I, Kramer X (2021) From injunction and settlement to action: collective redress and funding in The Netherlands. In: Uzelac A, Voet S (eds) Class actions in Europe. Holy grail or a wrong trail? Springer, pp. 97–130. https://doi.org/10.1007/978-3-030-73036-9_5
Whalen R (2022) Defining legal technology and its implications. Int J Law Information Technol 30(1): 47–67. https://doi.org/10.1093/ijlit/eaac005

Legal Landscape of Online Advertising: An Interpretative Approach

Aura Elena Amironesei

Abstract The exponential growth of online advertising has transformed the global commercial communication landscape, generating a rapid shift from traditional to digital media. Fueled by consumer migration to online environments, the Internet has overtaken traditional channels in advertising spending. However, Romania's legal framework remains fragmented, combining outdated provisions not originally tailored to digital contexts, recent EU-driven adaptations, and guidance from multiple regulatory authorities. This fragmentation generates uncertainty for advertisers, consumers, publishers, and platforms. Recent EU legislative initiatives, notably the Digital Services Act (DSA) and the Digital Markets Act (DMA), add new compliance obligations for both domestic and foreign operators in local markets. This chapter maps the legal framework governing online advertising in Romania, identifying key legislative instruments, institutional actors, and enforcement practices. Employing doctrinal legal analysis, complemented by comparative insights, case law, and regulatory practice, it offers a critical overview of the current regulatory landscape and explores future prospects in light of evolving forms of online advertising and emerging EU standards.

1 Introduction

The recent unprecedented and speedy growth of online advertising has impacted the commercial communications' landscape all over the world, and Romania is not an exception. As during the last year digital platforms and social media networks became the main vehicles for marketing, the related regulatory framework shall

A. E. Amironesei (✉)
Faculty of Law, 'Alexandru Ioan Cuza' University of Iași, Iași, Romania
e-mail: elena.amironesei@uaic.ro

I. Maria Costea (ed.), *Legal Interpretation in Motion*, Ius Gentium: Comparative Perspectives on Law and Justice 144,
https://doi.org/10.1007/978-3-032-32948-6_12

evolve accordingly. Online advertising in Romania has expanded rapidly in recent years, following the global trend, with the Internet now surpassing the traditional media in advertising spending; this trend has been even more accelerated by the consumer migration to online environments.

Despite the aforementioned advertising's growth, Romania's legal framework of online advertising ecosystem remains quite crumbled, comprising old laws (not originally designed for digital media), recent adaptations derived mainly from European Union law, and guidance from various regulatory authorities (mainly soft law). This creates uncertainty for all the stakeholders, namely advertisers, consumers, publishers and online platforms. In addition, global legal developments, in particular those coming from the European Union (hereinafter, the 'EU'), such as Digital Services Act (hereinafter 'DSA') and Digital Markets Act (hereinafter, 'DMA'), introduce new compliance obligations for both national and foreign entities operating in Romania and advertising themselves online.

This chapter focuses on mapping the Romanian legal landscape applicable to online advertising, emphasizing the key legislative instruments and institutional actors. Methodologically, this chapter employs doctrinal and legal analysis, supported by a brief comparative perspective and references to case law and regulatory practice. The chapter seeks to inform scholars and practitioners in the field of law and/or marketing about the current state and future prospects of online advertising regulation in Romania within the EU context, taking into consideration the newest forms of online advertising.

2 Conceptual and Legal Definition of Online Advertising

Advertising is said to be 'the backbone of the Internet and the core of most digital monetization models' (Pachauri and Bharti 2018, p. 1120). In both Romanian and EU's regulatory context, online advertising encompasses a broad range of digital marketing techniques, performed via the Internet (European Commission 2008, p. 6) [desktop or mobile (Bundeskartellamt 2018, p. 1)] aimed at promoting goods, services, or brand identity. Unlike traditional advertising channels, online advertising relies, obviously, on the Internet, and also on a complex web of intermediaries—including ad networks, data brokers, social media influencers, and automated ad exchanges; all these participants are to be explained further. Online advertising is characterized not merely by its occurrence within the digital environment, but fundamentally by its reliance on Internet connectivity. It is directed specifically at Internet users, and advertisements cannot be delivered or displayed when a user is offline. Online advertising also provides better targeting mechanisms (Ungureanu and Popescu 2022, p. 122), in particular when encompassing new technologies.

2.1 *Defining Online Advertising from a Marketing Perspective*

As previously noted, online advertising, as the term online implies, refers to advertising carried out via the Internet. While the notion of 'online' is relatively unambiguous, the term 'advertising' is less clearly defined. Consequently, the primary challenge lies not in defining online advertising per se, but in establishing a precise definition of advertising itself.

Although certain definitions of advertising have been sketched within the legal doctrine, they have mostly emerged from the necessity to delineate the scope of legislation governing advertising. Without a clear understanding of what constitutes advertising, it becomes difficult to determine the conditions under which the law should be applied (Kerr and Richards 2020, p. 2). The situation differs in the field of marketing, where debates do exist regarding the notion of advertising and its scope. Although, at a general level, most individuals can recognize advertising and distinguish it from other types of content, particularly when it is neither deceiving nor subliminal, finding a precise definition proves challenging for many (scholars included). This difficulty extends even to marketing professionals, as we have noticed in the literature.

Starting with the etymology of the word advertising, we can step by step pave the way to defining it. The notion of advertising comes from the Latin word *advertere* which means 'to turn the minds of towards'(Rathi 2021, p. 6779). Hence, one of the first characteristics of advertising is the capacity to persuade, to convince, to catch/draw attention. One paper in the literature even draws a parallel with the serpent from the Garden of Eden, suggesting that he could be regarded as the first advertiser for persuading Eve to partake of the forbidden apple (Vangelov 2023, p. 182); of course, in this case, none of the advertising definitions provided by the Romanian law would be applicable because there is no economic or commercial purpose. This perspective, however, highlights another fundamental role of advertising: influencing behavior and persuading consumers to engage in commercial transactions or undertake specific actions. Nevertheless, in our view, the conduct of the serpent in the Garden of Eden does not meet the criteria for considering advertising. According to another author, advertising can also be considered 'the process of calling user's attention to a product or service by way of paid announcements' (Ungureanu and Popescu, p. 121), hence outlining two essential elements of advertising: (i) the scope of capturing the attention of the consumer and (ii) its paid/remunerated nature.

One author from the marketing literature defines online advertising as 'deliberate messages placed on third-party web sites including search engines and directories available through Internet access' (Ha 2008, p. 33). However, we find this definition to be too narrow, as the types of online advertising extend beyond the basic activity of placing messages on third-party websites. Such examples are influencer and giveaway marketing. Also, online advertising might also be placed on the website of the advertiser himself. A more detailed and complex definition has been recently proposed, as follows: 'Advertising is paid, owned, and earned mediated communication, activated by an identifiable brand and intent on persuading the consumer to make some cognitive, affective or behavioral change, now or in the future' (Kerr and Richards 2020, p. 16). However, a limitation of this definition lies in its use of the term 'consumer.' While advertising is often directed at consumers, it also targets traders and potential business partners. Consequently, advertising cannot be confined solely to communications addressed to consumers. In the context of international trade law, the promotion of goods and services frequently excludes consumers altogether, yet advertising activities persist.

Another definition which outlines the commercial nature of advertising is 'Advertising may be the paid form of non-personal communication to spread business information in target audience via some medium' (Rehman ur et al. 2019, p. 129). An important and noteworthy aspect of this definition is its emphasis on the fact that advertising is always conducted for a price, which does not necessarily refer exclusively to monetary compensation. The consideration for advertising may take various forms; the essential point remains that advertising is never gratuitous but is invariably carried out in exchange for something of value (goods, services, etc.). However, there are also definitions that completely oversee the potential payment for advertising and do not take it into consideration when discussing the characteristics of advertising. Such an example would be basic definitions such as 'advertising is to give public notice or to announce publicly' (Rathi 2021, p. 6780), which does not refer at all to any price or consideration. In addition, from the very same definition, we can also conclude that the content of advertising should be non-personal, so with a commercial nature. This conclusion is also supported by the fact that it is considered that advertising is used for 'communication business information to the present and prospective customers' (Rathi 2021, p. 6780).

ICC Advertising and Marketing Communications Code (hereinafter, 'ICC Code 2024') provides under the section of 'Definitions' (ICC 2024) that 'advertising' means 'any form of marketing communications carried by the media', typically in return for payment or other valuable consideration'. Based on our research, we conclude that there is a blurred line between concepts such as advertising and marketing; however, marketing appears to be the broader notion, encompassing advertising within its scope. This conclusion is further supported by the definition of marketing communications provided by the ICC Code 2024, which states: '"marketing communications" includes advertising as well as other techniques, (…)'.

Finally, the simplest and straightforward definition we came across comes is from American Marketing Association (AMA), as follows: 'Advertising is a business practice where a company pays to place its messaging or branding in a particular location'.[1] Once again, this definition highlights the commercial nature of advertising, which is invariably carried out for consideration.

In conclusion, advertising is undoubtedly a form of commercial communication that may assume various formats, written text, images, video, or audiovisual content, aimed at promoting a brand, services, or goods, and at times encouraging the viewer to engage in a commercial transaction, such as purchasing goods or

[1] Available at: https://www.ama.org/marketing-vs-advertising/.

participating in a promotional offer. According to multiple scholars, as a rule, advertising activities involve consideration from the benefiting party and are not carried out gratuitously.

2.2 *Definitions of Online Advertising Under Romanian Law*

Despite the title of this section, Romanian law does not contain a clear provision defining online advertising. However, Law No. 158/2008 on Advertising, which transposes Directive 2006/114/EC of the European Parliament and of the Council concerning misleading and comparative advertising, provides a general definition of advertising, set forth in Article 3:

> publicitate - orice formă de prezentare a unei activităţi comerciale, industriale artizanale sau liberale, în scopul promovării vânzării de bunuri ori servicii, inclusiv bunuri imobile, drepturi şi obligaţii [a) advertising - any form of presentation of a commercial, industrial, artisanal or liberal activity, for the purpose of promoting the sale of goods or services, including immovable property, rights, and obligations].

Nevertheless, this general definition is media-neutral and does not address the specificity of online, in particular algorithmically targeted or AI-targeted advertising. At the same time, as the law does not distinguish between types/categories of advertising, we deem it is applicable to all forms of advertising. A similar general definition of advertising can be found in Law No. 185/2013. However, this definition differs in that it also emphasizes the role of advertising in informing consumers and supporting their right to be informed, a right closely linked to freedom of expression, which generally protects commercial speech and, by extension, advertising activities. Law No. 185/2013 defines advertising as follows:

> advertising — the entirety of specific methods and tools used to facilitate consumer awareness and appreciation of certain products or services, or to inform the public about events, the purpose of certain spaces, product launches, store openings, and similar activities, as well as any form of presentation of a commercial, industrial, artisanal, or liberal-profession activity aimed at promoting the sale of goods and services, rights, and obligations.

Other Romanian norms applicable in the field of advertising, such as Law No. 365/2002 on electronic commerce, provide a definition of commercial communications, which could arguably be considered equivalent to advertising. Law No. 365/2002 is tangentially relevant to the online environment, as it addresses advertising in the context of electronic commercial communications. According to Article 1 para. 8 of Law No. 365/2002, commercial communications are defined as:

> any form of communication intended to promote, directly or indirectly, the products, services, image, name, designation, trade name, or emblem of a trader or a member of a regulated profession. The following shall not in themselves constitute commercial communications: information allowing direct access to the activity of a natural or legal person, in particular a domain name or an electronic mail address; and communications relating to the products, services, image, name or trademarks of a natural or legal person made by an independent third party, especially where done free of charge.

Once again, we notice that the central element encompassed by the notion of advertising is the intention or purpose of promoting a trader or aspects related to economic activity. Under Romanian legislation, the defining characteristic of advertising is the objective to promote a trader and any elements associated with that trader, including brands, services, products, locations, name, and business activities.

The promotional objective of advertising is similarly reflected in the definition of audiovisual commercial communications provided by the Romanian Audiovisual Law No. 504/2002, which transposes the EU Audiovisual Media Services Directive (AVMSD). However, the application of Law No. 504/2002 is generally limited to licensed broadcasters and on-demand audiovisual media services, and not all online platforms fall within its regulatory scope. Nevertheless, major platforms that provide substantial online advertising services, such as Facebook, Google, YouTube, and Instagram, fall within the scope of this law, as evidenced by the fact that they can be sanctioned by the competent authorities under Law No. 504/2002 for engaging in prohibited practices regulated by the same law.[2] According to Law No. 504/2002, commercial communications are defined as:

> audiovisual commercial communications, including advertising, product placement, political advertising, and teleshopping'. Further examining the law, we find the definition of audiovisual commercial communications: ‚images, with or without sound, intended to promote, directly or indirectly, the goods, services, or image of a natural or legal person engaged in an economic activity, these images accompanying or being included in a program or in user-generated video content in exchange for payment or remuneration similar to payment, or for the purpose of self-promotion. Forms of audiovisual commercial communication include, among others, broadcast or televised advertising, sponsorship, teleshopping, and product placement.

2.3 *Digital, Online, and Virtual Advertising: Conceptual Boundaries Under the Romanian Law*

Although the notion of 'digital advertising' is sometimes used interchangeably with 'online advertising', the two notions are definitely not equivalent. Online advertising constitutes a subcategory of digital advertising, as it utilizes digital means;

[2] See, for example, National Audiovisual Council (CNA), Decision No. 396 of 15 May 2025 ordering action against illegal content disseminated on the online platform TikTok, concerning audiovisual material uploaded and distributed on TikTok via the user account "Mihai Paiu Mihai". Published on 4 June 2025. Available at: https://cna.ro/a-decizia-nr-396-din-15052025-xy3v4qun05iv8snckvvhyjr7/; National Audiovisual Council (CNA), Decision No. 996 of 16 December 2025 ordering action against illegal content uploaded and distributed on the online platform Instagram. Available at: https://cna.ro/c-decizii-continut-ilegal-online-lhc3wh2kvf5obt8747lzu2pu/; National Audiovisual Council (CNA), Press release: CNA public meeting of 12 March 2025. Sanctions imposed include a fine of RON 5000 against România TV and decisions ordering the removal of certain audiovisual materials from YouTube and Facebook. Published on 12 March 2025. Available at: https://www.cna.ro/a-comunicat-de-presa-sedinta-publica-a-cna-din-12032025-gnciw6uiflrc3bund1sk577w/.

however, the scope of digital advertising is considerably broader. A clear example is digital out-of-home (DOOH) advertising, such as the famous digital billboards in New York's Times Square, which illuminate the area even during the darkest nights. This form of advertising is digital, but not online, as it targets viewers in public spaces without requiring Internet access or an online presence to be seen. The concept of digital advertising is partially captured in Law No. 185/2013, which provides a definition for the 'digital mesh', a medium of digital out-of-home (OOH) advertising. According to Article 3, a digital mesh is defined as 'a large-scale advertising support displayed on the exterior surface of a building, using an electronic display mode for advertising'. It is crystal clear from this definition that the digital mesh refers to digital OOH advertising, which is not online, as it is physically installed on-site in the real world, without involving Internet access or an online environment.

Online advertising is sometimes mistakenly confused with virtual advertising. However, the definitions of virtual advertising cover, in our opinion, a much broader area. Virtual advertising can refer either to advertisements digitally superimposed onto real-life footage or to advertising that takes place within virtual or virtual reality environments. The latter is often referred to as 'immersive advertising' when it has the capacity to engage and introduce the consumer in the advertisement's environment (or, more generally, the brand environment's). It is also sometimes labelled as 'interactive advertising', particularly when it incorporates features that allow user engagement, a characteristic easily achieved within virtual reality. The immersive advertising is usually performed through technologies with immersive capabilities (Bhowmik and Das n.d., p. 3), such as AR (augmented reality), VR (virtual reality), mixed reality (Sands et al. 2024, p. 284), 360 imaging, the Internet of things (IoT) (Bhowmik and Das n.d., p. 3), and, more recently, even artificial intelligence (Tran 2024, p. 15). Another, more poetic, perspective on the technologies used for this type of advertising is that they 'blend the real and virtual worlds' (Sands et al. 2024, p. 284). Immersive or interactive advertising provides the viewer not only with a visual depiction of the advertisement, but also with a product or brand-related experience which connects more with the potential consumer, making the advertisement an engaging experience (Bhowmik and Das n.d., p. 4).

Coming back to the first meaning of 'virtual advertising', which is also the most used nowadays, it is worth mentioning that Law No. 504/2002 also provides a definition of 'virtual advertising', defining it as ‚a technique for broadcasting televised advertising that consists of processing the image, during event transmissions, by replacing the images of advertising panels displayed at the venue with advertising messages inserted by the broadcaster, or by superimposing new images containing such messages over any area of the transmitted image'. In doctrine, virtual advertising is also defined as 'a form of digital technology that allows advertisers to insert computer-generated brand names, logos, or animated images into television programs or movies' (Barfield 2006, p. 154). For example, during the live broadcast of a sports event, the advertisements physically displayed on the perimeter fences may be virtually replaced or covered in real-time. The spectators who are present at the venue will see the original, real-time, out-of-home (OOH) advertisements that are displayed there, while television or online viewers will see advertisements digitally inserted over by the broadcaster, which may differ from the actual advertisements present at the event; the TV spectators will not be able to appreciate that the advertisements they see to be shown on the real-life premises are not real (Lewis Silkin 2020, p. 3). Of course, this technique offers several advantages. It can significantly enhance advertising revenue, as a single real-time advertisement can be virtually replaced by multiple advertisements for television viewers, allowing multiple advertisers to pay the publishers (the broadcaster) for exposure rather than only one. Additionally, it facilitates compliance with national advertising regulations; for instance, if a product advertised on-site is prohibited in a particular jurisdiction, viewers in that jurisdiction can instead be shown a different advertisement. Furthermore, virtual advertising enables content customization, allowing advertisements to be adapted to the viewers' language or cultural background; for example, replacing a single English-language advertisement with localized translated versions for audiences in different countries watching the same international event. In general, the virtual advertising is customized by region (Lewis Silkin 2020, p. 7), and not necessarily by country. Notably, at its beginnings, virtual advertising was banned in multiple countries, including France, Portugal and Norway (European Commission 2004).

3 Types of Online Advertising in Practice

Now that we have shed some light on the notion of online advertising and on potential equivalents or other terms that are mistakenly used to designate it, in order to accurately determine which Romanian regulations are applicable to online advertising, it is necessary to also outline the various forms and formats that online advertising can take, as some may not be clear-cut or immediately apparent. It should be emphasized from the outset that not all the advertising forms identified are necessarily lawful or regulated; some may fall within a grey area.

In our view, the existing forms of online advertising can be classified into two categories: (i) types based on pre-existing online tools specifically designed for advertising purposes, and (ii) types developed through human creativity by utilizing online tools that were not originally intended for advertising. In the first category, we find the standard key modalities of online advertising, which can be identified based on the manner in which online advertising services are delivered: display advertising, search advertising, social media advertising, behavioral (targeted) advertising, and native advertising. Falling under the second category are practices such as giveaways on social media platforms, influencer marketing, electronic word-of-mouth (e-WOM) (through posts, comments, reviews, likes, and reposts), and the creation and use of social media pages. In-between, we have the dark patterns, which, as their name suggests, operate in the dark zone of law. In what follows, we will briefly describe each of these forms.

Display advertising refers to visual advertisements placed on websites and applications, encountered by users as they navigate web pages or use apps. In this way, the user is provided with upfront information about a brand, its products or its services (Thakor 2019, p. 56). Display advertising services are offered, for example, by Meta on its platforms Instagram and Facebook; in general, display advertising involves, in addition to the publisher and advertiser, many intermediaries (Choi et al. 2020, p. 569) that facilitate the advertising services provided by a publisher and which make the offer of a publisher to meet with the request of an advertiser and also help to optimize and improve the advertising services and the performance of an advertisement (Devaux 2023, p. 2). Search advertising, also known as search engine marketing (Jafarzadeh et al. 2015, pp. 1–2), involves the promotion of products or services through paid positioning in search engine results. When a user searches for a particular product or service, paid advertisements appear among the top results, overriding the organic, algorithm-driven hierarchy that would otherwise govern the order of search results. In this way, search advertising allows for brands to buy their ranking/position (Jafarzadeh et al. 2015, p. 3) in the hierarchy of the results displayed following an user's search.

Social media advertising encompasses promotional content that appears exclusively on social media platforms (Deng 2025, p. 1). This may include display advertising or other advertising formats, provided the content is of course paid for. One of the greatest advantages of social media advertising is that it provides the possibility for an advertisement to go viral (Pelet and Ettis 2022), benefitting thus from a tremendous success and popularity, and reaching an incredibly large number of potential consumers. Behavioral (targeted) advertising refers to advertisements shown to specific users based on their personal preferences, determined based on their collected personal data; hence, this type of advertising allows for a customised (personalized) advertising content (Priyanka and Siraj 2024, p. 231), which is considered to lead to ‚the most relevant and efficient advertisements' (Priyanka and Siraj 2024, p. 231)Finally, native advertising involves branded content designed to mimic the editorial content into which it is integrated, making it incredibly difficult for users to distinguish the advertising from organic content; hence, it will appear that there is no advertising content on that website. In essence, this type of advertising is designed to match ‚the look, feel and function of the media environment in which it appears' and, against the basic characteristics of advertising, it does not force any particular attention from the users (IAB Europe 2021a, b, p. 5). Native advertising can take any form, including, for examples GIFs available on the Internet for the users to use (IAB Europe 2021a, b, p. 5).

It is important to note that all the advertising types briefly described above are not mutually exclusive, on the contrary, often they overlap. For example, social media advertising can take the form of targeted display advertising, thereby combining elements of three different advertising modalities in a single one.

With respect to forms of advertising not originally designed by online advertising service providers, we consider that the primary types are: giveaway marketing, influencer marketing, and electronic word-of-mouth (e-WOM) (Dwivedi et al. n.d.,

p. 3) or user-generated content. More recently, dark patterns have also emerged within the advertising landscape, representing a new form of illicit advertising.

Giveaway marketing is based on promotional contests in which a product or service is offered as a gift [free of charge (Syahputra et al. 2022, p. 527)] to users who choose to participate in the contest under specific terms and conditions. Giveaways are conducted exclusively in the digital environment, typically on social media platforms, and they are meant to generate a higher user involvement (Choudhary et al. 2024, p. 434) and to increase the overall engagement of the users with the brand. Giveaways also lead to brand loyalty (Choudhary et al. 2024, p. 434). Generally, the rules for participating in a giveaway require users to engage in activities specific to social media, which promote the goods, services, or overall brand organizing the giveaway. Giveaways may be organized directly by brands or by third parties, such as influencers or other type of endorsers. The actions that are commonly required to be performed by the users include sharing the brand's post(s), following the brand's social media page(s), and/or commenting on the post while eventually tagging additional friends. For transparency, fairness and consumer protection, a giveaway must include clear rules outlining the conditions for participation and, equally important, the time, criteria and method for selecting and announcing the winner(s). A software program is typically used to select the winner, who is then announced through the channels specified in the giveaway's official rules (generally via social media posts). Giveaways are also addressed in Article B6 of the ICC Code 2024, which provides guidelines on how to conduct/organize them.

Influencer marketing is defined as 'marketing communications in which influencers promote a brand's offerings on their own social media pages' (Belanche et al. 2021, p. 2); therefore, it is carried out through influencers, primarily via social media platforms. Influencers are addressed in the ICC Code 2024, where they are defined as 'individuals, organisations, or machine-created or controlled representations, i.e., avatars, who primarily use social media platforms to communicate and interact with their audiences, including followers. In that context, they may shape audience attitudes for commercial purposes based on brand partnerships. However, they can also act independently of such arrangements, for instance, when promoting their own brands and products. In such cases, they can be considered marketers. Individuals who meet this definition are covered by it regardless of the designation they use, such as creator or brand ambassador. The definition also includes those with a relatively small number of followers'. We consider this definition to be one of the most comprehensive currently available, as it fully captures the role of influencers within marketing. The fundamental characteristics of an influencer are the existence of a community of followers on social media and the authenticity (Ebben and Bull 2023, pp. 2–3). This authenticity differentiates influencers from traditional celebrities, who often lack the same level of genuine engagement. Influencers build, in theory, a personal bond with their community, enabling them to exert real influence over their audience. However, as an influencer's follower base grows, it becomes increasingly difficult to maintain a strong, individualized connection with all followers and to ensure alignment between the influencer's content and the audience's expectations. Nevertheless, at such a scale, any content posted is seen by a large number of individuals, thereby significantly contributing to brand awareness and the dissemination of commercial messages across broad audiences.

Electronic word-of-mouth (e-WOM) conducted by the Internet users takes various forms, including reposts, comments, likes, reviews, and ratings on social media platforms, as well as on specialized review platforms or search engines. For example, Google's review and rating system contributes significantly to the promotion and visibility of certain businesses.

Another form of online advertising is based on the pages that brands maintain on social media platforms, through regular posts consisting of images or videos. A brand's constant presence online inevitably enhances its brand awareness and contributes to the promotion of the goods and/or services it offers. However, this form of promotion is more accurately characterized as organic advertising.

Although all of these practices represent in our view different forms of online advertising, most are not directly regulated under Romanian law. Instead, they are indirectly addressed through the consumer protection legal framework and applicable data protection regulations. Importantly, not all general advertising regulations extend to every type of advertising. As will be demonstrated, certain advertising laws regulate only advertising conducted by traders, excluding cases where advertising is carried out by users who are not influencers. In such instances, advertising can be either intentional or unintentional, paid or unpaid, although, as we have previously noted, most marketing definitions consider advertising to involve a paid component.

Finally, we arrive at dark patterns, a highly debated and increasingly concept, not only in Europe, but also in jurisdictions such as the United States.[3] India,[4] and Australia.[5] Although dark patterns have existed for some time, they have recently attracted heightened attention and have simultaneously evolved into more diverse forms. We discuss them as they also occur in advertising (OECD 2022, p. 9).

In the EU, dark patterns are defined as ‚tricks used in websites and apps that make you do things that you didn't mean to, like buying or signing up for something' (European Parliamentary Research Service 2025). Alongside intelligent advertising (or AI-powered advertising), dark patterns represent some of the latest and most complex legal topics in the field of advertising. While intelligent advertising is generally regarded as lawful, dark patterns are consistently classified from the very beginning as illicit practices. They are deemed unfair commercial practices

---

[3] See, for example, Federal Trade Commission, Bureau of Consumer Protection, Bringing Dark Patterns to Light. Staff Report, September 2022. Available at: https://www.ftc.gov/system/files/ftc_gov/pdf/P214800+Dark+Patterns+Report+9.14.2022+-+FINAL.pdf.

[4] See, for example, Advertising Standards Council of India (ASCI), Dark patterns: The new threat to consumer protection. Discussion document, November 2022. Available at: https://www.ascionline.in/wp-content/uploads/2022/11/dark-patterns.pdf.

[5] See, for example, Baumeister J, Park J-Y, Cunningham A, von Itzstein S, Gwilt I, Davis A and Walsh J, Patterns in the Dark: Deceptive Practices in Online Interactions. Landscape Assessment—A report to the Data Standards Chair. Adelaide, Australian Research Centre for Interactive and Virtual Environments, University of South Australia, 2024. Available at: https://dsb.gov.au/sites/dsb.gov.au/files/2024-11/report-patterns-in-the-dark.pdf.

under consumer protection law and are widely considered unethical due to their manipulative nature (Mildner et al. 2023a, b, p. 1); however, we will postpone the discussion of the legal framework applicable to dark patterns and will first focus on explaining what dark patterns are and providing examples to clarify their nature and content.

Dark patterns take on various forms and manifestations within both marketing and legal literature. In theory, they are often described as design techniques embedded in user interfaces (Mildner et al. 2023a, b, p. 1) of a platform or website which negatively and purposefully influence the behavior and decision-making of the consumer, in a manner against their normal will (and even against their own private interests).

Beyond the marketing sphere, a clear example of a dark pattern is the cookie consent banner that appears on websites (Mildner et al. 2023a, b, p. 1). These banners are often designed in a way that baits (Burkell and Kelly 2024) the data subject toward clicking 'accept', typically through visual techniques such as a larger, more prominently colored 'accept' button, contrasted with a less visible 'reject' option (and also, the accept button is the first one displayed on the page, while the reject option is always the second). In addition, if the user clicks on 'reject,' a list of options may appear that must be manually deselected, thereby increasing the effort required from the consumer and further discouraging rejection. This unethical design seeks to persuade, distract, or frustrate the user into making the choice intended by the deployer of the dark pattern, specifically to click on the 'accept' button. Naturally, the outcomes of such manipulation are unfavorable to the consumer, but advantageous to the controller or designer responsible for implementing the dark pattern. It is widely acknowledged that dark patterns are present throughout the online advertising ecosystem, appearing in environments ranging from social media platforms to online games. In the field of advertising, there are similar practices; moreover, the dark patterns associated with cookie consent mechanisms are as well more than relevant to online advertising, as personalized advertising usually relies on data collected through cookies. Examples of dark patterns in advertising include the use of ,speculative technologies targeting users with specific advertisements using public displays' (Mildner et al. 2023a, b, p. 2). Other examples of dark patterns with a high impact on online advertising are the practices of preventing users from closing or even deleting their social media accounts (Kelly and Rubin 2024), so their attention on social media to be continuously commercialised.

In our opinion, it can be argued that even the concept of TikTok embodies elements of a dark pattern by default and by design, as its design subtly encourages users to continue scrolling and 'consume' content and embedded advertisements without full awareness, having at the same time a negative impact on their attention (Chen et al. 2022, pp. 1–2); at the same time, infinite scrolling, which sits at the core of TikTok, is also deemed to be a dark pattern itself (Cara 2019, p. 108). Dark patterns may also include practices such as hard to cancel, forced enrollment (Mildner et al. 2023a, b), hidden costs, 'pay to skip' models, 'play by appointment' strategies, pre-delivered content, social pyramid schemes, bait-and-switch tactics, hidden legalese stipulations, forced actions, mandatory registrations, immortal accounts, information milking, perpetual data retention ('we never forget'), captive audiences, attention grabbers, restricted functionality, interruptions, obfuscation, forced continuity, shaming, disguised advertisements, 'sneak into basket' techniques (Ukgoda 2024, p. 104), urgency (e.g. countdown timer indicating the expiry of a deal) (Organisation for Economic Co-operation and Development (OECD) 2022, p. 8) Just as advertising, one of the goals of advertising is getting consumers to purchase (more or for the very first time) (Organisation for Economic Co-operation and Development (OECD) 2022, p. 8).

4 Romanian Legal Framework Applicable to Online Advertising

As shown in the previous sections of this chapter, online advertising takes a wide variety of forms, some of which were not initially intended for advertising purposes. With the direct support of human creativity, pre-existing tools on online platforms have been adapted and exploited for promotional activities, transforming them into advertising practices. Given this diversity and the innovative nature of advertising methods, it is challenging for the law to anticipate and regulate all types in a detailed manner. Furthermore, due to the intrinsic differences among these practices, a single regulatory instrument cannot comprehensively encompass the entire voluminous and ever-changing spectrum of online advertising.

In Romania, online advertising is regulated by a mosaic of general and sector-specific laws. However, as previously explained, none of these legal instruments comprehensively regulate the full scope of modern online advertising, particularly in areas involving advertising algorithms (e.g., for real-time bidding advertising), influencer marketing, and behavioral profiling. Nevertheless, we will next outline the Romanian general legal frameworks and briefly examine some of the specific regulations applicable to online advertising. In the next chapter, to provide a comprehensive overview of the legal provisions applicable to online advertising in Romania, we will also briefly examine the relevant European Union legal framework, with particular emphasis on regulations that explicitly address online advertising activities.

4.1 Romanian General Framework for Advertising Regulation

The most general and principal Romanian legal instrument which regulates advertising nationally is Law No. 148/2000 on Advertising. This law applies to all forms of advertising, regardless of its type/means, as it does not establish a specific scope, following the Latin maxim *ubi lex non distinguit, nec nos distinguere debemus*. However, the law has been substantially amended in time, particularly following the adoption of sector-specific advertising legislation. Law No. 148/2000 primarily regulates advertising from a consumer protection perspective, seeking to establish a framework that safeguards consumer interests.

The beforementioned law sets forth general principles applicable to all advertising content and communications. Pursuant to Article 5, advertising is required to be decent and accurate and to be designed in a spirit of social responsibility. This provision is complemented by Article 20, which details the procedures for verifying and enforcing the accuracy of advertising content. Under Article 20, the advertiser bears the burden of proof in respect of the accuracy of the information contained in the advertisement, and the competent authority is entitled to require the submission of documentary evidence substantiating the claims. Failure to provide the requested documentation within 7 days, or the submission of insufficient evidence, may lead to a finding that the advertisement is inaccurate, in which case the advertiser may incur administrative liability and be subject to fines.

Article 6 enumerates the principal general prohibitions applicable to advertising content and practices. Under this provision, advertising is prohibited if it makes use of subliminal techniques; undermines respect for human dignity or public morals; involves discrimination based on race, sex, language, origin, ethnic identity, or nationality; prejudices religious or political beliefs; harms the image, honor, dignity, or private life of individuals; exploits superstition, naivety, or fear; endangers personal safety or incites violence; encourages behavior that harms the environment; or promotes products or services that are contrary to the law.

Chapter III of Romanian Law No. 148/2000 establishes a set of advertising restrictions that primarily target the products and services being advertised, with particular emphasis on tobacco and alcohol products. Although most restrictions are not directed exclusively at advertising activities, several provisions may nonetheless affect online advertising practices. For instance, under Article 13, it is prohibited to advertise tobacco and alcohol products in ways that suggest therapeutic, stimulative, or sedative effects; imply that these products can resolve personal or private problems; portray abstinence negatively; emphasize the alcohol content to encourage consumption; or link alcohol consumption to driving. Article 13 also imposes compelled commercial speech obligations on tobacco advertisements, a mechanism encountered in other jurisdictions, typically justified by public health policy objectives. Interpreting Article 13, which restricts advertising methods for alcoholic beverages, it can be concluded that such beverages cannot be promoted through online advertising. In addition, the advertising of narcotic and psychotropic substances is absolutely prohibited, regardless of the medium, including online environments. As regards medicinal products, online advertising is strictly limited to over-the-counter (OTC) medicines and is subject to the prior approval of the advertising content by the Romanian National Agency for Medicines and Medical Devices.

Another general legislative instrument relevant to advertising in Romania is Law No. 185/2013 on the placement and authorization of advertising media. However, this law primarily regulates physical advertising media, and its scope cannot be easily extended to online advertising, despite Article 2 stating that it applies to 'economic advertising' without any specific distinctions or additional mentions.

Nevertheless, some of its provisions could arguably be applied to advertising disseminated online.

Under Romanian law, explicit advertising for tobacco products, electronic cigarettes, and nicotine pouches is strictly prohibited on television and radio, as well as on public transport tickets. Moreover, the advertising of alcohol products is prohibited when conducted through editorial means (e.g., newspapers and magazines) and on public transport tickets. In addition, the advertising of tobacco, electronic cigarettes, and alcohol is prohibited, by any means, within educational and medical institutions or in their immediate vicinity. Although Law No. 185/2013 was not originally intended to regulate digital platforms, its broad definitions may nonetheless allow for a technical application to online advertising formats, such as banner advertising, influencer marketing, and native advertising. In practice, the enforcement of these provisions in relation to digital platforms has been limited, owing to jurisdictional ambiguities, an insufficiently delineated scope of application, and the absence of modernised enforcement mechanisms.

The final general legislative instrument applicable to all forms of advertising, including online advertising, is Law No. 158/2008 (republished) on Misleading and Comparative Advertising, implementing Directive 2006/114/EC on misleading and comparative advertising. As stated in the Directive, the primary objective of the law transposing it is to protect traders against misleading advertising and to lay down the conditions under which comparative advertising is permitted. The law also clarifies that commercial audiovisual communications qualify as advertising; however, it expressly provides that they fall outside its scope and are instead governed by the Romanian Audiovisual Law, namely Law No. 504/2002. Although the law does not explicitly define commercial audiovisual communications as advertising, the very need to exclude them from its scope implies that, under normal circumstances, they would be considered a form of advertising subject to the general rules established by Law No. 158/2008.

Law No. 158/2008 essentially prohibits all forms of misleading advertising, which are assessed by reference to all elements of the advertisement, in particular the characteristics of the goods or services (such as availability, nature, functionality, origin, and expected results), the price and the method of its calculation, as well as the nature and rights of the advertiser, including identity, qualifications, and intellectual property. Under the same law, comparative advertising is permitted only if it meets cumulative conditions: (i) it must not be misleading; (ii) it must compare goods or services serving the same needs or purposes; (iii) it must objectively compare relevant, verifiable, and representative characteristics, including price; and (iv) it must not discredit or denigrate competitors or their distinctive signs. Furthermore and finally, it must not unfairly exploit the reputation of a competitor, present imitations of protected products, or create confusion between traders, their trademarks, or their goods and services.

4.2 *Sectoral Romanian Legislation Applicable to Online Advertising*

As discussed earlier, the Romanian legal framework governing online advertising encompasses both general advertising provisions and rules laid down in sector-specific legislation. The last category of laws focuses on specific fields; however, since these fields are connected to online advertising, the respective legal instruments also contain provisions relevant to advertising. The following section will focus only on those laws that contain a more substantial set of provisions on online advertising and that significantly contribute to the applicable legal framework.

4.2.1 Law No. 365/2002 on Electronic Commerce

Romanian Law No. 365/2002 on Electronic Commerce transposes the EU's eCommerce Directive (Directive 2000/31/EC of the European Parliament and of the Council of 8 June 2000) and governs commercial communications transmitted by electronic means. Article 5 imposes disclosure obligations on service providers, requiring certain information to be made available to consumers. In our view, this obligation extends to advertisers' websites and social media pages, insofar as these platforms are used to offer services and simultaneously serve an advertising function, enhancing brand visibility and awareness.

Article 6 prohibits unsolicited commercial communications via electronic mail unless prior consent has been obtained, thus aligning Romanian law with the opt-in standard. Although traditionally associated with emails, the concept of 'electronic mail', as defined in Law No. 506/2004, encompasses all electronic messaging services, including Instagram chat, Facebook Messenger, and WhatsApp. Consequently, any unsolicited advertising transmitted via these messaging services is subject to the anti-spam regime.

Additionally, Article 6 requires that all commercial communications constituting information society services be clearly identifiable as such, with the advertiser's identity transparently disclosed. This effectively establishes a general disclosure obligation applicable to all forms of online advertising, including influencer marketing. Nonetheless, the law does not specifically regulate newer forms of advertising, such as influencer marketing or algorithmically personalised advertisements, which, although disseminated via information society services, do not qualify as commercial communications by electronic mail and therefore fall outside the scope of these specific provisions.

4.2.2 Law No. 506/2004 on Personal Data and Privacy in the Electronic Communications Sector

Romanian Law no. 506/2004 sets conditions to guarantee individuals the right to private life and the lawful processing of personal data within the electronic communications sector. Transposing the ePrivacy Directive (Directive 2002/58/EC of the European Parliament and of the Council of 12 July 2002), it complements the GDPR (Regulation (EU) 2016/679 of the European Parliament and of the Council of 27 April 2016) in areas such as the use of cookies, tracking technologies, and device fingerprinting, provisions particularly relevant in the context of behavioural (targeted) advertising, which relies on personal data collected through cookies.

Article 4(5) of Law no. 506/2004 establishes the requirement of prior informed consent for the storage of, or access to, information (cookies) on users' devices. Valid consent must be based on clear, complete, and accessible information, specifying the purposes of data processing. Moreover, users must be provided with the means to refuse access by third parties and the ability to delete stored data. By interpreting Article 4(6), these requirements extend to online advertising practices based on data collected via cookies, unless the user has explicitly requested to receive targeted advertisements, a highly improbable scenario in practice.

Additionally, Article 12 of Law no. 506/2004 prohibits unsolicited commercial communications via automated means, including electronic mail, unless the user has given prior explicit consent. An exception exists where the user's email address was obtained in the context of a sale; in such cases, further use for direct marketing is permitted provided that an accessible and straightforward opt-out mechanism is available, such as the commonly used 'unsubscribe' link included in commercial emails.

These obligations are reinforced by the GDPR, which, as an EU regulation, is directly applicable in Romania without requiring transposition into national law, pursuant to the Treaty on the Functioning of the European Union. The Romanian Data Protection Authority (ANSPDCP) has issued several decisions regarding the improper use of cookies, underscoring that passive behaviours such as scrolling or inactivity do not constitute valid consent. Notably, a fine was imposed on SUDREZIDENȚIAL Broker S.R.L. for unlawfully collecting personal data through cookies without obtaining user consent.[6] ANSPDCP has also issued fines for the use of non-compliant cookie banners (such as the absence of a 'reject' option), the deployment of third-party analytics tools without obtaining proper consent, and the failure to provide clear and accessible privacy information regarding advertising technologies.

[6] National Supervisory Authority for Personal Data Processing (2022) *A new sanction for the infringement of the GDPR*. Press release, 22 December 2022. https://www.dataprotection.ro/?page=Comunicat_Presa_22_12_2022.

4.2.3 Audiovisual Law No. 504/2002

Romanian Law No. 504/2022 governs both traditional television services and on-demand audiovisual content. At the intersection of online advertising and the Audiovisual Law, short video formats such as Instagram Reels and YouTube Shorts emerge as particularly relevant. Evidence of the law's applicability in the digital environment is reflected in the investigations and sanctions imposed by the Romanian National Audiovisual Council (CNA).

According to Article 1 of the Audiovisual Law, online platforms such as Instagram, Facebook, and YouTube qualify as 'video-sharing platform services' as they provide users with access to user-generated videos or programs without holding editorial responsibility over the content, while content organization is managed by the platform provider through automatic means, particularly algorithms. The sequence in which users view content is thus determined by the platform's algorithmic curation.

In this context, the Audiovisual Law is clearly applicable to online advertising when the content qualifies as 'audiovisual commercial communication', defined as images, with or without sound, intended to promote, directly or indirectly, the goods, services, or image of a natural or legal person engaged in economic activity, where such images accompany or are included in a program or user-generated video in exchange for payment or similar consideration, or for purposes of self-promotion. However, the law's applicability is conditioned on the content being disseminated through a video-sharing platform.

The law imposes specific obligations on audiovisual commercial communications, including transparency requirements for sponsorships, product placement regulations, and prohibitions on certain types of content. While platforms like YouTube fall under the scope of the Audiovisual Law in specific contexts, most user-generated content and influencer marketing materials on social media remain outside its reach unless the platform qualifies as a video-sharing platform service.

Clear evidence of the law's direct applicability to online audiovisual advertising can be seen in the enforcement actions undertaken by the National Audiovisual Council, including the removal of content from platforms such as TikTok and Facebook in 2025.[7]

[7] National Audiovisual Council (2025) *Press release: CNA public meeting of 10 March 2025.* Sanctions—decisions ordering the removal of certain audiovisual materials from TikTok and Facebook. Press release, 10 March 2025. https://www.cna.ro/a-comunicat-de-presa-sedinta-publica-a-cna-din-10032025-qoa7mtxhx3r5ol1lpv4f5m95/.

4.2.4 Law No. 363/2007 on Combating Unfair Commercial Practices in the Relationship Between Traders and Consumers and Harmonizing Regulations with European Consumer Protection Legislation

Romanian Law No. 363/2007 transposes Directive 2005/29/EC on unfair commercial practices. The law provides a general framework for protecting consumers against misleading and aggressive practices in commercial relationships, aiming to ensure a high level of consumer protection and the proper functioning of the internal market.

In the context of online advertising, the law is particularly relevant as it prohibits any practice that is likely to materially distort the economic behavior of the average consumer. This includes misleading actions and omissions, aggressive commercial practices, and the failure to clearly disclose the commercial intent behind marketing communications.

Given the law's broad applicability, it captures a wide array of online marketing strategies, including influencer marketing, native advertising, and targeted advertising, requiring transparency and honesty in all consumer-facing communications. In two previous articles, we have shown that on social media there are several practices, with an advertising purposes, that can be qualified as unfair commercial practices either towards the consumers (in the B2C relation between brands and consumers), either towards the other competitors (in the B2B relations). Finally, dark patterns are also considered to fall within the scope of unfair commercial practices and are therefore prohibited under the regulatory framework established by Law No. 363/2007.

4.2.5 Government Ordinance No. 99/2000 (Republished) on the Marketing of Products and Market Services

Last but not least, Romanian Government Ordinance No. 99/2000, in our view, comprehensively regulates giveaway marketing practices. In theory, under Articles 41, 42 and 43, it regulates advertising lotteries. Traditionally, as defined in the ordinance, an advertising lottery is ‚a promotional mechanism organized by a trader, in which participation is conditional on the purchase of goods or services, and winners are selected randomly, offering participants the chance to obtain prizes without additional payment beyond the transaction itself'. By analyzing this definition, it becomes evident that it is applicable to giveaway marketing, as the ordinance does not differentiate between online and traditional advertising environments, nor does it specify the medium in which the promotional mechanism must occur or the precise manner of participation and winner selection. The definition closely aligns with the structure of giveaway marketing: a promotional mechanism organized by a trader on social media platforms, offering users the opportunity to win prizes without any additional payment beyond completing certain required actions, such as commenting, following the brand, or reposting branded content.

What distinguishes Government Ordinance No. 99/2000 in relation to advertising lotteries is the requirement that the rules governing such lotteries be authenticated by a notary public prior to their commencement. This measure aims to protect participants by ensuring the integrity of the promotional mechanism: the rules cannot be altered once authenticated, thereby safeguarding participants against potential abuses by the trader and ensuring the fulfilment of the promised conditions. Notarization facilitates the verification of the rules' authenticity and prevents amendments from being made without public disclosure.

However, there are opinions suggesting that the requirement for notarial authentication is rooted in the traditional structure of advertising lotteries, where participation is typically contingent upon the purchase of a good or service. By contrast, social media giveaways generally do not require a financial transaction; rather, participation is based on completing actions specific to the platform, such as reposting, commenting, following a brand, or tagging friends.

We do not share this view. Consumer protection should remain paramount, irrespective of the medium or the form of consideration. It cannot be argued that social media actions lack economic relevance. If such actions held no value, traders would have no incentive to organize giveaway marketing, nor would it have evolved into a widely adopted marketing strategy among brands with an online presence. These actions directly contribute to brand visibility and consumer engagement, thus carrying clear economic significance. If the notarization requirement is not respected, the entire giveaway marketing initiative may be deemed invalid. Participants who suffer harm as a result may seek reparation for their damages under general principles of civil liability, enshrined in the Romanian Civil Code.

5 Short Overview and Resume of EU Regulation Applicable to Online Advertising

Romanian law, as briefly presented in the previous sections, is supplemented by EU's regulations and directives, with the former being directly applicable and the latter transposed into national legislation. It is important to highlight that, while Romanian legislation does not directly regulate specific types of online advertising, certain EU legal instruments do provide explicit regulatory frameworks in this regard.

5.1 GDPR and Personal Data Use in Online Advertising

Arguably, one of the most impactful EU's legal instrument shaping online advertising is the General Data Protection Regulation (hereinafter, ‚GDPR'), which is directly applicable in Romania, as in all the EU Member States. Online advertising, in particular behavioural/targeted advertising, typically involves the massiveprocessing of personal data, including, for example, past online acquisitions, IP addresses, geolocation information, browsing behavior (on search engines), and profiling based on user interactions.

Several fundamental GDPR principles have a notable impact on online advertising practices. While we will not explore this topic in depth (given the extensive body of scientific literature thoroughly examining the various facets of GDPR as it relates to online advertising, including works dedicated to specific issues), we will briefly highlight the relevance of the GDPR in the context of online advertising. Additionally, we will outline the primary legal considerations that interested parties should be fully aware of, which, naturally, can be further explored upon analysing the existing scholarly work on the same subject.

Under Article 6 of GDPR, a lawful basis for data processing is required, with consent being the predominant ground for ad targeting activities, unless a legitimate interest can be demonstrated. Thus, even data processing for advertising purposes requires a lawful basis before proceeding with the data processing. In the context of online advertising, consent (Vo Trung 2025) and legitimate interest (IAB Europe 2021a, b, p. 5; Galli et al. 2022) are generally the most commonly invoked legal grounds. However, we will not delve into a discussion of these choices or evaluate their actual legal compliance; it is worth noting, though, that the use of legitimate interest as a basis for online advertising has sparked considerable debate and raised significant questions regarding its lawfulness.

Transparency obligations, set out in Articles 13 and 14 of the GDPR, require that users be provided with clear, accessible information regarding the purposes and methods of data collection and processing. Consequently, whenever a data subject's personal data is processed for online advertising purposes, the data subject must be thoroughly informed about the entire data processing policy, which should include legal grounds for processing, purposes, methods, storage of data information, the rights of the data subject under the GDPR etc.

Article 22 governs profiling and automated decision-making, imposing that users be informed when significant decisions are made based solely on automated processing of their data. Additionally, the principles of data minimization, a core principle (Access Now 2021, p. 4), and purpose limitation demand that data processing for targeting purposes remain proportionate, necessary, and specifically justified in relation to the intended advertising objectives. There is considerable debate regarding the actual effectiveness of these principles, particularly given the difficulty of defining a minimum set of data necessary for personalisation. It is also debatable whether the collection and processing of ever larger volumes of data would not, in practice, enhance user profiling and improve the targeting of advertisements. From this perspective, the principles of data minimisation and necessity risk losing their practical relevance, as it becomes increasingly difficult to argue that there can be 'too much' data when the objective is to construct detailed user profiles for targeted advertising.

5.2 EU Regulation on Fairness and Transparency in Online Platforms (2019/1150)

Although at first glance Regulation (EU) 2019/1150 may not appear to be directly related to online advertising, a closer look at its scope, as outlined in Article 1, and the definitions provided in Article 2, makes it clear that the regulation applies to online intermediation services and online search engines, such as Meta and Google, major online advertising service providers. Consequently, the rules set forth in this regulation inevitably extend to online advertising activities.

Firstly, with regard to terms and conditions, Article 3 of the Regulation imposes several requirements, including that they be drafted in clear and intelligible language, made available at the pre-contractual stage, and contain provisions regarding the ownership and control of business users' intellectual property rights. Given that business users engage in online advertising and maintain a presence on social media platforms, where online advertising activities occur, and considering that these platforms operate under terms and conditions, it follows that the terms and conditions governing the provision of online services must comply as well with the requirements set out in the Regulation, in particular in Article 3.

Secondly, one of the most significant provisions of the Regulation in the context of online advertising concerns ranking. Article 5 imposes obligations on providers of online intermediation services to clearly outline in their terms and conditions the main parameters that determine ranking, as well as the reasons for the relative importance of these parameters compared to others. This requirement is particularly relevant for online advertising conducted through search results or recommendation systems. Notably, Article 5(3) directly addresses advertising services, highlighting the paid nature of ranking in search engine results: 'Where the main parameters include the possibility to influence ranking through any direct or indirect remuneration paid by business users or corporate website users to the respective provider, that provider shall also set out a description of those possibilities and the effects of such remuneration on ranking in accordance with the requirements set out in paragraphs 1 and 2'.

Finally, equally important in the context of online advertising is Article 7, which addresses the issue of differentiated treatment. It requires providers of online intermediation services to include in their terms and conditions a description of any differentiated treatment given to goods or services offered to consumers, whether by the provider itself or by business users controlled by the provider, compared to other business users. This description must reference the main economic, commercial, or legal reasons behind such differentiated treatment. This provision is particularly relevant in light of criticisms directed at companies like Meta, which has been accused of favouring large advertisers. Allegedly, major companies face less scrutiny regarding ad compliance with Meta's policies, experiencing fewer rejections and quicker resolutions, whereas smaller advertisers often endure ad rejections, prolonged review processes, and more complex procedures to contest these decisions.

5.3 Digital Services Act (DSA) and Digital Markets Act (DMA)

The DSA and DMA have been the focus of extensive online discussions and numerous scientific and legal articles. They are also the subject of book chapters and comprehensive research papers. Therefore, we will merely review the relevant obligations in the context of online advertising, which are equally applicable in Romania.

5.3.1 DSA and Online Advertising

According to its preamble, Regulation (EU) 2022/2065 (hereinafter, ,DSA') aims to create a safer and more transparent online environment, and it includes important rules for online advertising, especially for platforms engaging in ad services. The DSA differentiates between very large online platforms (VLOPs) and other platforms by imposing additional, higher-standard obligations specifically on VLOPs. Thus, the general obligations apply to all platforms, while the additional and more restrictive requirements are reserved exclusively for VLOPs.

One of the most important sets of obligations, applicable to all the online platforms, concerns transparency requirements imposed on online advertising providers, which obliges platforms to ensure that the users are clearly informed when they are being presented with an advertisement. Being compliant with the transparency obligations, includes clear labeling, disclosure of the advertiser and disclosure of targeting criteria.

When it comes to VLOPs, such as Facebook, Google, Instagram, YouTube, and TikTok, the number and complexity of obligations are significantly increased, as they are subject to additional and substantial requirements involving not only legal, but also considerable technical efforts. VLOPs are required to maintain a publicly accessible repository of advertisements, often referred to as an ad library, allowing the public to access data related to the performance and transparency of ads. Furthermore, VLOPs must conduct risk assessments of their advertising systems, with particular focus on systemic risks such as political manipulation or the spread of disinformation through advertisements. In addition, VLOPs are obliged to implement user empowerment measures, providing users with the ability to adjust their ad targeting preferences or to opt out of ads based on profiling.

One last obligation imposed for VLOPs is to explain how their recommendation systems work, particularly when those systems are used to serve targeted advertisements. Users must have access to information about the key parameters of the algorithm and the option to opt for a non-personalized experience; as noticed lately, the last option might imply additional costs for the users.

5.3.2 Digital Markets Act and Online Advertising

Regulation (EU) 2022/1925 (hereinafter, 'DMA'), targets gatekeepers, the large online platforms that act as important gateways for business users to reach consumers, and addresses unfair practices in digital markets, including online advertising. Under the DMA, gatekeepers that provide advertising services, such as Google and Meta, must provide advertisers and publishers with information about the price paid for each ad and the fees deducted for their services.

Similarly to DSA, DMA also introduces obligations of transparency, this time in relation to the performance metrics of advertisements, in order to ensure the correction of information asymmetry because until now, advertisers often had no clear insight into how their ads performed or how auction mechanisms worked. Gatekeepers are prohibited to conduct any self-preferencing activities (promoting themselves by virtue of their power to control the promotion channels), which means they are not allowed to favour their own advertising services or businesses in rankings.

Of paramount importance in the context of online advertising, particularly behavioral or targeted advertising, is the restriction placed on gatekeepersto refrain from combining personal data from different sources without the explicit consent of the data subject (the user). This limitation significantly affects their ability to develop highly details user profiles for ad customization/targeting. Previously, the common practice was to collect data from various sources (multiple third parties) and websites to build highly accurate profiles, thereby maximizing the personalization and effectiveness of advertisements.

5.4 Intelligent Advertising Under the EU AI Act

The AI Act is particularly relevant to online advertising given the emergence of a new form of advertising that integrates artificial intelligence -intelligent advertising. In online advertising, AI systems can be employed for user targeting, content personalization, dynamic pricing, content generation, marketing strategy development, and predictive analytics for ad placement.

The AI Act, the EU's pioneering regulation on AI systems and one of the first of its kind globally, is fully applicable to intelligent advertising. AI Act classifies AI systems into categories based on their associated risk levels, with specific obligations imposed for each category. In this context, we will briefly outline the relevant obligations.

The two primary categories are high-risk and limited-risk AI systems. Additionally, the AI Act defines a category of prohibited AI systems, encompassing those that are entirely banned. High-risk and limited-risk systems, by contrast, are permitted but must comply with specific regulatory requirements depending on their classification.High-risk systems include AI that significantly affects people's choices or behaviors in sensitive areas, while limited-risk systems include AI systems that interact with users (*e.g.*, chatbots) and require transparency obligations.

When it comes to online advertising, AI used for profiling and targeting users with ads may fall into either limited or high risk AI systems. As already mentioned, limited-risk systems mainly require transparency, more specifically for the user to know they are interacting with an AI system. The same system might be qualified as high-risk if the AI system uses advanced profiling techniques, that could manipulate consumer behavior in a significant way, particularly if it affects vulnerable consumers.The transparency obligations includes, among others, clear labeling when content is AI-generated or AI-optimized, notification of obligations when profiling or targeting is based on AI decisions.

5.4.1 Relevant Prohibited AI Practices Under AI Act[8]

In February 2025, the European Commission issued guidelines regarding prohibited AI practices under Article 5 of the AI Act (European Commission 2025), which have direct relevance for AI-powered online advertising. The first and foremost prohibition applicable to intelligent advertising is the one enshrined in Article 5 (1) (a), which bans all the AI systems deploying:

> subliminal techniques beyond a person's consciousness or purposefully manipulative or deceptive techniques, with the objective, or the effect of materially distorting the behaviour of a person or a group of persons by appreciably impairing their ability to make an informed decision, thereby causing them to take a decision that they would not have otherwise taken in a manner that causes or is reasonably likely to cause that person, another person or group of persons significant harm

More specifically, in AI-powered advertising cannot be used subliminal techniques and neither techniques that are manipulative or deceptive on-purpose and which eventually lead to affecting negatively the consumer decisions. For example, if an advertiser places online advertisements that rely on AI systems to subtly manipulate users' emotions or unconscious biases through personalised yet imperceptible adjustments, such AI systems, together with the corresponding advertisements, should fall within the scope of the prohibitions established by the AI Act.

The second prohibition relevant when it comes to intelligent advertising is the one enshrined in Article 5 (1) (b), which bans the AI systems:

> that exploit any of the vulnerabilities of a natural person or a specific group of persons due to their age, disability or a specific social or economic situation, with the objective, or the effect, of materially distorting the behaviour of that person or a person belonging to that group in a manner that causes or is reasonably likely to cause that person or another person significant harm

---

[8] Regulation (EU) 2024/1689 of the European Parliament and of the Council of 13 June 2024 laying down harmonised rules on artificial intelligence (Artificial Intelligence Act) and amending certain Union legislative acts.

In its guidelines from February 2025, the European Commission even exemplified how this prohibition is directly applicable in the field of advertising: an AI-predictive algorithm can be used to target with advertisements for predatory financial products people who live in low-income post-codes and are in a difficult financial situation, thus exploiting their susceptibility to such advertisements because of possible despair and causing them significant financial harm.[9]

Finally, less likely applicable, but still potentially relevant is the prohibition enshrined in Article 5 (1) (c) which refers to social scoring. Based on its provisions, any AI system that ranks or scores individuals based on personal characteristics for advertising advantages (*e.g.*, offering different ad experiences based on social status) should be banned.

6 Conclusions

Businesses should adapt to the new environment where consumers spend an extensive amount of time online because that is where their attention span is. Nowadays, it is uncommon to find a company without a virtual presence, as this could be equated with the gradual demise of a corporation due to a lack of visibility. OOH advertising (traditional, physical advertising) does not necessarily ensure brand awareness in an era characterised by speed, multitasking, and high mobility, as individuals are constantly on the move and tend to pay limited attention to their surroundings. Online advertising is the nucleus of modern business, which is why understanding its legal framework is crucial also from an economic perspective.

Due to unprecedented levels of digitalization and technological advancement, the graphic depicting the shift from traditional to online advertising takes the shape of a sharp slope in recent years. Regretfully, the legal landscape did not undergo a similar transformation; instead, its upward trajectory was more gradual, and its slope was more rounded. The degree of on-line advertising and the level of legal requirements fluctuate slightly as a result, and this is also true in Romania. However, does this not mean that current regulations that are generally relevant to advertising can't also be applied to online advertising, even though national legislators did not create legislation specifically for the new forms of online advertising. Simultaneously, EU lawmakers have taken important measures to update EU law to reflect the modern digital and technology environment, which tends to close some of the gaps in Romanian legislation.

Romanian advertising rules closely adhere to EU regulations, especially as some of them are derived from EU directives that have been transposed. Even though certain specific forms of online advertising are not covered by Romania's extensive

[9] European Commission (2025) Commission publishes the Guidelines on prohibited artificial intelligence (AI) practices, as defined by the AI Act. Policy and legislation publication, 04 February 2025. https://digital-strategy.ec.europa.eu/en/library/commission-publishes-guidelines-prohibited-artificial-intelligence-ai-practices-defined-ai-act.

advertising laws, the fundamental rules still apply. It should be noted that when specific forms of advertising are regulated, some general advertising regulations, not just for Romania, but for most countries that control advertising, become more specific. But fundamentally, the rules are still the same. The AI Act, which forbids the use of subliminal techniques in advertising and the ban on subliminal advertising, which is found in most jurisdictions (including Romania), are the best examples. Theoretically, subliminal advertising of any kind is illegal, even in the absence of the AI Act's ban.

Advertising should not be treated as the exclusive subject of an analysis of online advertising legislation. A comprehensive legal assessment must also consider the broader regulatory implications in adjacent fields with which advertising intersects, such as competition law, digital services and markets regulation, data protection, consumer protection, and data governance. The types of advertising that may not always be initially classified as advertising or may be the result of the advertisers' creativity, making them a combination of various online tools and the legal regimes applicable to those tools (such as the giveaway) can make a legal analysis of online advertising and its regulation more difficult at times. Finally, we consider that the rapid development of artificial intelligence, together with the continuous evolution of digital technologies, will give rise to new forms of advertising. Given Romania's EU membership and the Union's expanding digital regulatory agenda, future rules on online advertising are likely to be adopted primarily at EU level, with national law playing a diminishing role.

References

Access Now (2021) Data minimization: key to protecting privacy and reducing harm. Access Now, New York. https://www.accessnow.org/wp-content/uploads/2021/05/Data-Minimization-Report.pdf

Barfield W (2006) Commercial speech, intellectual property rights, and advertising using virtual images inserted in TV, film, and the real world. UCLA Entertain Law Rev 13(2): 154–185 https://escholarship.org/content/qt26b704xs/qt26b704xs_noSplash_489a8ac646c81e09a2b9eacf4182bcbf.pdf

Belanche D, Casaló Ariño LV, Flavián M, Ibáñez Sánchez S (2021) Understanding influencer marketing: the role of congruence between influencers, products and consumers. J Bus Res 132:186–195. https://doi.org/10.1016/j.jbusres.2021.03.067

Bhowmik K, Das D (n.d.) The emergence of immersive advertising. Infosys BPM. https://www.infosysbpm.com/offerings/functions/bpm-analytics/insights/documents/the-emergence-of-immersive-advertising.pdf

Bundeskartellamt (2018) Online advertising. Series of papers on "competition and consumer protection in the digital economy". Bundeskartellamt, Bonn. https://www.bundeskartellamt.de/SharedDocs/Publikation/EN/Schriftenreihe_Digitales_III.pdf

Burkell J, Kelly D (2024) Identifying and responding to privacy dark patterns. Final report to the Office of the Privacy Commissioner of Canada (contributions program 2023–2024). The University of Western Ontario, London. https://uwo.scholaris.ca/server/api/core/bitstreams/2a4e861c-72b0-4049-97ea-8b21b66a6fb5/content

Cara C (2019) Dark patterns in the media: a systematic review. Network Intelligence Stud VII(14):105–113. https://seaopenresearch.eu/Journals/articles/NIS_14_3.pdf
Chen Y, Li M, Guo F, Wang X-S (2022) The effect of short-form video addiction on users' attention. Behav Inform Technol. 42(16): 2893–2910. https://doi.org/10.1080/0144929X.2022.2151512
Choi H, Mela CF, Balseiro SR, Leary A (2020) Online display advertising markets: a literature review and future directions. Inf Syst Res 31(2):556–575. https://doi.org/10.1287/isre.2019.0902
Choudhary P, Banerjee SP, Singh A (2024) Assessing the effectiveness of social media context and giveaways in driving virtual engagement and positive customer perception in Verma S M et al. (eds.), Proceedings of the 9th International Conference on Synergizing Sustainable Technologies and Management Practices (STAMP 2024), Advances in Economics, Business and Management Research 321. https://doi.org/10.2991/978-94-6463-682-6_29
Deng L (2025) The impact of social media advertising on consumers' purchasing decisions. SHS Web Conf 215:01012. https://doi.org/10.1051/shsconf/202521501012
Devaux R (2023) Display advertising: How context matters? Working paper. https://papers.ssrn.com/sol3/papers.cfm?abstract_id=4352475
Dwivedi YK, Kapoor KK, Chen H (n.d.) Social media marketing and advertising. https://publications.aston.ac.uk/id/eprint/40400/1/Social_media_marketing.pdf
Ebben M, Bull E (2023) Constructing authenticity: Social media influencers and the shaping of online identity. In Online Identity—An Essential Guide. https://doi.org/10.5772/intechopen.1002607
European Commission (2004) Commission interpretative communication on certain aspects of the provisions on televised advertising in the "television without frontiers" directive (2004/C 102/02). Off J Eur Union C 102:2–11. https://eur-lex.europa.eu/legal-content/EN/TXT/HTML/?uri=CELEX:52004XC0428(01)
European Commission (2008) Commission Decision of 11 March 2008 declaring a concentration to be compatible with the common market and the functioning of the EEA Agreement (Case No COMP/M.4731—Google/DoubleClick). https://ec.europa.eu/competition/mergers/cases/decisions/m4731_20080311_20682_en.pdf
European Commission (4 February 2025) Guidelines on prohibited artificial intelligence (AI) practices as defined by the AI Act. Policy and legislation publication, Brussels, European Commission. https://digital-strategy.ec.europa.eu/en/library/commission-publishes-guidelines-prohibited-artificial-intelligence-ai-practices-defined-ai-act
European Parliament, European Parliamentary Research Service (EPRS) (2025) Regulating dark patterns in the EU: towards digital fairness. At a glance—digital issues in focus. European Parliament, Brussels. https://www.europarl.europa.eu/RegData/etudes/ATAG/2025/767191/EPRS_ATA(2025)767191_EN.pdf
Galli F, Lagioia F, Sartor G (2022) Consent to targeted advertising. Eur Bus Law Rev 33(4):485–512. https://doi.org/10.54648/eulr2022023
Ha L (2008) Online advertising research in advertising journals: a review. J Curr Iss Res Advertising 30(1):31–48
IAB Europe (2021a) GDPR guidance: legitimate interests assessments (LIA) for digital advertising. IAB Europe, Brussels. https://iabeurope.eu/wp-content/uploads/IAB-Europe-GDPR-Guidance-Legitimate-Interests-Assessments-LIA-for-Digital-Advertising-March-2021.pdf
IAB Europe (2021b) Guide to native advertising. IAB Europe, Brussels. https://iabeurope.eu/wp-content/uploads/IAB-Europe-Guide-to-Native-Advertising_2021-1.pdf
International Chamber of Commerce (2024) ICC advertising and marketing communications code, 11th edn. ICC, Paris. https://iccwbo.org/wp-content/uploads/sites/3/2024/09/ICC_2024_MarketingCode_2024.pdf
Jafarzadeh H, Aurum A, D'Ambra J, Ghapanchi AH (2015) A systematic review on search engine advertising. Pacific Asia. *J Assoc Inf Syst* 7(3):1–32. https://doi.org/10.17705/1pais.07301

Kelly D, Rubin V (2024) Identifying dark patterns in user account disabling interfaces: content analysis results. Soc Media Soc 10(1). https://doi.org/10.1177/20563051231224269

Kerr G, Richards J (2020) Redefining advertising in research and practice. Int J Advert. https://doi.org/10.1080/02650487.2020.1769407

Mildner T, Freye M, Savino G-L, Doyle PR, Cowan BR, Malaka R (2023a) Defending against the dark arts: recognising dark patterns in social media. In: Proceedings of the designing interactive systems conference (DIS '23). ACM, Pittsburgh. https://doi.org/10.1145/3563657.3595964

Mildner T, Savino G-L, Doyle PR, Cowan BR, Malaka R (2023b) About engaging and governing strategies: a thematic analysis of dark patterns in social networking services. In: Proceedings of the 2023 CHI conference on human factors in computing systems (CHI '23). ACM, Hamburg. https://doi.org/10.1145/3544548.3580695

Organisation for Economic Co-operation and Development (OECD) (2022) Dark commercial patterns: draft background report. OECD, Paris. https://one.oecd.org/document/DSTI/CP(2021)12/FINAL/en/pdf

Pachauri V, Bharti V (2018) Behavioral advertising: challenges and opportunities for online advertisers. Int J Acad Res Dev 3(2):1120–1124. https://www.researchgate.net/publication/377575639_Behavioral_advertising_Challenges_and_opportunities_for_online_advertisers

Pelet J-É, Ettis SA (2022) Social media advertising effectiveness: the role of perceived originality, liking, credibility, irritation, intrusiveness and ad destination. Int J Technol Hum Interact 18(1):1–19. https://doi.org/10.4018/IJTHI.2022010106

Priyanka, Siraj S (2024) The online behavioural advertising tripod: understanding the linkages between users' knowledge, privacy concerns and customers' attitude. Jordan J Bus Admin 20(2):229–243. https://doi.org/10.35516/jjba.v20i2.2009

Rathi PK (2021) Misleading advertisement and Indian laws: an overview. Turkish Online J Qualitative Inquiry 12(8):6779–6785. https://tojqi.net/index.php/journal/article/view/7485/5310

Rehman ur F, Javed F, Yusoff RM, Harun A, Khan A, Ismail F (2019) What is advertising? A short review of historical development. Acad Res Int 10(4):128–136

Sands S, Ferraro C, Demsar V, Cohen J, Gvirtz A (2024) Immersive advertising—a review and research agenda: potential effects of and considerations for AR, VR, and MR advertisements. J Advert Res 64(3):284–300. https://doi.org/10.2501/JAR-2024-018

Silkin L (2020) Virtual advertising: cutting through the regulation. Proposing a way forward. White paper. Lewis Silkin, London. https://d1xyy3yiuu5xkq.cloudfront.net/wp-content/uploads/2020/09/09092823/Supponor-Whitepaper-2020-FINAL.pdf

Syahputra R, Sutoyo, Ariska E (2022) Promotional practices with giveaway as attraction of consumer interest in Islamic economic perspective (case study of Instagram account @ Fatim_Kids15). Jurnal Ekonomi 11(3):527–531. http://ejournal.seaninstitute.or.id/index.php/EkonomiJurnal

Thakor SD (2019) Everything about display advertising. Int J Res All Subjects Multi Lang 7(3) https://www.raijmr.com/ijrsml/wp-content/uploads/2021/03/IJRSML_2018_vol07_issue_03_Eng_16.pdf

Tran MT (2024) Immersive marketing and advertising information systems. In: Metaverse Driven Intelligent Information Systems. Springer, Cham, pp 15–28. https://doi.org/10.1007/978-3-031-72418-3_2

Ukgoda H (2024) The dark side of social media: analysing dark pattern combinations and their impacts. Indonesian J Inf Education 8(2):101. https://doi.org/10.20961/ijie.v8i2.91666

Ungureanu A, Popescu D-L (2022) Online advertising – History evolution and challenges. *Revista Economica* *74*(3):121–130. https://doi.org/10.56043/reveco-01010110.56043/reveco-2022-0031

Vangelov N (2023) Advertising: in search of a definition. A critical review. In: Communication and Media of the 21st Century: Educational and Professional Challenges (Proceedings of the International Scientific Conference), pp 182–192. https://doi.org/10.60060/GRCW3600

Vo Trung H (2025) Consent to processing personal data in online behavioural advertising as per the GDPR and experience in Vietnam. Access Justice Eastern Europe 8(2):179–202. https://doi.org/10.33327/AJEE-18-8.2-a000101

The Application of the Undue Influence in the Matter of Liberalities Overinterpretation Versus Underinterpretation

Codrin Macovei

Abstract This chapter examines how contemporary analyses of dol theory are reflected in legal approaches to suggestion and captation in the Romanian law of wills and estates. Some theorists point to the risks of continuing to over-interpret the dol in the matter of liberalities. This equation risks oversimplifying matters, which could compromise the understanding of the ways in which the will of a testator or a donor can be tampered with. There is also a risk of overlooking the harm that may be suffered by those who are victims of undue influence. A more nuanced approach posits that vulnerability is a common human trait that cuts across social identities and experiences and must be correctly identified and protected.

1 The Regulation of the *dol* in Romanian Legislation

To be legally effective, the consent given for the conclusion of a legal act must be the result of an enlightened and free will. If one of the parties has not decided to conclude the act knowingly or has been subject to pressure, his consent, without being non-existent, is vitiated and the contract is annullable. One of the vices of consent is the dol, its legal regulation being found in the Romanian Civil Code (in force since 1.10.2011), in Art. 1214.

The word "dol" evokes the general idea of bad faith. It can be encountered at two times in the legal act: either on the date of its conclusion or on the date of its execution. This Article is concerned with the date of the conclusion of the legal act and not the fault in the performance of the obligations. We mean by "dol" in concluding the legal act any trick, cunning, cunning, deception, manoeuvre or workmanship used to induce a person into error to induce him to contract. This definition allows a relationship between dol and error to be seen. Thus, the dol does not achieve its purpose unless it creates an error. This is how consent is corrupted. Compared to the

C. Macovei (✉)
Faculty of Law, 'Alexandru Ioan Cuza' University of Iași, Iași, Romania
e-mail: mcodrin@uaic.ro

I. Maria Costea (ed.), *Legal Interpretation in Motion*, Ius Gentium: Comparative Perspectives on Law and Justice 144,
https://doi.org/10.1007/978-3-032-32948-6_13

penalty of error, the nullity that protects the party who has undergone the grievous man works is easier to obtain by judicial means because it is easier to prove: It materializes through external actions, while the error is a purely internal phenomenon of the person's intellect. Thus, we realize that the Romanian legislator proves to be more protective of the contractor who is the victim of a dol, than of the contractor who is in error. The latter was wrong spontaneously and must do it himself. The subject of undue influence has been deceived, which implies an agent of deception. We find in the face of undue influence the protohistory of a civil crime. Each time the constituent elements are fulfilled, the penalty is applicable (Nicolae 2018).

Art. 1214 paragraph (1) the Romanian Civil Code presents us with the constituent elements of the dol. We need to record the presence of manipulations, fraudulent manoeuvres. We can infer that the dol includes both a material element, a psychological element and an unjust element, an injustice.

The material element seems the easiest to identify. It is all about any observation of the manoeuvres of a charlatan, of a machine, of a staged, which manifests cunning. But even the simple lie, without being accompanied by external acts, can be a dol, without qualifying itself as an extortion. It is even admitted that reluctance, that is, deliberate silence concerning a circumstance which the other contractor would have had an interest in knowing, is a form of undue influence (Bigwood, 1996).

The psychological element presupposes the existence of the intentional element, which involves the intention to mislead the other side (Boroi & Anghelescu, 2021).

The unjust element implies the ethical judgment, that of morals. To explain better, this appreciation differentiates between *dolus malus* and *bonus dolus. Bonus is* the exaggeration of the merchant, the boastfulness of the seller. Do not allow for nullity. *Dolus malus* is a serious lie that exceeds the capacity of his scepticism *bonus pater familias. Dolus malus* justifies the action for nullity (Ciucă 2015).

The grievous works must come from the contractor or from the third party. The debt from a third party cannot be sufficient for the annulment of the act, unless it acts as the representative of the contractor or the party is an accomplice of the third party (Article 1214 paragraph (3), as referred to in Article 1215 paragraph (1) Civil Code). However, with an exceptional character, according to art. 1038 paragraph (2) the civil code may trigger the annulment of the will even if the grievous works were not committed by the beneficiary of the testamentary dispositions and were not known by him.

Grievous man works must be determined, not only by facilitating that leading to the conclusion of the contract. Thus, the dol must be the principal, as opposed to to the incident one, which affects only secondary aspects of the parties' understandings. Even without the incident undue influence, the party would still have contracted, although perhaps in better conditions. Only the principal lien justifies the cancellation of the contract, while the incidental dole can only motivate the granting of damages.

The penalty of undue influence is the relative nullity of the contract (Article 1251 Civil Code), which can be requested by the tricked contractor. It may also obtain damages if it has suffered damage which the cancellation has failed to repair (in its entirety). It also benefits from the option of maintaining the contract if it considers the option favourable to it, with only compensation, which can, for example, translate into a reduction in the price of the sale.

2 Extrapolation of the dol in the Matter of Liberalities

In Romanian law, according to Article 963 (1) of the Civil Code, the inheritance is due, in the order and according to the rules established, to the surviving spouse and relatives of the deceased, namely his descendants, ascenders and collateral, as the case may be. As is apparent from Article 984 paragraph (2) of the Civil Code, liberalities can be made only by donation or by the binding contained in the will. According to Article 986 of the Civil Code, the legate is the testamentary disposition by which the testator stipulates that, upon his death, one or more legatars acquire his entire patrimony, a fraction of it or certain specified goods. According to Article 985 of the Civil Code, donation is the contract by which, with the intention of gratifying, a party, called a donor, irrevocably disposes of an asset in favour of the other party, called a donee (Codrea, 2016).

Upon the death of a natural person, his patrimony is transferred to the legal heirs or testamentary heirs, according to Art. 955 Civil Code.

Being a legal act, in the sense that it includes the manifestation of the will of a person with the intention to produce legal effects, the will must meet, in order to be valid, the substantive conditions provided by law for any legal act (consent, capacity, object and cause), as well as the specific liberalities.

In this regard, according to Article 1038 paragraph (1) of the Civil Code, the will is valid only if the testator has had discernment and his consent has not been vitiated.

As can be seen from the texts presented above, the Romanian Civil Code does not mention any adaptation of the undue influence in the matter of liberalities. There are also no particular forms of undue influence in this matter.

However, the Romanian doctrine has used since the 19th century, with the adoption of the French Civil Code (1864), the notions of captation and suggestion, concepts derived from French law prior to the codification of Napoleon, (l'Ancien Droit) and borrowed from the contemporary doctrine of this codification (Grimaldi 2000).

Thus, the idea has been perpetuated that in the matter of liberalities, the dol appears in the specific forms of captation and suggestion, by which the disposer can either be inspired by hatred of his natural heirs or instill in the profit of someone an affection founded on artificial causes (Rauschi 2000).

It follows from the above-mentioned legal provisions that the dol necessarily involves the use of grievous manworks, that is, fraudulent means that must consist in the execution of manoeuvres to direct situations, the use of lies or the preservation of a grievous silence. Moreover, it is required that these fraudulent mantransactions be the determining factor in the preparation of the will or donation, in the sense that without their exercise the disposer would not have sought the act of liberality (Bob-Bocşan, 2022).

In conclusion, the void in the matter of liberalities should be understood as any manoeuvre arising from the cupidity, whereby, unfairly, a person is persuaded to alter the common order of succession or to create or change the destination of his generous intentions (Pawlowski, 2018).

3 The Consensus of Disuse of Suggestion and Captation

Both suggestion and captation have independent definitions in the doctrine.

The Suggestion consists of hidden and tendentious means used for the purpose of planting in the mind of the disposer the idea of donating which he would not have made on his own initiative.

The Captation, consists of grievous mantras and fraudulent means used to gain the confidence of the disposer and to deceive the good faith of the disposer, to plant in the mind of the disposer the idea of making a donation or a connection which he would not have made on his own initiative (Rauschi 2000).

It is argued that there is a different intensity that would characterize the two forms of undue influence in the matter of liberalities. Thus, the captation involves more direct and brutal cunning means (removal of the disposer of relatives and friends, abuse of authority and influence), while the suggestion is characterized by more subtle manners (minicnous statements about relatives, speculation of certain feelings or conceptions (Deak and Popescu 2026).

The meanings revealed correspond, faithfully, to the very meaning of the two words in the common language. Thus, the suggestion is "the influence exerted on one's will; control and direct one's will," while captation is "gaining a person's goodwill."

However, it is argued in recent legal literature that these definitions create confusion (Bob 2001). We understand that the means to clearly delineate between the two types of undue influence in the matter of liberalities are lacking. The intensity of the grievous works would be difficult to delineate and to classify in the absence of any legal assessment criterion. In addition, it is noted that all the doctrinal definitions of the two sides of the undue influence are stereotyped, empty phrases, which do not help the lawyer in understanding and practical identification.

Starting from these caveats of the impossibility of clear differentiation, some modern authors choose to treat the void in terms of liberalities only as a by-product or claiming the futility of preserving these shades of undue influence (Chirică 2017) in the matter of liberalities.

4 The Unequal Dimension of Judicial Practice

In relation to the seemingly undisputed conclusions of the doctrine in the sense that the forms of undue influence in the matter of liberalities have lost their meaning, judicial practice finds an abundance of cases in which suggestion and captation are invoked in order to annul some liberalities.

We look at some relevant cases.

In a first case (Judgment No 9392/2024 of 23.12.2024, code RJ g84eg93ed, https://rejust.ro/juris/g84eg93ed), the applicant claims to the court that the son of the deceased is deceased, so that the will concerning him has become obsolete and the will of the deceased has not been free, has been altered by dole in the form of a suggestion, in the sense that the beneficiaries of the private legate subject to the authenticated will have used the cunning to influence the deceased, made false claims against the applicant, they speculated the feelings of affection of the deceased in order to induce him to test in their favor the entire share of the common property he had acquired during his marriage with the applicant, in violation of her reserved share. The applicant also pointed out that the fraudulent handling used had a decisive role, resulting in the alteration of the testator's will, their intention being to induce him to order in the sense that he would not have done so on his own initiative.

In a second case (Judgment No 3707/2025 of 20.03.2025, code RJ 5934d776, https://rejust.ro/juris/5934dd776), the applicant stated that at the time of the conclusion of the will, the deceased testator was in an advanced state of illness and was unable to dispose of being fully mental, lack of discernment and the physical and mental capacity necessary to perform and conclude valid legal acts that meet the legal conditions. The legal acts concluded had the consent vitiated by the dol, in the form of captation, the testator being induced in an error caused by the bereaved, fraudulent manoeuvres of the party to induce him to conclude an act that in other circumstances he would not have performed. The defendant and his wife infiltrated the life of the 95-year-old uncle, initially by performing various activities (transport of goods), later suggesting to him, and finally to convince/compel him to leave all his movable and immovable property by concluding an authentic will, without losing any opportunity prior to its conclusion, when in difficult health situations, to ask him to leave all his assets. There were times when the deceased told the applicant that the two spouses were trying to remove him from their relatives by telling him that they wanted to poison him, not to trust the applicant.

In a third case (Judgment No 35/2025 of 12.02.2025, code RJ 6267884e6, https://rejust.ro/juris/6267884e6), the appellate court held in its reasoning that in order to analyze the merits of the action it was necessary to determine 'whether the deceased's will was to revoke the will, without being influenced, obliged, this implies that the reasons for this revocation should also be noted.' It was considered that the decision was given with the wrong application of the rules of substantive law, the court of appeal not analyzing from the perspective of the elements specific to the captation and suggestion, as specific forms of dol in the matter of liberalities. Just as it has been held in practice and doctrine that, in the matter of liberalities, the dol which takes the form of captation and suggestion causes less a false representation of reality and more a manipulation of the disposition of the disposer.

In a fourth case (Judgment No 1339/2024 of 19.12.2024, Code RJ 7288g5728 (https://rejust.ro/juris/7288g5728), the court notes in fact that according to the undisputed claims of the parties, they met in 2015 and after about 6 months began a relationship, living together. On 16.09.2016, the donation contract authenticated under no. 880 was concluded between the applicant as a donor and the defendant as a donor, by which the applicant gave the defendant the share of 5/16 of his property X. the contract provided for a clause establishing the prohibition of extradition, encumbrance and rental in favor of the donor on the property.

On 10.05.2018, the donation contract authenticated under no. 424 was concluded between the applicant as a donor and the defendant as a donor, by which the applicant gave the defendant the share of 10/48 of his property Y. the contract provided for a clause establishing the prohibition of extradition, encumbrance and rental in favor of the donor on the property.

The court notes that in law, according to Article 1214 of the Civil Code, (1) consent is vitiated by the Dol when the party was in an error caused by fraudulent misrepresentations of the other party or when the latter fraudulently omitted, to inform the contractor of circumstances which he ought to disclose to him. (2) the party whose consent was vitiated by the Dol may request the cancellation of the contract, even if the error in which it was found was not essential.

The court noted that informed consent is an essential condition for the transposition into life of the principle of equity, since only a person duly informed of his obligations can be obliged to perform them correctly and completely. Thus, the legal will must be in accordance with the concrete and real circumstances at the time of the conclusion of the civil legal act, otherwise there is a risk that the manifestations of will of the participants in civil law relations will not correspond to their true material or spiritual needs, but be subject to chance, to the exploitation of naivety by the co-contractors, to lack of experience or knowledge in a certain area relevant to the concluded legal act.

The court points out that the Romanian legislature expressly regulated in Article 1214 C.civ. The institution of undue influence as a defect of consent, requiring the nullity of a civil legal act to intervene when the party was in an error caused by the other party's fraudulent misrepresentations or when the latter omitted, fraudulently, to inform the contractor of circumstances which it was appropriate to disclose to him.

Generally speaking, in terms of liberalities, the dol manifests itself in the form of captation and suggestion. In addition, the court makes the classification of the two forms. Thus, the captation consists of grievous mantras and fraudulent means used in order to gain the confidence of the disposer and to deceive his good faith in order to induce him to donate a good to the one who used it or to gratify it by will. Suggestion, on the other hand, is exercised by hidden and tendentious means in order to plant in the mind of the disposer the idea of making a donation or of constituting a link which he would not have made on his own initiative. Freedom may be annulled only if fraudulent manners have resulted in the alteration of the will of the disposer in the sense that, without their exercise, they would not have done the act (Deak, 2018).

By suggestion, therefore, the idea is to be born in the mind of the disposer to make a liberality, and by captation the induced decision is directed, to gratify a certain person in a concrete way. In the case of captation, tougher means are used, such as: removal of the testator's relatives/friends, interception of correspondence, creation of an appearance of total dependence of the disposer in a state of illness, on the person who asks for the liberality, while, in the case of suggestion, the means are more subtle and insidious, such as speculation of feelings, lying statements against close persons/ relatives, etc. Last but not least, the two specific forms of undue influence in this matter will have to be tested as such and obviously cannot be confused with the manifestations of compassion and natural help.

In that regard, the Court of first instance held that the applicant claimed that her consent had been vitiated by the dol, which takes the form of captation and suggestion, since the defendant agreed to move with her to her home provided that she was assured of a certain security, asking him to transfer some of his property to the building, since they will remain together definitively, as husband and wife.

With regard to the revocation of consent by the Dol, in order to induce the applicant to conclude the two contracts, the court of first instance held that, according to the provisions of the Code of Civil Procedure, the person making a claim before the court must prove it.

The court notes that from the evidence administered in the case, it could not be held that there were grievous manworks performed by the defendant in order to determine the applicant to draw up the two donation contracts in authentic form.

Thus, according to the interrogation administered to the applicant, it follows that the relationship with the defendant was natural, they knew each other's parents, went on holidays, at birthdays, aspects confirmed by the statement of a witness, who stated that the relationship between the parties was like in movies, the applicant waiting to marry the defendant. Regarding the two donation contracts, the witness stated that he learned about them at the time he was informed that he would be a witness in the trial.

In his replies to the interrogation, he denied that he had asked the applicant to donate part of the apartment to him, that he had proposed to her in marriage or that he had plans for marriage. According to WhatsApp conversations filed on the file, the defendant sent him a message with the following text: "I feel the need to have something, to be quiet for my future. I want to stay with you, I feel good about you."

This message sent by the defendant does not lead to the conclusion that the defendant attempted to induce the applicant to conclude any of the donation contracts, which could also be the house they were building together or that they were going to marry.

The court points out that the parties had a beautiful relationship, similar to a relationship between the spouses, given its duration of about 6 years, as well as the fact that they lived together.

At the same time, the Court of first instance held that both the nature of the contracts, namely donation contracts, and their terms, are rendered in clear and accessible language, capable of removing any doubt as to the issues claimed by the applicant.

Given that the existence of the undue influence had not been demonstrated at the time of the conclusion of the two donation contracts, the court dismissed the applicant's request for summons, in contradiction with the defendant, as unfounded.

Against the above civil sentence, the applicant appealed, seeking annulment of the sentence and referring the case back to the first court, and, alternatively, changing the sentence to allow the action.

The appellant further argues that what should have been proved and proved in the present case are the following. The use of cunning means by the defendant fraudulent mantras, cunning, lies in order to mislead the applicant in the category of cunning means to speculate on the affection and passion of a person in order to induce him to make a liberality, in this case the fact that he will marry her, that they will be a family partially materialized through the 6-year relationship The intention of the author of the respective complaint of the defendant to mislead the applicant in order to induce her to conclude the two donation contracts. It follows from those conditions that the provocation of the error presupposes bad faith on the part of the author of the complaint, given that he knew the situation of the applicant and the legal situation of the subject-matter of the liberalities, that the applicant had a child who inherited from his father the share of the property that was the subject of the contracts of donation.

The dol does not necessarily and exclusively materialize in a single fact and concomitant with the conclusion of the legal act, the rough manners can last for years, the essential thing is that these manners are prior to the conclusion of the legal act, to cause an error in the mind of the disposer that persists at least until the conclusion of the legal act and to give consent to its conclusion. Hence the conclusion that the dol as a vice of consent is discovered after the conclusion of the legal act from the discovery of the dol, following the limitation period.

It follows that it is irrelevant that the appellant read and signed the donation contracts by declaring that she understood their content as the first instance misapprehended because there was *animus donandi at that time*, the applicant had not discovered the dole, the act, the act, the act, the act, the act, the documents, the documents, the documents, the documents and the documents. the act of generosity on her part being motivated by the defendant's promise to marry her, the verbal promise being also accompanied by facts such as the defendant's presentation of the applicant's family and vice versa as the life partner with whom the defendant declared that he wanted to spend the rest of his life, his intention to enage the minor child at that time, of the applicant, trips to the relatives of the defendant abroad, the fact that the applicant cared for the defendant in his home after undergoing heart surgery and other aspects resulting from the evidence administered in the substance.

The appellant then claimed that if the appellate court considers that the Court of Appeal has decided on the substance of the case, it is requested that it be found that the applicant has proved the void both in terms of material and subjective elements.

The material element materialized in external manifestations both in the form of suggestion and captation, with the emphasis that it is not mandatory for the dol to manifest in both forms. In the present case, the marriage is to win the applicant's affection for the sole purpose of gratifying the defendant, who acknowledged at the interrogation that in reality he had never intended to marry the applicant with whom he could not form a family because of his age. The suggestion in the present case is psychological manipulation and emotional influence on the applicant, the defendant manipulating her through gestures, vacations, gifts and false promises of marriage. Specifically, before the conclusion of the first donation contract, the defendant moved to the applicant's house where he did not act as a guest or tenant, promised the applicant that they would marry, presented it to his family, parents and sister, went with the applicant to his parents, all these are sufficient arguments to prove the dol.

The court of judicial review, the General Court, notes the following aspects that interest the subject matter of our chapter. In the reasoning of the request, the applicant claimed that she met the defendant in September 2015 and they soon moved together with plans to marry. He showed that the donation contracts are struck by relative nullity, his consent at their conclusion being vitiated by the dol. He mentioned that the conditions of undue influence were met, namely the error caused by the defendant was essential, consisting in the fact that he promised him that they would marry, start a family and provoke his son, these promises were made in order to give their consent at the conclusion of the two donation contracts. The General Court considers that the internal will must be free and conscious, because only thus can a contract be legally valid. The vices of consent express the situation in which the internal will exists but is not free and conscious. The General Court finds that the judge of first instance examines each element which must be proved in order to find that, in the case, the applicant's consent to the conclusion of the two donation contracts had been obtained by means of the Dol, that is, the existence or non-existence of the objective element consisting in the use of cunning means to mislead the subjective element, namely the intention to mislead a person, in order to induce him to conclude a civil legal act. The judge correctly held that the parties had a beautiful relationship, similar to a relationship between the spouses, given its length of approximately 6 years, as well as the fact that they lived together. But that, as well as the fact that the applicant claimed that she had not read the documents and signed them, since she trusted the defendant, cannot lead to the conclusion that there is a mistake caused (which is essentially the wrong) and in relation to the conditions under which the act was concluded, which led to the conclusion of the contract, contrary to the real will of the person whose consent was vitiated. A normal relationship of love and friendship cannot produce harmful legal effects for the persons involved in that relationship. A normal relationship cannot be transformed after its termination into an abnormal one that produces effects such as the cancellation of donation contracts, the parties of the contract involved in the concubinage relationship being practically guilty only of having that relationship. Affirms that the applicant's act of generosity was motivated by the defendant's promise to marry her, the verbal promise being also accompanied by facts such as the defendant's presentation of the applicant's family and vice versa as the life partner with whom the defendant declared that he wanted to spend the rest of his life, his intention to engage the minor child at that time, of the applicant, trips to the relatives of the defendant abroad, the fact that the applicant cared for the defendant in his home after undergoing heart surgery and other aspects resulting from the evidence administered in the substance.

The General Court notes that in order to have a so-called dol, the alleged ill-intentions of the defendant must be proved at the time of the conclusion of the donation contracts or the potential existence of another relationship that the respondent had or a similar element that would create a potential doubt about it his so-called bad intentions. From the evidence administered in the case, the incidence of grievous manopies exercised by the defendant in order to determine the applicant to draw up the donation contracts was not retained. At the time of their conclusion, the defendant was employed in relation to the appellant, became co-owner of the house and also purchased a land in the locality X. the fact that their relationship later broke does not automatically imply that there was any dole at the time of the conclusion of the donation contracts, the defendant has no hidden intention at any time during the relationship,

In his first-instance questioning, the defendant noted that there was never any promise of marriage or adoption of the applicant's son and that he never asked the applicant to transfer ownership of the house to him. Therefore, she did not commit any grievous mantras to mislead the applicant appellant. The witness proposed by the applicant stated that she was not aware of the engagement or of any proposal for marriage. The appellant is the only one who claims the opposite. As for the WhatsApp conversations filed in the file, which resulted in the defendant sending the applicant a message with the following text: "I feel the need to have something, to be quiet for my future. I want to stay with you, I feel good about you" this message sent by the defendant does not lead to the conclusion that the defendant tried to persuade the applicant to conclude any of the donation contracts, it could also be the house they were building together or that they were going to get married. Significant is the fact that the defendant had income between EUR 2000 and EUR 10000 per month, which is why he had no economic or material reason to speculate in any way the applicant's feelings of affection in order to obtain the conclusion of the two contracts. Also from a financial perspective, the defendant has the prohibition of alienation, encumbrance and renting of the property. The General Court concludes that if the defendant pursued a potential economic interest he would not have accepted the insertion of such a term in the contracts. The Court therefore holds that no evidence of the elements of the undue influence has been provided.

5 Synchronous Developments in Canada

The Romanian and, perhaps, French experience of interpreting the dol in its action in the field of liberalities may seem equivocal. Is suggestion and captation merely a false echo of Roman law? Perhaps experience in a common law state, Canada, can indicate a firmer answer.

Undue influence in common law, comparable to captation (sometimes referred to in its English translation as "fraudulent captation") in civil law, refers to situations where the person who draws up a will—the testator—acts according to the wishes and according to the coercive pressure of the other. In such courts, since the coercive force determining the legal act does not reflect the testator's will, a court will be entitled to annul the will. Freedom of will, recognized in the common law system, is not considered unduly compromised because, in such scenarios, the law perceives the will intention as being overtaken by the actions of another.

Suggestion and captation can have a critical impact on the resulting will, and there is no lack of jurisprudence addressing this issue. Thus, the equitable doctrine of undue influence was established to prevent "the use of any special capacity or opportunity that may exist or arise to affect the will or freedom of judgment of the donor" (Tyson 1997) at the same time, the roots of this doctrine in common law succession law preceded and were distinct from those of the doctrine which developed in connection with inter vivos transfers. In order to establish undue influence in common law testamentary contexts, it is not necessary to demonstrate abuse or bad faith on the part of the beneficiary, even if the latter is normally perceived as someone who manipulates or coerces a testator in order to promote his own interests. Thus, the unjustified influence was associated with the notion of "moral guilt." It has also been likened to coercion, in the actions of the testator while under the control of the testator are not aligned with the testator's own intentions or choices. It is sufficient for the party that disputes the validity of the liberal will to demonstrate that the nature of the relationship between the testator and the respondent beneficiary was such that it was possible for the beneficiary to dominate the will of the former, and that such domination actually happened (Geffen v Goodman Estate, 1991 2 SCR 353 at 377–78, 81 DLR (4th) 211).

Another response to the legislation, this time, to suggestion and captation, comes from the Restoration (second) of Torts (Restoration). This reads in § 774B (1979): "One who by fraud, duress or other tortious means intentionally prevents another from receiving from a third person an inheritance or gift that he would otherwise have received is subject to a liability to the other for the loss of the inheritance or gift." Therefore, here the resolution is a tortuous one, similar to the provisions of the Romanian civil code that entitles the one who suffered damage to the repair of this. However, the common law doctrine criticizes this solution because it makes the matter of tort a rival to solutions that protect the consent of the party (Campbell 2021).

With regard to the standard applicable to the understanding of suggestion and captation and the burden of proof in common law of undue influence in testamentary contexts, there has been considerable uncertainty over several decades, some of which have been clarified by the Supreme Court's Vout v Hay decision (Vout v Hay, 1995 2 SCR 876 at para 16, 125 DLR (4th) 431). The Court stated that the common law presumption of the validity of the will benefits the party defending it before a judicial appeal. Even where there is evidence that there have been "suspicious circumstances" that call into question the validity of a will, this presumption persists where such circumstances refer to potential undue influence. In other words, there is no presumption of undue influence in testamentary contexts even where circumstances of undue influence are present. The Court identified three types of circumstances that could be considered "suspicious" in testamentary contexts: Those related to the circumstances of the formation or preparation of the will, those related to the quality of the testator and those related to the possible presence of fraud or undue influence. In the first two contexts (formation of will and capacity), evidence of suspicious circumstances may defeat the presumption by favoring the validity of the will, and the burden then changes to the detriment of the heirs to prove that the will was legitimately consented and/or that there was testamentary capacity. However, the burden of proof does not change where undue influence is at issue (Poyser 2019).

In conclusion, suggestion and captation strongly overlap with legal concepts developed within separate legal traditions. Their main distinction is that the continental legal system is more explicitly anchored to the notion of fraud. Therefore, the dol in the matter of liberalities requires evidence of intention and pernicious outcome, while the same is not true, at least in theory, for the concept of undue influence in the common law. However, even in cases where the dol is invoked before the Court of Quebec, judicial assessments may refer to the language and concept of undue influence. Likewise, while malicious intent is not a necessary element of undue influence in the common law, the conduct and reasons of the party alleged to have engaged in undue influence are usually challenged on a moral basis and ordinary courts will assess such claims accordingly (Banton v BANTON, 1998 CanLII 14926 (ON SC), [1998] 164 DLR (4th) 176 at 189; Elder Estate v Bradshaw, 2015 BCSC 1266 at para 93; Tribe v Farrell, 2003 BCSC 1758 at para 9, 2006 BCCA 38).

6 Conclusions

Interpreting the undue influence in a broad manner, allowing its autonomy in the matter of liberalities, without any formal support of any legal text, would be, according to the contemporary Romanian doctrine, desirable to cease. The futility of preserving the extended nuances of undue influence in the matter of liberalities appears for some authors precisely through the subjectivism of overinterpretation. Apparently, the benefits of the legal categories of suggestion and captation would only apply to victims weakened by age or illness who make liberalities without recourse to legal advice from a notary. However, we hope that we have succeeded in proving through the jurisprudence presented in this chapter that the problem of undue influence in the forms of suggestion and captation is a perfectly current one. And the field of action goes far beyond the examples of sick or elderly people. Critical questioning demonstrates the relevance of understanding that all of us—at one point or another—are vulnerable. This universalist approach requires lawyers to move away from the preconceptions that some social groups are particularly vulnerable, deserving our exclusive focus on the question of who deserves special vigilance and support. Care must be taken to protect those facing risks of harm while avoiding violations of their dignity and autonomy of will. At the same time, efforts are needed to identify vulnerability circumstances that may not be obvious. And what better starting point do we have if not the doctrine of suggestion and captation? A more applied approach to the nuances of suggestion and captation should facilitate legal efforts to achieve the delicate balance of the preservation of testamentary liberties, while protecting the interests of all those whose will has been influenced by undue influence. Therefore, we conclude that we are not in a situation of free extension of the limits of the interpretation of the provisions of the Civil Code in the matter of undue influence.

References

Bigwood R (1996) Undue influence: impaired consent or wicked exploitation. Oxford J Leg Stud 16:503-515

Bob-Bocşan MD (2001) Considerations on the undue influence in the field of liberalities. Law no./2001

Bob-Bocşan MD (2022) Elementary manual of private Romanian law. Universul Juridic Publishing House, Bucharest

Boroi G, Anghelescu CA (2021) Civil law. The general part, 3rd edn. Hamangiu Publishing House, Bucharest

Campbell A (2021) Vulnerability and volition in the testamentary law of undue influence and captation. Revue générale de droit 51(1):67-95

Chirică D (2017) A civil law treaty. Succession and liberalities. Hamangiu Publishing House, Bucharest

Ciucă VM (2015) Roman law. Teachings, vol I. University Publishing House "Alexandru Ioan Cuza" Iaşi

Codrea C (2016) The donation in European law. Comparative law. Universul Juridic Publishing House, Bucharest

Deak F (2018) Treaty of civil law. Special contracts, vol III. Universul Juridic Publishing House, Bucharest

Deak, Fr., & Popescu, R. (2026). *Treaty of inheritance law. Vol. II: Testamentary inheritance. Universul Juridic Publishing House, Bucharest*

Grimaldi M (2000) Droit civil. Libéralités. Partages d'ascendants, Editura Litec, Paris

Nicolae, M. (2018). *Civil law. General theory. Vol. II: The theory of civil subjective rights. Solomon Publishing House. Bucharest*

Pawlowski M (2018) Undue influence: towards a unifying concept of unconscionability. Denning Law J 30(1):117-126

Poyser JES (2019) Capacity and undue influence, 2nd edn. Thomson Reuters, Toronto

Rauschi, Şt., Popa, Ghe., & Rauschi, Şt.-a. (2000). *Civil law. Junimea Publishing House, Iaşi*

Tyson M (1997) An analysis of the differences between the doctrine of undue influence with respect to testamentary and inter vivos dispositions. Aust Prop 5:38-43

Guidelines for Legal Interpretation of Compensation in Early Consumer Loan Repayment Under EU Regulations

Luiza Cristina Gavrilescu

Abstract This study addresses the issue concerning the admissibility of the bank creditor's claim to oblige the consumer debtor to pay compensation in the event of early repayment of the contracted debt. Although the creditor cannot restrict the debtor's right to repay the borrowed amount in advance, it is considered that the exercise of this right is onerous. This requires, however, that a fixed interest rate has been agreed or early repayment to occur within a period in which the borrowing rate is fixed. Compensation may not exceed the amount of interest that would have been paid during the period between early repayment and the agreed termination date of the credit agreement. The granting of this compensation will be conditioned by compliance with the limitations imposed by the new European regulations established by Directive (EU) 2023/2225 of 18 October 2023, which is to be transposed into the legislation of the member states. The impact of these regulations consists in the application of a uniform legal cap (at the level of all EU member states) for the maximum value of early repayment compensation.

1 Introduction

Opinions regarding the recognition of the bank creditor's right to claim compensatory indemnity from the consumer for amortizing the loss caused by the repayment of the contracted loan before the due date have been divided. In doctrine, arguments have been expressed for invalidating the bank creditor's right to compensate for the uncollected interest as a result of early repayment. The proposed solutions were justified by the fact that the interest charged covers lucrum cessans for the creditor, so the additional early repayment fee is no longer legally justified. It is not permissible for the professional creditor to attempt to claim an obligation to pay a sum as a fee for the debtor's execution of the principal obligation to pay the loan instalments.

L. C. Gavrilescu (✉)
Faculty of Law, 'Alexandru Ioan Cuza' University of Iași, Iași, Romania
e-mail: luiza.gavrilescu@uaic.ro

I. Maria Costea (ed.), *Legal Interpretation in Motion*, Ius Gentium: Comparative Perspectives on Law and Justice 144,
https://doi.org/10.1007/978-3-032-32948-6_14

However, the new regulations developed at the European level recognize the creditor's right to obtain compensation for the damage caused by the deprivation of the amounts they could have collected if the loan contract had been executed for the full duration initially agreed upon by the parties. Thus, the recognition of the debtor's right to discharge their payment obligation earlier through unilateral expression of will and implicitly to benefit from a reduction in the cost of the loan, is balanced by the admission of the creditor's right to request compensation to partially cover the loss caused by this change in the contract execution provisions.

2 Basis of the Consumer Debtor's Right to Early Repayment of the Loan

The consumer debtor is legally entitled to repay the debt at any time, without being conditioned by a certain number of instalments or a specific payment amount, being able to repay the loan in advance, either in full or in part.

According to the provisions of Article 40 paragraph (3) of Government Emergency Ordinance no. 52/2016, most recently amended by Government Emergency Ordinance no. 15/2024, the consumer has the right, at any time, to fulfil their obligations in whole or in part under a credit contract before its termination.

2.1 Justification for the Exception to the Waiver of the Benefit of a Contractual Term

The potestative right of the consumer to opt for early execution, before maturity, of some of the payment obligations incumbent upon them under the contract is not conditioned by obtaining the bank creditor's consent. The consumer's right to early repayment of the amounts borrowed under credit contracts is considered an essential right from the perspective of the provisions of Directive 2014/17/EU.[1]

The logical arguments and legal foundations for this right of the consumer debtor are supported by the general principles of civil contractual law. Starting with the observation that the primary obligation of the debtor in a credit contract is to repay the borrowed capital, it can be considered that a creditor who refuses to accept full payment of the debt is at fault.

Thus, it can be argued that the debtor has a right to opt for full or partial repayment of the amounts owed before the due date established according to the loan

---

[1] Directive 2014/17/EU of the European Parliament and of the Council on credit agreements offered to consumers for residential immovable property and amending Directives 2008/48/EC and 2013/36/EU and Regulation (EU) no. 1093/2010 was transposed into domestic law by G.E.O. no. 52/2016 on credit agreements offered to consumers for immovable property; as well as for amending and supplementing G.E.O. no. 50/2010 on credit agreements for consumers.

agreement. The particularities of exercising the right to early repayment and the practical difficulties related to the associated legal effects derive from the stipulation of the contractual repayment term, in the case of fixed-term loans, for the benefit of both parties, both the creditor and the consumer debtor. The debtor cannot be penalised for voluntarily executing the obligation early. Given the vulnerable position of the consumer debtor, it is considered that the repayment term is stipulated primarily in their interest, to avoid early forced execution (Ţiţ 2020, pp. 91–110).

Regarding the professional creditor's interest in maintaining the initially agreed term for collecting remunerative interest, this is positioned on a secondary level, as the early collection of the borrowed capital allows the creditor to reinvest those amounts by granting other loans, which will generate new civil fruits to their benefit, substituting those that would have been generated by the liquidated loan.

2.2 *Delimitation of Waiver of the Contractual Term from Termination of the Contract*

Since the credit contract is concluded for a fixed term, its termination cannot be done unilaterally but involves the agreement of both parties. However, termination by the consumer debtor is admitted by exception based on the law due to the inferior position they occupy in relation to the professional creditor.

The potestative right of the consumer to early repayment of the loan should not be confused with the potestative right of the consumer to unilaterally terminate the credit contract, even if there are partial similarities between the legal effects of exercising these rights. Thus, the potestative right to early repayment of the loan is recognised for the debtor based on the principle that the creditor cannot prevent the voluntary execution by the debtor of the principal payment obligation generated by the loan agreement for consumable goods. On the other hand, the debtor's option to unilaterally terminate the credit contract is based on the principle that the consumer debtor is in an inferior position and should benefit from additional protection (Goicovici 2022, p. 394).

The right of withdrawal is established by Directive (EU) 2011/83 on consumer rights (as amended by Directive (EU) 2019/2161 and transposed into national legislation by Government Emergency Ordinance no. 58/2022 for amending and supplementing certain normative acts in the field of consumer protection). Thus, a consumer has the benefit conferred by the Union legislator to exercise their potestative right of withdrawal from the consumer credit contract without invoking any reason, under the conditions of Article 14 of Directive (EC) 2008/48, within a period of 14 calendar days calculated either from the day of conclusion of the consumer credit contract or from the day the consumer is informed of the contractual terms and conditions if that day is later than the date of the contract's conclusion.

2.3 *Derogatory Nature of Consumer Law Rules from Common Law Norms*

Due to the vulnerable position of the debtor, the need to substitute formal balance with real balance has been identified. Union legislation is oriented towards reducing the risk of over-indebtedness of individuals through the contracting of financial credit services and towards encouraging the quickest possible discharge of payment obligations assumed by consumers in credit contracts through voluntary execution (Gavrilescu 2020b, pp. 33–39). The interpretation rule established by Article 77 of the Consumer Code is that obscure or ambiguous clauses are invariably interpreted in favour of the consumer (Duivenvoorde 2019, pp. 219–228).

3 Benefits Obtained by the Debtor as a Result of Early Repayment

A consumer who has paid in advance is entitled to a reduction in the total cost of the credit, this reduction consisting of the interest and costs related to the amount repaid in advance for the period between the date of early repayment and the date provided for the termination of the credit contract.

The debtor's right to obtain a reduction in the cost of the credit as a result of early repayment is due to the lack of proper information provided to the debtor regarding the circumstances on which the determination of the appropriate repayment period depends. Thus, the occurrence, during the execution of the credit contract, of unforeseen events at the time of the contract's conclusion, which may facilitate the fulfilment of the payment obligation in a shorter period than initially estimated, may determine the debtor to make an early payment (Gavrilescu 2021, pp. 103–123).

The continuation of contractual relations after (total or partial) early repayment is mentioned in Article 41 paragraph (2) of Government Emergency Ordinance no. 52/2016: "In the case of partial early repayment, the consumer has the right to choose between: a) maintaining the value of the monthly instalment and reducing the initial credit period; b) reducing the value of the monthly instalment and maintaining the initial credit period; c) reducing the value of the monthly instalment and reducing the initial credit period".

3.1 *Establishing the Concept of Total Cost of Credit*

The total cost of the credit includes all the costs associated with concluding and executing the credit agreement, namely the costs related to providing the main service contracted by the debtor, such as interest and fees on the borrowed capital, as well as the costs generated by ancillary services provided by the creditor for the establishment of the credit, which are executed from the date of the contract conclusion. Thus, while the premiums depend on the duration of the contract, the others are independent of it, with the payments already made from the date the credit is granted.

3.2 *Partial Refund of Credit Fees*

Regarding the expenses incurred for granting the credit, a distinction must be made between those that were made to fulfil the legal obligations regarding the granting of the credit, such as those related to the file analysis, the conclusion of mandatory insurance contracts, and those that were made at the debtor's request, such as fees for special financial advice, optional additional insurance, etc.

In one opinion, it was considered that the right to a refund should not include the amounts paid for granting the credit, which were collected before the execution of the contract began. However, it was found that by limiting the debtor's right to a refund of payments made in advance for services related to the period after the early payment and until the initially agreed contract termination date, proves to be economically inefficient (Józon 2020, pp. 909–930).

More precisely, given that the creditor considers that, in the event of early repayment by the debtor of the borrowed amount, they will only have to refund the interest and fees for the residual period, there will be a tendency to artificially increase the costs of establishing the credit file, as long as these are completely exempt from the obligation of repayment. For this reason, in the CJEU Lexitor Case C-383/18, a more pragmatic solution was identified, namely the delineation of mandatory expenses for file creation, which can partially form the object of the refund claim in the event of early repayment, and optional expenses, which were made at the debtor's choice, based on the principle of autonomy of will, which cannot be refunded (Baffi and Parisi 2021). Therefore, compensation cannot be granted for ancillary services provided at the express request of the debtor: financial advice expenses, optional insurance.

4 Legal Grounds for the Bank Creditor's Right to Claim Compensation for Covering Damages

The professional creditor cannot prevent the debtor consumer from fulfilling their obligation to repay the borrowed capital early. However, in cases where the credit was contracted for a fixed period and is onerous (capital that generates income), the creditor has the right to receive compensation for early repayment, within legal limits.

In Romanian consumer law, clauses that provide for the collection of compensation for early repayment in the matter of credits intended for real estate investment are currently prohibited. The creditor does not have the right to apply penalties, charge compensation, or any other costs from the consumer in the case of early repayment, according to Article 41 paragraph (3) of Government Emergency Ordinance no. 52/2016.

Nevertheless, in other categories of contracts, it has been considered that granting compensation to the creditor could be justified on grounds of economic equity (Akon 2024, pp. 77–104).

4.1 Invoking the Principle of Preserving Contractual Balance

In fixed-term credit contracts concluded with consumers, the final repayment term is not established solely for the benefit of the consumer, so that they can waive the term by early repayment without costs, exercising a right to fully repay the borrowed capital without incurring expenses. The consumer's right to early repayment remains valid, as it represents the fulfilment of the debtor's main obligation.

However, since this right counteracts the effects of the contractual term, its exercise will involve costs, and the creditor is entitled to objective compensation, according to the provisions of Article 67 of Government Emergency Ordinance no. 50/2010 on credit agreements concluded with consumers,[2] amended by Government Emergency Ordinance no. 52/2016 on credit agreements offered to consumers for immovable property and for amending and supplementing Government Emergency Ordinance no. 50/2010 on credit agreements for consumers.

The onerous nature of the debtor's waiver of the benefit of the term is due to the reciprocity of the obligation of the parties to the credit contract and the requirement to respect the binding force of the contract. This argument is based on the assertion that the risk of maintaining the amounts collected in advance in a state of "non-accrual" must be counterbalanced.

4.2 Adapting the Principles of Civil Liability to the Specifics of Consumer Law Relations

In common civil law, compensating for the unrealized benefit due to early repayment is permitted, but in consumer law, this has been viewed with caution.

Adapting solutions from the sphere of classic civil relations to the realm of banking credit services concluded with consumers is required due to the radically different premises of the two categories of relations, characterized by an inequality of power between the contractual parties (Ginestri 2023, pp. 375–393). An argument

[2] G.E.O. no. 50 of 9 June 2010 on credit agreements for consumers (published in Official Gazette no. 389 of 11 June 2010) with subsequent amendments and completions.

of opportunity and legal technique is invoked in this regard, focused on the idea of the inappropriateness and inadequacy of resorting to common law (civil/commercial) norms to solve the issue of compensating the element of lucrum cessans for the bank creditor.

To avoid transferring arguments from common law to consumer law, the principle of *specialia generalibus derogant* must be applied. Thus, if in the territory of real estate crediting, the pre-eminence of prohibitive consumer norms excludes the possibility of granting such compensation to the professional creditor, for other types of consumer credits, the issue continues to subsist (Goicovici 2022, pp. 118–120).

Although some similarities are noted between the two categories, the solutions applicable in the case of civil loan contracts where early repayment, total or partial, occurs, regarding the creditor's request for compensation for the unrealized benefit due to the cessation of interest accrual on the returned amounts, are not compatible with the particularities of bank credit contracts granted to consumers.

Therefore, it is necessary to analyse how the distinction between actual damage suffered and unrealized benefit is reflected in the creditor's compensation claims.

5 European Guidelines for Improving Member States' Legislation

The European Parliament has proposed interventionist measures regarding the recognition of the creditor's right to obtain compensation for the loss caused by the breach of contractual provisions related to the agreed period for contract execution.

It can be noted that the provisions of Directive (EU) 2023/2225 of 18 October 2023 on consumer credit agreements[3] and repealing Directive 2008/48/EC[4] allow for the granting of early repayment compensation, but permit member state legislators to limit, within the scope of consumer credits, the possibility of creditor compensation under certain conditions.

[3] Directive (EU) 2023/2225 of the European Parliament and of the Council of 18 October 2023 on consumer credit agreements and repealing Directive (EC) 2008/48, published in OJ L 2023/2225, 30.10.2023, p. 1, corrected and republished in OJ L, 2023/90205, 22.12.2023. In accordance with the provisions of Article 47 of Directive (EU) 2023/2225, "Member States shall adopt and publish, by 20 November 2025, the laws, regulations and administrative provisions necessary to comply with this Directive. They shall apply those provisions from 20 November 2026".

[4] Directive (EC) 2008/48 of the European Parliament and of the Council of 23 April 2008 on credit agreements for consumers and repealing Council Directive (EEC) 87/102 (published in OJ L 133, 22.05.2008, pp. 66–92). As regulated by Article 47 of Directive (EU) 2023/2225, "Directive (EC) 2008/48 is repealed with effect from 20 November 2026". Directive (EC) 2008/48 was transposed into national legislation by G.E.O. no. 50 of 9 May 2010 on consumer credit agreements (published in Official Gazette no. 389 of 11 June 2010). https://eur-lex.europa.eu/legal-content/RO/TXT/PDF/?uri=OJ:L_202302225.

6 Contracts Exempted from Compensation Benefit

Creditors are prohibited from charging an early repayment fee in cases where they could not rely on the equitable nature of the early repayment compensation. Amounts charged under this title must be fully refunded to the debtor, including legal interest for the period between the payment of these amounts to the creditor and the actual refund to the consumer.

6.1 Real Estate Credits

In the European Standardized Information Sheet, provided to the consumer at the time of contract formation to clarify the conditions under which the debtor can repay the credit early, in full or in part, it is specified in section no. 9 of Part B that "In the section regarding liquidation costs, the creditor informs the consumer that, in the case of early repayment, no compensation is paid.". Therefore, in credit contracts for real estate investments, any clauses regarding the creditor's right to compensation for unrealized benefit due to the non-collection of interest on amounts recovered early would be considered unwritten.

Regarding this exception, some reservations have been formulated in the doctrine (Goicovici 2017). Thus, it has been appreciated that the provisions of Article 68 of Government Emergency Ordinance no. 50/2010 should be interpreted in the sense that the bank creditor, in the matter of credit products for financing the acquisition, consolidation, extension of immovable property, would have the right to charge compensation for early repayment, within the legal ceiling, even in situations where the interest rate charged is variable. It has been pointed out that it would constitute an omission of the Romanian legislator not to mention in the content of Article 68 of the ordinance that real estate investment credits granted to consumers are exempted, in which the creditor's right to charge early repayment compensation would operate in all situations, regardless of the method of determining the interest rate (fixed or variable). For example, the legislation in Serbia mentions in Article 36 of Law no. 73/2012 for the protection of consumers of financial services, that compensation for early repayment cannot be charged in situations where early repayment occurs during a period when the interest rate on the credit is not fixed, except for real estate investment credits, in which case charging compensation is permitted regardless of the type of interest, within the legal ceiling. It has been considered that such an explicit mention would have been useful in Romanian legislation regarding real estate investment credits contracted by consumers, so that the provisions of Article 68 of Government Emergency Ordinance no. 50/2010 on credit agreements concluded with consumers, with the amendments brought by Government Emergency Ordinance no. 52/2016 on credit agreements offered to consumers, which prohibit professional creditors from charging early repayment compensation in the case of a variable interest rate, would be circumscribed to cases of consumer credits, respectively for unnamed personal needs without real estate guarantees.

6.2 *Variable Interest Rate Credits*

In cases where early repayment of the loan occurs during periods with a variable interest rate, charging early repayment compensation is prohibited, as the lending bank has objective mechanisms to adjust the interest rate according to the reference indices clearly mentioned in the contract, without being able to subsequently transfer the financial losses resulting from the early recovery of the capital onto the consumer. Since the variable interest rate is recalculated whenever the reference indices mentioned in the contract change, the creditor is protected against financial imbalances arising from changes in credit conditions, while the consumer remains exposed to the risk of these fluctuations.

Granting compensation for missing out on variable interest during the time intervals eliminated as a result of early repayment of consumer credit is not admissible also because it would not be possible to transparently estimate its evolution.

Therefore, the creditor cannot obtain compensatory amounts if the debtor makes an advance payment during a period when the interest rate on the credit is not fixed, as stated in Article 68(c) of Government Emergency Ordinance no. 50/2010.

6.3 *Non-Payment Risk Insurance Contracts*

In cases where repayment was made as a result of executing an insurance contract aimed at covering the risk of non-payment, Article 68(a) of Government Emergency Ordinance no. 50/2010 prohibits charging compensatory amounts for early repayment. The rationale is that in this scenario, early repayment is not voluntary and does not occur at the debtor's initiative, but as a result of the occurrence of the non-payment risk (debtor's insolvency) based on the existence of an insurance contract against the risk of non-payment between the bank and an insurance company.

6.4 *Overdrafts*

In cases where repayment has been made as a result of executing a credit contract granted in the form of an "overdraft," Article 68(c) of Government Emergency Ordinance no. 50/2010 prohibits charging compensatory amounts for early repayment.

The rationale for the prohibition is that, in cases where the credit contract is granted in the form of an overdraft facility, the essence of the overdraft is that partial or full payments made by the consumer do not extinguish the debt but can be immediately reused by the consumer as available amounts under the credit agreement. Therefore, the mechanism of early repayment—which involves the total or partial extinguishment of the debt through payment—is incompatible with the structure.

The credit granted in the form of an overdraft involves making the borrowed capital available, within the established limit, with each payment made by the consumer. The function of the payment is not to extinguish the debt but to make available to the debtor, for the duration of the contract, the contractually capped funds that exceed the credit balance of the debtor's current account. As a result, early repayment cannot be discussed, as the creditor has committed to keeping these amounts available to the debtor for the agreed duration. On this basis, it can be concluded that early repayment compensation cannot be charged in the case of an overdraft.

7 Conditions for Compensation Established by European Regulations

7.1 Value of Early Repayment

The creditor is entitled to compensation only if the value of the early repayment exceeds the threshold provided in domestic law, which cannot exceed 10,000 EUR over a 12-month period, according to Article 29 paragraph (4)(a) of Directive 2023/2225. Thus, the granting of early repayment compensation is limited to situations where the amount repaid within a 12-month period exceeds a certain minimum threshold. This compensation shall not apply to small amounts or to amounts below the threshold. The minimum value will be determined by national legislation—threshold below the amount of 10,000 EUR (Rott 2023a, pp. 1–14).

7.2 Fixed Interest Rate of the Credit

For the compensation to be granted, early repayment must occur during a period when the interest rate on the credit is fixed. The justification is that only in the case of a fixed interest rate can a clear evaluation of the potential missed benefit be made (Esposito and Grochowski 2022, pp. 1–31).

7.3 Burden of Proof

In the case of early repayment by consumer debtors, the presumption of the rapid appreciation of the repaid capital by professional creditors should operate. Therefore, it is up to the bank creditor to prove both the existence of the damage consisting of the uncollected interest benefit and its extent.

8 Components of the Right to Compensation

8.1 Compensation for Actual Damage Suffered

In recital (70) of Directive 2023/2225, it is specified that early repayment compensation in consumer credit matters can be admitted "for costs directly related to early repayment," an expression that seems to exclude unrealized benefits from the scope (Arroyo Amayuelas 2024, pp. 1–24).

These costs include expenses involved in readjusting contractual relations due to early payment, such as reissuing a new repayment schedule or releasing copies of documentation that proves the extinguishment of contractual obligations.

In the matter of real estate investment credits, recital (66) of Directive 2014/17/EU "on credit agreements offered to consumers for residential immovable property" establishes the possibility for the creditor to charge early repayment compensation, provided that its value does not exceed the level of economic loss suffered by the creditor due to early repayment. Additionally, Article 25 paragraph (3) states that member states may provide that the creditor has the right, when justified, to fair and objective compensation for any costs directly related to early repayment of the credit, but does not impose a penalty on the consumer. In this regard, the compensation does not exceed the financial loss borne by the creditor. Under these conditions, member states may provide that the compensation cannot exceed a certain level or may be permitted only for a certain period. Thus, European regulation establishes the principle of correlating the level of compensation with that of "costs directly related to early repayment of the credit," which seems to target the price of ancillary services related to readjusting contractual relations due to early repayment.

8.2 Compensation for Unrealized Benefit

The compensation to which the creditor is entitled for unrealized benefit shall cover at most the value of uncollected interest due to the exclusion of the period during which the credit agreement would have been in effect in the absence of repayment, i.e., from the date of early payment until the initially agreed maturity of obligations.

The compensation for elements in the category of lucrum cessans envisages in the analysed situation the compensation allocated to the creditor who loses the right to collect the interest that would have been generated by the borrowed capital if the initially stipulated interval for the contract effects had been maintained within the initially agreed parameters.

However, given that the credit institution's business activity involves the circulation of money, such as reinvesting deposited amounts in granting loans or financial placements, the idea of causing damage through early repayment of the credit has been received with reservations. Practically, by early collection of the borrowed amount, the bank can almost automatically cover the unrealized benefit by reinvesting the money in other profit-generating activities.

The argument of missing out on the benefit of collecting interest on amounts repaid early has been deemed as irrelevant in consumer credit relations.

9 CJEU Guidelines on the Interpretation of European Regulations in Case C-536/22 VR Bank Ravensburg-Weingarten[5]

In cases where discrepancies in the interpretation of European regulations are found, recourse is made to CJEU decisions aimed at reconciling them.[6] A controversial aspect referred to whether the debtor's right to reduce credit costs based on early payment includes amounts that do not depend on the duration of the contract, such as the expenses related to the formalities for establishing the credit.

In interpreting the provisions of Article 25 paragraph (3) of Directive 2014/17, it is noted that for evaluating the compensation to which the creditor would be entitled for covering the unrealized benefit due to early repayment, a determined element will be the financial loss borne by the creditor, materialized in the residual contractual interest that will no longer be collected. It also mentions the limits resulting from the equitable nature of the compensation and the principle of prohibiting the penalization of the consumer for voluntarily early execution of their obligation, respectively capping the compensation at the level of the financial loss correlated

[5] CJEU, 5th Chamber, judgment of 14 March 2024, in the case C-536/22, ECLI:EU:C:2024:234, https://curia.europa.eu/juris/document/document.jsf?text=&docid=283830&pageIndex=0&doclang=ro&mode=lst&dir=&occ=first&part=1&cid=1427172.

[6] CJEU, Dec. of 30 Apr. 2014, in Case C-26/13, ECLI:EU:C:2014:282 (Kásler); CJEU, Dec. of 26 Feb. 2015, in Case C-143/13, ECLI:EU:C:2015:127 (Matei); CJEU, Dec. of 23 Apr. 2015, in Case C-96/14, ECLI:EU:C:2015:262 (Van Hove); CJEU, Dec. of 20 Sept. 2017, in Case C-186/16, ECLI:EU:C:2017:703 (Andriciuc); CJEU, Dec. of 20 Sept. 2018, in Case C-51/17, ECLI:EU:C:2018:750 (OTP Bank v Ilyés and Kiss); CJEU, Dec. of 5 Jun. 2019, in Case C-38/17, ECLI:EU:C:2019:461 (GT/HS); CJEU, Dec. of 3 March 2020, in Case C-125/18, EU:C:2020:138 (Gómez del Moral Guasch); CJEU, Dec. of 16 Jul. 2020, in Joined Cases C-224/19 and C-259/19, ECLI:EU:C:2020:578 (Caixabank and Banco Bilbao Vizcaya Argentaria); CJEU, Dec. of 12 Jan. 2023, in Case C-395/21, ECLI:EU:C:2023:14.

with the cessation of interest accrual on the capital or the sequences of the borrowed capital repaid early.

10 Limits Imposed on the Extent of the Right to Compensation

The establishment of limitations on the extent of the right to compensation aims to avoid the dissuasive effect that the application of the compensation clause would have on the consumer debtor's intention to free themselves in advance from the obligation to repay the borrowed amounts.

The legal provisions in Union consumer law regarding capping the auxiliary service fees charged to the consumer in the event of early reimbursement represent a benchmark for national legislations.

Thus, the early repayment fee must be set at a maximum level of 0.5% x the amount repaid early for credits contracted for a duration less than 12 months and a maximum of 1% x the amount repaid early for credits contracted for a duration exceeding 12 months, according to Article 29 paragraph (2) of Directive 2023/2225.

The creditor may exceptionally claim higher compensation if they can prove that the damage suffered due to early repayment exceeds the amount established in accordance with paragraph (2).

If the compensation requested by the creditor exceeds the actual damage suffered due to early repayment, the consumer has the right to a corresponding reduction. In this case, the damage consists of the difference between the initially agreed credit interest rate and the interest rate at which the creditor can lend the amount subject to early repayment at the time of the respective repayment and takes into account the effect of early repayment on administrative costs.

It should be noted that the phrase used in the text of the Directive about the "actual damage" generated as a result of early repayment, actually covers the component of unrealized benefit, with the European legislator imposing the condition that its extent be assessed on objective, neutral, transparent grounds, correlated with the actual manner in which these amounts could have been revalorized by the creditor (Luzak Junuzović 2019, pp. 97–107).

The maximum legal ceiling imposed by the provisions of the Directive can eventually be reduced by the national legislator, but not increased. It is shown by prohibitive norm that the amount of compensation mentioned in paragraph (2) and paragraph (4)(b) does not exceed in any case the amount of interest that the consumer would have paid in the period between early repayment and the agreed date for termination of the credit agreement—according to Article 29 paragraph (5) of Directive 2023/2225.

11 Principles for Transposing European Standards on Compensation

The principles applicable for establishing the compensation owed to the creditor are outlined in recital (70) of Directive 2023/2225: (i) the principle of transparency and the intelligibility of the clauses that provide the method of calculating the compensation; (ii) the selected calculation method should not present an excessive degree of complexity but should be easy to apply; (iii) the facilitation of control or supervision of the compensation determination mechanisms (control carried out by the competent authorities).

The transposition of European provisions into national legislation must be done in the spirit of respecting the limitations imposed on the discretionary exercise of the creditor's right to charge an early repayment fee.

With the exception of the cases provided for in Article 29(3), lenders are entitled to compensation, which Member States can limit (Recital 71, Article 29(4)(a)).

Thus, in legislations where such a cap is instituted only for the fee charged for readjusting the repayment schedule or, in the case of full repayment, releasing the documentation that attests to the extinguishment of contractual relations, it must be applied, through an extensive interpretation, also to the compensation claims for the creditor's unrealized benefit. Otherwise, there would be a risk of circumventing these legal prohibitions by the creditor converting the qualification of the fees charged in such a way as to avoid their reduction. For example, they could artificially raise the repayment costs on interest and fees associated with the principal debt under conditions where these would not be subject to legal limits.

Early repayment must logically lead in all cases to a reduction in the total cost of the credit for the consumer, so the compensation set by the bank cannot exceed, but only may be equal to at most the value of the interest that the consumer would have paid in the respective interval. For fixed-rate credits, the bank lender can collect fair compensation to offset part of the losses recorded at the interest level.

Regarding the determination of the legal ceiling base that will establish the maximum value of early repayment compensation, the fixed interest value will be taken as a reference, not the APR (annual percentage rate), considering that the total cost may also include the bank fees charged for the provision of additional or ancillary services by the bank creditor in the respective interval. As a result of early repayment, these ancillary services will no longer be provided to the consumer for the number of months for which early repayment of the credit occurs, meaning that these fees will not be owed by the consumer. Since the rationale for early repayment compensation is to cover part of the financial loss resulting from the non-collection of civil fruits (the actual interest) that the borrowed capital would have generated according to the contract in the established interval, and the APR includes costs for services practiced by the bank (such as the bank account management service), and through early repayment, this service is no longer necessary, the rationale for additional compensation is excluded for these.

This excludes compensation in the case of variable interest rates, which is understandable, but in these cases, lenders should also be able to claim for administrative costs incurred by early repayment (Arroyo Amayuelas 2024, pp. 1–24). Perhaps this is not because these costs are thought to have been largely passed on in interest rates, but this should have been clarified (Álvarez Olalla 2022, pp. 217–218).

12 Obligation of the Bank Creditor to Inform the Consumer in the Pre-Contractual Phase About the Existence and Extent of the Right to Compensation

The creditor has the obligation to inform the consumer about the right to early repayment. To maintain a high degree of transparency and avoid abuses related to the establishment of compensation for early repayment of debts, it is necessary for these obligations to contain precise information about the calculation methods and limits of compensation imposed by bank creditors, taking into account professionalism standards. The transparency with which bank creditors communicate, at the contract formation stage, the limits and calculation methods of compensation for early repayment can stimulate competition between banks and reduce the total cost of credit on the interbank market (Fungačova and Weill 2017, pp. 104–120). Additionally, this can facilitate attracting new clients, assuming that consumer debtors prefer credit products with clearly displayed final costs, including early repayment compensation.

Bank creditors and, if applicable, credit intermediaries have the obligation to provide consumers with the necessary information, based on specific credit clauses and conditions, to compare multiple offers and make an informed decision regarding the conclusion of a credit contract, including the amount of early repayment compensation.

The rules regarding capping the value of compensation to which the creditor is entitled in the event of early repayment are imperative; deviation through contractual clauses that would tend to exceed the maximum legal ceiling is not permitted.

12.1 Requirements for Fulfilling the Obligation to Inform

For informing the consumer in the pre-contractual phase about the possible imposition of early repayment compensation, the provisions of Article 10 paragraph (5)(j) of Directive 2023/2225 will be considered. It is necessary for the information provided to allow the consumer to clarify the determining economic implications, specifying the selected method for calculating the compensation (Cherednychenko 2021, pp. 183–206).

12.1.1 Substantive Requirements

The professional creditor has the obligation to inform the consumer from the pre-contractual phase about the method of calculating the compensation; the method must be clear, transparent, and easily verifiable based on objective elements.

Thus, the consumer is entitled to have the calculation mechanism used for determining the compensation owed in case of early repayment described in the contract. The contractual provisions must be presented to the consumer in the pre-contractual phase, to give them the opportunity to examine in detail the terms included in the contract, to carefully evaluate the contractual conditions, and to make an informed decision about contracting after a clear analysis of the assumed consequences (Goicovici 2023, pp. 497–527).

From the perspective of the *rationae materiae* scope of the provisions regarding the professional creditor's obligation of transparency in determining the amount of early repayment compensation, the notion of misleading action or misleading omission, as forms of unfair commercial practices, can materialize both in an omissive and commissive manner (Rott 2023b,pp. 871–893).

Omissive acts consist of neglecting to mention information, in the pre-contractual phase and at the time of signing the credit contract, regarding the objective method of calculating the value of early repayment compensation.

Commissive acts can materialize in misleading actions, such as using non-transparent calculation formulas based on ambiguous elements, such as clauses regarding the "monetary policy of the bank creditor" (Cherednychenko 2024, pp. 241–270).

12.1.2 Formal Requirements

The requirements of the informative formalism refer to the provisions which expressly establish that the inclusion in the content of the credit agreement is mandatory, according to art. 21 para. (2) letter (s) of the European Directive. The transparency of the clauses implies that the text proposed to the adherent must be intelligible, both grammatically and linguistically. Additionally, formal transparency is also assessed through the accessibility of the contractual terms, for their consultation by the consumer in the pre-contractual stage (Loos 2023, pp.281–299).

In the context of digital asymmetry, the consumer is particularly susceptible to practices that exploit power differences to their detriment, generating a constant state of vulnerability known as digital vulnerability, specific to the online environment characterized by constant monitoring and manipulation of consumers (Drazewski 2021).

Therefore, it has been highlighted that, in conditions of digital asymmetry, the creditor has a duty of diligence to ensure that the consumer's decision-making autonomy is not affected by their commercial practice. Specifically, the creditor's duty of diligence is materialized in Directive (EU) 2023/2225 in the form of the obligation to inform the consumer, regulated in a much more rigorous, harmonized manner compared to the previous regulation [Directive (EC) 2008/48]. Thus, pre-contractual information must be provided to the consumer through the "European Standard Information on Consumer Credit" form, provided in Annex I, visibly and as much as possible on the first page of the form, and if this is not possible, at least the main elements must be displayed in the first part of the form, on no more than two pages. It has therefore been considered that the requirement for the presence of the form represents a "model" of the creditor's diligence (Vâlcu 2024).

12.2 Consequences of Failing to Fulfil the Obligation to Inform

Member states must provide effective and proportional measures in case of violation of the rules adopted, based on the Directive regarding pre-contractual information (De Elizalde 2019,pp. 147–149).

Regarding the proof of fulfilling the transparency obligation and the duty to inform, incumbent on professionals, the following characteristics are noted:

- an absolute, irrefragable presumption of good knowledge of the domain operates, so contrary evidence of insufficient knowledge of the norms of the domain in which they operate is inadmissible. Therefore, exoneration of the bank creditor from liability for non-execution of the pre-contractual information and transparency obligation is not possible.
- the burden of proof regarding the execution of the duty to inform and of the transparency obligation is reversed, since the consumer would not be able to prove the negative fact that the execution of the responsibility to inform was not met.

Thus, the burden of proving enforcement, lies with the bank creditor, who will be required to provide proof of proper execution of the pre-contractual information or banking transparency obligation if they intend to rebut the legal presumption. Admissible means of proof include pre-constituted documents that attest to the proper execution of the legal duty to inform the consumer (Helberger et al. 2022, pp. 175–200).

The lack of transparency of contractual provisions that establish the obligation to pay compensation for early repayment allows the consumer debtor to invoke the unenforceability of unclear clauses and implicitly eliminate them as abusive (Mišćenić et al. 2023, pp. 346–374). The finding of such violations also attracts the application of contravention fines to the bank creditor.

13 The Abusive Nature of the Clause Waiving the Application of Imperative Legal Norms Regarding Compensation Capping

Contractual stipulations by which the professional creditor proposes to the consumer to waive one or more of their legal rights, including the right to early repayment of the credit and the application of imperative legal norms regarding the capping of the creditor's compensation for early repayment, are null and void.

13.1 Nature of the Nullity of the Waiver Clause

Regarding the type of nullity (absolute or relative), the legislator has not explicitly qualified the type of nullity, which generates the need to qualify it through the application of interpretation rules (Gavrilescu 2020a, pp. 59–77).

Thus, the opinion that qualifies this nullity as relative points out that, generally, cases of absolute nullity are expressly mentioned by law, and absolute nullity represents an exceptional situation. By using grammatical interpretation arguments, starting from the elliptical expression of the legislator "are null and void," combined with the teleological argument extracted from the nature of the protected private interest—the legitimate economic interests of the consumer debtor—it could be concluded that the provisions of Article 80 paragraph (1) of Government Emergency Ordinance no. 50/2010, as amended by Government Emergency Ordinance no. 52/2016 regarding credit agreements offered to consumers for immovable property, establish a case of relative nullity.

On the other hand, the opinion that qualifies this nullity as absolute counters the solution of relative nullity with the *per a contrario* argument, starting from the prescriptible nature within the general term of 3 years of the right to the annulment action, which would be calculated from the date of signing the contract containing the annullable clause, which would lead to illogical solutions in the case of consumers who decide to exercise their right to early repayment (which is not extinguished by signing the abusive early waiver clause) and who exercise this right after a period of more than 3 years of contractual credit relations (Pavillon 2023, pp. 65–80).

Thus, it will be noted that, although the protected interest has a private and not a public nature, the consumer's action to suppress the abusive early waiver clause of the consumer's rights recognized by the imperative provisions of the law is imprescriptible, and the appropriate sanction would be to consider the clause as unwritten.

13.2 Consequences of the Nullity of the Waiver Clause

The nullity of abusive bank clauses is, as a rule, a partial nullity, affecting only the clause itself, which will be deemed as unwritten or removed from the contractual field. Therefore, the contractual relations will continue to be carried out, as long as the cause of these relations is not affected (Goicovici 2024).

14 Conclusions

The issue of recognizing the bank creditor's right to receive compensation from the consumer debtor in the event of early repayment of the borrowed amount must be analysed in relation to several variables. Firstly, the admissibility of such a request is circumscribed to the domain of consumer credits for personal needs, since in the case of real estate loans there are prohibitive rules in this regard.

From the category of consumer credit contracts, overdrafts and those executed contracts based on non-payment risk insurance are excluded. The right to compensation can only be granted in cases where the repayments exceed the minimum threshold set at the level of 10,000 euros or more. Regarding the compensation granted to the creditor, a distinction is made between actual damage suffered and unrealized benefit. The first category includes expenses incurred by the contract modification requested by the debtor, such as issuing a new repayment schedule in the case of partial payment or issuing proof of credit liquidation in the case of full repayment.

The amount of compensation will be capped at a variable percentage depending on the duration of the loan: an amount of 0.5% of the repaid amount for amounts repaid within a maximum of 12 months, respectively 1% of the repaid amount for a period longer than 12 months. In this case, only periods when the interest rate is fixed will be considered, and compensation cannot be charged for non-collection of variable interest. If the creditor proves that the actual damage suffered exceeds the level of expenses occasioned by early payment, he may claim that these ceilings are exceeded. Regarding the unrealized benefit, the difference between the interest rates on credits that the creditor will be able to obtain at the payment date and those initially provided in the contract, which the creditor would have normally collected, is considered. At the debtor's request, the compensation reclaimed by the creditor can be reduced. The level of compensation granted to the creditor cannot exceed the value of the interest that could have been collected between the reference interval from the date of early payment to the due date.

The European legislative framework will be harmonized by adopting the provisions of Directive 2023/2225.

References

Akon T (2024) The unfairness of personalised price terms in consumer credit products. Eur Rev Contract Law 20(1):77–104. https://doi.org/10.1515/ercl-2024-2003

Álvarez Olalla P (2022) Contratos de crédito al consumo. Tarjetas de crédito. In: Santos Morón MJ, Mato Pacín Ma N (coords) Derecho de consumo: visión normativa y jurisprudencial actual. Tecnos, Madrid: 217–218

Arroyo Amayuelas E (2024) A third directive on consumer credit. Eur Rev Contract Law 202, 20(1):1–24. https://doi.org/10.1515/ercl-2024-

Baffi E, Parisi F (2021) Early repayment of loans under EU law: The Lexitor Judgment. 7 227, available on-line

Cherednychenko OO (2021) The proposal for a new EU Consumer Credit Directive: towards responsible lending in the digital age? Law Financ Markets Rev 15(3–4):183–206. https://doi.org/10.1080/17521440.2022.2153611

Cherednychenko OO (2024) On the bumpy road to responsible lending in the digital marketplace: the new EU Consumer Credit Directive. J Consumer Policy 47:241–270. https://doi.org/10.1007/s10603-024-09564-z

De Elizalde F (2019) Partial invalidity for unfair terms? CJEU in Abanca – C-70 & 179/17. J Eur Consumer Market Law 8(4):147–149

Drazewski K (2021) Protecting fairness and consumer choice in a digital economy. EU Consumer Protection 2.0, BEUC, Brussels

Duivenvoorde B (2019) The upcoming changes in the unfair commercial practices directive: a better deal for consumers? J Eur Consumer Market Law 8(6):219–228

Esposito F, Grochowski M (2022) The consumer benchmark, vulnerability, and the contract terms transparency: a plea for reconsideration. Eur Rev Contract Law 18(1):1–31. https://doi.org/10.1515/ercl-2022-2035

Fungačova Z, Weill L (2017) Does bank competition reduce cost of credit? Cross-country evidence from Europe. J Bank Finance 83(3):104–120

Gavrilescu LC (2020a) Evaluarea condiţiilor exercitării controlului caracterului abuziv al comisioanelor de întocmire/analiză dosar şi de gestionare/administrare a creditului de către instanţele naţionale în sensul interpretării unitare a legii în lumina reperelor jurisprudenţiale stabilite de C.J.U.E. Annals of the "Alexandru Ioan Cuza" University, Iaşi, vol LXVI: 59–77.

Gavrilescu LC (2020b) Invocarea moratoriul legal al rambursării împrumuturilor bancare în vederea evitării intrării în insolvenţă a debitorilor. Phoenix Insolvency Magazine 74(4):33–39

Gavrilescu LC (2021) Măsuri adoptate la nivel european de flexibilizare a reglementărilor bancare în vederea susţinerii continuităţii activităţii antreprenorilor. Revista Română de Drept al Afacerilor 1: 103–123.

Ginestri M (2023) Equality or superiority of the weak party? Consumer protection and the issues at stake. Eur Rev Contract Law 19(4):375–393. https://doi.org/10.1515/ercl-2023-2022

Goicovici J (2017) Consideraţii privind dreptul consumatorului de rambursare anticipată şi sancţiunile aplicabile creditorilor profesionişti în contractele de credit, Studia Iurisprudentia, no. 4.

Goicovici J (2022) Dreptul relaţiilor dintre profesionişti şi consumatori. University Course, Hamangiu Publishing House, Bucharest

Goicovici J (2023) Faţetele bunei-credinţe a profesionistului în evaluarea clauzelor abusive din contractele de credit încheiate de consumatori. In: Almăşan A, Zamşa CE [coord.], vol II, Hamangiu Publishing House, Bucharest: 497–528

Goicovici J (2024) Beneficiul ratat si comisionul datorat de catre debitorul consumator creditorului bancar pentru rambursarea anticipata a capitalului imprumutat, dupa decizia CJUE în cauza VR Bank Ravensburg-Weingarten. Universul Juridic Review 5:87–109. https://heinonline.org/HOL/P?h=hein.journals/univjurid2024&i=879

Helberger N, Sax M, Strycharz J, Micklitz H-W (2022) Choice architectures in the digital economy: towards a new understanding of digital vulnerability. J Consumer Policy 45:175–200. https://doi.org/10.1007/s10603-021-09500-5
Józon M (2020) Judicial governance by unfair contract terms law in the EU: proposal for a new research agenda for policy and doctrine. Eur Rev Private Law 28(4):909–930
Loos MBM (2023) Crystal clear? The transparency requirement in unfair terms legislation. Eur Rev Contract Law 19(4):281–299. https://doi.org/10.1515/ercl-2023-2018
Luzak J, Junuzović M (2019) Blurred lines: between formal and substantive transparency in consumer credit contracts. J Eur Consumer Market Law 3:97–107
Mišćenić E, Tereszkiewicz P, Infantino M (2023) The interplay between the CJEU and national courts in the case law on unfair contract terms in foreign currency loans: a comparative overview. Eur Rev Contract Law 19(4):346–374. https://doi.org/10.1515/ercl-2023-2021
Pavillon C (2023) Effective judicial protection, private enforcement and the reshaping of substantive remedies. In: Micklitz H-W, Twigg-Flesner C (eds) The transformation of consumer law and policy in Europe. Hart Publishing: 65–80
Rott P (2023a) Small credit through online platforms. Law Financ Markets Rev15(3–4):207–220 https://doi.org/10.1080/17521440.2023.2167523
Rott P (2023b) The balance in consumer protection between substantive law and enforcement. Eur Rev Private Law 31:871–893. https://doi.org/10.54648/erpl2023032
Ţiţ NH (2020) Încuviinţarea executării silite a debitorului consumator-exigenţe europene, realităţi naţionale. Sci Ann Alexandru Ioan Cuza Univ Iaşi, Leg Sci Ser 66(2):91–110
Vâlcu EN (2024) În ce măsură exigenţele Directivei (UE) 2023/2225 garantează consumatorilor în contractele de credit de consum, drepturi adecvate erei digitalizării. Revista Română de Dreptul Afacerilor (4)

Public Authority, Responsibility and Resources

Interpreting the Liability of the Members of the Government in the Constitutional Jurisprudence of Romania and France

Ioan Dumitru Apachiţei

Abstract The jurisdiction of the Constitutional Court of Romania in matters regarding the criminal liability of Government members is based on the provisions of Article 109, paragraph (2) of the Constitution, which establishes procedural protection mechanisms granted to these members, without constituting immunity. Within Romanian constitutional jurisprudence, this protection extends even after the termination of the mandate, while also allowing accountability for acts committed during the exercise of governmental duties. The entire system of criminal liability is fundamentally grounded in the guarantee of the individual freedom of Government members, which is ensured through specific constitutional procedures. On the other hand, in France, following the 1993 reform, constitutional jurisprudence allowed expanded access to prosecution procedures for Government members through the creation of the Court of Justice of the Republic, an institution that enabled citizens to file complaints. The 1993 constitutional amendments aimed to balance the criminal liability of Government members with protection against procedural abuse. Decisions of the French Constitutional Council and relevant rulings, such as the "contaminated blood" case, have reflected the fundamental principle of equality before the law, in accordance with international norms.

1 General Considerations Concerning the Accountability of Government Members

One of the essential conditions for holding Government members accountable is political will. In this regard, French legal literature has noted that, ultimately, the use and effectiveness of constitutional mechanisms depend on the political context ("Les mécanismes constitutionnels dépendent largement pour leur utilisation et pour leur efficacité du contexte politique…" (Favoreu et al. 2019, p. 817)).

I. D. Apachiţei (✉)
Faculty of Law, 'Alexandru Ioan Cuza' University of Iaşi, Iaşi, Romania
e-mail: ioan.apachitei@uaic.ro

I. Maria Costea (ed.), *Legal Interpretation in Motion*, Ius Gentium: Comparative Perspectives on Law and Justice 144,
https://doi.org/10.1007/978-3-032-32948-6_15

Moreover, in a landmark decision of the Constitutional Court of Romania, the distinction between political accountability and criminal liability that may apply to Government members was analyzed (Mâţă 2022, pp. 208–209; Deaconu 2018). Thus, based on the analysis of Article 109 of the Romanian Constitution (adopted on 21 November 1991, published in the Official Journal no. 233 of 21 November 1991, and entered into force on 8 December 1991), the Court ruled in Decision No. 270/2008 (published in the Official Journal no. 290 of 15 April 2008) that "it is not by chance that the constituent legislator regulated both political and criminal liability within the same provision, as they intervene, on the one hand, due to the breach of the mandate of trust granted by Parliament, and on the other hand, for the breach of the act of appointment of the Government by the President of Romania based on this mandate. As has been shown, paragraph (2) of Article 109 of the Constitution establishes that only the Chamber of Deputies, the Senate, and the President of Romania have the right to request the initiation of criminal proceedings against Government members. From the analysis of the text, it results that the term 'only' means 'no one' else but these three public authorities can request prosecution, and that prosecution cannot be initiated in the absence of a request from either the Chamber of Deputies, the Senate, or the President of Romania, as applicable. While criminal investigation bodies may carry out various acts preceding the initiation of prosecution under the law, they may not continue without notifying one of the three public authorities to request criminal prosecution. In such situations, the Public Ministry—the Prosecutor's Office attached to the High Court of Cassation and Justice—is obliged to notify the Chambers of Parliament or the President of Romania, as appropriate, regarding the information and data in their possession indicating the possibility of initiating criminal prosecution against a Government member, as these are the only authorities competent to decide on this procedural act. As for the conjunction 'and' in the text of Article 109 paragraph (2), it marks the end of a list, which grants each of the three authorities its competence. The constitutional text excludes both cumulative competence of requests from the three public authorities and alternative competence among them (…) the provisions of Article 109 paragraph (2) first sentence of the Fundamental Law establish the absolute right of each of the three public authorities to request prosecution, and the exercise of this right by one of them cannot be made to the detriment of the others, nor is the right of one conditioned on the rights of the others."

The notion of "Government members" must be understood in relation to the provisions of Article 102 paragraph (3) of the Romanian Constitution, which states that "the Government is composed of the Prime Minister, ministers, and other members established by organic law." The organic law referred to by the Constitution is Emergency Ordinance No. 57/2019 on the Administrative Code (published in the Official Journal no. 555 of 5 July 2019), which, in Article 18, defines the "composition of the Government." Thus, the Government of Romania is obligatorily composed of the Prime Minister and the ministers, while optionally it may also include Deputy Prime Ministers, State Ministers, Delegated Ministers, and Ministers with special duties attached to the Prime Minister.

2 Political Accountability of Government Members

The Cabinet's collective responsibility involves both the acceptance or dismissal in group of all Government members and the obligation of each minister to adhere to the general orientation established by the Government. Most often, the constitutions of European states explicitly enshrine the principle of collegiality, for example: Article 68 of the Constitution of the Czech Republic, Article 115 of the Constitution of Croatia, Article 28 of the Constitution of Ireland, Article 190 of the Constitution of Portugal, Article 114 of the Constitution of the Slovak Republic, and Article 108 of the Constitution of Spain. In Italy, the Constitution explicitly enshrines the principle of collegiality (Article 95); however, this is tempered by the fact that ministers are individually responsible for the acts adopted by their respective ministries (Favoreu et al. 2019, p. 707).

The provisions of Article 109, paragraph (1) of the Romanian Constitution define the political accountability of the Government, in the sense that it is to be exercised only before Parliament. Each Government member holds joint (collegial) accountability with the other members, both for the activity of the Government and for the acts it adopts, an essential feature of parliamentary systems (Chryssogonos and Stratilatis 2012, p. 27). Similarly, the provisions of Article 20, paragraph 3, in relation to Article 49, paragraph 1, of the French Constitution stipulate the Government's accountability before the National Assembly (Thiébault 2006, p. 325), a mechanism known as the "question of confidence" (la question de confiance). From this perspective, the wording of Article 49, paragraph 1, has been criticized on the grounds that it should have explicitly referred to the Prime Minister's option to assume responsibility, since the constitutional provisions may otherwise imply a mandatory assumption of responsibility (Hamon and Troper 2014, p. 552). In another interpretation, it has been suggested that the French Government is obliged to assume responsibility for the governmental program and may optionally do so for its general policy (Favoreu et al. 2019, p. 812).

In this regard, through Decision No. 76-72 DC of 12 January 1977 (published in the *Journal Officiel de la République Française* of 13 January 1977, p. 343), the Constitutional Council held that the Fundamental Law tends to give similar meaning to the notion of "program" and the expression "general policy statement." To date, no negative vote has ever been cast under Article 49, paragraph 1 of the French Constitution regarding a general policy statement (Favoreu et al. 2019, p. 813).

The political accountability of the Government involves some notable differences between the French and Romanian systems, primarily determined by the procedure for appointing Government members.

Thus, the Romanian Constitution sets out in Articles 85 and 103 the procedure by which the Government is invested, which includes three stages: (a) The President of Romania designates a candidate for the position of Prime Minister, following consultations with the party holding an absolute majority in Parliament (such a scenario did not occur between 1991 and 2025) or, if such a majority does not exist, with all parties represented in Parliament; (b) The person designated for the position of Prime Minister has a period of 10 days from the designation to obtain a vote of confidence from Parliament on the government program and the list of ministers, both Chambers of Parliament, in a joint session, will vote by absolute majority to grant confidence to the Government; (c) If the Government receives the vote of confidence, the Prime Minister and the ministers are then appointed by the President of Romania.[1] This mechanism for appointing Government members justifies the provision in Article 109 paragraph (1) of the Romanian Constitution, in the sense that the Government is politically accountable only to Parliament.

Notable differences can be observed regarding the procedure for appointing the French Government, where the primary role belongs to the President of the Republic. According to Article 8 of the French Constitution, the President appoints the Prime Minister, and the appointment of the ministers is made by the President at the proposal of the Prime Minister (Constantinesco and Pierré-Caps 2006, p. 352). In this respect, the French Constitution does not require the Government to be invested or to receive a vote of confidence from the National Assembly (Thiébault 2006, p. 334; Hamon and Troper 2014, p. 552).

As for the stability of Government members, neither the Romanian nor the French Constitution provides for the possibility of the president unilaterally causing the Prime Minister's or ministers' resignation. Thus, from a legal perspective, both the President of France and the President of Romania may dismiss the Prime Minister only if the latter has requested to be relieved of office, provided they still enjoy the confidence of the legislature and intend to remain in office (Hamon and Troper 2014, p. 553).

The political responsibility of Government members is indirect, meaning that it does not apply individually but collectively, through the adoption of a motion of no confidence. Like the French one, the Romanian Constitution does not provide for an individual motion (Thiébault 2006, p. 335; Toader and Safta 2015, p. 264). In this respect, the Constitutional Court of Romania has ruled in Decision no. 148/2007 (published in the Official Journal no. 162 of 7 March 2007) that, in terms of effects on the Government and its members, there are substantial differences between the two types of motions. Thus, the Government is invested, according to Article 103 paragraph (3) of the Constitution, by being granted confidence through the vote of most deputies and senators, following a joint session debate of both Chambers on the program and list of the Government. The withdrawal of confidence in the Government is carried out under Article 113 paragraph (1) of the Constitution, by adopting a motion of no confidence in a joint session of both Chambers, with the vote of the majority of deputies and senators. Unlike a simple motion, the adoption of a motion of no confidence has the direct legal effect of dismissing the Government in its entirety.

The third type of motion, known in the legislation and practice of several countries as the individual motion, is not provided for in the Romanian Constitution. The

[1] This presidential power also represents an obligation; the President cannot refuse to appoint Government members.

individual motion has legal effects similar to those of the motion of no confidence, but not on the entire Government, only on certain specifically named members. Thus, submitting a request for the dismissal of a Government member within a simple motion cannot create legal obligations for the Government, the Prime Minister, or other people.

The dismissal or appointment of a minister may be carried out exclusively by the President, upon the proposal of the Prime Minister, a condition that applies under both Romanian and French constitutional law (Thiébault 2006, p. 335). In this regard, both the Prime Minister of France and the Prime Minister of Romania have the exclusive power to terminate a minister's mandate.

Regarding the two types of motions, the motion of no confidence and the simple motion (also referred to as a provoked motion), it should be noted that they apply under different conditions. For example, in its jurisprudence, the Constitutional Court of Romania has held that parliamentary oversight is generally without sanction in the Romanian constitutional system, as in most other countries. The only exception in which parliamentary oversight carries a sanction is when it is exercised through a motion of no confidence, whose adoption results in the dismissal of the Government. The Court also found that the notion of the "simple motion" was introduced into the Constitution during its revision, when Article 112 paragraph (2) was redrafted to expand the scope of motions: the Chamber adopting the motion may express its position not only on a matter that was the subject of an interpellation, but also on other issues of domestic or foreign policy.

The simple motion provided members of the Parliament with a more effective instrument for exercising the parliamentary oversight function over the Government. However, adopting a simple motion does not have the direct legal effect of revoking a Government member. Therefore, the lack of such legal effect does not nullify its political impact, since, if the executive ignores the simple motion, the two Chambers of Parliament may, if necessary, resort to the motion of no confidence (Decision no. 148 of 21 February 2007, published in the Official Journal no. 162 of 7 March 2007).

The constitutional provisions of France regulate in Article 49, paragraph 2, the motion of no confidence (la motion de censure/spontanée), and in paragraph 3 the provoked motion (motion de censure provoquée). On this matter, the Constitutional Court of Romania highlighted in Decision No. 609/2020 (published in the Official Journal no. 980 of 23 October 2020) that the Romanian Fundamental Law "does not regulate two categories of motions of no confidence; on the contrary, the motion of no confidence as a legal institution is a single one, governed by Article 113 of the Constitution; the specific elements related to the motion of no confidence initiated in the context of the Government's assumption of responsibility reveal only two procedural particularities (the context of initiation—after the presentation of the program, the general policy statement, or the legislative proposal subject to the assumption of responsibility—and the constitutional possibility of initiation—regardless of whether its signatories have already submitted a motion of no confidence during the same parliamentary session under the provisions of Article 113 of the Constitution), as well as one substantial particularity (in the case of rejection of the motion of no confidence, the program, general policy statement, or legislative proposal is deemed adopted), which cannot qualify the motion of no confidence under Article 114 of the Constitution as a distinct parliamentary oversight instrument from the motion of no confidence governed by Article 113 of the Constitution. [...] it follows that, by voting on a motion of no confidence, regardless of whether it was submitted under Article 113 or Article 114 of the Constitution, parliamentary oversight is exercised, and the withdrawal of confidence in the Government occurs, which has the effect of dismissing it."

According to Article 49, paragraph 2 of the French Constitution, the motion of no confidence is the means by which the National Assembly questions the Government's responsibility. In French legal doctrine, it has been noted that this method of holding the Government accountable is so strictly regulated that it has only been successfully adopted once, on October 5, 1962, to denounce the irregularity of a constitutional revision[2] (Acquaviva 2016, p. 215). The motion of no confidence is initiated by one-tenth of the members of the National Assembly, and the vote must take place within 48 hours of its submission. The motion is adopted by an absolute majority (Hamon and Troper 2014, p. 553) of the members of the National Assembly, and only votes cast in favor of the motion are considered; thus, members of parliament who are absent or who abstain are deemed to be opposed to the motion.

Each deputy may present no more than three motions of no confidence during an ordinary session and only one during an extraordinary session.

In practice, the motion of no confidence regulated by the French Constitution no longer represents an effective means of sanctioning Government members; rather, it is seen as a tool through which the parliamentary opposition generates political debate to express disagreement with the Government's policies publicly (Favoreu et al. 2019, p. 814).

According to Article 49, paragraph 3, which regulates the Government's assumption of responsibility, this procedure could be applied without limitation prior to the constitutional revision of 23 July 2008; currently, its use is restricted to matters related to public finances or the funding of the social security system (Acquaviva 2016, p. 216). These provisions allow the Prime Minister, after deliberation within the Council of Ministers, to commit the Government's responsibility before the National Assembly for the purpose of passing a bill. The bill is considered adopted if, within the next 24 hours, no motion of no confidence is introduced, or if a motion of no confidence is introduced but not adopted. French legal doctrine has noted that the provisions of Article 49, paragraph 3 of the French Constitution are designed to circumvent parliamentary opposition that might otherwise introduce amendments aimed at delaying the adoption of a legislative proposal. The Government's assumption of responsibility thus avoids debate and results in the adoption of the bill without a formal vote (Acquaviva 2016, p. 216). The cited author also observed that the provisions of Article 49, paragraph 3 have consistently worked in the Government's

[2] By comparison, in Romania, between 1993 and 2021, over 44 motions of no confidence were submitted, of which 6 led to the dismissal of the Government.

favor, as no motion of no confidence under this article has ever been adopted[3] (Acquaviva 2016, p. 216). Equally, this procedure can be useful in situations where there is insufficient legislative support for the bill or when the parliamentary majority does not wish to trigger a change in Government members[4] (Thiébault 2006, p. 338). Essentially, the Government does not seek parliamentary support but merely a lack of formal opposition.

In both the French and Romanian Parliaments, there is no legal mechanism to prevent the Government from assuming responsibility. In this regard, Romanian constitutional jurisprudence has affirmed that once the procedure of assuming responsibility has been initiated, "Parliament cannot prevent the Government from continuing the procedure in question, as this would lead to unacceptable situations in which a minority Government could never assume responsibility, which would flagrantly violate Article 114 of the Constitution. Furthermore, the Government itself cannot withdraw its request to assume responsibility, as it is an irrevocable act. In this constitutional context, the submission of a motion of no confidence signifies the initiation of parliamentary oversight over Government activity and, mutatis mutandis, constitutes an irrevocable act marking the beginning of such oversight; it is a tool generally available to the parliamentary opposition and, not least, a form of expressing dissent regarding the measures adopted by the Government." (Decision no. 1525/2010, published in the Official Journal no. 818 of 7 December 2010).

A particular case concerning the application of Article 49, paragraph 3 of the French Constitution, occurred during the adoption of the finance law for the 2023–2027 period (*Loi de programmation des finances publiques pour les années 2023 à 2027*) once during an extraordinary session and once during an ordinary session, which prompted a referral to the Constitutional Council. In Decision No. 2023-857 DC of 14 December 2023 (published in *Journal Officiel de la République Française* (JORF) no. 0293 of 19 December 2023), the Council held, on the one hand, that the Prime Minister may use the procedure provided by Article 49 paragraph 3 of the Constitution for successive readings of the same bill during different sessions (first in an extraordinary session, then in an ordinary session), and on the other hand, that the Prime Minister may delegate to a minister the task of informing the National Assembly of the Government's assumption of responsibility.

A similar conclusion was reached by the Constitutional Court of Romania, which noted that "no constitutional provision prohibits the submission of a motion of no confidence outside ordinary sessions. Parliamentary oversight is not exercised intermittently only during the ordinary sessions of Parliament, but continuously (…). The fact that Article 113 paragraph (4) of the Constitution expressly provides that 'If the motion of no confidence has been rejected, the deputies and senators who signed it may not initiate another motion of no confidence during the same session,

---

[3] Since the beginning of the Fifth Republic, over 50 laws have been adopted under Article 49(3) of the French Constitution.

[4] In French legal doctrine, it is said that the Government was "overthrown" (*renversé*).

except when the Government assumes responsibility in accordance with Article 114' does not mean that deputies or senators who have signed or submitted a motion of no confidence during an ordinary session could not initiate one outside of these sessions. Moreover, the text under analysis does not stipulate that deputies and senators may initiate a motion of no confidence only during ordinary sessions; rather, it refers solely to the prohibition of initiating more than one motion of no confidence within the same session." (Decision of the Romanian Constitutional Court no. 609/2020, published in the Official Journal no. 980 of 23 October 2020).

In a more general interpretation, the French Constitutional Council held in Decision No. 89-269 DC of 22 January 1990 that, in exercising the prerogatives granted by Article 49, paragraph 3, the Prime Minister is not subject to any conditions other than those outlined in the constitutional text itself. Furthermore, in paragraph 6 of the same decision, the Council clarified that the interim Prime Minister exercises their role from the moment the President signs the decree and has the same powers and rights as the full Prime Minister, including with respect to the application of Article 49, paragraph 3 of the French Constitution. A relatively similar approach is found in the Romanian context, where it has been stated that "the interim Prime Minister enjoys full competence, identical to that of the acting Prime Minister, for a maximum period of 45 days; however, the absence of a duly appointed Prime Minister beyond this period results" (Decision of the Romanian Constitutional Court no. 538/2018, published in the Official Journal no. 1076 of 19 December 2018) in the termination of the Government's mandate, in accordance with Article 110 paragraph (2) of the Romanian Constitution.

3 Criminal Liability of Government Members

The Constitutional Court of Romania has developed consistent jurisprudence on the application of constitutional provisions concerning the criminal liability of Government members, as set out in Article 109, paragraph (2) of the Romanian Constitution. According to this constitutional provision, "Only the Chamber of Deputies, the Senate, and the President of Romania have the right to request criminal prosecution of Government members for acts committed in the exercise of their duties. If prosecution is requested, the President of Romania may order their suspension from office. The indictment of a Government member entails their suspension from office. Jurisdiction belongs to the High Court of Cassation and Justice." These constitutional provisions establish a distinct procedural mechanism designed to protect the exercise of governmental office without preventing the application of the principle of criminal liability.

Article 109, paragraph (2) of the Romanian Constitution contains three scenarios. The first clause provides that when the Government member also holds the status of deputy or senator, the request for criminal prosecution may only be made by the Chamber of Deputies or the Senate, depending on which Chamber the person belongs to. Additionally, if the Government member does not have parliamentary status, the President of Romania requests that criminal proceedings be initiated. The second clause of Article 109, paragraph (2) provides the President of Romania with the discretionary power to order the suspension of a Government member from office. Finally, the last clause assigns jurisdiction for adjudication to the High Court. For offenses committed by a Government member that are unrelated to the exercise of their duties, they are subject to liability under the general criminal law (according to Article 7(2) of Law no. 115/1999, republished in the Official Journal no. 200 of 23 March 2007). Furthermore, criminal liability for acts committed in the exercise of their office applies from the date of taking the oath until the termination of office (according to Article 11 of Law no. 115/1999).

The reasoning retained in the decisions handed down by the Romanian Constitutional Court can be summarized as follows:

a) The Romanian Constitution does not establish governmental immunity but rather an objective procedural protection mechanism. This measure remains applicable even after the end of the mandate, with regard to acts committed during the mandate. Specifically, the Constitution provides a form of protection for the mandate exercised by Government members, which has the legal nature of a constitutional procedural guarantee (Decision of the Romanian Constitutional Court no. 93/1999, published in the Official Journal no. 300 of 28 June 1999);
b) The Government member benefits from the guarantee of individual freedom through the protective measures established by the Constitution (Decision of the Romanian Constitutional Court no. 799/2011, published in the Official Journal no. 440 of 23 June 2011);
c) Parliamentary status is compatible with holding the position of Government member, which is why the Chamber of Deputies or the Senate has the right to request the criminal prosecution of a Government member for acts committed in the exercise of their official duties. The request from the public prosecutor must be submitted to the Chamber of Parliament to which the individual belongs (Decision of the Romanian Constitutional Court no. 270/2008, published in the Official Journal no. 290 of 15 April 2008);
d) The decision to approve or reject the request for criminal prosecution of a Government member who is also a deputy or senator lies exclusively with the plenary of the Chamber of Parliament to which they belong. The legal committee of that Chamber does not have decision-making competence in this regard (Decision of the Romanian Constitutional Court no. 548/2015, published in the Official Journal no. 717 of 23 September 2015);
e) For a Government member who does not hold the status of deputy or senator, the request for criminal prosecution must be made by the President of Romania (Decision of the Romanian Constitutional Court no. 270/2008, published in the Official Journal no. 290 of 15 April 2008);
f) No member of the Parliament or minister can be held liable for political opinions or actions carried out in the process of drafting or adopting a piece of legislation. Immunity accompanies the legislative decision-making process. The absence of legal liability for legislative activity serves as a guarantee for the exercise of the

> mandate of a member of the Parliament or a minister. This immunity contributes to ensuring independence and security in the performance of their rights and obligations (Decision of the Romanian Constitutional Court no. 68/2017, published in the Official Journal no. 181 of 14 March 2017).

Unlike the constitutional framework in Romania, the French legal system concerning the liability of Government members is based on different premises. Thus, many of the aspects regulated by Article 109, paragraph (2) of the Romanian Constitution and further developed in Romanian constitutional jurisprudence are not applicable in French law. In Romania, the constitutional provisions are based on the premise that holding the position of Government member is compatible with holding parliamentary office. In contrast, in France, Article 23, paragraph 1 of the Constitution explicitly establishes the incompatibility of the two roles, stating that "the position of Government member is incompatible with the exercise of a parliamentary mandate."

In France, the criminal liability of Government members is governed separately by Article 68-1 of the Constitution, which states that they are liable "for acts committed in the exercise of their functions and classified as offenses at the time they were committed." Prior to the 1993 constitutional revision, the rules governing the liability of Government members were the same as those governing the liability of the President of the Republic for high treason, and prosecution required a vote by both Chambers of Parliament (Favoreu et al. 2019, p. 559; Apachiţei 2025, pp. 314–337). This procedure made it difficult to initiate criminal liability, which led to the adoption of the constitutional law of 27 July 1993. That reform established the Court of Justice of the Republic[5] and introduced a more accessible procedure for the prosecution of Government members (Carcassonne 2011, p. 326).

The need for constitutional amendments regarding the criminal liability of French Government members was prompted in particular by the case known as the "contaminated blood" scandal. The victims had been infected with the HIV virus as a result of blood transfusions and sought to sue certain Government members, who were accused of failing to provide the necessary information to prevent the use of contaminated blood supplies. At the time, the victims could not initiate proceedings themselves, as this power rested exclusively with the parliamentary assemblies (Favoreu et al. 2019, p. 560; Chantebout 2009, p. 513).

The 1993 amendments regulated Title X of the Constitution, concerning the criminal liability of Government members. In the first stage, it was established that the initiation of proceedings no longer depended on the parliamentary assemblies. A person who considered themselves the victim of a crime or offense committed by a Government member could file a complaint with a "Petitions Commission" composed of magistrates from the Court of Cassation, the Council of State, and the Court of Auditors. The commission would decide whether to reject or accept the complaint. In the second stage, if the commission decides to proceed, the case file

[5] The functioning of the Court of Justice of the Republic is regulated by Organic Law no. 93-1252 of 23 November 1993.

will be referred to the Court of Justice of the Republic, which consists of 15 members (12 members of the Parliament and 3 judges from the Court of Cassation). The Court of Justice of the Republic issued its first ruling in 1999 in the "contaminated blood" case (Favoreu et al. 2019, p. 560). In 2013, a proposal to revise the French Constitution was introduced, which included, among other things, the abolition of the Court of Justice of the Republic and the transfer of jurisdiction over criminal cases involving Government members to the ordinary criminal courts, following a preliminary filtering stage (Bell 2000, pp. 66–68). We can therefore observe that the procedure for engaging in criminal liability for French Government members has gradually come closer to the procedure established by Romanian law.

In Decision 98-408 DC of 22 January 1999 (published in *JORF* no. 20 of 24 January 1999), the Constitutional Council held that Articles 26, 68, and 68-1 of the Constitution were inconsistent with Article 27 of the Treaty on the Criminal Court, which provides that criminal liability must apply equally to all individuals (Rousseau et al. 2016, p. 431; Oellers-Frahm 2005, pp. 112–113).

3.1 Civil (Pecuniary) Liability of Government Members

At the constitutional level, there are no significant differences between France and Romania regarding the civil (pecuniary) liability of Government members. It is established that, in France, if a minister causes harm outside the exercise of their official duties, they are liable under general civil law, like any other citizen. Similarly, if the damage is caused in the exercise of official duties, the rules of administrative law apply, and the minister is held liable in the same way as any other public official (Acquaviva 2016, p. 163).

4 Conclusions

A comparative analysis of constitutional jurisprudence in Romania and France regarding the liability of Government members reveals notable similarities in how the balance between the protection of public office and criminal liability is regulated. In both systems, the criminal liability of Government members is interpreted not only through the lens of general legal provisions but also through the perspective of protecting the mandate, to ensure a stable institutional framework. The Romanian Constitutional Court has reinforced the principle of safeguarding governmental office, emphasizing that this procedural mechanism remains applicable even after the end of the mandate.

In France, the 1993 reform marked a turning point by establishing a more accessible mechanism for initiating the criminal liability of Government members through the creation of the Court of Justice of the Republic and by enabling victims of alleged offenses to initiate criminal proceedings. These constitutional amendments ensured greater transparency and fairness in the prosecution of Government members, based on adherence to international principles of equal treatment under the law.

Although the legal frameworks of the two states differ depending on their constitutional architecture, both systems guarantee the right of access to justice and uphold fundamental principles of legal accountability in the face of abuse of power. Thus, Romanian and French constitutional jurisprudence play an essential role in ensuring effective oversight of Government members, while maintaining a balance between the protection of public office and the need for accountability for actions committed during their term of office.

References

Acquaviva JC (2016) Droit constitutionnel et institutions politiques. 19th edn., Gualino editeur, Paris

Apachiţei ID (2025) Infracţiuni contra securităţii naţionale, Hamangiu Publishing House. Bucharest

Bell J (2000) The criminal liability of politicians in France. Camb Yearb Eur Leg Stud 3:65–78. https://doi.org/10.5235/152888712802859150

Carcassonne G (2011) La constitution introduite et commentée. 10th edn. Editions du Seuil. Paris

Chantebout B (2009) Droit constitutionnel, 26th edn. Dalloz, Paris

Chryssogonos K, Stratilatis C (2012) Limits of electoral equality and political representation. Eur Const Law Rev 8(1):9–32. https://doi.org/10.1017/S1574019612000028

Constantinesco V, Pierré-Caps S (2006) Presidential elements in government France: the quest for political responsibility of the President in the Fifth Republic. Eur Const Law Rev 2:341–357. https://doi.org/10.1017/S1574019606003415

Deaconu S (2018) Răspunderea miniştrilor în constituţiile române: relaţia dintre răspunderea politică şi răspunderea juridică. Revista Dreptul, no. 10/2018

Favoreu L, Gaïa P, Ghevontian R, Mestre JL, Pfersmann O, Roux A, Scoffoni G (2019) Droit Constitutionnel, 21st end. Dalloz, Paris

Hamon F, Troper M (2014) Droit Constitutionnel. 35th edn. LGDJ Lextenso, Paris

Māţă D.C. (2022), Drept administrativ, Vol. I, 4th edn. Universul Juridic Publishing House, Bucharest

Oellers-Frahm K (2005) Italy and France: immunity for the prime minister of Italy and the president of the French Republic. Int J Const Law 3(1):107–115. https://doi.org/10.1093/icon/moi007

Rousseau D, Gahdoun PY, Bonnet J (2016) Droit du contentieux constitutionnel, 11th edn. LGDJ, Paris

Thiébault JL (2006) Delegation and accountability. In the Fifth Republic. In: Strøm K, Müller WC, Bergman T (eds) Delegation and accountability in parliamentary democracies, comparative politics. Oxford University Press

Toader T, Safta M (2015) Dialogul judecătorilor constituţionali, Universul Juridic Publishing House, Bucharest

From Apparent Minimalism to Genuine Simplicity: Contouring the Concept of Budget Through Interpretation

Ioana Maria Costea

Abstract This study explores the evolution of the concept of "budget" from its apparent minimalism in everyday language to its genuine complexity within legal structures. It examines budgetary law through both axiological and deontological lenses, highlighting how legal norms are deeply intertwined with societal values and are determined by Sovereign's role as Legislator, creditor, and debtor. The analysis begins with semantic definitions of "budget" across English, Romanian, and French, tracing its historical and normative development. The work then delves into the legal facets of budgetary law, focusing on constitutional and statutory definitions, the structure of the budgetary system, and the principles that underpin public finance regulation—such as universality, unity, annuality, balance, and publicity. Interpretative tactics in budgetary law are scrutinised, revealing that interpretation is often routine and structured, with administrative and judicial actors playing distinct roles. Case-law examples illustrate the practical outcomes of interpretation, emphasising the predictability and universality of budgetary legal solutions. Ultimately, the chapter argues that budgetary law is a systemic, public-oriented field, governed by strict regulatory and interpretative techniques, making its subjects constant beneficiaries of external norms, often without explicit awareness.

1 Introduction: Budgetary Law Between Axiology and Deontology

In classical, simplistic normative theories of contemporary origin, all legal mechanisms are based on axiological sources. These are most evident in the criminal law register, where the legal norm protects a social value and ensures pragmatic mechanisms for Sovereign's reaction to the infringement of that value; in the ECHR case-law, where the standard of protection is exploited in the register of '*fundamental*

I. M. Costea (✉)
Faculty of Law, Alexandru Ioan Cuza University of Iași, Iași, Romania
e-mail: ioana.costea@uaic.ro

I. Maria Costea (ed.), *Legal Interpretation in Motion*, Ius Gentium: Comparative Perspectives on Law and Justice 144,
https://doi.org/10.1007/978-3-032-32948-6_16

values in a democratic society' and even at the level of primary normative sources in European Union law, such as Article 2 TFEU, "*These values are common to the Member States*" (Costea and Ilucă 2023, p. 68). This results in a consequential and even an inter-determined link between legal norm and values, since the norms explicitly enshrine traditional values and confirms emerging ones. The normative process absorbs the axiological structure of the legislating societal frame translated through the voice of the Sovereign (Laiu-Tincu 2024, p. 180); it even includes a priority order with legal consequences echoed by fundamental texts such as treaties, statutes, constitutions, by secondary legislation and even by tertiary norms.

In an axiological frame, regulation regarding public finances finds its own place with multiple determinants: the Sovereign has a triple role: He is regulator, He is both creditor and debtor; He is the depository of societal trust and exponent of values entrusted throughout electoral processes. The public funds mechanism is not entirely original; it reflects a traditional *modus operandi* created and tested in the private sector in the field of companies (Ungureanu 2018, p. 56), where through two consensual tools: the association contract between shareholders and the mandate contract amid their joint will and the administrator(s), the common purpose is put into practice and pursued to its end. Hence common values, expectations, and interests are followed mobilizing joint resources, skills, and purposes through an implicit trust liaison generating a common will. A similar mechanism is put in place for managing public finances as election processes sift a common frame of values entrusted to a representative decision-making corpus. Since the stake is higher than any other as it regards society as a whole, and a traditional consensual link is logistically impossible to put in operation, the Sovereign is entrusted with a broader, generic, and stable role; He is both regulator and part of this social construct; He disposes regulations affirming and safeguarding these common values through legal norms from constitutional ones (at national level) and treaty norms (at European Union level) to administrative law in its finest Kantian categorical imperative form. The most available example that comes to mind is the Regulation (EU, Euratom) 2020/2092 of the European Parliament and of the Council of 16 December 2020 on a general regime of conditionality for the protection of the Union budget stating:

> The Union is founded on the values of respect for human dignity, freedom, democracy, equality, the rule of law and respect for human rights, including the rights of persons belonging to minorities, enshrined in Article 2 of the TEU (…) Whenever Member States implement the Union budget, (…), and whatever method of implementation they use, respect for the rule of law is an essential precondition for compliance with the principles of sound financial management enshrined in Article 317 of the TFEU.

Therefore, sets of rules regarding budgetary context at various levels are crystalizing in an axiological frame. Since we witness a web of normative acts, one can state that we are in the presence of a legal domain: budgetary law or public finance law. This legal corpus emerges from and is subdued to the core etiologic, societal consensus, not as a part of natural order but rather as a more sophisticated, evolving subset of values. This would clearly represent the overture on budgetary or public finance law, where Law through the will of the Sovereign puts into text a set of values, in a reactive dimension and sets the stage for a functioning society.

Under a different lens, law is also a proactive tool, as it transposes into instruments and procedures a common purpose, not only as a source but also as a destination. Budgetary law derives, as mentioned above, from the purest form of power and crosses layers of regulation from heterogeneous power's sources—European Parliament, national parliament, regional or local regulatory bodies—to its beneficiary—nationals, citizens, residents. A certain input in these regulatory layers will not only promote a common preexisting value but also determine or support the emergence of new common values. The most circular example is given by the provisions of Article 86 TFEU, deriving from a political construct generating a European budgetary frame and secondary a common value: the protection of the financial interest of the EU including through criminal law instruments. This common value emerged as a side effect of implementing a European public finances frame determining the necessity to shape and craft secondary tools for fighting certain unwanted behaviors and even tertiary instruments to repress unwanted conducts. This orienting role is innately mobile, evolving and shapeshifting; this inherent transformation is part of the process of lawmaking.

2 The Notion of Budget(s) as a Simple Noun

Since we have established that a legal norm is attached to a social relationship, with the inherent meanings derived from the ante-legal order of the societal mechanism, an interpretative approach in the field of public finances would naturally start from the identification of the common, usual meanings, from the everyday language of the terminology addressed.

2.1 *Basic Definitions*

A sound legal interpretative approach will almost automatically start from a semantic assessment. We will proceed in such manner and evoke the definitions in English (as long as our text is written in this language), Romanian (as we are scholars of Romanian legislation) and French (as French law is a traditional legal system).[1]

> According to the Cambridge dictionary, in English, there is a semantic distinction between nouns: budget and the Budget; the first is a plan to show how much money a person or organization will earn and how much they will need or be able to spend, while the second (in the UK), is the official statement that the Government elaborates about how much it will collect in taxes and spend on public services in the future.
>
> According to Romanian dictionary, the common noun, *budget* designates/designated: (2009) the record of income and its allocation to expenditure categories over a certain

[1] https://dictionary.cambridge.org/dictionary/english/budget; https://dexonline.ro/definitie/buget/definitii; https://www.cnrtl.fr/definition/academie9/budget.

period (usually a year) for a state, organization, family etc.; (1998) the balance sheet of income and expenses of a state, enterprise, etc. over a determined period; (1955) plan including the calculation or monetary expression of the probable income and expenses of a state, enterprise, or institution, etc. over a determined period (usually a year), based on financial experience, i.e., on the balance sheet of the expired year.

According to Dictionnaire de l'Académie, in French, the noun *budget* has three meanings: *état des recettes et des dépenses prévues par une collectivité, un organisme, une entreprise, pour une période déterminée, généralement pour un an; acte de prévision des recettes et des dépenses annuelles de l'État, qui fait l'objet d'une loi de finances votée par le Parlement; ensemble des revenus et des dépenses d'une personne, d'une famille.*

Before correlating these semantic variations, it is worth mentioning that according to the same sources, the noun was borrowed from English into French in the fifteenth century with an archaic version of the contemporary meaning, while at its origin the term derives from a French noun *bougette*, small leather bag.

This simple, basic interpretative approach illustrates a fluidity at the border of legal and non-legal semantics, as the noun in different languages and different social orders tends to adjust, contract, extend or restrict its meaning. From these definitions to the normative text and back, a multitude of interferences bring a multitude of considerations. For example, the notion of *budget* verifies a state function by designating the mechanism invoked by us at the beginning of this study, from which civil and even purely private functions radiate, when we talk about the budget of a company or the budget of a family. This register is a socio-cultural one that remains at an informal level as it is not confirmed by a concern of the Legislator to regulate material norms and procedural stages regarding non-public budgets.

Hence, in this tri-level semantics, there are norms regulating public budget—legally an almost tautological paraphrase, since the term *budget* is used mainly in regulations regarding public finances with some nuances we will underline further in our analysis; norms regulating financial administration in private associative entities—companies, associations, trusts, cooperatives—which have a similar annual financial plan, forecast, prognosis, extracted from their accounting, generally referred to as *annual accounts*[2] and a common ground frame regulating personal finances, where no budgetary standards are applicable. Some form of balancing revenues and expenses derives from a human need for predictability The commonality to all these planning strategies is control, residing in a general interest, hence proper budgets are public, transparent, unique, universal, mandatory, annual and balanced; private associative entities are ruled also by forms of transparency correlated to information relevant for stakeholders, employees, fiscal authorities, financial markets or creditors but are not essentially public, nor balanced; personal finances are generally opaque, non-systemized, fragmented and administrated in a continuum, not balanced nor unique.

A secondary note is relevant as the Romanian dictionary fluctuates in the definitions' content in time; this fluctuation is very natural; concepts are alive and

[2] Council Regulation (EC) No 2157/2001 of 8 October 2001 on the Statute for a European company (SE) OJ L 294, 10/11/2001, pp. 1–21.

subject to evolution but a diachronic approach especially in the Romanian historical context allows us to underline the pro-active effect of regulation. One can easily notice the shift between definition from the 1950s implemented in the core era of the newly installed communist regime and previous or contemporary definitions. An immersive study (Dascălu 2016, pp. 19–21) reveals that the concept is in use since the middle of the nineteenth century and a certain semantic circularity is to be observed determined by the string of political options succeeding, placing the concept in relation to political doctrines, macro-economic options and structural legal theories.

In a mundane note, we would notice that the semantic family also contains the verb *to budget* connecting financial resources to a certain purpose, as the action to allocate resources to a certain project and the adjective *budget* describing a very cheap good or service, intaking the effect of a public procurement procedure searching for the cheapest offer.

2.2 Who, When and How Is Using the Noun Budget?

In the life of an ordinary legal subject, there is very little budgetary presence in correlation to public finances; private finances are more defined, conceptualized and acknowledged as they provide or participate in the resource management, as a tool for survival. The concept of *budget,* like all legal concepts, is transposed in series of legal norms with varying legal force constituting budgetary law. This semiotic connection from a concept to a branch of law is rather common: family-family law; contracts-contract law; crime-criminal law (Dunea 2019, pp. 107–122) etc., yet we will underline that in the analyzed sector, legal schools polarize in various degrees this correlation and affirm explicitly the existence of such a legal field. For example, central and eastern Europe doctrine (Marková 2015, p. 282) is attuned to a more structured theory of secondary branches of public law: administrative law, financial law, budgetary law, viewing the latter as part of the financial law system (Tsindeliani 2017, p. 15). In different approaches (Lienert 2013, p. 68; Bates 1915, p. 76), budget is a function of the constitutional-administrative-financial order with accents deriving from constitutional case-law (Laze 2019, p. 39).

In determining the relation to budgetary law, we will construct our approach on the subjective legal theory proposed by professor Codrea that differentiates between the subject and the subject of law; in *Logică juridică*, addressing the relation between law and life itself, professor Codrea asserts:

> The taking care of social values from fields that indirectly target the human, the religious, the moral or customary, with the immediate consequence of the fact that the law relates indirectly, mediated to those values, as a container, decanter or protector, places the law in a secondary position compared to the normative fields that still enjoy a special aura and that the law merely takes care of (...) We do not refer to parents as ascendants within the mean-

> ing of civil law, we do not interpret the fact that we are raised and protected by parents in terms of the execution of a legal maintenance obligation until the age of majority, we do not understand our children in their legal capacity as legal or testamentary successors, we do not marry considering the partition procedure etc. (Codrea 2023, p. 369)[3]

Like in A Major key musical piece, the subject and the legal subject are driven by a contingent of common valuations, in which life is the subject's field of expression, and the normative attenuates it, when in acute measures, from a role designated by the cited author as indirect, mediated, secondary. In the intimate, private circle, there is rarely any place for the interference of law; the scarce and occasional turbulences shift the melodic line to G Minor giving place to an external intervention. Hopes, dreams and faiths are reduced to strategies, budgets and costs; confidence and balance are replaced by fragility and destitution. Assistance lies within the other, distributed on statistical grounds; I becomes We as in we will build a wall, we will go to war, we will punish, we will cure, we will educate, we will nurture. The public intervention evoked in any register from theocratic to democratic—based epistemologically upon various justifications from Divine mediation to administrative appeal—will offer a standard, average shaped action from a public agent, financed by public resources. One can imagine a calm, Chopinesque night, and clearly not foresee the rhythm of a military polonaise; in one's home, with the loved ones, we do not project ourselves as subjects of budgetary law. Nevertheless, if we add to this frame an exceptional event such as a medical emergency, a wildfire or an airstrike, the tone shifts dramatically as one is anticipating and even demanding a salvatory intervention. This intervention, generated spontaneously by community's solidarity in other historical eras, is nowadays managed by a public service, using public finances as a medical team, a firefighter's brigade or a military defensive action is called upon and is expected to arrive in due time. It is not the service that adds an unavoidable layer to our existence, since not all subjects nor simultaneously nor successively will access all public services. It is its accessibility, its availability. Hence, against all subjective positions or projections, we are never external to the budgetary law; we are never a non-subject of budgetary law. Depending on age, constitutional status, administrative structure, political constructs, this thread may vary in intensity and tension; it may underline the relation between the objective position—taxpayer—and the subject dimension—human in need; it may strike a correlation chord and make it audible.

This awareness probability is indeed embedded with subjectivity; one cannot be forced to hear, comprehend or acknowledge the external intervention. Here lies the

[3] Original text "Luarea în grijă a unor valori sociale din câmpuri care vizează în mod nemediat umanul, cel religios, moral sau cutumiar, cu consecința imediată a faptului că dreptul se raportează indirect, mediat la acele valori, ca recipient, decantor sau protector, plasează dreptul într-o poziție secundară față de câmpurile normative care încă se bucură de o aură aparte și pe care dreptul doar le ia în grijă (...) nu ne raportăm la părinți ca la ascendenți în sensul legii civile, nu interpretăm faptul că suntem crescuți și ocrotiți de părinți în termenii executării unei obligații legale de întreținere până la vârsta majoratului, copiii nu ni-i înțelegem în calitatea lor juridică de succesori legali sau testamentari, nu ne căsătorim având în vedere procedura partajului etc."

answer to the questions raised in the title of this section: the noun *budget* will be spoken in rare occasions against its silent omnipresence.

3 Legal Facets

In a continental legal system, it is only natural to observe a plurality of normative confirmation of budgetary law; the same omnipresence is identifiable in European law as consequence of a positivist approach to framing a supra-statal entity. Hence both the Romanian Constitution and the Treaty on the functioning of the European Union enclose provisions—organized as a specific section on the budgetary matter.

3.1 Normative Definitions

The Romanian Constitution dedicates Title IV to the matters of *Economy and public finances*, detailed in seven articles focusing on: *economy, property, financial system, public national budget, taxes and other contributions, the Court of Auditors* and *the Economic and Social Council.*

In this frame, the noun *budget* is being used eighteen times; in a profane reading of the text, one can try to identify a definition of the term and its main attributes. Not so much to our surprise, at constitutional level the term has no definition; the noun is used in locutions, determined by adjectives in order to underline the meaning of the word mainly by article 138: the *National Public Budget, the State Budget, the State Social Security Budget; the Local Budgets of Communes, Cities And Counties* where the initial concept is the gender including the other as species. One can conclude that the concept of *National Public Budget* is exhaustive and all-encompassing because the enumeration uses the constructive technique known as limitative regulation; thc *National Public Budget* is tripartite with a variable distribution criterion: the subject, hence there are mentioned two national budgets and a third category: local budgets, fragmented upon the type of local administrative unit and the object, hence two of these budgets are all-round purposed and assure the functioning of national and local administrations and the third has an axiological dimension as a frame for social security policies.

Articles 137 and 139 RC maintain almost the same focus points, but each include prophetic variables: the first mentions public institutions (a generic term used in plural form) discussing *financial resources of the state, administrative-territorial units and public institutions* and the second in para. (3) introduces the concept of *contributions to the setting-up of (some) funds* (a non-articulated noun, used in plural, with undefined article). Hence, our initial trio seems to be performing the main arias, but other voices are to be given ear to.

Further investigation, down the chain of normative sources will confirm the initial trio, as each tenor has its own score: Law No. 500/2002 regarding public finances; Law No. 273/2006 regulating local public finances and Law No. 360/2023 regarding the public pension system. These infra-constitutional normative acts are not budgetary laws; they do not include substantial provisions regarding public revenues nor expenses; these texts have a procedural content and ensure the procedural line accompanying a budget throughout its life stages.

To affirm its object, Law No. 500/2002 defines and uses the phrase *system of budgets* through the normative technique of exhaustive and limiting enumeration.

Art. 2 pct. 38 Law No. 500/2002—1) central budgets: a) the state budget; b) the state social security budget; c) the budgets of special funds; d) the state treasury budget; e) the budgets of autonomous public institutions; f) the budgets of public institutions financed in whole or in part from the state budget, the state social security budget and the budgets of special funds, as the case may be; g) the budgets of public institutions financed in whole from their own revenues; h) the budget of funds originating from external credits contracted or guaranteed by the state and whose reimbursement, interest and other costs are ensured from public funds; i) the budget of non-reimbursable external funds; 2) local budgets.**Legal**

In a structural approach, announced by the constitutional provisions, we can derive a first conclusion regarding the object of budgetary law, that it regulates or more precisely it creates a system of budgets, defined by plurality, autonomy, differentiated by competences, object, sources of financing and even destination of expenses. This autonomy is not absolute, nor in relation to its legal regime, nor in relation to its financing sources. Hence, this system of budgets presents itself as a solidary orchestra, where resources are transferred from one component to another, from strings to brass, woodwind or percussion; an in-depth analysis shows that the state budget fuels both social security budget and local budgets (Gherghina 2024, pp. 140–158), which do not lose their autonomy; some public institutions are financed by separate lines from state or local budgets, and some have their own revenue sources. It is fair to acknowledge that the state budget is the violin section, it is omnipresent, widespread and rather flexible. This fluidity might distort the overall image on the dimensions of the budgetary system, as resources leaving from one budget to fuel another budget will be recorded both as revenues and expenses twice (Bostan et al. 2018, p. 55). The solution to avoid such a falsification of the budgetary system dimension is mathematical and consists of consolidating these components by recording them twice as positive and negative numbers. This treatment gives us a new legal concept—*general consolidated budget*:

Art. 3 par. 2 Law No. 69/2010—the set of budgets that make up the budgetary system, including the state budget, the state social insurance budget, the budgets of special funds, the centralized general budget of the administrative-territorial units, the budget of the State Treasury, the budgets of autonomous public institutions, the budgets of public institutions financed in whole or in part from the state budget, from the state social insurance budget and from the budgets of special funds, as the case may be, the budgets of public institutions financed entirely from own revenues, the budget of funds from external loans contracted or guaranteed by the state and whose reimbursement, interest and other costs are ensured from public funds, the budget of non-reimbursable external funds, as well as of other entities classified in public administration, aggregated, consolidated and adjusted according to Regulation (EU) No. 549/2013 to form a whole.**Legal**

This holistic approach is systemic, strategic and embedded with political decisions. It is transposed in a normative frame to endow it with Kantian attributes as a categorical imperative beyond traditional normative limitations, as it is so intertwined in the fiber of social functionality that it involves all stakeholders as an interstatal and a supra-statal command. Its generality, universality and moral dimension are intrinsic to functioning of the budgetary system; *the general consolidated budget* exists as a mere concept, an abstract and deontic instrument that ensures an over-all functionality of public resources beyond strict and limitative normative positivism. Hence, this norm is transcending budgetary legal positivism.

Returning to a more pragmatic level of regulating budgetary law, we can underline that in contradiction with the conceptual dimension of the general consolidated budget, unitary budgets, components of this concept are subject to a legal definition.

Art. 2 par. 6 Law No. 500/2002—document through which revenues and expenditures or only expenditures are provided and approved each year, depending on the financing system of public institutions.**Legal**

Art. 2 par. 7 Law No. 273/2006—document that provides and approves, annually, the revenues and expenses of the administrative-territorial units.

Hence, a budget has a physical existence, it's a document that materializes the Sovereign's power as Legislator to regulate public resources; it has a field of action limited by subject—state budget, local budget, public institution budget—and by legal force. Deriving from its deontic range, budgets are normative acts emanating from various forms of Legislators: European Union budget is a declaration of the President of the European Parliament;[4]; state budget is a law *stricto sensu* as primary normative act of the Parliament[5]; local budgets are Decisions of County or Local Councils; all public institutions adopt a budget as an administrative normative act. Their normative course has some particularities: budgets are annual, public, based solely on the proposal of the executive branch (Roş 2009, p. 100), don't contain general provisions, are addressing a single passive subject.—the executive branch, have different regulatory force, are differently subject to judicial review and are prescribing a future conduct, establishing goals to be attained. So, a budget is a legal act, a financial plan, a command to be executed.

3.2 Transversal Attributes Deriving from Normative Principles

If the above approaches, corresponding to a grammatical and teleological interpretation, allowed us to narrow down the content of the concept, and to address its key elements, a further reading in the systematic method would add relevant elements, by "*reading an individual legal provision in light of the broader legal order to which it belongs*".[6] A stylistic tactic, admitting that there is a certain stylistic of legal normative acts, allows us to treat the body of text in this matter as a pyramidal construct, under both the force of the normative texts—as shown above from constitutional provisions to normative administrative acts—and the course of the texts. Hence, we can assert legal texts within budgetary law follow a pyramidal structure addressing definition, principles and procedural matters—competence and stages of the budgetary process—, and that these layers of regulation refine the concept.We will also add a tertiary component to our method, as the subject is distinctively approached in national, local and European Union regulation.

Following the legislative stepladders, one may notice that the point of the pyramid—the legal definitions—lies on a secondary segment of regulation containing principles regarding budgetary frame. These principles confirm a significant degree of normative condensation as regarded transversally within the budgetary system through identical solutions: universality, publicity, unity, annuality, specialization, monetary unity, balance. These principles assure a plentiful normative space for a systemic interpretative reading with a clarifying contribution to the purpose of the interpreter.

We will operate under the presumption that each of the principles has its own unique content, revealed by its definition. Since the purpose of our study is to clarify the concepts of *budget* and *budgetary law*, we will extract from these principles an attribute of the budget and use it as a mark of specificity in the broader spectrum of

---

[4] http://publications.europa.eu/resource/cellar/1e65e12a-f4ac-11ef-b7db-01aa75ed71a1.0006.03/DOC_1.

[5] https://legislatie.just.ro/public/DetaliiDocument/294638.

[6] See supra Codrea, Chapter II.

the semantic method. This condensation from principle to attribute will keep us closer to the concept and allow us some distance from the procedural aspects, which exceed the purpose of the current study.

We can notice a series of semantic marks of singularity: universality, unity, monetary unity, specialization (Gherghina 2024, pp. 63–94). From these marks, we can extract relevant attributes of the budget as a legal concept:

- the budget includes all revenues and expenses; therefore, it behaves differently from its distant cousin the "private budget" which is purpose oriented: *a vacation budget, a do-it-yourself budget, a wedding budget* etc.;
- the budget is included in a singular document; this characteristic is a conditional one, there is no document including the *general consolidated budget* and surely there is no document including both national and European budget. This attribute is to be read under the sign of administrative autonomy, under the *adagio* "for each public institution": thus the state has a singular budget, so does the European Union, each local authority and broadly each public institution.
- the budget is constructed on the same "mathematical" unit of measure, the same currency therefore, it behaves differently from its distant cousin the "private budget" which can combine different currencies or even choose the currency used as unit of measure; companies and natural persons have the liberty to build upon any currency, technique used in long term projects where more stable currencies are elected;

Secondary, one can notice some marks of rigid limitations; the budget is annual and balanced:

- annuality is a temporal constraint grouping volumes of revenues and expenses in a limited timeframe, which ensures predictability, obeys repetitive needs in a cycle-based approach and allows comparisons between identical timeframes;
- balance is a double faceted attribute; it will measure the correspondence between revenues and expenses and avoid deficit. In the broader budgetary symphony, deficit is the untuned instrument, the supreme fault, a form of deficiency translatable in spending future resources today. Balance is not perfect; in fact, state budgets are constructed in a deficient manner (Gherghina 2024, p. 207); the controlled deficit is a tool of foreseeing a surplus of expenses, like within the frame of the EU the Stability and Growth Pact (SGP);
- specialization ensures a unique reading key for all budgetary operations; any entity conducting a budget will draft it under the same coded sources of revenues and destinations for expenses. The budget is constructed on a very strict matrix: *the budget classification*; this matrix is comparable if not even derived from accounting techniques, where the financial reflection of any patrimonial legal act is recorded with its value as an active or passive element. This duality is a common mark of accounting and budgetary frame and a tool for surveillance: self-control, control of stakeholders, of public authorities and even community.

Thirdly, and probably the most characteristic attribute of a true budget, is its publicity; budgets are public in all phases of their existence, as they are formed of public resources. This publicity allows a societal control on the actions of the executive power in administrating public means. The drafting, the execution and the result of a budgetary cycle are all public; public access to information is a key feature of budgets, demarcating this instrument from other planning financial tools. Individuals do not have a true budget as their financial life does not undergo this publication process; companies are held to make public only some of their financial information especially if they operate in financial markets, which are accessible to the broader public.

4 Interpretative Tactics in Budgetary Law

Our working hypothesis is that budgetary law does not follow traditional interpretative paths, and despite using the same interpretative tactics to define the concept, the applicatory cases are scarce, almost inexistent in relation to the variety and vastness of relevancy of such texts. We will try to assert the role of interpretation in this legal field, to identify the actors of such an interpretation and finally to assess the existence and the unknotting of aporias in budgetary law.

4.1 The Role of Interpretation

Interpretation of a legal text is traditionally a tool to address variables in a legal context; it will allow the enforcer of a certain text to read a certain factual context and to give it not only a qualification, but also a trajectory. Legal interpretation is as all interpretations are an attempt to pin the meaning of a text, not for sterile purposes, nor bare esthetics, but for the pragmatic purpose of a binary nature to establish if a certain rule is applicable or not to a certain factual context. Interpretation is a routinary exercise, as it addresses a vastity of factual cases—see for example, the obligations amongst spouses or parents and children—and it becomes visible against the backdrop of a conflict, whose intensity and stake accrue the interpretative relevance.

As shown above, in a controlled environment—the definition of the budget as a concept—all classical methods of legal interpretation—grammatical, systematic, historical, and teleological—are almost instinctively accessed in a research frame and will guide the author of the interpretation—the scholar in the first part of the study—in their endeavor. But research-oriented legal interpretation is a rather rare exercise; it tends to serve a systematization purpose and to favor a sterile structured legalism,[7] qualifiable easily as a "non-authentic" interpretation. In this controlled

[7] See supra Codrea, Chapter II.

environment, the iterative hermeneutics is almost inexistent; the legal text is disconnected from the specific contexts and the scholar, as interpreter, is rarely engaged in applying the text to a mature, alive context.

Hence, to test and assess the role of legal interpretation in budgetary law, one should emerge in the third layer of regulation, hence the administrative and judiciary procedural norms and identify the content of the fields of application of such norms and the disruptions within these fields.

4.2 The Interpreters

When answering the question who is called upon to perform legal interpretation in budgetary matter, the image of a pianist playing a sonata arises, maybe a Chopin's Nocturne or the Beethoven's Mondscheinsonate; the judge, as a solitary mind and keeper of the function and instruments to achieve such a task, will play its prescribed role with solemnity, discretion and irrefutable force responding to "a robust, judiciary protected serial subject, with a derivative legal coherent story about itself which can be patched any time by a tertium through some form or another of symmetrical compensation" (Codrea 2018, p. 25). This accrued visibility of the soloist is rather symbolic; it steals the stage lights, since his interventions are addressing legal conflicts, which are rarer than the contextual applications of a certain legal text on budgetary issues. Additionally, his interpretative intervention is a summative one; he is called upon to evaluate a context that has already been read by the involved parties, whose readings on the same provision are colliding.

Thus, if we were to give a more precise answer, we would state that the prime interpreters of the budgetary legal texts are its own subjects, which we would identify in a broad manner as public entities and public service beneficiaries. All legal texts regulate a social relation, which customarily has two subjects, the active subject and the passive subject. In budgetary law, the role distribution is rather a combination, either G2G, G2B or G2C relationship. Hence, the interpreter might be a public servant, as agent of a Government structure in relation to another governmental structure; an entrepreneur (Amironesei 2022, p. 137) in relation to a public institution or a citizen in relation to a public body, *lato sensu*, as beneficiary of a public service, regardless of its nationality.

Abilities in performing such an interpretative task vary within these categories of interpreters upon their professional competences, their role—to collect, distribute and to use resources (Government), to provide goods and services or labor (enterprises or public servants) or to demand and receive public services (citizens, private legal entities and even other public entities).

4.3 The Interpretative Paths

Each subject has a particular standpoint in relation to public resources, their content and legal regime. Each subject is an interpreter, user of legal logic[8] tools as it traces, through its own reading of the context a relation between budgetary law and his own contextual reality. This applicative exercise is performed daily, in thousands of contexts, in almost an intuitive manner:

- G2G: money is transferred for one account to another; grants are awarded; authorizing officers commit, validate or authorize items of expenditures from potatoes to nuclear reactors;
- G2B: professors enter class, firefighters start their shifts, constructors contract and execute highways, hospitals, schools; fabricators deliver sheets, chalk, yogurt, motor oil etc.;
  – G2C: students enter class; patients present themselves in the doctor's office; newborns receive birth certificates and newlyweds their marriage documents; convicted fellows are eating their lunch; petitioners address the judge and at any moment, all inhabitants are at peace, watched by an unseen military force etc.;

In this budgetary law construct, as in all administrative matters, the most at hand interpretative path would be a structured legalism one, as the interpretative process is directly or indirectly assured under the state authority; hence an interpretation "*reduced to the act of identifying the preexisting meaning of the legal norm*"[9] is almost mandatory. The premise that legal texts are all-embracing, sufficient and clear is at ease in administrative structures. A non-monotonic logical approach is entirely excluded, not by an obtuse approach of the administration since at this level the true variety of contexts addressable by a legal text unfolds plenary, but by the nature of administrative interpretation that does not contain the force to implement principles and especially as "*the principle that legal reasoning must remain open to exception, revision, and reinterpretation*".[10] The contextual variables are takeable into account in an approach derived from deontic logic, which accommodates "*both the structured command theory ... and the layered, context-sensitive duties*".[11] We admit that elements of semantic logic intervene at this level of interpretation, as legal terms are in use in all legal relationships, regardless of the level of interpretation and of the subjects involved and "*legal terms acquire content across varying contexts*"[12] including administrative ones. Such is the case of qualifying an expenditure as acquisition of goods, investment or acquisition of a service; determining what a force majeure event is in an administrative contractual bond; adjusting the

[8] See supra Codrea, Chapter II.

[9] See supra Codrea, Chapter II

[10] See supra Codrea, Chapter II,.

[11] See supra Codrea, Chapter II

[12] See supra Codrea, Chapter II.

VAT quota for a certain taxable operation or determining which citizens fall under the provisions of a certain text: students from a single-parent family, vulnerable person or exempted taxpayer etc.

In certain contexts, these first-hand tools might prove themselves insufficient; the G2B or G2C relationship could reveal a more tense fabric resisting a traditional cut. Therefore, a one- step interpretation implemented by the administrative body is insufficient to ensure conformity; the other subject advances a different interpretative approach with a different result generating the binary positions that the subjects in a conflict hypothesis assume. More sophisticated means of interpretation are called upon to extinguish the deriving conflict; the intervention of the judge is increasingly necessary. The administrative interpretation is replaced by the judiciary, throughout the phase of the prior complaint (Costea and Ilucă 2018, p. 365); the *soft subject*—the private law subject (Țiț 2014, p. 146), the citizen, the subordinated public entity—will access a contentious path, firstly before the administrative body, in a prior complaint, then before the specialized judge. An array of argumentation theory tools is set in motion, evoked by the complaint, the response to the complaint and the administrative or judicial resolution. These argumentative notes are equal in pure legal judicial approach, under the principle of equality of weapons and gain the supplementary force necessary to induce a solution only through a secondary reading given with public force, by the judge after "*weighing competing claims, resolving conflicts, and determining the justificatory force of interpretations*".[13] In judicial context, dynamic epistemic logic or paraconsistent logic approaches are seldom encountered towards budgetary law, as courts might advance interpretive shifts or solve internal contradictions of the budgetary legal system.

4.4 The Interpretative Outcomes

One may state that not all legal interpretation falls under a deontic approach, but law itself is a deontic construct as the Legislator pursues a certain type of social effect and dedicates the text to this purpose. Surely, our statement is subdued to a limited, positivistic view on law; it is impossible for us at this point to derive a budgetary premise from *jus naturalis*. Even if we consider a fundamental value within the natural law such as the right to live, it is hard to conceive a system of statutory and protective norms including budgetary means of doing so, without admitting that these norms are purpose oriented and the result of an intervention from the Legislator through administrative and judicial bodies using public resources is essential. We will defend our premises that public resources are the result of a creative process, regardless of the means of fulfilling this purpose—democratic, autocratic or even

[13] See supra Codrea, Chapter II.

totalitarian—and that the process in itself is essentially deontic, even if the general public is not aware of the forces involved in this process.

Hence, in budgetary law, outcomes of interpretation are dual.

One set of interpretative maneuvers will question and determine the extent of budgetary law, the realm of public resources; it will delimit the tuning for the ouverture and ensure that the strict, specific legal regime is forcefully implemented when administering public money. The issue is vital to the existence of a given legal order, as budgetary law is the key of any administrative composition; supranational, statal, regional or local. The rules for collecting and distributing revenues and operating expenditures are, as shown above, universal, hence applicable to all items falling under public authority. This legal regime is omnipresent as an *obstinato*, it will follow resources from entering the administrative pipe-like system and will require consistency in applying the mandatory regime for the management, distribution and usage of public money. This omnipresence is proof of the significance of qualifying as budgetary a certain patrimonial frame, hence any conundrum in answering this question will require an elitist, refined interpretative approach, as we will see in the next section.

Another set of interpretative operations will address with less refined instruments very pragmatic day-to-day questions, like coverage of medical insurance, funding for a certain form of education, salary rights for public servants or military pensions, performance and compliance within a construction contract or the price of a service in a public procurement procedure. This fragmentation of the budgetary process brings forward an array of interpreters and an almost infinite number of contexts all submitted to a rather limited number of legal texts with almost identical legal solutions for drafting, approving, executing and auditing a budget. The universality and unity of this regulation is pretentious, it claims legitimacy for the very core of structured legalism; not only norms are hierarchically structured, but also the prime interpreters, hence the administrative system should function without deviation based on an internal axiomatical set of regulations and interpretative approaches. This general and omniscient system of budgets—the general consolidated budget - should be operated yearly, with an unruffled rhythm, *andante* and *con accuratezza;* any note out of tune would be addressed by straightforward, simple interpretative procedures of administrative source and the judiciary would rarely emerge. If we were to qualify the legal nature of this emergence, we cannot state that it is essentially budgetary by nature, except maybe in G2G litigation,[14] but rather of a secondary nature given by the budgetary chapter that contains it: a pension claim is not by nature a budgetary issue, but rather a social security litigation; a salary claim for a public servant is a matter for labor law jurisdictions; a contractual dispute over compliance or price is a litigation amongst professionals.

In a broader line, all interpretative interventions related to a legal text will aspire to a binary solution: to pair or not to pair a certain context to a certain norm. The

[14] For example, in the litigation following an audit of the Court of Accounts that invalidates the decision of an authorizing officer regarding a certain expense.

solution of this process is usually offered by the *strong party* of the legal relationship and usually responds to the claim of the *soft party*. In our preliminary approach, we evoked the context of a medical emergency, a wildfire or an airstrike as the space where budgetary law becomes visible in relation to a certain individual; upon the call for medical aid, the emergency operator swiftly implements a process of legal interpretation that will result in the decision to send or not an ambulance to the aid of the claimer. This ordinary, even prosaic example could seem rather far from the legal and even judiciary order and certainly from any budget-related apprehension; this spatiality does not legitimate the question on the existence of such a public finance frame, but rather proves the ubiquity, even if not lucid, of the G2C relationship.

5 Some Case-Law Advances

Case-law examples in budgetary matter are rather scarce; to identify such cases, the easiest way is to point out some G2G relationship, deriving either from the *a priori* control exerted by the legislative power on the budgetary law—hence a constitutional control - or from the control phase of the budgetary process, namely the aporias generated by clashing interpretation from the public authority and the Court's of Accounts.

In jurisprudential notes, the Constitutional Court found it appropriate to define the budget or the budgetary system through what appears an interpretation directed towards a positivist, norm-generating result, adding to the plain, basic and even insufficient constitutional definition.

Example "The budget is constituted as a financial plan of the state, approved by law, which provides for the public revenues and expenditures established each year, necessary for the fulfillment of the functions and tasks of the state"—Constitutional Court of Romania, Decision No. 1657/2010.[15]

Some Highlights We could underline some shortcomings in this interpretative intervention: the budget is not a plan *per se* but rather a mathematical display of possible future revenues and expenses; it does not function exclusively at the state level; not all budgets are approved by law.

Example "The author of the exception shows that the national public budget, as defined in the Constitution (a.n.) … includes "the state budget, the state social insurance budget and the local budgets of communes, cities and counties", a limited and clear list, not being possible to further extend it through other legal texts. It shows that art. 1 para. (2) of Law No. 500/2002, which establishes to which budgets its provisions apply … includes in letter e) the budgets of autonomous public institutions, and in letter g) the budgets of public institutions financed entirely from own

[15] Monitorul Oficial al României, Partea I, No. 33 from 13.01.2011.

revenues… The Financial Supervisory Authority claims that its budget has never been part of the consolidated general budget… Law No. 72/1996 was replaced by Law no. 500/2002 on public finances … which introduced a new formula, that of "budgetary system" which substitutes the phrase "national public budget" … The Court finds that the locutions "national public budget" and "budgetary system" are synonymous, as they include all the budgets that are drawn up and carried out in a financial year, at the level of a state, through which a permanent control is exercised over the establishment, distribution and use of public funds, as well as over the companies that have relations with the national public budget."—Constitutional Court of Romania, Decision No. 633/2015,[16] para 14–19.

Some Highlights The Constitutional Court undertakes a rather creative interpretative path, guided by the historical method combined with Dynamic Epistemic Logic components, which highlights a red line in budgetary law, and connects (we would name this connection a synonymy with rather equivalent functions) the archaic constitutional provisions with current regulation.

Example "Therefore, … it follows that the Government considered the obligations resulting from Article 126 TFEU in drafting the 2019 State Budget. Any infringements of Article 126 TFEU shall be established in the context of the excessive deficit procedure, provided for in the above-mentioned text of the TFEU, and not through a review of the constitutionality of the State Budget Law. … It should be emphasized that the state budget is a financial plan of the state, it cannot predict with absolute accuracy the economic developments during a budget year but outlines the main directions of the state's action from a budgetary perspective. Any imbalances that may arise during the budget year may be corrected by normative acts of the force of law. … The Court ruled that the financing of budgetary expenditures is made from financial sources allocated in the budget, and that the increase of some expenditures is financed either by supplementing the budgetary allocations from the budgetary reserve fund at the disposal of the Government, or by budget rectification…"—Constitutional Court of Romania, Decision No. 127/2019, para 98–100.[17]

Some Highlights The Constitutional Court ensures a systemic interpretation addressing not the concept, but rather the inherent distribution of competences deriving from the functioning of such system.

In jurisprudential notes, specialized Courts are rarely called upon to deliver systemic developments and are more prone to address questions deriving from the budgetary procedure, ensure interpretation on precise matters, involving a rather static context and a limited number of legal provisions.

Example "Thus, any payment from public money must be based on a supporting document, and it is not allowed to make payments in the absence of documents to

[16] Monitorul Oficial al României, Partea I, No. 904 from 07.12.2015.

[17] Monitorul Oficial al României, Partea I, No. 189 from 08.03.2019.

support them. Financial and budgetary legislation … requires that any payment from public funds be accompanied by supporting documents. This is a legal requirement, not just a recommendation, and failure to comply with it can attract various sanctions, in relation to the deviations found. Only by having documents attesting to the services provided and paid for, verifications can be carried out to show how public money was spent. Supporting documents are essential in the audit process, allowing the traceability of funds and the identification of possible irregularities. … The appellants' claim that by the fact that the laying work and implicitly the "soil" material is a work actually executed and not contested, it can be considered that the related article "road transport of topsoil" was implicitly executed, cannot be accepted, the execution of any operation paid from public funds being necessary to be proven by supporting documents"—Cluj Court of Appeal, 3rd section AFC, Decision No. 815/2024[18]

Some Highlights Cluj Court's of Appeal decision is relevant through its universal and unitary approach on public expenditures, as it states for any public expenditure, hence confirming a structural interpretative approach with no room for exemptions, expansions or even analogies through budgetary enactment procedures.

Example "The irregularity found against the City ## is represented by the violation of the provisions of art. 5 para. 1, 8 and 9 of G.O. No. 80/2001. The ministries, the other specialized bodies of the central public administration, the local councils of communes, cities, municipalities, sectors of the municipality of Bucharest, the county councils and the General Council of the Municipality of Bucharest, as well as all public institutions subordinated to them, apply the expenditure norms for equipping with cars and for consuming of fuels provided in Annex no. 3, within the limits of the approved budgetary expenditures; para. 8 prohibits public authorities and institutions, regardless of the financing and subordination system, to purchase cars, …, with a cylinder capacity of more than 1,600 cc and whose price exceeds … the amount of 18,000 euros including VAT. By exception to the provisions of para. 8, the institutions in the field of defense, public order and national security may purchase (such) cars … with the approval of the chief authorizing officer … Violation of the provisions of art. 5 para. 8 of G. O. No 80/2001 cannot be justified by the fact that the expense incurred with the purchase of the Volkswagen car was approved by the Decision of the local council 118/2013, (that the expenditure) is located in the income and expenditure budget for 2013 and in the list of investment objects, …, neither in the light of the fact that the Mountain Rescue Service is an institution in the field of defense, public order and national security, nor in the light of the existence of well-justified cases, these two requirements being necessary to be fulfilled cumulatively"—Ploieşti Court of Appeal section AFC, Decision No. 1470/2019[19]

---

[18] RJ Code 865432666 (https://www.rejust.ro/juris/865432666).

[19] RJ Code 577d9888 (https://www.rejust.ro/juris/577d9888).

Some Highlights Ploieşti Court's of Appeal decision uses a very simple interpretative path, as it combines the grammatical reading of two normative definitions, regulation of the object and the exemption, and concludes that all elements of the rule stating text are identified in the factual context and that the elements of the exemption stating text are not.

6 Conclusions

The premises of our analysis seem to be confirmed: public law, especially in its core frame addressing public finances, is subject to strict regulatory and interpretative techniques. The adaptation in this field derives not only from the object of the norms, but also from the context of their application and from the voice of the interpreter.

The interpretative intervention follows, more than ever, a structured, limited path and delivers universal solutions. This generality does not take away the relevancy of the interpretation, but rather makes it a specific process deontically oriented, classic in its core, with layered intervention from the Legislator, the Government and the Judiciary.

Budget appears as a systemic concept, all-encompassing regarding its object: public finances and its subjects: Government, entrepreneurs, citizens. This generality is derived from the public nature of budgetary law, and hence it stays within the frame of public law where texts, contexts and interpretative paths are separated from private law. This seclusion applies both at objective and subjective level and processes the methods of interpretation in a specific key.

The result of interpreting and applying budgetary legal texts is and ought to be like a highly predictable musical piece, remarkable by its internal repetition and rhythmic *ostinatos* like Erik Satie's *Vexations*, with its 840 repetitions of a short phrase. This predictability confirms in the end a routinary existence, making its subjects constant and unaware beneficiaries of an external norm.

Acknowledgments This research has been conducted with the support received through the project 'City: Future Organisation of Changes in Urbanisation and Sustainability' (CF 23/27.07.2023), financed by the Ministry of Investment and European Projects through the National Recovery and Resilience Plan (PNRR-III-C9-2023 - I8_round 2).

References

Amironesei A-E (2022) Siluetele juridice din influencer marketing. Analele Ştiinţifice ale Universităţii Alexandru Ioan Cuza din Iaşi, SSJ 68(3):137–155

Bates FG (1915) Budgetary laws. Am Polit Sci Rev 9(4):759–762

Bostan I, Toderaşcu C, Florentina GA (2018) Challenges and vulnerabilities on public finance sustainability. A Romanian case study. J Risk Financ Manag 11(3):55. https://doi.org/10.3390/jrfm11030055

Codrea C (2018) The Deadly Game. Deciphering duel and its impossible legal prohibition through Nietzsche and Hegel. Postmod Open 9(2):15–25
Codrea C (2023) Logică juridică. Hamangiu Publishing House, Bucharest
Costea IM, Ilucă D-M (2018) First step in a conflicting dialogue: preliminary procedure in budgetary and fiscal litigation. EUFIRE Proceedings. Alexandru ioan Cuza University Publishing House, Iaşi: 365–385
Costea IM, Ilucă D-M (2023) The conditionality regime for protecting the European Union budget: between dialogue and institutional monologue. Dreptul 34:78–89
Dascălu D (2016) Tratat de drept fiscal. Hamangiu Publishing House, Bucharest
Dunea M (2019) Poenalia sunt strictissimae interpretationis?(I). Analele Ştiinţifice ale Universităţii Alexandru Ioan Cuza din Iaşi, SSJ 45(2):107–122
Gherghina S (2024) Drept financiar public, 4th edn. Universul juridic Publishing House, Bucharest
Laiu-Tincu M (2024) Reprezentanţii suveranităţii naţionale şi principiul predictibilităţii în materie fiscală. Scie Ann „Universităţii Alexandru Ioan Cuza din Iaşi„. Jur Scrie Ser 70(1):179–191
Laze M (2019) La natura giuridica della legge di bilancio: una questione ancora attuale. Rivista della Associazione Italiana Costituzionalisti 2:17–64
Lienert I (2013) The legal framework for public finances and budget systems, The international handbook of public financial management. Palgrave Macmillan UK, London: 63–83
Marková H (2015) Place of budgetary law in legal system. System of financial law general part. Acta Universitatis Brunensis. Iuridica. Editio Scientia 514:282–292
Roş V (2009) Drept financiar. Sistemul bugetar. C.H. Beck Publishing House, Bucharest
Ţiţ N-H (2014) Conceptual distinctions regarding the notion of enforcement. J Public Adm Finance Law, special:146–153
Tsindeliani I (2017) System of budgetary law. Norwegian J Dev Int Sci 9:15–18
Ungureanu CT (2018) Dreptul comerţului internaţional. Hamangiu Publishing House, Bucharest

MIX
Papier aus verantwortungsvollen Quellen
Paper from responsible sources
FSC® C105338

If you have any concerns about our products,
you can contact us on
ProductSafety@springernature.com

In case Publisher is established outside the EU,
the EU authorized representative is:
Springer Nature Customer Service Center GmbH
Europaplatz 3, 69115 Heidelberg, Germany

Printed by Libri Plureos GmbH
in Hamburg, Germany